Twentieth Century
Architecture
A Visual History

Other books written or edited by Dennis Sharp:

Modern Architecture and Expressionism (1966)
Sources of Modern Architecture (1967)
Planning and Architecture: Essays for Arthur Korn (1968)
The Picture Palace and other Buildings for the Movies (1969)
Manchester Buildings (1966, 1969)
The Bauhaus (1970)
Glass Architecture and Alpine Architecture (1972)
Henri van de Velde: Theatres 1904–14 (1974)
Form and Function: A Source Book for the History of Architecture and Design 1890–1939 (with T. and C. Benton, for the Open University, 1975, 1980)
The Rationalists: Theory and Design in the Modern Movement (1978)
Hermann Muthesius's 'The English House' (1979, 1987)
Contemporary Architects (with M. Emanuel, 1980)
Sources of Modern Architecture: A Critical Bibliography (1981)
Building to the Skies: The American Architecture of Alfred C. Bossom (1984)
Dictionary of Architects and Architecture (General Editor, 1991)

Manfredi Nicoletti, Lucio Passarelli, et al, *Premiated Scheme, Acropolis Museum*, Athens, Greece, 1991; view towards the Acropolis

TWENTIETH CENTURY
ARCHITECTURE
A Visual History

DENNIS SHARP

Facts On File
New York • Oxford

Copyright © 1991 Dennis Sharp

Facts On File, Inc.
460 Park Avenue South
New York NY 10016

Library of Congress Cataloging-in-
Publication Data
Sharp, Dennis
Twentieth century architecture: a visual
    history/by Dennis Sharp.
432p. 32cm.
ISBN 0-8160-2438-3 (alk. paper)
1. Architecture, Modern – 20th Century.
I. Title.
NA680.S517   1990
724′.6–dc20

Facts On File books are available at special
discounts when purchased in bulk
quantities for businesses, associations,
institutions or sales promotions. Please call
our Special Sales Department in New York
at 212/683-2244 (dial 800/322-8755 except
in NY, AK or HI).

Text design by Pickerill and Trodd.
Manufactured by The Bath Press.
Printed in Great Britain.

CONTENTS

PREFACE

This is a presumptuous book. It presumes that most people know about architecture from built examples and are perhaps less interested in unbuilt and drawn schemes. The latter are probably better appreciated by architects, by scholars, historians and students of architecture, although admittedly many drawings of buildings are works of art in their own right. In a way, unbuilt architecture presents a parallel and complementary history to the one this book adopts. But it is a different history and only touched upon here in parenthesis.

When the first edition of this book appeared in 1972 it was generally well received and translated into a number of foreign language editions. In a sense, it reflected a particularly strongly held view about what the Modern Movement meant to twentieth-century architecture. It took into account the changing international scene and hinted at the eventual demise of the so-called 'International Style' without actually mentioning the post-prandial term (Post-Modernism) that gained most publicity and notoriety at the time (see Introduction to the 1980s decade).

Although one or two attempts were made to re-issue the book during the 1980s the growing disaffection with Modernism and the high cost of printing mitigated against it. Then came a rash of post-Modernist titles from other hands.

The death of Modernism was announced. But it would not lie down. Many attempts were made to rename it and to start up something else: post-Modernism, post-post Modernism, Late Modernism, Late-classic Modernism, Neo-Modernism, the 'New' Modernism, and so on. The boughs of this particular tree soon grew heavy and – like Mondrian's apple tree – Modernism changed its shape, abstracted its programme and began to express a vivid new vocabulary. It was a movement that built on Frank Lloyd Wright's organic and democratic traditions, that drew upon nature, resurrected Le Corbusier the all rounder, Aalto the abstractionist, and Expressionism, and that created new, platonically solid Modern geometries. It was helped by the growth of internationalism and by the widely acknowledged and substantial achievements of the pioneer phases of the Modern Movement proper.

The phenomenal growth of interest in the work and ideas of C. R. Mackintosh, Otto Wagner, Gunnar Asplund, Adolf Loos and Frank Lloyd Wright – to name just a few of the most popular architects – over the past two decades has led to a much wider level of general public interest than was the case in the reticent days of the early 1970s. Architectural history (or fiction?) is now a formidable industry. It is destined to become increasingly so with specialist architectural centres, museums and archives springing up almost everywhere. Much greater prominence has been given too to vernacular, regional and indigenous cultural views about architecture and the built environment.

This new edition attempts to chart that development through built examples, and the whole framework of the book has been re-examined in order to tighten up presentation and, occasionally, to reflect changed attitudes and values. A few errors have been corrected. A number of new and better illustrations have been added or substituted.

Through the addition of new material on the 1970s and 1980s, the important changes that have occurred in the architecture of the past two decades are shown. After the gradual demise of the Modern Movement in architecture in the 1970s, the growth of historicist experiments were reinforced in a period of revisionist 'Post-Modernism'. A return to the Neo-Classical language of architecture occurred and a new interest grew up in nature and organic architecture. The book indicates too the revival of the so-called Expressionist tendencies. The introductory texts that act as decade openers for the two new sections chart some of the many changes of emphasis – particularly on aspects of pluralism and regionalism – in the architectural ideas of the past two decades. Side by side with fundamental changes that have occurred in national architectural attitudes and styles there has also been a remarkable growth in international connections, exchanges and experiments as well as in the proliferation of ideas through magazines, books and computer graphic techniques and other means of communication. The text and pictures chosen for the new sections of this revised edition of the volume reflect these international tendencies and the material is once again organised in the familiar contextual and chronological fashion.

The original pages of the book and the new sections both support the case for the twentieth century as one of the greatest periods of architectural innovation, creative revolution and spatial exploration. The century opened with a precursory, pioneer and heroic period and we can now see that that was followed by a transitory stage which in turn adjusted to the inevitability of evolutionary change and the reaffirmation of the well worked out basic principles of the 'New' and Modern Architecture.

Dennis Sharp
Epping Green, Hertford, UK 1991

PREFACE TO THE ORIGINAL EDITION

This book examines pictorially the architecture of the twentieth century. It has been designed in such a way that the non-specialist reader will be able to follow through in the buildings actually built the changes which have occurred over the last seventy years. The book does not ignore the many unbuilt, projected schemes, but in order to trace the development of twentieth-century architecture by built examples, the schemes have been isolated in the introductory sections. It is not possible, of course, to include every building of major importance that has been erected in the world over these seventy years, nor is it necessary to do so. The aim has been to underline the importance of those buildings which themselves have influenced successive structures and which have provided acceptable, and often highly original, solutions to specific design problems.

To a very large degree, therefore, this book differs from previous publications, particularly those illustrated books which concentrate on presenting a selection of buildings and unbuilt projects to prove a particular theory about the growth of the modern movement in architecture. It also differs from those books which have featured the work of individual architects. Those methods of historical analysis are both important and useful, but neither method adequately fulfils the need for a *visual* record arranged in chronological sequence. By juxtaposing buildings of the same date, regardless of their country of origin, many lessons can be drawn and a more accurate assessment can be made of a building's importance in relation to preceding and succeeding structures. Thus the generic importance of certain buildings becomes more obvious and pedigrees more clearly delineated.

I believe that it is only by a careful analysis of a building within the contexts of time, circumstances and motivation that its creative significance can be judged. Architecture is not like painting where a general consensus can be obtained on the validity of individual works by their popularity, critical acclaim and market price. With architecture, the basis of judgment is essentially experimental and, in the last analysis, the best guides to a building's performance and acceptability are probably provided by those people who react to it most strongly – the client-consumer, the occupant or the visitor. The reactions of these people may be at variance with the intentions of the designer, who is more likely to be viewing his work in relation to that of his colleagues.

Further than this, buildings which exist as physical objects – and not simply as designs on paper – can also be assessed from photographs, films and critical descriptions by independent critics and historians, and their success measured to some extent by referring to the aims and aspirations of their designers. I have attempted to use, whenever possible, all these methods in order to arrive at my own conclusions. In a number of cases I have had the opportunity of seeing the buildings at first hand, although far fewer than I would have liked.

The final selection of examples proved immensely difficult and purely external limitations had to be accepted in order to complete the book. I had originally intended to cover many more examples, but the limitation set by the publisher on the number of illustrations to be used was accepted as one criterion which imposed a not entirely unwelcome restriction on what could be incorporated in this survey. The publisher has not imposed any restrictions on the choice of subject or illustrations and the book, therefore, is essentially a personal selection based on my own reading and interpretation of the changing architectural scene over this century.

One of the chief difficulties which occured in assembling the main pictorial sections for this book was concerned with dating. The accurate dating of a building is a hazardous business and in many other publications serious mistakes have been made by the acceptance of loose dating. I have chosen the *completion* date as the most significant, but, wherever possible, have also indicated against each entry the date span for individual schemes from inception to completion, in parenthesis after the completion date itself. This overcomes to a large degree the confusion caused by 'date scrambling'.

The actual layout of the book is easy to follow: in most cases a building of major significance is illustrated by more than one picture and in many cases is accompanied by a plan or section. There are, however, a few obvious omissions caused either by the inaccessibility of the buildings or the unavailability of photographs of them or because they were of a temporary nature or have now been demolished or altered out of all recognition.

This book will be viewed as a personal anthology and some of my readers may well consider that I have been too partisan and far too speculative. During the time the book has taken to compile, I have been acutely aware of the shifts in emphasis in architectural thinking, of changes in fashion, of new discoveries and of rediscoveries of buried talent, as well as only too aware of the growing conviction among architects and students that the rug of 'modernism' has been pulled from under their feet. I am becoming more and more convinced that when the historian moves in to assess a period he is taking on the rôle of a removals man busily packing and labelling objects for storage. The 'heroic' period of the modern movement is not yet finally consigned to the warehouse but it is certainly on its way in the pantechnicon. So many fundamental changes took place in the 1960s in ideological and polemical positions among architects, students and critics that they have invalidated much of the work of the earlier part of the century. Even those bright architects who looked for inspiration within the restricted confines of the functional aesthetic of the pre-war period were accused of dabbling with Historicism, or at best engaged in some unholy rhetoric. The current situation is still confused, even chaotic, split by numerous arguments over values and meaning, styles, life-styles, manners, methods and mannerisms as well as complexities and contradictions about the rôle of the architect and the needs of the society in which he works. On top of all this, fundamental questions are being asked about the methods used by designers, about the techniques and the materials employed in building and the effect the designer's work has on the ever-widening definition of mans' environment.

I have attempted to stress in this book some of these shifts in emphasis, at least in so far as they can be interpreted through actual buildings. However, behind all this, I have attempted to indicate the particular kind of architecture that has emerged this century, which even today in many quarters is still misunderstood. It was founded on what Walter Gropius in 1936 called 'a new conception of building, based on realities' which brought with it 'a new conception of space' and 'superior technical resources' and embodied principles and practices that lead to its characteristic appearance.

Dennis Sharp
St Albans, 1972

INTRODUCTION

'It is the forms, the shapes and the patterns of architecture which everyone first apprehends and which also have survival value.'

Henry-Russell Hitchcock

The Derivation of Ideas in Twentieth-century Architecture

In reviewing a period of rapidly changing ideas, fashions and tastes the difficulty is that of finding the point in time at which to start the analysis. This difficulty faces anyone tracing the development of architecture in the twentieth century. What, in essence, is twentieth-century architecture? Is it different from previous architecture and, if so, in what way? What is meant by 'modern' architecture? Is its almost continuous use in the second half of the nineteenth century any different from the more portentous usage it gets today?

In attempting to provide a record of this century's architecture, I have purposely chosen examples which have had some generic importance or have played some innovatory part in architecture over the past ninety years. I use 'modern' as a keyword, synonymous with 'avant-garde'. It is an elastic term. As 'architectural modernism' it can be stretched to include the tangled progress of many revivals – neo-Baroque, neo-Liberty or the more recent 'new vernacular' – as well as the idiosyncrasies of inconsistent designers. What it does not cover is as pertinent as what it does: I have omitted the blubber of Edwardian Britain's magnificent but largely irrevelant edifices and their continental counterparts, the illiterate revival of interest in Classicism by Fascist states and the middle-of-the-road meanderings of government architects and public works departments around the world.

The buildings featured here are therefore not the only important buildings of their day, nor necessarily the ones that excited the most comment at the time. But I would argue that they do represent a forward-looking attempt to alter attitudes and conventions towards architecture. Why then should one isolate these buildings of the twentieth century if they tell only a partial story of what has been known since the 1830s as 'modern architecture' – an architecture, that is, which belongs to the modern age and is thus different from the architecture of all previous epochs? The answer to my own question is in a quotation from Professor E. Laube: 'Every definition or theory of architecture represents a certain kind of architecture. Every definition or theory of architecture gives an answer to what is architecture. Every manifestation of architecture favours the growth of a new definition or theory of architecture.' The Victorian 'moderns' sought for a change in kind. A change in terms of definition and theory was to take much longer.

The nineteenth century was an age of rapid growth and unprecedented expansion in virtually every field of human endeavour, in which new ideas shot from the heads of inventors, industrialists, philosophers and artists like the sparks from an early electric generator. The simile can be taken further: in the arts and architecture the nineteenth century was an 'electro-dynamic' age in which the forces excited by one fashionable current had an effect on others. Architecture was in a rut. With the ever-increasing knowledge of past styles, buildings no longer had to conform to established patterns or to the dictates of a patron or a region. With the demand for completely new types of building – railway stations, hospitals, universities and other educational buildings, as well as mass housing for industry's new

settlements – architects themselves became confused over matters of style, status and method.

A liberation of ideas and a common revolutionary feeling characterized the second stage of Modernism at the end of the nineteenth century, when the 'enemy' had been identified as revivalism and eclecticism. There was a conviction that whatever came after the battle had been won would represent a new order, a new aesthetic, a new sensibility, the hope of a new world. Ruskin, Morris, Darwin and Freud all contributed to the new sensibility. So, too, did British nuts-and-bolts specialists like Joseph Paxton, the engineer who built the sensational glass palace for the exhibition of 1851 in London, and W. H. Barlow, the engineer of the St Pancras train shed – the longest span arch in the world in 1864 – and countless other engineering innovators who transformed the world of solid, four-walled architecture into one depending on lightness, spectacular open spaces and structural adventure.

Rational Materials

The generally accepted view by architectural historians that the introduction of new materials almost miraculously caused a breakthrough on every sector of the design front is a myth. Virtually all the materials used, and most of the technical developments introduced by architects even well into the twentieth century, were known and had certainly been tried years before in the previous century while the more conventional techniques and materials, such as timber, stone, brick and concrete, go back to antiquity. The material that the engineers so confidently and prophetically handled was, of course, iron, both cast and wrought. It was not by any means a new material, but through improved methods of manufacture it had taken on the characteristics of a tough, all-purpose substitute for masonry and brick. Without the precedent set by the nineteenth-century engineers, the modern movement in architecture might have been very different, but few indeed were the architects who saw in iron engineering any real possibilities for a new architecture. Viollet-le-Duc, the French restorer, architect, theorist and encyclopædist, saw ways of producing the effects of stonework more economically and, above all, more rationally, with iron, but as John Summerson points out in an essay in his book *Heavenly Mansions*, 'Viollet-le-Duc's rationalism did not succeed, any more than the English fumbling with styles'.

Over a period of time, however, the influence of Viollet-le-Duc, of the Viennese architect and teacher Otto Wagner, of the Dutchman H. P. Berlage and of the German neo-Classicist Karl Friedrich Schinkel, manifestly created a climate of opinion in which a 'modern' architecture could emerge. A complex process of cumulative influences engendered the 'new art and architecture' which eventually manifested itself under the blanket term Art Nouveau, the French-inspired counter-part to the *fin-de-siècle* movement which spread through Europe like a bush fire after 1885. The effects of newness and originality were not tied to any one technological advance or new aesthetic idea, but were produced by a general sense of liberation from the repressive routines of for ever having to pour new wine into old bottles.

There is, however, one important technical discovery which does impinge on any discussion of the new architecture, and that is the developments in reinforced concrete from the 1890s onward. This artificial monolithic material derived from the combination of steel and concrete became possible because of the tensile and compressive qualities of the respective materials. It offered undreamt-of possibilities for architecture. It was a material as solid-looking as stone, but it overcame the problems of dead loads; it was relatively elastic, flexible and economic to produce; it was self-finishing, speedily erected, fireproof and easily calculable. The repercussions of reinforced concrete construction on twentieth-century architectural design were of paramount importance in establishing a new appearance to buildings. This plain-surfaced material, which did not easily respond to ornamentation either carved into or added to its faces, allowed for an architecture of plain wall surfaces with roofs like billiard tables, exactly along the lines predicted by the *fin-de-siècle* prophets.

Architecture and Ornament

Another myth is that of the plea for an architecture freed from ornamentation, an argument which is to be found in the writings of all the important modern-age theorists and architects during and after the Art Nouveau period. It is well known that Adolf Loos, the Viennese architect and journalist, equated ornament with crime, and that later architects such as Walter Gropius, Le Corbusier, J. J. P. Oud and Mies van der Rohe, carefully eliminated it from their work, only to replace ornament with the use of surface textures, the application of colour, the articulation of surfaces and the employment of precise geometrical shapes. The battle over ornament was related to the victory over eclectic mannerisms of previous architectural styles, particularly the superficial fripperies associated with the decorative revivals throughout Europe at the end of the century. The 'no ornamentation' arguments were part of a much wider plea for freedom in life. It was motivated by deep aesthetic desires for structural honesty and clearly defined volumes. This plainness of surface was provided by the very few examples of buildings erected by the leaders of the new school of thought. The impact of these must have been almost as shocking as the first glimpse of full frontal nudity on the stage a few years ago. The public and the critics responded to the new, 'naked' architecture of Loos, Hoffmann and Le Corbusier with a measure of revulsion – without realizing that here was the invention of a new form of architectural expression which depended on a simple building envelope, a dynamic aesthetic based on the grouping of masses, spatial interpenetration and hard surface edges.

In the past, ornamentation had implied an obscurity of contours and a softening of edges, but in spite of some critics the past itself was not anathema to all the new designers. Hans Poelzig write in 1906: 'We cannot do without the past in solving the architectural problems of our own day', particularly 'on the mastery of tectonic problems'. Where ornamentation had played an important part in the great periods of the past it was justifiable; it was not justifiable when applied surface deep and spoiled the 'organic clarity' of an architectural solution. According to Poelzig and his colleagues, the new architecture would be ruled by objective considerations rather than simply artistic ones, and would be characterized by a want of confusion over its tectonic purpose.

At the opening of this century, the attempt was being made to establish a connection between architectural theory and practice. It is, therefore, appropriate to consider here in some detail the theoretical aspects of the pictorial survey which follows, and to continue the discussion, serial fashion, in the introductions to the successive decades. It is, of course, a dangerous piece of ground on which to tread, and I am only persuaded to put my foot on it in the hope of dispelling some curious notions which have grown up over the years among the public, among architects, and among architectural students about 'style', the ambivalence of architecture as a science or an art, and making qualitative judgments about buildings. What may appear to one section of the public as 'square and oblong, angular structures', without the 'vestige of grace and nobility, elegance and charm' – as one recent newspaper editorial put it – may appear to another part to be a fitting representation of the present age. To both sections, what is being considered is the final *look* of a project. In doing so, one need not devalue the social importance of a building, nor the technical developments implied in it, nor any wider environmental issues that may impinge upon it. These are other ingredients in the architectural mix. But I am convinced that what the layman looks for in a building is far more fundamental and simplistic than most designers are prepared to admit. Liking or disliking a building is an instant decision made almost entirely on acceptable or non-acceptable features. The configuration of a building has an immediate impact. A well-qualified eye might be able to deduce from its exterior the organization and even the use of the building. But few people see more than the outside of the average non-public building, whether or not it purports to be good architecture, and as for its organization or use, that hardly comes into it.

It is not surprising that many of the younger generation now seek alternatives to the structure that polarizes its functions on a limited site. An open, participatory architecture, in which nodal points of concentrated human activity are linked, rather than as at present dispersed into separate compartments, augurs well for an urban society that has turned in on itself. Unfortunately, the experiments that have been made in this direction are still limited and chiefly confined to paper. Land values and availability still very largely rule the way that architecture has to go, and for most of the world's practitioners commissions are still 'one-off': a client (it may be one person or a vast institution) wishes to build and an architect is appointed to provide a building which will have aspirations to being 'architecture'. The problems to be solved will be not only those of appearance, scale, proportion and compatibility, but also of finance, function, space, enclosure, materials, finishes, servicing and structure. Many of these issues are at bottom theoretical ones, concerned with the aesthetics of architecture as interpreted by currently acceptable standards.

Architecture: A Social Art

These 'acceptable standards' and the wider problem of 'style', are what the aesthetics of architecture are about. The question of stylistic analysis has become confused, and matters have not been made any easier by the dismissive attitude of several generations of theorists who considered aesthetic speculation in architecture as unnecessary, if not a downright intrusion. This blind acceptance of architecture as an entirely skin-and-bones, or materials-and-function, art in which creative, social and and personal factors have little part to play is to me untenable. Architecture is a social art that impinges on man's primitive and cultural requirements. It is the consequence of existence within an identifiable place of

A, B: Joseph Paxton, *The Crystal Palace*, Hyde Park (later at Sydenham), London, 1851; at the time the greatest covered area in iron and glass and mostly prefabricated. Largest span 22m.
C, D: W. H. Barlow and R. M. Ordish, *Train Shed*, St. Pancras Station, London, 1888; the widest spanning structure in the world – 73m – until superseded by the *Gallerie des Machines.*

shelter. The aesthetic part of architecture is no less essential than any other aspect. It may be the fault of the historians that the professional aestheticians have largely ignored architecture in their discussions: architectural history having long been treated like some minor offshoot of the natural sciences, with branches, divisions, styles and sub-styles, as if responding to some sort of evolutionary pattern. Or perhaps because its data is less readily accessible than that of more limited and 'finer' arts? However, there is evidence that methods are changing, and that historians have lately been moving towards an enterprising method of analysis borrowed from the currently in vogue 'structuralist' theory in linguistics and anthropology which allows a wider displacement of subject-categories (such as 'value' and 'meaning') and appears to overcome some of the worst drawbacks of the chronological or progressive approach to history.

The fundamental aesthetic issues involved in the art of architecture still need to be elucidated. Whenever a designer puts pencil to paper he raises questions about space, enclosure, geometric organization, the treatment of surfaces and the use of materials. What the final physical artefact expresses must by its nature reveal an aesthetic attitude as well as technological, psychological and social ones. This exposes two basic approaches to design, one of them deriving from rationalism and seeing the creation of order as imperative, the other insisting that we recognize the complexity of any artefact.

The German architect and theorist, Hermann Muthesius, stated the rationalist, 'machine-conscious' viewpoint as early as 1901: 'Let the human mind think of shapes the machine *can* produce,' he wrote. 'Such shapes, once they are logically developed in accordance with what machines can do, we may certainly call artistic. They will satisfy, because they will no longer be imitations of handicraft, but *typical* machine-made shapes.' Type art became, for Muthesius and a number of his colleagues in the Deutscher Werkbund up to 1914, the highest ideal of art, in which everything was to be brought under the domination of a recognizable form.

Perception gives us our awareness of the phenomenal world, and an architectural theory has grown up which distinguishes between typical art and a vocabulary of forms based on an understanding of order *and* variety. 'Generally we judge and act on the basis of a few representative phenomena,' Christian Norberg-Schultz wrote in his book *Intentions in Architecture*, 'that is, we have an incomplete and superficial idea of the world of objects.' We are forced, Norberg-Schultz argues, to reorientate and change our existing attitude if we are to become more perceptive. We need to train our minds to understand complex and simple objects equally, and to train our eyes in such a way that they will influence our judgment in terms of patterns, shapes, forms and spaces. All is not what it seems – as most perceptualists like to demonstrate. Illusion abounds. Two silhouettes on a ground can look distorted. Two lines of equal length can be laid out in a way that makes them appear unequal. Architectual aesthetics, in the wide sense, is concerned with perceptions like these.

Unlike the study of history, the study of aesthetics is not just a method of chronological analysis. It stresses the recurrence of certain tendencies in art. It involves objective comparison and investigation of the forms and characteristics of works of art. The experience that is called aesthetic, Ogden and Richards point out in their book *The Foundations of Aesthetics* (1922), is bound up with contemplating, enjoying, admiring and appreciating an object. Aesthetics is concerned with problems of taste, artistic imagination, stylistic differences and similarities as much as with the nature and variation of forms.

Changing Aesthetic Concepts
Much writing on aesthetics has been and still is concerned with the definition of the primary concepts 'beauty' and

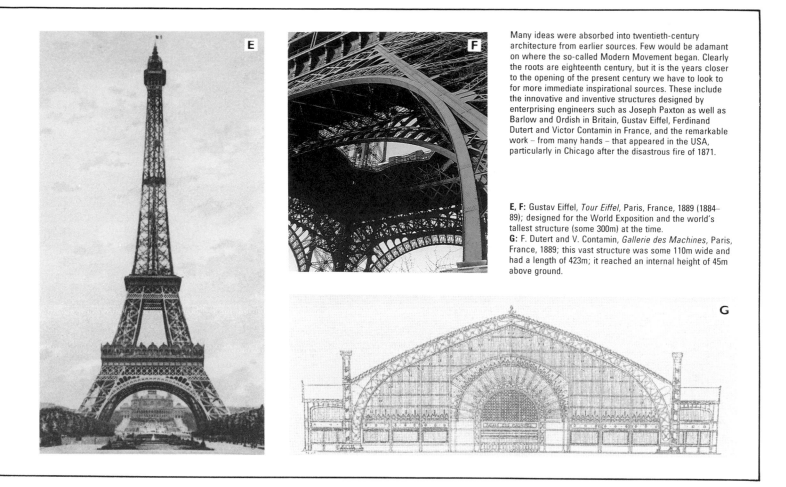

Many ideas were absorbed into twentieth-century architecture from earlier sources. Few would be adamant on where the so-called Modern Movement began. Clearly the roots are eighteenth century, but it is the years closer to the opening of the present century we have to look to for more immediate inspirational sources. These include the innovative and inventive structures designed by enterprising engineers such as Joseph Paxton as well as Barlow and Ordish in Britain, Gustav Eiffel, Ferdinand Dutert and Victor Contamin in France, and the remarkable work – from many hands – that appeared in the USA, particularly in Chicago after the disastrous fire of 1871.

E, F: Gustav Eiffel, *Tour Eiffel*, Paris, France, 1889 (1884–89); designed for the World Exposition and the world's tallest structure (some 300m) at the time.
G: F. Dutert and V. Contamin, *Gallerie des Machines*, Paris, France, 1889; this vast structure was some 110m wide and had a length of 423m; it reached an internal height of 45m above ground.

'truth'. Each age will reinterpret the forms and aims of works of art in terms of these changing concepts. Such definitions are transitory and often lack common validity. The value of studying aesthetics comes in the evaluation of the art productions of an epoch. Such evaluations are uncomfortably difficult to make, they are gropings with the mysteries of art experience, and have caused numerous polarities to be invented, such as Romantic/Classic, Dionysian/Apollonian, Emotion/Reason, Instinct/Intellect, Expressionism/Functionalism. They only add to the confusion.

At the beginning of the century, a great deal of thought on architectural aesthetics was still concerned with problems of style and with those that identified the forms of art and architecture with human forms and movements. For instance, Lipps's theory of empathy was applied to architecture, in which 'specific architectural forms, from the Greek column to the Gothic pointed arch, to the modern cantilever girder, represent frozen human movements'. This analogy, which linked both problems, was deceptive, though not useless. Empathy can be interpreted as 'the power of projecting one's own personality into – and so fully comprehending – the object of contemplation'. The state of mind of the observer of a work of art is stressed, and the prompting of mental responses which have an origin in human activity. This accords with the view of T. E. Hulme that 'any work of art we find beautiful is an objectification of our own pleasure in activity. Worth of line and form consists in the value of life which it contains for us.' It is obvious that the theory of empathy would be popular with architectural theorists. Its popularity runs from August Endell's exposition of Lippsian views (he had trained under the philosopher) within Munich 'secessionist' circles to the enigmatic English scholar, Geoffrey Scott, who published his 'Study in the History of Taste', *The Architecture of Humanism*, in 1914.

In Geoffrey Scott's beautifully written, yet wilfully romantic book, we find empathic thinking translated into an architectural context. *The Architecture of Humanism* influenced thinking about whether a building should 'express' its purpose or its structure, or 'express' the ethical qualities of truth, beauty, sincerity or even the personality and emotional approach of the architect. Unfortunately for Scott, it later became the concern of many architects to rationalize architecture in terms of the machine and of mechanistic theory. Side by side with the view that great architecture must always be efficient and fit for its purpose, this left most of the bodily metaphors far behind. It is, however, of interest to compare Scott's views with those of Endell, who wrote at the turn of the century that 'many forms give us pleasure. Rising forms arouse feelings other than those engendered by descending or spreading ones. The first ones (rising forms) own force and energy; the second ones, a certain light liveliness. A curve holds potency, a straight line sharpness and speed.'

'Space' and 'volume' – categories which were of concern to many aestheticians – existed as little as the idea of 'function' for the empathic theorists, although by the end of the first decade of this century the common identity of form with what Paul Zucker called 'dynamic empathy' (*dynamische Einfühlung*) was coming to be recognized. The implied basis of empathy is indicated by Reyner Banham in his book *Theory and Design in the First Machine Age*, and he sees a gradual fusion of the empathic theory with French academic ideas in the development of modern architectural theory: 'the change-over from the Lippsian idea of space (as felt volume), which is the sense it has in the writings of e.g. Muthesius, to the later concept of space as a three-dimensional continuum, capable of metrical sub-division, without sacrifice of its continuity, appears to depend largely for its assimilation to the Blanc/Gaudet (French academic) idea of composition' and to the 'extension of that idea to operate in three dimensions instead of the two dimensions of the building-plan or the picture surface, both of which are two-dimensional fields metrically subdivided without sacrifice of their continuity'.

Related to the empathic view, but by no means identical with it, was the intuitive theory of Benedetto Croce, 'in which art is defined as the expression of sentiment, a pure but vital act of the imagination'.

R. G. Collingwood, the Cambridge art theorist, whose book *Principles of Art* was well known to architects, first developed his ideas along Crocean lines, but he later discarded them. It was an important decision. He felt that art could not be just imaginative activity; the artist is the one who utters what everyone else feels or senses but cannot express. Art is the faithful transcription of surrounding events and transactions and the welding of collective intimations into individual images. This leads on inevitably to considering the image in terms of symbolism – an area of thought which has been developed by the American philosopher, Suzanne Langer, in relationship to music. Architecture, as articulate form in her definition, must become a self-sufficient image, an expression of feeling, not simply a stimulus to it.

The Question of Style

Buildings, as things made by man, as artefacts, are conditioned by their designer's knowledge and inspiration and by prevailing trends in construction techniques and in aesthetics. An inadequate designer might like to dodge the issue of aesthetics, but he could hardly do his job satisfactorily without recourse to acceptable standards of construction and technical feasibility. Then when the architectural historian comes along to assess a building for its merit, he will consider it in relation, in time, to earlier and later buildings, and in place, to the cultural context of the place in which it was built. A broad analysis is then possible across national frontiers, in relation to the exchange and dissemination of ideas. The more obviously recognizable qualities that are found in works of art, in the work of architects and in groups of buildings are often described as 'style'.

Already, the modern movement in architecture has been parcelled up and carefully labelled by experts and pigeon-holed in the categories 'International style', 'Expressionism', 'Elementarism', 'Constructivism', 'Futurism' and 'Functionalism'. These can be useful labels, and I employ them in this book, but it would be misleading for the reader to see in them more than a convenient classification when discussing characteristics and families of forms.

Use of the word 'style' is also based on the conviction that it helps to elucidate the correspondences between various buildings, and heightens an awareness of the positions held in common by various designers and groups. A succinct definition of 'style' has been provided by Meyer Shapiro, and on it I base my own ideas: 'the constant form – and sometimes the constant elements, qualities and expression – in the art of an individual or group . . . above all, a system of form with a quality and a meaningful expression through which the personality of the artist, and the broad outlook of a group, are visible'. In writing of literary style, John Middleton Murray further extends the etymology of 'style': 'a true style . . . must be unique', idiosyncrasy therefore 'appears to be essential to style'. The architecture of the past ninety years bears this out. The prefacing of a new stylistic framework often occurred through the idiosyncrasies of certain creative designers or theorists. But the designer and the theorist make awkward bedfellows, and at the beginning of this century they were on either side of the mattress.

The 'Beaux-Arts', or French academic, approach to design was, at the turn of the century, the strongest single influence on theoretical writings by both architects and critics of architecture, but in practice, however, important theoretical and visual changes were taking place which were unrelated to any 'formal' concepts. These changes were due to the activities of a small number of people, mainly those involved in the revolutionary atmosphere of Art Nouveau.

In France, the academic teaching of the Ecole des Beaux-Arts, and the firmly established rationalist interest in struc-

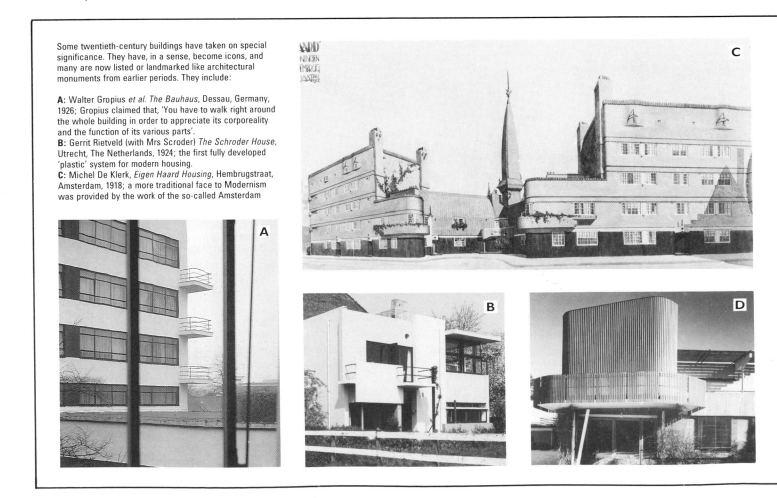

Some twentieth-century buildings have taken on special significance. They have, in a sense, become icons, and many are now listed or landmarked like architectural monuments from earlier periods. They include:

A: Walter Gropius *et al. The Bauhaus*, Dessau, Germany, 1926; Gropius claimed that, 'You have to walk right around the whole building in order to appreciate its corporeality and the function of its various parts'.
B: Gerrit Rietveld (with Mrs Scroder) *The Schroder House*, Utrecht, The Netherlands, 1924; the first fully developed 'plastic' system for modern housing.
C: Michel De Klerk, *Eigen Haard Housing*, Hembrugstraat, Amsterdam, 1918; a more traditional face to Modernism was provided by the work of the so-called Amsterdam

ture outlined in Auguste Choisy's *Histoire*, lasted well into the twentieth century. The Beaux-Arts attitude was based on principles which the English architect Alan Colquhoun has defined as 'principles of plan organization and form composition whose foundations went back to eighteenth-century theories of psychological response, and to that recurrence of Neoplatonic doctrine which had been enshrined in the academies'. It would be too long a task to describe the effect of the Ecole and its subsidiaries, as its tendrils stretched to almost every educational establishment teaching architecture throughout the world. I do, however, want to establish here that it was at the point where academic education met, or in Colquhoun's words, 'collided' with the 'revolutionary new structural techniques and new social consciousness' that modern architecture was born.

The immediate effect of the collision was to widen the divergence between practice and theory, producing a dichotomy that was only finally overcome by the international acceptance of the functional aesthetic in the late 1920s and early 1930s. This dichotomy was pronounced in Germany, where the basic concepts of the theorists seemed, at the beginning of the century, to contradict the prevailing trends of the creative artists and architects. One of the rare examples of a man who combined the practical with the theoretical concept was August Endell, already mentioned. He commanded a unique position. That the aesthetics of modern architecture were developed pragmatically after practical experiments had been successful was indicated in an article by Paul Zucker (*Journal of the Society of Architectural Historians*, 1951), and it was here that the foundations of the so-called modern movement were perhaps weakest. The erection of socio-functional theory on that basis was doomed to collapse. Paradoxically, the architects themselves had designed their footings on a substratum of fashionable trends.

I do not mean that Functionalism, material Functionalism, as a concept has been proved incapable of making good architecture. That would be completely wrong. But the facts seem to point to the conclusion that, except for the work of the really 'advanced' modern architects such as Loos, Gropius, Le Corbusier, Mies van der Rohe, Mendelsohn and, later, Duiker, Rietveld, Oud and Stam, and their finest interpreters and disciples, there has been little understanding of the purpose and concepts of the 'new architecture' itself. For lesser men, it skeletonized the idea of the conceptual whole and produced the dry bones of plagiarism. Dissatisfaction with plagiarism has inevitably led back to an emphasis on the differences and misunderstandings that arose in Germany and Holland during the formative years of the 1920s, when the aesthetic contest was one of function, form and/or space *versus* expression – a contest in which the Expressionist argument was forced to yield to the Objectivist. Both had, in fact, more in common than is generally conceded, and although such out-and-out romantics as Mendelsohn, Häring and Scharoun resolutely pursued individualistic, free-form courses, their ideas were essentially orientated towards function.

Form and Space
The real duality existed in the contrast between the technical, social and functional basis, as initially propounded by Adolf Loos and later adapted by Le Corbusier, and the theorist's concern for problems of space and form, questions of 'perceptual form' (*Wirkungsform*) and 'actual form' (*Daseinsform*) and arguments about the 'formation of space' (*Raumbildung*). In spite of such differences on basic issues, both theorist and practising architect met to overcome their common enemy, nineteenth-century revivalism and eclecticism.

The aesthetic qualities of space, volume and form and their visualization interested the theorists, while the preoccupation of the practising architects was with form, material, technique and function. To underline the divergence of ideas, it is worth

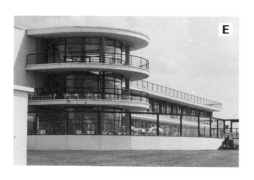

School, who widely employed the use of brickwork and stone detailing.
D: Alvar Aalto, *Villa Mairea*, Noro, Noormarken, Finland, 1938–9; Aalto's finest attempt in the pre-war period to humanize his Modern architecture and, indeed, to link it to regional materials.
E: Serge Chermayeff and Eric Mendelsohn, *De La Warr Pavilion*, Bexhill on Sea, 1936; in the *diaspora*, German Modernism came to Britain. This is probably the best example of that cultural integration.
F: Hans Scharoun, *Schminke House*, Lobau, Germany, 1929; one of the most successful of all the early functional/organic buildings.
G: Felix Candela, *Restaurant*, Xochimilco, Mexico, 1958; the engineering aesthetic transferred to thin shell concrete construction.
H: Aldo Van Eyck, *Orphanage* (now Berlage Institute for Architecture), Amsterdam, 1960; the flagship of post-war modern architecture, Van Eyck's 'icon' was in danger of demolition in 1980. It now has a new and useful life.
I: R. Piano and R. Rogers, *Pompidou Centre*, Paris, 1976; few buildings display such a close involvement of theory and practice as the famous Parisian art centre, nor for that matter the growing internationalism in architecture.

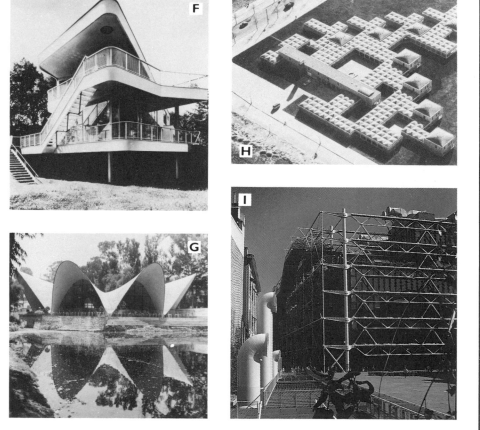

mentioning that it was Schmarsow's least important theory – purpose and function influencing form – that came closest to practising architects' aims. Though even here, as Zucker indicates, architects were satisfied if the purpose was functionally expressed in the layout and then simply transferred to the façade, while Schmarsow argued that the creation of space itself was the decisive factor. Schmarsow implied that the organization of the plan was only a natural symptom of all human activity.

Before the stagnant years of the First World War, the 'theorists' were concerned with problems of the aesthetic meaning of space and volume (inner and outer space) and their inter-relationship, as well as with the symbolic and cognitive character of architecture. At the same time, the work of Frank Lloyd Wright in America was concerned with what he referred to as the 'dissolution of inner space into outer space'. Wright's ideas, and Mies van der Rohe's immediately after the war, were both towards simplicity. Mies aimed at a classical purity which was later made explicit in his buildings and in such epigrams as 'less is more'. Wright strove for 'organic simplicity'.

Other German theorists interested in architecture abruptly denied the functional implications of architectural form. Leopold Ziegler presented a theory with little constructional emphasis and pleaded for 'a necessary minimum of structural elements'. It was possible for theorists to take their stand at various points along the architectural fence, considering architecture to be either 'space' or 'volume', or a combination of the two. Such categories would be again subdivided to express some individual opinion, usually in relation to a particular and acceptable definition. Many German architects of the 1920s considered 'space' to be the essence of architecture, so it was a 'twofold creation of space' limited by 'volume' – function being relegated to a secondary role. Architecture was thus represented as the relationship of interior space, volume (which determined interior as well as exterior space) and the general exterior space.

From this summary it can be seen that the theorists were generally agreed on a minimalization of functional expression, and were chiefly interested in the spatial and symbolical approach. The decisive contribution of the practising architect was in the expression of a building's function in its façades, and in the whole new working otu of an aesthetic based on the symbolism of the 'machine' idea.

The Machine Aesthetic
By 1925, having absorbed outside influences such as the technical innovations of engineering, the spatial ideas of the architectural theorists and of the painters, the ideas of the new generation of scientists, and the visionary ideas of its own Expressionist phase, architecture clearly expressed the aspirations of the Functionalist formulators. The leaders of the modern movement had absorbed the painterly concept of inter-penetration, the De Stijl-Elementarist spatial organization as well as the Wrightian principles of outer and inner space, and conceived an architecture in three-dimensional terms, freed from the principles that had been inherent in previous architecture. Academic concepts of voume and space still played some part in the new, rational attitude – as one can see in the work and theory of Le Corbusier, Gropius and Mies – but the dominant aesthetic considerations related to functional organization on plan, and to what could be described as the visual extension of a mechanistic analogy, the so-called 'machine aesthetic'. This did not mean that architects envisaged blowing up simple machines to the size of a building, but rather that they drew their analogies in terms of format, shape and efficient use from the products of engineering.

Elements of Cubism and Futurism were also to be found in the architecture, especially the housing, of the early 1920s. This was far more than just a simple-minded attempt to apply art forms to building design (although some projects produced in Czechoslovakia, Poland and even Denmark possess a curt, Mediterranean geometricality that was both stark and insipid, and totally out of keeping with the traditions of those countries). Sigfried Giedion made a valiant attempt to make out a watertight case for Cubism in architecture in his book *Space, Time and Architecture*. He wrote: 'The method of presenting spatial relationships which the Cubists developed has furnished the plastic principles of the present-day visual approach.' His case seems to be backed up all the time by the knowledge that Le Corbusier had joined with Ozenfant and Dermée in 1917 and produced their own kind of puritanical Cubism which they called 'Purism'.

'Purism', says Giedion, coming from French soil, 'was the closest of all to the aim of Cubism and, at the same time, to architecture.' That is a half-truth only. While Le Corbusier and Ozenfant were innovators in painting, *French* Cubism itself had very little to do with architecture and those aspects of architectonic form that Giedion and other historians allude to. It was a different matter in its exported form. For the Dutch 'De Stijl' group, Cubism was, according to H. L. C. Jaffé, 'the most essential phase' in its development. Van Doesburg refers to it as 'the critical point in evolution'. But why? Probably because Cubism 'raised to the first rank those elements which, in illusionistic painting, had held a secondary place (such as plane, colour, proportion)'. Jaffé goes on to say: 'This *Umwertung* (revaluation) of plastic qualities from secondary into primary factors is, indeed, the only essential expression of relations'. The same could be said for architecture. Van Doesburg conceived his well-known exploded house plan as a pattern of relationships between vertical and horizontal planes, in which space is cut, shaped and heaved through and over the planar surfaces. Translated into actual building, as in Rietveld's house for Mrs Schröder-Schräder of 1924, the De Stijl aesthetic takes on a significance denied it in the two-dimensional world of painting and drawing. Here was a new plastic system, complete in itself, 'modern' in substance and appearance, validation of a designer's ability to create a distinct form-language appropriate to his age.

After 1927, the utilitarian aspect of the international Functionalist movement further underlined the universality of the rectangular, hard-edged system. It looked as if it was technologically correct for the age, and the theory which backed it up appeared to support the words of Bruno Taut that 'necessity is by far the greatest incentive to inventive activity'.

Up to the period in the 1950s, when building work started again in earnest throughout the world, the concept of an architecture of necessity prevailed. Utility and austerity were virtues enhanced by the Second World War as a penance for the wasteful luxury of expending men's lives and subsidizing a destructive technology. Architecture only fulfils its rôle in enriching men's minds and a nation's culture in times of peace. The world has seen so many changes since the 1950s that architecture no longer fits comfortably into an evolutionary scheme. The consistency of expression with each era, the occurrence and repetition of artistic and design trends during the first half of this century have given way to a more anarchic situation, and to a greater awareness among architects of the social context of their work, and to the desire to synthesize what Nervi has called the 'characteristic feelings of (our) own time' into 'forms valid for everyone'. Architecture has no single goal, the architect himself no isolated brief. The architect's design responsibility is, in the last analysis, shared with the society in which he works, and is itself a reflection of that society's changing needs, values and standards.

Decade 1900

Hector Guimard. *Métro entrance*, Paris, France. 1900
Detail of one of the glazed pavilions (see page 15)

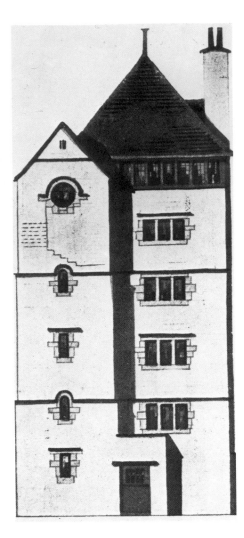

At the beginning of the new century, Art Nouveau provided the transition from the eclecticism prevalent in nineteenth-century art and architecture to the new attitudes and experiments that were to form the basis of twentieth-century architecture and design. Art Nouveau may have evoked nineteenth-century sensibilities, but it was also a powerful purging force. It produced a 'gloss' art of surface application and decoration which unhinged the doors of perception to a wilder, exaggerated and vital body of forms and means of expression. It also enlarged the audience for works of art, for Art Nouveau was a *popular* art style, the unwitting progenitor of participatory people's art (for example, posters, book covers, theatre costumes), an artistic mechanism through which the energizing influence of popular culture and national myths was released.

Art Nouveau might be viewed as an all-purpose extending ladder put up within the structure of 'Fine Art' and used by designers to climb out of stylistic formalism into a period of expressive freedom. During the period, which runs from the 1880s to well into the first decade of the twentieth century, the chords of individualism were touched. A disparate, and often confusingly divergent, body of theory emerged that attempted to link national Romanticism with progressive and aesthetically 'scientific' ideas – naturalism with 'arts and crafts', rococo images with bourgeois life-styles. But whereas the spirit of rococo forms was that of an exuberant hybrid writhing within the framework of Classicism, Art Nouveau exuded a wilder impulse, in which freedom, individuality, sex and pleasure were to play an important part. The 'gay', abandoned 'nineties gave way in a seemingly effortless way to 'Eros Modern Style' and to decadence. The seriousness found in the writings of social reformers after the middle of the nineteenth century was replaced by an infectious jollity and bohemianism in the capital cities of Europe. Is it any wonder that in this atmosphere the curvaceous linearity of interiors, objects and even buildings should follow?

The apotheosis of the Art Nouveau was reached in 1900 at Paris. At the World Exposition of that year held on the banks of the Seine, the 'new art' designers worked side by side with extreme pseudo-revivalists who were getting out of their bloodstreams the most grotesque parodies of previous styles. Oddities such as Binet's Château d'Eau and the cockleshell entrance portal to the exhibition pushed Rococo to a point of absolute, if splendid, absurdity, while Samuel Bing's exhibit of six 'rooms beautiful' brought about the realization of the full, mature Art Nouveau style.

In Paris, too, during Exposition year, the stations on the Métropolitain underground system, designed in a remarkable vegetal manner by Hector Guimard, were opened, taking the excesses of the 'new art' to the man in the street.

In other parts of Europe, new developments continued unabated. The Glasgow Four (Charles Rennie Mackintosh, Margaret and Frances Macdonald and Herbert MacNair) began to make an impact on the artists of the Vienna Secession. Hendrik Berlage, the important Dutch architect and theorist, completed his work on the

Above:
Elevation of Tower House, Bognor, Sussex by
C. F. A. Voysey

Above:
H. P. Berlage (1856–1934)
Above right:
Hector Guimard (1867–1942)
Otto Wagner (1841–1918)
Right:
Competition design for a rail terminus at Karlsruhe,
Germany, by Rudolf Bitzan, 1905

Amsterdam Exchange and exerted a considerable influence on the generation of architects whose work began to appear before the end of the decade. Seemingly quite independently, Antonio Gaudí in Barcelona continued to erect the most remarkable and technologically advanced buildings of the day. Although all were contemporaries of continental Art Nouveau, these British, Dutch and Spanish personalities were only superficially connected with the mainstreams in Belgium, France and Germany.

It was at Darmstadt that the first fully worked-out group of buildings in what might be called an Art Nouveau style, or Jugendstil, appeared. The Austrian architect Josef Maria Olbrich, a pupil of Otto Wagner, was employed by the Grand Duke Ernst-Ludwig of Hessen to design a housing colony for artists and an exhibition centre, proposed for the city in 1899. In 1901 the main exhibition and studio house were opened and up to 1908 a number of adjacent buildings and houses, including the famous local landmark, the Hochzeitsturm by Olbrich, were added. One of the houses built in the first phase was by a young artist and book-illustrator, Peter Behrens, who up to 1901 had not tried his hand at architecture. Before the end of the decade, his was to become the best-known name in European architectural circles and his industrial buildings for the German electrical combine AEG were among the most admired buildings in Europe.

Behrens, his contemporary Hans Poelzig and the younger architect Walter Gropius (who spent some time as a pupil in Behrens's office) had entered a sphere of design that had been avoided by the *prima-donna* architects of the nineteenth century: industrial architecture. These Germans admired their own indigenous neo-Classicism, but they had also instinctively grasped opportunities to provide rational solutions to problems of factory design and of structures that previously would probably have been left to civil engineers. They dealt with water-mills and water-towers, machine sheds and storage buildings. By working on such problems, the architects of the twentieth century associated themselves with the splendid structures produced by the nineteenth-century engineers and the innovations – both technical and aesthetic – possessed by these constructions.

If Art Nouveau is seen as a nineteenth-century movement that overlapped the twentieth, then we can interpret engineering structures like Paxton's Crystal Palace, Eiffel's Tower, the succession of *Halles des Machines* at World Exhibitions and the countless train-sheds in Britain and on the Continent, in terms of twentieth-century ideas of lightness, economy, practicability and rationalism. The German Werkbund, founded in 1907 at Munich but conceived as early as 1901, brought about more clearly than any other contemporary association of architects, designers, craftsmen, industrialists and educationalists the fusion of the art of architecture and the science and technology of engineering. Born of high German idealism, its influence, both through the work of its members and in its publications, on architectural developments, and indeed 'cultural aims' generally, extended up to the Second World War.

Martin Nyrop, *City Hall*, Copenhagen, 1888–1905. One of the earliest examples of Scandinavian National Romanticism in brickwork

The social and utopian settlements at the turn of the century in England had repercussions throughout the world. The garden city ideas were discussed in Cadbury's Bourneville, nr Birmingham in 1901. The Green at Bourneville with Rest House.

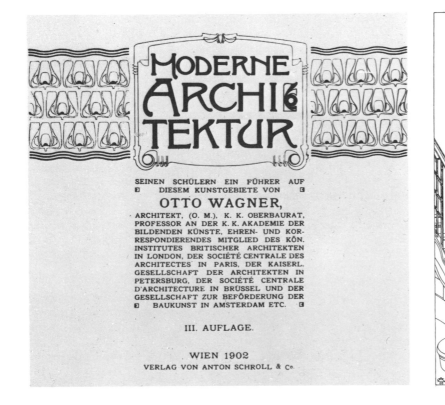

Left:
Title-page of Wagner's *magnum opus*
'Jugendstil' detail of a baluster for a house, Posen (Poznan), by Alfred Grenander, 1905

Above:
Kallio Church, Finland, by Lars Sonck, an exponent of National Romanticism

To the Werkbund, as well as to other organizations like the Vienna Werkstätten (Workshops), machinery provided a stimulus to standardization and the mass-production of objects which can be seen as anticipatory of the simple, geometric aesthetic of the new architecture. The simplified forms of machine-made objects were also acknowledged as having evolved from 'the spirit of the machine itself'.

Beside these technological and *Maschinenstil* aims, the Werkbund also shared with its sister organizations a great admiration for the domestic architecture and design work produced in England around the turn of the century, as well as an interest in the education establishments for designers that had been set up in London, in particular Lethaby's Central School of Arts and Crafts, which had opened in 1894.

Even after the virtual eclipse of British leadership in the arts by 1905, the cumulative effects of the English Free Architecture movement and the Glasgow school were still being felt throughout Europe. A definitive three-volume work, *Das Englische Haus* (1904–05) by Hermann Muthesius, had done much to popularize the more advanced designs of English domestic architects. In particular, the work of the individualistic and somewhat idiosyncratic architect C. F. A. Voysey appealed to the Germans with its clean lines, simple white interiors and functional organization. Indeed, up to the Second World War, Voysey's work was interpreted as that of a pioneer modern architect, a claim which the architect himself vigorously denied in an issue of the *Architects' Journal* in 1935: 'I have no claim to anything new. . . . Steel construction and reinforced concrete are the real culprits responsible for the ultra-modern architecture of today.' Earlier, with equal zest he had described the classical tradition so often pillaged by his contemporaries in England as a 'crutch for fools'. Ambivalent though Voysey may have been, there was in his buildings a certain recognizable and associative theme that possessed qualities of originality and newness. Muthesius himself recognized Voysey as the most important member of what he called the 'Norman Shaw Group'. Some years later, Henry-Russell Hitchcock underlined the generic importance of Voysey's own house, The Orchard at Chorley Wood in Hertfordshire, completed in 1900, as a model 'parodied *ad infinitum* first by architects and then by builders'.

A further, and more tenuous, connection with the English domestic tradition can be found in the work of that other important innovator of the first decade, the Viennese architect Adolf Loos. His modern movement pedigree is recognized not only in his stark, classically inspired buildings but also through some of the pithiest epigrams of his generation, advocating a utilitarian basis for living. His essay that equated ornament with crime, first published in 1908 and later republished in French in Le Corbusier's magazine *L'Esprit Nouveau*, is a key document of twentieth-century architectural thinking, while his house on Lake Geneva of 1904 can be viewed as a remarkable prototype of the modern house.

France, too, had its early innovators, notably the engineer/architect Auguste Perret and a young student Tony Garnier. Garnier's main contribution to ideas emerged in a plan he drew up between 1901 and 1904 for an industrial city. Although not officially published until 1917, this plan at the time it was drawn incorporated the most advanced ideas on 'zonal' planning and the typical buildings it incorporated virtually prophesied the standard features of the reinforced concrete architecture of the 'twenties and 'thirties. On top of this, a number of technical innovations that were years ahead of their time, such as electric heating systems and service ducts, were included in the scheme.

Perret's inventive work in the use of reinforced concrete has been obscured by the common accusation of more recent historians that he developed into an Academic Formalist later in his career. His importance to twentieth-century architecture cannot be overlooked, for his early buildings were of enormous significance. The apartment block in the rue Franklin (1903) and the Garage Ponthieu (1906), both in Paris, were imaginative steps towards disciplined and 'honest' reinforced concrete construction. And in the Paris of that day they formed a suitably elegant contrast to the accelerated ageing-process that Art Nouveau had undergone after 1905. They really were an expression of French 'new art and architecture', in contrast to the ineffective, commercialized plagiarism that became rampant in art circles after the days of the individualistic designer were over and the new art itself had been transferred into machine production to meet the ever-growing needs of the market-place.

Art Nouveau was soon reduced to what Erich Mendelsohn, one of Van de Velde's most admiring disciples, later referred to as a 'marketable excrescence'. For architecture, it had, however, alongside other divergent ideas and disparate innovations, served its transitional purpose. It had created a climate of opinion for experiment, creativity and that popular sport of later years, avant-gardism, and thus paved the way for the emergence of a new and more dynamic stage of development during the next decade.

1900

Hector Guimard. *Métro entrances,* Paris, France.
1900 (1898–1900)
Right: the open-pavilion type
Below: the fan-shaped half-pavilion type of Métro
entrance
Centre right: the enclosed type of pavilion entrance

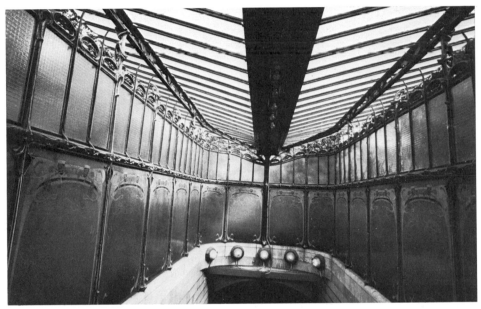

René Binet. *Château d'Eau,* Exposition, Paris, France. 1900
Bottom Right: general view

Although the Métropolitain was not completed until 1901, the most spectacular
entrances and pavilions designed by Guimard had been seen by a large number of
visitors to the Paris Exposition in 1900.
Guimard called himself an 'architecte d'art',
creating in his work a strict structural bias
based on naturalistic principles related to
the kind of ornamentation found in the
paintings, sculpture and graphics of the
Art Nouveau. The sensuous forms, the
repetitive panelling and the elongated,
stalk-like structural supports were, in the
Métro designs, combined in a number of
ways, in some cases to provide enclosed or
half-closed pavilions, in other cases open-
topped entrances. A few examples still exist.

The brilliance of Guimard's innovations
is beyond question but it is useful to
juxtapose his work with that of Binet's
Château d'Eau – the most spectacular
exhibit at the Exposition – for this clearly
shows the contrast between a gestating
modernism and a wild, woolly nineteenth-
century eclecticism.

1900

Victor Horta. *Hôtel Solvay*, Brussels, Belgium. 1900
(1894–1900)
Right: recent photograph of the façade on Avénue Louise

Victor Horta. *Hôtel Aubecq*, Brussels, Belgium. 1900
(1899–1900) (Demolished)
Below: general view
Right: detail of the glazed roof above the staircase

C. A. Voysey. *The Orchard* (architect's own house),
Chorley Wood, Herts., England. 1900 (1899–1900)
Above: staircase and entrance hall
Right: the architect's elevational drawing
Bottom: general view of The Orchard

Horta and Voysey were both highly
original architectural designers and both
contributed a great deal to the changing
sensibilities of the period. Neither, however,
can be regarded as essentially twentieth-
century architects. The form-language is
eclectic in the case of Horta, and pleasantly
English-rural in the case of Voysey. What
they contributed to twentieth-century architecture may, therefore, well have been
fortuitous. With Horta it was a confident
use of structural elements and glass as well
as a freedom of surface, with Voysey a
marked simplicity of treatment right
throughout his building. The house at
Chorley Wood, an expanded suburb of
London on the Metropolitan line, was built
by Voysey for his own occupation. The plan
was rectangular and subdivided into the
usual domestic rooms, but with the addition
of a school room. Upstairs, under the low,
oversailing roof, there were five bedrooms
situated around a central staircase. The
simple white interior caught the imagination
of the architectural world by its frugality as
well as for its 'fitness' of purpose (a favourite
phrase of the architect). Here in essence was
the root of the mechanistic and 'efficient'
aesthetic.

Horta's town-houses served a more
artistic purpose.

1901

Victor Horta. *L'Innovation Department Store,* Rue Neuve,
Brussels, Belgium. 1901 (Destroyed in 1967)
Right: the main street façade
Below: exterior and interior detail of the ironwork

Josef-Maria Olbrich. *Ernst-Ludwigs-Haus,* Darmstadt, Germany 1901 (1899–1901)
Above: main entrance porch and doorway
Below: plan of the Artists' Colony at Darmstadt

Peter Behrens. *Own house,* Darmstadt, Germany. 1901
Left: general view of the Behrens House
Below: Behren's own drawing of the front elevation

Horta's Grands Magasins à L'Innovation is a building without a direct precedent in the history of architecture, but not without relatives. Working towards this unique structure over many years, Horta produced a remarkable collection of iron and glass buildings which are clearly related to the great nineteenth-century Parisian store interiors, and probably to the covered arcades and galleries that sprung up throughout Europe during that century. But this example is a fully mature art nouveau building, comprehensive down to its last iron, glass or granite detail. That it should have been allowed to be destroyed in 1966–67 is deplorable. The decoration wavers between obvious naturalism and evidences of abstract form.

The building had four storeys and was divided horizontally into three bays. The wide central bay ran through two storeys, topped by the vault that appears as a decorative feature on the 'fairground' frontage.

The setting up of an Artist's Colony at Darmstadt brought to the city the noted Austrian architect J.-M. Olbrich and the virtually unknown designer Peter Behrens. Both men were to have an immense influence on the course of twentieth-century architecture. The Olbrich building exhibits the flat surfaces and simple forms of the modern movement and represents the continuation of an approach begun in Vienna. Behrens began his architectural career with his own house.

Many buildings were added at Darmstadt and some of these are referred to on later pages.

1901/2

C. H. Townsend, *Whitechapel Art Gallery* (formerly East End Gallery), London, 1901 (1895–1901)

C. H. Townsend. *The Horniman Free Museum,* Forest Hill, London, England. 1902 (1900–02)
Right: contemporary view of the Horniman Museum

Henri van de Velde. *Interior design of the Folkwang Museum,* Hagen, Germany. 1902 (1900–02)
Below left: the staircase to the upper gallery
Below right: the entrance hall

Occupying a narrow, sloping site, the Horniman Museum in south London was designed in 1900 but not completed until 1902. Designed by Townsend, who had earlier produced the interesting White-chapel Art Gallery, the Horniman is a good example of English 'Free School' work of the period, and is complementary to the continental Art Nouveau work. It, too, is simple yet with historical connotations. The long, rectangular building is contrasted with a tower feature that bears the hallmarks of *fin de siècle* individualism.

Art Nouveau by 1902 had come to the Ruhr in the hands of one of its founders, Henri van de Velde, and to the private museum of Karl Osthaus at Hagen in West-phalia. For the Folkwang Museum, Van de Velde created splendid new spaces inhabited by nymph-like figures in the elongated style.

The wilder impulses of Art Nouveau can be seen in the incredibly plastic, almost neo-Baroque, version of the style in D'Aronco's Turin exhibition pavilion in 1902. The Viennese school's influence can be detected in the coupled columns on the ground floor, and there is the flamboyance of French exhibition architecture in the row of elegant ladies supporting the dome with out-stretched arms.

D'Aronco's design had won an open com-petition, and a leading historian of Art Nouveau, Henry Lenning, claims that this pavilion 'celebrated' the international triumph of the style.

The members of the Nancy school in eastern France were the real hand-craftsmen of Art Nouveau. Many of them trained as architects, and the outstanding architect among them was Emile André. The picture of the interior of the Maison Fernbach shows the impeccable craftsmanship and beauty of his furnishing and interior design.

Raimondo D'Aronco. *Central Pavilion,* International Exposition of Decorative Arts, Turin, Italy. 1902 (Demolished)
Above: general view

Emile André. *Maison Fernbach,* Nancy, France. 1902
Below: interior

1903

Right: original sketch of the new *Beurs* by H. P. Berlage

Below: interior of the Exchange

Herman Gesellius, Armas Lindgren, Eliel Saarinen, *Hvitträsk*, Kirkkonummi, Finland, 1903 (1901–1903)

Auguste Perret. *Apartments, 25-bis rue Franklin,* Paris, France. 1903 (1902–03)
Left: the street elevation with the twin concrete-framed balconies rising up the full height of the main front

Hector Guimard. *Castel Henriette,* Sèvres, France. 1903
Below: the south façade

Berlage, the Dutch master-architect of the turn of the century, prepared a number of designs for the 'Merchants' Exchange' on the Damrak, along neo-Renaissance lines. He won the competition for the building in 1897. The building erected stems from the final project designs of 1898.

A polyglot building finished in red brick, with stonework trimmings, which owes as much to Viollet-le-Duc's theories as it does to the long line of craft tradition in Holland, it had a profound and lasting influence on the whole of that line of architects and artists, collectively called the 'Amsterdam school'. They perpetuated a rich, and essentially more fantastical grammar of decorative

brickwork than Berlage's Exchange possessed, but the aspects of spatial organization and careful detailing in the building were of paramount importance.

The introduction of reinforced concrete as a structural material began in the 1890s in France, but the first extensive use of the material for domestic architecture was made in the Perret flats. It was not a structurally 'advanced' building, indeed its trabeated construction was reminiscent of previous timber and iron examples, but it was a prophetic building which incorporated the use of exposed frames, an open-well frontage (designed to meet local building code requirements) and a small roof garden.

Perret the Academic did not fall for the fripperies of Art Nouveau, which are seen in their historicist context in Guimard's Castel Henriette. Schmutzler, the Art Nouveau historian, writes that this pastiche of medieval robber-baron castles 'can scarcely be said to represent Art Nouveau at its best'. It does, however, indicate an allegiance to eccentric asymmetrical design which was to absorb many architects of the next generation.

Hvitträsk, once a house and studios for the Finnish 'famous three', is now a national monument. It retains its character and combines Jugendstil impulse with Arts and Crafts attention to detail and organic effect.

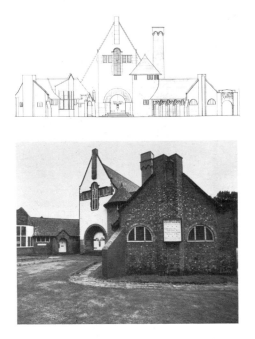

Edgar Wood. *First Church of Christ Scientist,* Victoria Park, Manchester, England. 1903
Top: a measured drawing of the main front of the church
Above: a recent photograph

G. P. Chédanne. *'Le Parisien' Offices,* Rue Réaumur, Paris, France. About 1903
Above: the upper part of the iron-framed 'Parisien' offices

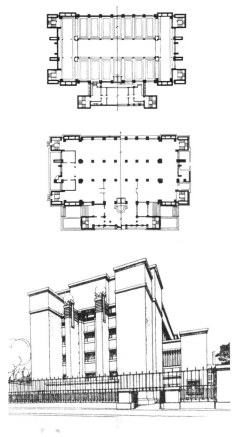

Frank Lloyd Wright. *Larkin Building,* Buffalo, New York, USA. 1905 (1904–05) (Destroyed)
Above: ground floor and a typical upper-floor plan, together with the architect's original drawing
Right: contemporary picture of the exterior of the Larkin Building

Edgar Wood, a Manchester architect of some note during the early part of the century, designed a number of highly original buildings in and around the city which were instrumental in generating copies throughout Europe. Wood's work was, like that of Voysey's, popular with German magazines such as *Moderne Bauformen*. The best known of his early buildings is perhaps the brick church in Manchester with its charmingly informal entrance forecourt and unpretentious detailing.

A more evocative example of modern building was to be found in Paris. Here Chédanne's offices continued the new interest in externalizing elemental engineering construction as a kind of Gothicky feature which is at once directly impressive and convincingly architectural.

Wright's Larkin Building was one of the important landmarks of the first decade, the first fully air-conditioned office block on record, with a central open-well of four storeys. It was sold to a wrecking firm for a paltry sum in 1949 and destroyed in 1950 – another moment of madness in America's war of cultural attrition. This office building holds a record for innovatory ideas, including stair towers (see, later, Gropius through to Kahn), modular metal and glass fittings and – which makes Wright a true prophet – the break-down of the box-like commercial building.

Sullivan, Wright's hero, was still working in the nineteenth-century ornamental vein, but with what showmanship and verve! With detail as intricate as a honeycomb and external lines as powerful as a battleship, the Carson, Pirie & Scott department store in its way represents the twentieth-century spirit of Chicago.

Louis H. Sullivan. *Carson, Pirie & Scott Department Store* (State Street addition), Chicago, Ill., USA. 1904 (1899-1904)
Above right: detail of the ornament added by Sullivan at the time of the 1903–04 extension to the original Schlesinger and Meyer Department Store
Right: general corner view of the Carson, Pirie & Scott Store

Auguste Perret. *Garage,* Rue de Ponthieu, Paris, France.
1906 (1905–6) (Destroyed)
Right: the street frontage

Otto Wagner. *Post Office Savings Bank hall,* Vienna,
Austria. 1906 (1903–06)
Below: interior, with its completely glass-covered vault

In all three buildings on these pages, glass plays an important part in their design. It is used as a vertical surface by Perret for the revolutionary façade for his garage, as a space enclosure and light source by Wagner for his public space and by Mackintosh as a feature and to allow generous light into a type of building that had earlier relied on small openings punched into masonry walls.

In Perret's simplified classical design, the windows fit into a grid offered by the column spacing and the elevation terminates, as do most classically inspired projects, with a cornice. Centrality is the essence of this design and the centre gangway inside finds direct expression on the exterior in the 'rose-petal' window. It was a new type of building built to garage the early automobiles and the plan is an ingenious invention that relies on the use of cantilevered parking spaces and new gadgets like lifts and rolling turntables.

Wagner's Post Office Bank was won in competition in 1903 and erected in two stages, 1904–06 and 1910–12. The Hall roof, completed as part of the first stage in 1906, was a major innovation although only a small part of the vast project. It covered the centrally positioned public space in the trapezoidal-shaped, six-storey building. The glazed vault was suspended from cables in the original competition design and a larger area was involved, but in the final design, a secondary roof was incorporated above the curved ceiling. The floor to the Hall was also finished in glass to allow light to penetrate rooms below.

Mackintosh's School is fairly conventional on plan but the use of light in what is essentially a solid Highland building is dramatic and highly original; the towering staircases are *tours de force*.

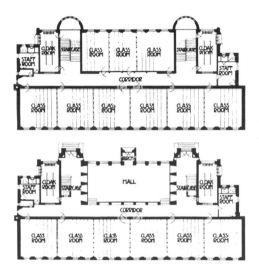

Charles Rennie Mackintosh. *School,* Scotland Street, Glasgow, Scotland. 1906 (1904–06)
Above: ground-floor and first-floor plans
Right: one of the twin staircase/entrance towers
Below: the architect's drawing of the road elevation

1907

Frank Lloyd Wright. *Unity Church* (Unitarian Universalist Church), Oak Park, Chicago, Ill., USA. 1907 (1904–07)
Right: the exterior to Kenilworth Avenue
Below and middle right: interior of the Temple
Bottom left: detail of main entrance
Bottom right: the architect's original drawing of the elevation to Lake Street

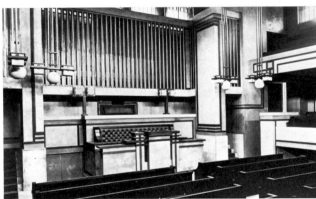

28

Greene and Greene (Charles and Henry Greene).
Blacker House, Pasadena, Calif., USA. 1907 (1906–07)
Top and above: general views of the house in its
beautifully contrived setting

Frank Lloyd Wright's celebrated Unity Church was first projected in 1904, virtually completed and dedicated in 1907 but not used officially until October 1908. Set in Oak Park, near to Wright's own house at the time of building, it was one of the first buildings in the world to be completed in raw monolithic reinforced concrete (covered over in 1961 by rendering). Elsewhere, only the French architect Perret had actually introduced the use of a fairfaced concrete finish externally, although the younger Frenchman Tony Garnier had proposed its use in his thesis for an industrial city.

Unity Church replaced an older timber building destroyed by fire in 1904. It was a revolutionary building in more than its treatment of materials: its interior designs based on rectangles, squares and planes coinciding and reacting with each other was of considerable importance to the

Dutch 'de Stijl' movement; its servicing systems were among the most advanced in the world, with hot-air heating integrated in the structure. The building is divided into two separate parts: the Temple or auditorium, which is more or less square, and a rectangular Parish House linked to the auditorium by a single-storey entrance loggia.

A whiff of eclecticism, a suggestion of Mexican influence, is to be detected in Wright's design. On the rapidly expanding west coast, a more obvious mixture of eclectic sources was apparent in the work of the brilliant house-designers Greene and Greene. 'Japonaiserie', Amerindian and log-cabin vernacular, Spanish Colonial and arts and crafts styles are combined in their two best-known Pasadena houses, the Blacker House (above) of 1907, and the Gamble House of 1908.

1907

Otto Wagner. *Church of St Leopold,* Am Steinhof, Vienna,
Austria. 1907 (1902–07)
Below: entrance front to St Leopold's
Right: the high altar in the church

Josef Maria Olbrich. *Hochzeitsturm and Exhibition
Buildings,* Artists' Colony, Mathildenhöhe,
Darmstadt, Germany. 1907 (1905–07)
Below: contemporary photograph of the 'Wedding Tower'
and surrounding buildings

Otto Wagner's church on the Steinhof seems to throw us back to the historical modes of the previous century. Indeed, designed in 1902, it is, on closer examination, very much a creation of its time – not so far removed from D'Aronco's Turin pavilion of 1902. But everything else is here too – the debt to Classicism, the flirtation with Romanesque, a sniff of Greek Orthodoxy and rudiments of Arts and Crafts. One of the most fascinating hybrids of the era, it is also one of Wagner's most inspired designs.

Less inspired, but designed by Wagner's most brilliant pupil, the Hochzeitsturm and exhibition galleries at Darmstadt were Josef Maria Olbrich's last contribution to this complex of buildings, which he had begun as early as 1899. A year later he was dead. Between 1899 and 1907 the scale of his buildings had changed, and the lightness, brightness and lucidity of the early Viennese school had gone. The overwhelming monumentalism of Prussian architecture seems to have taken over. But there were still flashes of inspiration from Olbrich, and the careful detailing of items in the Baroque park (gates, metalwork, etc.) indicated his continuing interest in craftsmanship.

What a contrast there is in Gaudí's Casa Batlló – as controlled yet freely moving as a well-set jelly – to the obvious struggle that Wagner and Olbrich had with the problem of external expression in their buildings! The interiors of this house seem to have pushed the lower part of the façade further out than it wanted to go, and great gaps appear in it, as if torn by some mad zealot and knotted together with concrete cords. The Casa Batlló was a remodelling of an existing apartment block six storeys in height, with an upper façade relatively under control and balconies such as one might find in the schemes of French Art Nouveau designers. But on top there is another crazy gesture: a 'hat' of Spanish tiles. The bony structure of the façade below reveals a strangely personal architectural statement.

A consumate granite structure, Tampere Cathedral helped consolidate Sonck's reputation as the leading architect of his generation. Won in competition in 1899, it has a square-shaped plan, but its compositional emphasis is towards the asymmetricality of the northern Art Nouveau or Jugendstil as is the interior.

Lars Sonck, *Tampere Cathedral*, Tampere, Finland, 1907 (1903–1907)

Antonio Gaudí. *Casa Batlló* (remodelling), Barcelona, Spain. 1907 (1905–07)
Top right: the strangely undulating façade of the Casa Batlló
Right: a drawing-room interior

1909

The designs for Glasgow School of Art were begun as early as 1896. That year, Mackintosh won the competition for a new school. It was early condemned as 'a reprehensible excursion into *l'art Nouveau*', and later praised as the most important early modern movement building in Britain. The Library wing, a masterpiece of craftsmanship and planning organization, was redesigned between 1906 and 1907 and is a remarkable contrast to the first part of the building, which was built in a spartan Scottish mode. The west façade is fresh and novel, with windows rising through the library space to a height of 25 feet, creating a dramatic effect on a steep hillside site.

Charles Rennie Mackintosh. *Glasgow School of Art, Library wing* (west façade), Glasgow, Scotland, 1909 (1907–9)
Right: the west façade from the south-west
Below: interior of the Library

Wright's Robie House had a tremendous impact on domestic design in the early part of this century. It represented a radical shift in emphasis. Stylistically it was different from other local examples and yet had little in common with main European innovations in house design. Its spatial planning was unique. Proportionally, too, it was considered in great detail, and special aspects of privacy and quietness played a part in the design. It was also one of the first designs to incorporate a garage as an integral part of the plan. Built for a progressive client, the house is distinguished still by its brick detailing and bold, oversailing roof lines, although today the full impact of the design is lessened by the juxtapositioning of an architecturally illiterate building behind it. The Robie House is now preserved as a building of historic significance.

Frank Lloyd Wright. *Robie House*, Chicago, Ill., USA. 1909 (1908–9)
Right: interior of the main upper-floor living-room
Below: general view of the street façade

1909

Peter Behrens. *AEG Turbine Erecting Shop*, Huttenstrasse, Berlin, Germany. 1909 (1908–09)
Below: the enormous neo-Classical façade to the Turbine Shop
Right: the Turbine Shop in relation to the other buildings in the AEG complex
Bottom: detail of the steel jointing of the columns in the side wall of the Turbine Shop

This enormously influential turbine shop was essentially a prestige building. Without doubt, it is Behrens's best-known work, and probably the most celebrated fusion of architecture and engineering of the first decade. It owes a lot to neo-Classicism as well as to production techniques. The scale of the building is breath-taking. Its heavy polygonal and curved ends act as a tremendous contrast to the lightweight construction of the three-pin arches along the length of the building and the carefully-detailed curtain walling. The architect returns to 'solidity, firmness', but less 'delight', with the rather incongruous two-storey, flat-topped wing on the side.

The largest non-domestic commissions for Wright, between his Unity Temple and the large Midway Gardens scheme of 1913, were these two buildings on adjacent sites. The Park Inn overlooked a local park, and the bank was situated on a corner site with offices over. Both buildings had longish, asymmetrical plans; both were dominated by great overhanging flat roof slabs. The bank itself was lit by clerestories reminiscent of those in the Unity Temple.

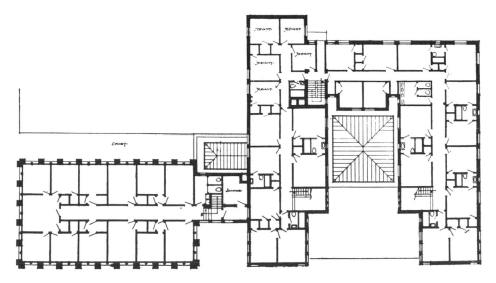

Frank Lloyd Wright. *City National Bank Building and Hotel*, Mason City, Iowa, USA. 1909 (1909–11) (Altered)
Left: general view of the bank
Top: entrance front to the hotel
Centre: second-floor plan and general perspective

Antonio Gaudí. *Parochial School*, near Sagrada Familia
Church, Barcelona, Spain. 1909
Right: view of the roof of the school from one of the
towers of the Sagrada Familia

Peter Behrens. *Schröder House*, Hagen-Eppenhausen,
Germany. 1909 (1908–09) (Destroyed)
Above: garden façade
Right: the road elevation, showing the adjacent
Behrens house for Cuno, completed in 1910

This small church building, somewhat over-
shadowed by the vast towers of the great
votive cathedral, is one of the most interesting of Gaudí's many structures. The curved,
wavy roof, which appears to be constructed
of reinforced concrete, was in fact built up
in traditional tile construction. The curving
walls, too – which enclose a double heart-
shaped plan on the centre of a triangular
site – were built in rough builders' tiles. The
building was meant for a short, useful life.
Fortunately, it was not demolished as intended, but has remained a sort of prophetic
gesture to the wavy-lined engineering
structures of modern Latin American
architecture.

The Schröder country house in a garden
suburb of Hagen, Westphalia, was built
during the period Behrens was consultant to
AEG. It was a solid-looking, symmetrically
organized villa of some character. It is
situated on a site next to the slightly later
Cuno House. The American critic H.-R.
Hitchcock has referred to these houses as
'Behrens' two finest works up to this time'.

Decade 1910

Hans Poelzig. *Milch Chemical Factory*, near Posen (Poznan, now Poland). 1912 (1911–12)

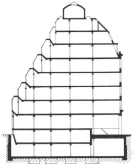

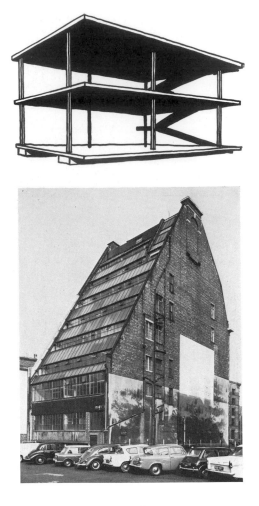

By 1910, much had been said and written on the characteristics of the new architecture that was emerging. The original Werkbund was giving birth to a comprehensive movement, having brought together for practical, educational, political and economic ends those who had represented an anti-machine attitude as well as the most progressive minds in Germany at this time. Behrens and Poelzig, the giants among the German pioneers, had created an initial vocabulary of flat surfaces, fully glazed walls, bold structural systems and expressive, typically Germanic, monumental forms.

Frank Lloyd Wright, whose work up to the beginning of this decade had received little publicity in European circles, also became a major influence on continental architectural developments. His buildings were illustrated for the first time in a sumptuous folio published by Wasmuth of Berlin in 1910 and had a profound effect on a number of German and Dutch designers. Berlage and Rob van 't Hoff, a young architect who was trained at the Architectural Association, London, and later settled in Holland, both saw Wright's work in the United States and helped to further what has been called Wright's 'peaceful penetration of Europe'.

It is worth emphasizing at this point one fact that is often overlooked by historians of modern architecture: the tremendous importance of photographic illustrations in books and magazines which, since the 1890s, had been disseminating the contemporary work of architects and designers throughout the world. The magazines in particular had replaced the traditional pattern-books and treatises used by architects and were a constant source of inspiration as well as a check-list on new tendencies. In the case of many of the more nationally important, commercial journals (not those produced by groups to propagate their own points of view), a change in editorial policy often meant a change within the architectural situation. It is reasonable to assume that the change of editor on the *Architectural Review* in 1905 had something to do with the demise of the influence of the English Free school and the rise of the middle-of-the-road conservatism from which British architecture suffered well into the 'thirties.

Many of the ideas current between 1910 and 1914 in continental architecture belong to what Reyner Banham has called the 'indoor revolution' that occurred in art circles throughout Europe and had been spread by means of art journals and exhibitions. The analytical tendencies introduced in painting by Cézanne (died 1906) and later by the Cubists (1908–14) had superseded traditional ideas of perspective and opened up an interest in the extension of the boundaries of space. Einstein's relativity theories (1905, 1915) extended the revolution of ideas to physics and philosophy.

There was much in Cubism to interest the architect searching for pure geometric shapes and overlapping spaces. Numerous attempts were made in the decade – even after the era of cubist painting itself was over – to translate cubist ideas into a building context. A whole 'school' of cubist architects developed in Prague, and the Dutch 'de Stijl' group established in Leiden in 1917 lent heavily on the cubist aesthetic. But the cube-like qualities of the Viennese buildings up to 1910 and after were not derived from French Cubism but probably go back to the architectural ideals of the period of the French Revolution, via the theory and teaching of Otto Wagner. Loos, Hoffman, Wagner and his pupils clearly exhibit neo-classical preferences in their late Secessionist buildings.

The Italian Futurist movement, too, absorbed from the Cubists ideas on simultaneity and deformation of the object in space. Between 1909 and 1912, they imbued the formal cubist pictorial techniques with their own notions of speed and dynamism. Futurism, a revolutionary art movement that sought to change every-

Above: Le Corbusier's 'Dom-Ino' house design, 1914
York House, Manchester, England, with section
Right: design for a villa at Bergen, Netherlands by
Staal, 1918

thing, had initially no architectural programme, even though its founder, the poet Marinetti, and his protagonists were obsessed with the problems of urban life. By 1914 a disciple had joined the futurist ranks with a previously prepared portfolio of visionary city projects – two years later he was killed in the war. This was Antonio Sant'Elia, whose work on a future metropolis had been displayed side by side with the work of his colleague Mario Chiattone at the first 'Nuove Tendenze' Exhibition in Milan in 1914. He was a unique figure in twentieth-century architecture, as important to the second decade as Antonio Gaudí and Tony Garnier were to the first. All three were men out of their time whose work has less significance to their own generation than to succeeding ones: Sant'Elia on Matte-Trucco, the architect of the Fiat factory in Turin in the 'thirties, on Henri Sauvage, the French architect of the 'twenties, and on the young generation of designers today; Gaudí on the whole line of expressionist architects from 1910 till now; and Garnier most of all on Le Corbusier and through him on city-planners everywhere in the world.

Sant'Elia's own modest manifesto of the architecture of the future, published at the time of the exhibition, was taken up and modified by Marinetti and published as the official 'Manifesto of Futurist Architecture'. Nothing was built during the decade that was essentially Futurist in concept, although a few projects surfaced on paper that included cascading ziggurat-shaped terraces. It was not until the next decade that Sant'Elia's message of the future finally got through.

The changes that occurred between 1910 and 1914 in building design were not insignificant. Walter Gropius and Adolf Meyer's Fagus factory at Alfeld is often referred to as the first truly *modern* structure that closed the pioneer phase and opened the new era. This is justifiable more in terms of its functional layout of the thin glass curtain wall that ambitiously wraps round unsupported corners (although somewhat paradoxically the windows at one end of the main block, behind which the toilets were situated, had to be painted over!) and of its simple construction. More importantly for twentieth-century architecture is the place this building holds in Gropius's own work: within this development its importance is indisputable. Again, a certain amount of wool has been pulled over our eyes about another pioneer building, Adolf Loos's Steiner House, Vienna, of 1910. One is made to believe that it is a simple cube building – as it appears to be from the garden elevation – and not the more conventional family house it can be seen to be from the road elevation. These, then, were indications of new tendencies at work in the realm of building, but it was the Werkbund that was yet to provide the impetus for the new architecture.

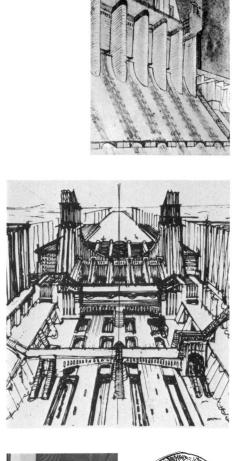

The culmination of Werkbund effort in the pre-war years resulted in a widely publicized exhibition on the banks of the Rhine at Cologne in 1914. At the exhibition all those associated with the German Werkbund from its foundation in 1907, including industrialists, artists, designers and 'friends of art', came together to review the work that had been done up to date and to proffer ideas on the future contact between art and industry. It was by no means an exhibition with a single goal but one which reflected the divided views of its participants.

At a conference in July 1914, held to coincide with the exhibition, attitudes had hardened to such an extent that a clash of personalities and ideologies became inevitable. A rift occurred between the respected leader of the Werkbund, Hermann Muthesius, and the arch-individualist and self-appointed founder of the *fin-de-siècle* Art Nouveau movement, Henri Van de Velde. Their arguments centred on the problems of standardization and artistic creation and were presented in the form of ten theses and ten counter-theses. Muthesius's theses included a fundamental

Above:
Two projects by Sant'Elia, 1913
Walter Gropius (1883–1969)
Paul Scheerbart (1863–1915) by Kokoschka
Below:
The Steiner and Scheu Houses, Vienna, by Adolf Loos, 1912

Above:
Designs for a cathedral, 1914, and a war memorial, 1918, by Mario Chiattone

Above:
Sketch for the Einstein Tower, Potsdam, Germany, by Mendelsohn, 1919

Above:
A sketch from 'Alpine Architecture' by Bruno Taut, 1919

futurological argument for the appropriateness of concentrating on machine production (typified by a standard repetitive product) for design objects which, he claimed, would 'make possible the development of a universally valid, unfailing good taste'. Van de Velde, in countering this point, raised the issue of artistic freedom and claimed that the artist will 'never subordinate himself to a discipline that imposes upon him a type, a canon'. The 'forms and decorations' that had been developed in keeping with the spirit of the age, Van de Velde also claimed, were still exploratory, and standardization was suggestive of a 'style' which could result only 'after the passage of a whole period of endeavours'. Clearly, however, Van de Velde was attacking not simply a premature solidification of style, he was also opposing the nationalistic overtones contained in Muthesius's ten theses and the commercially motivated desire to provide quality exports.

Progressive minds – and by all accounts Muthesius was a nationalistic evolutionist – were aware of developments in the new automobile and aircraft industries and of the commercial potential of die-stamped machine parts and even artistic goods. They also recognized the growing effectiveness of machine-made and machine-assembled armaments, and it is not surprising, therefore, that many of the industrialists who were associated with the Werkbund should look to designers within the organization for guidance on the manufacture of such items. This was reflected in the Werkbund's own Yearbooks, which featured articles and illustrations on vehicle design, airships, battleships, bridges and trains, as well as on *objets d'art*, buildings and posters. Underlying all this was a clear didactic aim: to provide exemplars and models across the board for objects for use whether they were pillows, plates, aeroplanes, posters or buildings.

The structures erected for the Cologne exhibition were as different from each other as were the viewpoints already mentioned. On the extensive site there were to be seen dull neo-Classical buildings by Muthesius, Paul, Kreis and Behrens, an Austrian pavilion in the late Secession style by Hoffman and three generic 'model' buildings by Walter Gropius, Bruno Taut and Van de Velde. The importance of the exhibition for European architecture was summed up in these latter buildings, each of which was a premonition of the architectural stances to be taken some four years later.

When the unproductive war years were over, it was to be clear that 'the mathematical beauty of industrial products' (a phrase of Bruno Taut's) would be recognized as a feature of post-war design. At the 1914 exhibition it was already a characteristic of the 'model' industrial building by Gropius and his partner Meyer, both of whom had been inspired by, and had worked for, Behrens, as well as of the small concrete and glass-domed pavilion called the 'Glass House' designed by Bruno Taut. The latter was for a display of products by the German glass industry and was intended to evoke a 'heightening of intensity' in the lives of the people. These buildings provided the tangible evidence that a new architecture existed.

Van de Velde's model theatre was in a separate category. It was a continuing reminder that, in the hands of an original designer, monumentality had a part to play in the architecture of the ensuing years. It represented a quality of plasticity that was not to be seen in the technological architecture of Gropius and Meyer, nor in the experimentalism of Taut.

At the beginning of the war years, Van de Velde's period at the Arts and Crafts School in Weimar drew to a close and in 1915 he nominated the young Gropius as his successor. In fact, by the time Gropius was able to accept an appointment at Weimar, he had developed his own views on design education and the future of the Weimar art training. In April 1919, he founded the Bauhaus in Weimar and began the most important experiment in design, art and, later, architectural education of the first half of the twentieth century.

Building, as the medieval overtones of the German word *Bauhaus* implied, was to become the core of the new educational system, but building was to have a much wider definition than hitherto. 'The ultimate aim of all the visual arts is the complete building!' Gropius declared in the first line of the Bauhaus Proclamation. It was not in terms of his own technological convictions that Gropius founded the Bauhaus, but more in line with the heterogenous nature of the Werkbund with its emphasis on craft training and creative ability. Initially, the Bauhaus suffered from a surfeit of contemporary Expressionism and paternalistic personalism, only to recover to find it had been taken over by constructivist aestheticians, and these in turn were rejected by modern movement militants, before the Nazis dealt a final blow. Gropius had been appointed Director of the Bauhaus at the same time that he, together with Bruno Taut and the Secretary of the Arbeitsrat für Kunst, had launched an 'Exhibition for Unknown Architects' in Berlin, consisting of sketches from the most advanced architects, artists and designers in Germany at that time. This exhibition was to provide the impetus for one of the most fantastic and visionary episodes in the history of modern architecture. It lasted from 1919 to 1923.

1910

Japanese influence ran deep in the United States and Frank Lloyd Wright's response is well enough known. The Greene Brothers and Maybeck were also conscious of its romantic appeal and, although local rather than international in stature, they did much to popularize an imaginative and 'friendly' eclecticism without resorting to slavish copying. This was of significance in American architecture right up to the mid-1920s. Maybeck's concrete, steel and timber church is the best of his many buildings, controlled down to its last hand-blocked ornament. In places, it contains hints of naturalism and Art Nouveau as witty counterpoints to the way nature itself was allowed to invade the building.

Bernard Maybeck. *First Church of Christ Scientist,* Berkeley, Calif., 1910
Right: the main frontage and entrance to the Church
Below: bird's-eye view of the Oriental-style roof shapes

Antonio Gaudí. *Casa Milá,* Barcelona, Spain. 1910
(1905–10)
Right: the elephantine columns of the lower part of the
Casa Milá
Below: ground-floor plan
Bottom: the building with its corner entrance and
bizarre roofscape

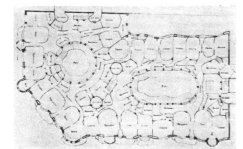

One of the strangest buildings in the world,
Gaudí's Casa Milá was designed in 1905–06
and finally completed under the direction
of his assistant architect in 1910. The
building is essentially Gaudí's and even the
modifications that have taken place more
recently do not obscure the elements of
originality introduced in this building during
the construction period. The freely planned,
seven-storey structure surrounding two more
or less circular courts was Gaudí's largest
and last residential commission. Its amorphous exterior is also reflected in the internal planning, which provides for a wide
variety of flat types and sizes.

The powerful exterior is in cut and ham-
mered stonework, laced round at balcony
openings with wild encrustations of vitalis-
tic wrought iron. The entire building is
related to curves – to vertical and horizontal
warped surfaces – that wrap themselves
dramatically round the imposing corner
and slip gently into the orifices required for
windows and doors. The roof space is a
terrain entirely founded on fantasy, conceived
years before Le Corbusier began to extol the
virtues of a 'second ground-level'.

Antoine Pompe. *Clinic for Dr van Neck,* 53 rue Waffelaerts,
St Gilles, Brussels, Belgium. 1910
Left: street façade in 1911
Below: the altered street façade today
Bottom: entrance hall in 1911

Brilliance of a totally different kind is to
be found in the Clinic for Dr van Neck by
Pompe, an architect whose work is hardly
known outside his native country. In this
clinic and apartment house (Dr van Neck
lived on the third floor), the designer was
concerned with creating a controlled environment. The gymnasium on the second
floor was protected from sun glare, noise
and neighbours by glass-brick screens. The
whole building was air conditioned and
the six pilasters that rise to the top of the
building are not strictly architectural
features but air-ducts which take the foul
air out of the building. The air entrance-
points are below the windows. The balcony
above the ironwork front door is removable.

1911

Josef Hoffmann. *Stoclet Palace,* Brussels, Belgium.
1911 (1905–11)
Right: garden façade
Below: street frontage

Hoffmann's impressive mansion at Brussels, designed for the Belgian industrialist Adolphe Stoclet in 1905, straddles the gap between nineteenth-century modes and manners and the new life-styles of the twentieth century which had germinated in *Fin de siècle* Vienna.

This Austrian building in an alien land is a full-blown repository of Secessionist arts and crafts – a *Gesamtkunstwerk* which included within its totality work by the creative spirits of the Viennese circle, including, notably, Gustav Klimt, whose famous mural decorates the long, low dining-room.

The Palais Stoclet is the last in the long line of great European town-houses built for luxurious living and sheer unadulterated 'aesthetic' pleasure. It owes much to Olbrich's Secession House in Vienna and to Otto Wagner. There is also a suggestion of the work of Mackintosh in its use of the rectangle as the primary generator of the forms of the house. Finished in white marble slabs boxed in by gilded metal borders, the asymmetrical building is dominated by the staircase tower.

Loos's Steiner House is the very antithesis of Hoffmann's mansion; it represents the other side of the Viennese coin. Loos was a utilitarian designer and it is the economical aspects of his forms that have won him the title of the 'father figure' of modern architecture. This garden elevation of the Steiner House has been used by many historians to prove the point. It is not entirely fair, as the road elevation, the planning, and the site restrictions have to be considered as well in the generation of the design.

The Poelzig Water Tower represents another kind of individualism, different from that of the Vienna school. Its strong monumental quality is obvious, but this is set against an expression of precise engineering forms in a building that had uses as a market hall, exhibition space and restaurant, all on floors beneath the huge water-tanks.

The Weimar art school's experiment in the first decade had an effect on architecture. Van de Velde, the head of the Kunstgewerbeschule, was commissioned to design his own buildings round his own requirements. The result was this small group of low buildings which were later adapted by Gropius for part of the Weimar Bauhaus premises.

Adolf Loos. *Steiner House,* Vienna, Austria. 1911 (Altered)
Above: garden elevation
Right: section and ground floor plan of the Steiner House

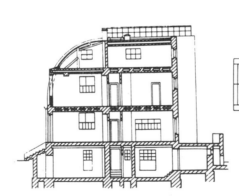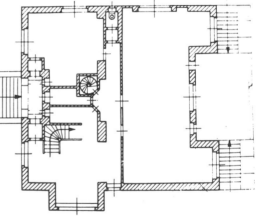

Hans Poelzig. *Water Tower,* Posen (now Poznan, Poland).
1911 (Demolished)
Below: general view
Bottom, middle: interior of the Tower at the exhibition
floor level

Henri van de Velde. *The School of Arts and Crafts,* Weimar,
Germany. 1911 (1905–11)
Above: external view of Van de Velde's school,
part of which later was used by the Bauhaus

Bruno Taut. *Steel Industries Pavilion,* Leipzig Fair, Germany.
1913 (Destroyed)
Below: contemporary view of the Steel pavilion

Hans Poelzig. *Office Building,* Breslau, Germany (now
Wroczlaw, Poland). 1912 (1911–12)
Bottom: general view of the corner office block

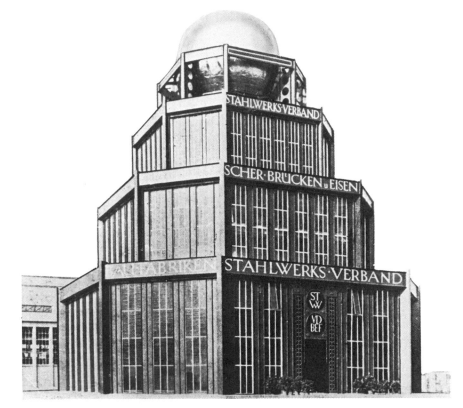

Josef Gočár. *The Spa Building,* Bohdaneć, Czechoslovakia.
1912 (1911–12)
Above: detail of the main entrance

Czech architecture after 1910 was characterized by a unique interest in the application of the Cubist aesthetic to architecture –
an original idea, implying that buildings
should be novel in the same way that Cubist
paintings were. 'Rondo-Cubism', as it was
called, had a mature artistic programme.
The movement had been inspired by Pavel
Janák, who expressed the notion of art being
governed by the 'creative idea'. He was the
theorist; a more representative practitioner
was Josef Gočár, who – unlike his colleagues
Chochol and Kroha – produced an architecture that was controlled, sculptural,
inventive and almost folkloric. His 1913 Spa
Building is a good example of this approach.
He later became an important member of
the Czech Functionalist movement.

Bruno Taut's Steel pavilion was but a pre-
lude to his glass architecture (see page 52),
a moment of inspiration that seems to link
the Viennese 'Secessionists' with the German
Werkbund (the dome motif had been used
by Olbrich for the Sezession House in 1898).

In Breslau in 1913, Hans Poelzig had swept
his dynamic office block round the corner of
the Junkerstrasse – a premonition of what
was to come from Mendelsohn and many
other architects of the following decades.

Quite independently, a creative mind of a
different order was at work in Switzerland.
After an abortive attempt to build a centre
for the anthroposophical movement in
Munich, Rudolf Steiner was able to erect
the headquarters of his new organization not
far from Basel. His entirely timber-clad
design was made in 1913. Building soon
began and the first Goetheanum was opened
in 1920. At the same time, strange edifices
connected with the movement grew up
around the new 'temple' in the grounds at
Dornach (see page 51). The Goetheanum
was burnt down on New Year's Eve, 1922/3
and was replaced by a new building in
reinforced concrete (see page 91). Steiner's
work falls into no stylistic category, its idio-
syncracies and originality makes it as unique
as the Czech phase of Rondo-Cubism.

Rudolf Steiner and others. *Goetheanum I* (Free High School
for Spiritual Science), Dornach, near Basel,
Switzerland. 1913 (1913–20; as the two Goetheanum
buildings were put up as funds became available, they are
illustrated at inception rather than completion dates)
(Mostly destroyed, 1922)
Above: the first Goetheanum with its timber domes and
concrete podium
Right: interior of the main timber-built auditorium of
Goetheanum I
Below: ground-floor plan and cross-section

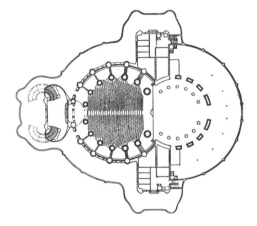

1913

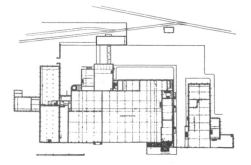

Walter Gropius and Adolf Meyer. *Shoe-last Factory (Fagus-Werke)*, Alfeld an der Leine, Germany. 1913 (1911–13)
Top: ground-floor plan of the Fagus factory
Above and right: two views of the administration wing (the picture above was taken recently)

Josef Chochol. *Villa,* Prague-Vyšehrad, Czechoslovakia. 1913
Below: front elevation

Josef Chochol. *Residential block* (three houses), Prague-Podolí, Czechoslovakia. 1913 (1912–13)
Above: elevation to the main road

48

One of the key buildings in twentieth-century architecture, Gropius's factory was designed to house the shoe-last machinery of Karl Benscheidt. Called at the time by Gropius 'an artistic and practical design', it appeared a somewhat radical departure from the more usual utilitarian structures that had gone up in Germany. It can be seen, in a way, as the logical extension of the factory aesthetic that had developed in Behrens's office. It was, indeed, Gropius's first independent commission after leaving that office. The epoch-making element in its design was the envelope of glass around the administration block.

The effect of Cubism and Purism on early modern movement buildings was nowhere more profound than in Czechoslovakia, and in that native style known as 'Rondo-kubismus'. This indigenous style, developed through its chief exponents Jiři Kroha and Josef Chochol, became fashionable and is not without influence on the work of some of the German expressionist architects of the 1920s. The 'pure' forms used are derived from reducing buildings to faceted geometrical parts. The blocky, abstract kind of architecture that emerged in the two designs on this page by Chochol is, of course, a kind of 'façadism' backed by idiosyncratic theory, which in its way was remarkably original and creative. Later he became far more committed to the principles of the so-called 'Rational school'.

The Century (or Centennial) Hall is also obsessive – the one major work by the Breslau City Architect that has created a niche in the history of world architecture. A concept on a grand scale, this vast domed hall was built to commemorate the centenary of the rising against Napoleon in 1813. It was the largest building of its kind anywhere in the world at the time of erection, and a clear indication that architect and engineer co-operation had made its mark. Dramatically constructed in heavy reinforced concrete, the Jahrhunderthalle's 213 feet diameter was far more impressive inside than out. Unable at the time to develop a system of glazing that would follow the curve of the dome, the designers constructed rings of windows at various intervals up the curve and a traditional lantern at the top.

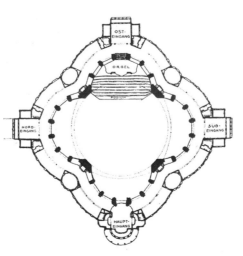

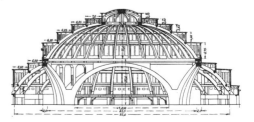

Max Berg. *Jahrhunderthalle* (Centennial Hall), Breslau, Germany (now Poland). 1913 (1911–13)
Top: interior of the great dome
Centre: the main entrance

Far left: layout of the Centennial Fair buildings
Left and below: plan and cross-section

1914

Antonio Gaudí. *Parc Güell,* Barcelona, Spain. 1914 (1900–14)
Right: the giant flights of steps that lead up to the doric hypostyle in Parc Güell

Eliel Saarinen (Gesellius, Lindgren and Saarinen), *Railway Station,* Helsinki, Finland. 1914 (1906–14)
Below: the main front, in the architect's original drawing

Frank Lloyd Wright. *Midway Gardens,* Chicago, Ill., USA. 1914 (1913–14) (Destroyed)
Above: the main interior court of the Gardens

Parc Güell was Gaudí's most important town-planning project. Originally planned as a type of Garden Village, it was still incomplete in 1914 when work terminated. Today it is a municipal park and consists of a bizarre collection of eccentric pavilions and virtuoso designs. The vaulted structure which meanders round the site is of especial interest with its leaning columns. A large public terrace is now situated above the hypostyle hall, although the original inten-

tion was for a Greek theatre here.

Gaudí's nationalism has been recognized and it is, therefore, interesting to compare his *parc* with a 'national romantic' building of the same date which is quite different in expression and formal treatment. Helsinki Railway Station did much for the elder Saarinen's international reputation. Won in competition in 1904, it was revised by Saarinen and built 1906–14. Like Wright's Mayan-inspired Midway Gardens of the

Rudolf Steiner. *Haus Duldeck,* Dornach, Switzerland. 1914
(1913–14)
Below and right: a general side view and a detail of
Haus Duldeck

same year, it was a confident essay in monumentalism.

This spread emphasizes the elements of difference, and even of discordance, during that traumatic period just before the First World War. It was a great period of individualism. Ignored at the time, but now seen retrospectively to be of some significance, are the smaller structures by Steiner around the Goetheanum (page 47), of which the Duldeck House is the most exciting.

Berlage's only British building, Holland House in the City of London, designed for the Müller Shipping Company, was technically far in advance of the others and introduced the use of movable partitions for office flexibility and sophisticated service systems. It was the first building designed by a pioneer continental modern movement architect in London.

H. P. Berlage. *Holland House,* Bury Street, London,
England. 1914
Left: a recent photograph of the Bury Street façade
Above: interior of the entrance hall; photograph taken
in 1914

1914

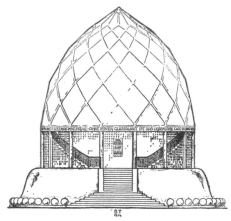

DER GOTISCHE DOM IST DAS
PRÄLUDIUM DER GLASARCHITEKTUR

Bruno Taut. *Glass House,* Werkbund Exhibition, Cologne,
Germany. 1914
Above: elevation of the Glass Pavilion with a Scheerbart
aphorism, 1914
Right: the entrance side of the Glass House
Below: interior of the lower water court of the
Glass House. The dome can be seen through the small
circular opening in the ceiling
Middle right: the architect's original plan

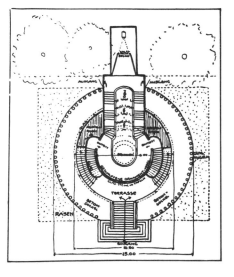

The efforts towards better design standards within the Deutscher Werkbund culminated in the organization of an exhibition at Cologne in 1914. The burning topic that occupied the organizers and the delegate members of the Werkbund, who came together at a conference during the exhibition, was the validity of standardization or 'type' design (for buildings, products or artistic objects) versus individual creativity. It came to a head in a now famous clash between Hermann Muthesius and Van de Velde, the designer of the Model Theatre; the question was left unresolved.

The exhibition buildings represented many different viewpoints, by no means the majority of which were positively twentieth-century in either concept or execution. However, the new and experimental was to be found alongside propagandistic, individualistic and didactic pavilions. Exhibitions are arranged to influence opinion, to teach and to promote by example. Taut's Glass House was of exceptionable significance: it promoted the use of glass and thereby the German glass industries that paid for it, and it created a novel environment of glass, concrete, water, colour and sound.

Gropius's factory, following closely on the heels of the Fagus design, was probably the first conscious attempt to produce a building by a division of functional areas, white-collar workers in the flashy (and Wright-inspired) office block, and a courtyard dividing this from the blue-collar workers' factory space. It was a model for efficient production and demarcation.

The theatre – again a didactic structures but without issue – was a masterpiece of simplicity, traditionally organized in the German auditorium manner but with an apsidal stage end. It was this kind of stage that was to influence the designers of the post-war proletarian theatre.

Henri van de Velde. *Model Theatre,* Werkbund Exhibition,
Cologne, Germany. 1914
Above: the front elevation of the theatre
Right: ground-floor plan

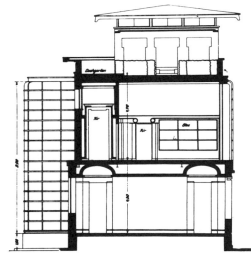

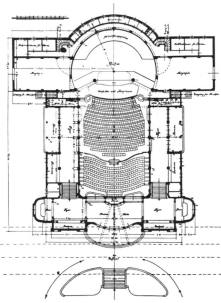

Walter Gropius and Adolf Meyer. *Model Factory,*
Werkbund Exhibition, Cologne, Germany. 1914
Below: general external view with the administration
block at the front, the courtyard behind and the
manufacturing area beyond. The Deutz Pavilion is to the
left of the picture
Left: section of corner tower

Antonio Gaudí. *Colonia Güell,* Santa Coloma de Cervelló,
near Barcelona, Spain. 1915 (1898, 1908–15)
Right: interior of the porch to the church
Below: crypt of the Colonia Güell chapel

Irving Gill. *Dodge Residence,* Los Angeles, Calif., USA.
1916 (1915–16) (Demolished)
Left: the garden elevation

Robert van't Hoff. *Villa,* near Huis ter Heide, Utrecht,
Netherlands. 1916
Below: the frontage of Robert van't Hoff's villa

J. M. van der Meij (Project architects: Piet Kramer and
Michel De Klerk). *Het Scheepvaarthuis* (Shipping House),
Amsterdam, Netherlands. 1916 (1911–16)
Bottom: corner tower of the Scheepvaarthuis

Although not completed until 1915, Gaudí's
Colonia Güell chapel was begun in 1899.
Technologically brilliant and structurally
sound, it combines the magic of traditional
religious architecture with the originality of
an isolated genius. Nothing else like it exists
– the crypt *is* a mysterious place, with seats
as fanciful as the thrusting structure. The
porch consists of a series of connected
columns taking down the load of isolated
pieces of roof or wall.

The Dodge Residence has been called one
of the first modern movement buildings in
the USA. It was a two-storey, white cuboid
house with recessed rectangular window
openings and a flat roof – as pure in architectural terms as anything conceived by contemporary Europeans.

At roughly the same date, Van't Hoff
introduced a variation of Wright's architecture to Holland and produced one of the
first concrete-framed houses in Europe.

Although Wright had not used concrete in
quite the same way, the symmetry and
architectonic qualities of the house show a
near-literal translation of his 1906 concrete
house, published in Holland. Van Doesburg
called it 'clear plasticism created by purely
architectural means'.

The Shipping House in Amsterdam began
an episode of fantasist or expressionist work
in Holland. The joint product of the three
who were to lead the so-called Amsterdam
school, it still holds the charm and brilliance
of that era.

1917/18

J. F. Staal and others. *Housing Estate, Park Meerwijk,* Bergen, near Alkmaar, Netherlands. 1918 (1916–18)
Right: the entrance to the estate with the small pavilion by Staal in foreground
Below: the original drawing for the layout of the estate by Staal
Centre right: 'Noah's Ark' by Margaret Kropholler
Bottom: the row of linked houses by Staal
(now altered)

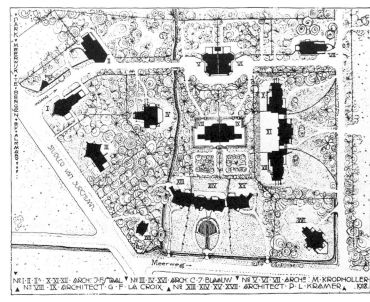

Willis Polk. *Hallidie Building,* San Francisco, Calif. 1918
(Demolished)
Right: street frontage

Jiří Kroha. *Montmartre Night-club,* Prague,
Czechoslovakia. 1918 (Demolished)
Bottom: interiors of the Montmartre

Park Meerwijk is an odd estate, but an
important departure in Dutch domestic
design at the time it was built. It was described on completion in 1918 as an 'exceptional architectural experiment' which
provided an opportunity for a number of
architects – including Staal (the co-ordinator
of the project), Kramer, Blaauw, La Croix
and the first woman architect of any
distinction in Holland, Margaret Kropholler
– to develop an 'expressionistic' architectural
vocabulary for domestic work on the small
scale.

The idiosyncratic and romantic designs
for the seventeen houses all, in their own
way, paid lip service to the English domestic
design tradition, and it is not surprising
to find a reference in an essay on the estate
to the fact that the 'form-giving qualities'
of Norman Shaw's, Edwin Lutyens' and
Voysey's work had been recognized by the
designers. There was also an indigenous
vernacular interest displayed.

The estate was erected for a speculator
and inhabited mainly by writers and
artists escaping from the urban life in
Amsterdam to the fresh air and freedom of
a seaside villa. In 1918 it was isolated; today
it is hemmed in by all the subsequent
development that has taken place along the
northern Dutch coast.

The gothic trimmings on Polk's frontage
to the Hallidie Building tend to obsure one
of the finest and most uncharacteristic
façades to be erected on the west coast in
the late 1910s. The sheer wall of glass of this
eight-storey framed structure, which had no
columns on the exterior in order to provide
large areas of display space, was prophetic.
Of particular interest, too, are the small
projecting balconies on either side of the
wide front which have an unobtrusive
linking fire-escape.

Kroha's night-club is another typical
product of the 'fantastic' period. Obsessive
to the extreme, it should be compared with
van Doesburg's L'Aubette, that other
avant-garde 'niterie,' designed to produce
an 'artistic' atmosphere!

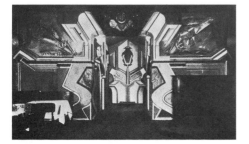

Hans Poelzig. *Grosses Schauspielhaus,* Berlin, Germany.
1919
Right and below: the interior transformed by the
sculptural hanging acoustical decorations of Marlene and
Hans Poelzig
Centre right: the architect's drawing of the exterior of
the remodelled theatre
Bottom right: a Max Reinhardt production c.1920

Poelzig's Grosses Schauspielhaus was one of
the few building schemes to be completed in
Germany immediately after the war. It was
not a new building but a reconstruction on
a grand scale of the old Zirkus Schumann.
Poelzig transformed the building into 'a
theatre for 5000' for the Kaiser of the Berlin
theatre world, Max Reinhardt. The interior
was enclosed by row upon row of stalactites
which lent a mysterious cave-like appearance
to the auditorium. To heighten the effect,
the whole was painted blood-red. The design was thoroughly eclectic, but in a
theatrical rather than an architectural sense.
Outside, the narrow arcades suggested
inspiration from the Roman amphitheatres;
the foyer smelt of Egypt and had lotus-
shaped columns carved by the architect's
wife; the interior was Poelzigian magic,
justified – of course – on acoustical grounds.

Decade 1920

City of the future, from Fritz Lang's UFA-film 'Metropolis'. Sets designed by Otto Hunte, Erich Kettelhut and Karl Vollbrecht. 1926

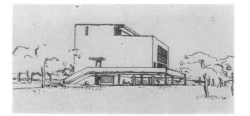

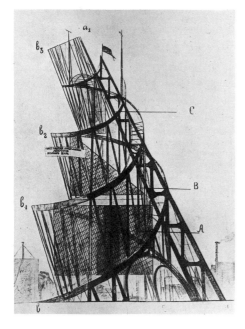

The nineteen-twenties were the most important years for the formation of the principles which controlled the modern movement in architecture up to the Second World War.

The individualism and experiments of the previous two decades were followed by the consolidation of viewpoints on what constituted the 'new' architecture. By 1926, the Swiss-French architect Le Corbusier was able to reduce its characteristics to five points:

the liberation of the ground floor by the introduction of free-standing supports; the independence of the structural skeleton of a building from the wall surfaces, which allowed the introduction of horizontal windows; the free plan; the free design of the façade; the introduction of a new 'free' level on the roof, the roof garden, which overcame the maintenance problems of flat roofs and offered the possibility of a new 'ground' level.

Le Corbusier had introduced these basic principles into his own designs – for example, the Citrohan (1921) and Monol house projects – but while the principles represented separate innovations that had, through him, been introduced elsewhere, the 'mere box', artistic or otherwise, became an articulated building. In projects and actual buildings, in manifestos and statements, the characteristics of this newly defined architecture were explicitly revealed. At the end of the decade, an American critic, Henry-Russell Hitchcock, was prepared to recognize the existence of a 'new tradition'.

At the beginning of the decade, the outlook had been very bleak for architecture. Europe, stunned by the debilitating effects of the worst war in the history of mankind, had almost come to a standstill. Little construction work was carried out because of lack of finance, labour and materials and, consequently, architects received few commissions. However, it was not an idle period but one of intense intellectual activity, during which architects seized the opportunity to promote new ideas, to establish certain priorities in the re-ordering of society and to dream up visionary projects.

The activities of the whole decade were permeated, too, by fervent left-wing revolutionary idealism which only faded in the last years of the decade through a common disillusionment with governments whose political programmes allowed no place for inventive architecture. The promise held out by Soviet architects was itself short-lived. Soviet Constructivism had its origins in the immediately pre-revolutionary period, but between 1917 and 1923, designs emerged that were a complete departure from precedent in their external appearance, planning and social programme. Vladimir Tatlin's project for a Monument to the Third International (1919–20) evoked through its interplay of spirals a new kind of architectural monumentalism, symbolic of the whole Constructivist movement. Other key innovations of the Constructivists were concerned with what were called 'social condensers' – building projects that took their form from notions about new styles of living. Unfortunately, these departures from convention proved to be too far advanced for the mass of the people and the political leadership.

In Germany, the post-war atmosphere of frustration and chaos had engendered a similarly revolutionary feeling among the active groups of visionary and utopian designers and artists. As in Soviet Russia, there was a heavy commitment among architects to social buildings and many projects had about them a familiar ring: imaginary buildings bearing titles like 'Workers' Club', 'People's Palace' and 'Cultural Centre'. But side by side with this in the German situation, there grew up a desire for an exploration of new shapes and new solutions to old problems as well as investigations into new materials and techniques of construction. Much was written and drawn up; hardly anything was built. Apart from the remodelling of the old Zirkus Schumann in Berlin by Hans Poelzig in 1920 to form the Grosses Schauspielhaus, and the small and somewhat perplexing Einstein Tower built at Potsdam by Erich Mendelsohn in 1919–21 (but not officially opened until 1924), the episode of 'fantastic' architecture has to be judged in terms of drawings and quasi-philosophical writings. Until a few years ago, the expressionist phase in architecture was considered an aberration and unworthy of consideration as generative of 'functional' architecture, but this is now no longer so. The so-called 'expressionist interlude' is seen as one of the main catalysts that sparked off the new architecture.

The theory that there was a continuous line of 'rational' architectural development, evolving from the clarity and precision of nineteenth-century engineering structures to a total acceptance of 'functionalist' architecture, has formed the basis of a number of historical interpretations of modern architecture. But the facts will not support it, unless one ignores the formative influence that Expressionism had on Walter Gropius, Mendelsohn, Mies van der Rohe and the latter part of Behrens's career. The Bauhaus itself, opened under the direction of Walter Gropius in 1919, was, until the injection of constructivist and Dutch 'de Stijl' ideas in 1923, almost entirely staffed by designers and artists committed to the expressionist line. Even as late as 1928, when Hannes Meyer, an arch-leftist and 'anti-art' architect, had taken over the directorship of the Bauhaus, he was still prepared, for cultural reasons, to bring in such an unequivocal Expressionist as Hermann Finsterlin.

There was, therefore, for most of the decade an overlapping of interests and a polarization of positions within the avant-garde itself. At no other point in twentieth-century architecture was such a proliferation of committed groups seen. Some of these groups provided the bridge from Art Nouveau, the 'Free schools' and Jugendstil to the expressionist episode which, in the post-war situation, represented the swan song of the 'artistic' or intuitive approach to architectural problems.

Out of this phase came designers such as Hans Scharoun, Hugo Häring and Hermann Finsterlin, whose buildings and designs contradict the doctrinaire approach of the rationalist architects of the next few years. Bruno Taut, himself the leader of the revolutionary, visionary groups in the immediate post-war period, abruptly and convincingly changed course after mid-decade. In 1918 he was referring to a building as a 'direct carrier of spiritual values, shaper of the sensibilities of the general public which slumbers today but will awake tomorrow. Only a total revolution in the realm of the spiritual can create this building . . .', but some ten years later he wrote 'Necessity is by far the greatest incentive to inventive activity.' He was referring to the notion which was to be found in the writings of many architects during the latter part of the decade when the work rules of a 'functional' architecture were finally defined.

Functionalism in itself was by no means a new doctrine, but its promulgation in the 'twenties as an aesthetic ideal laid a new emphasis on the clarity and mechanistic precision of external forms (the functional and efficiency aspects of machines was an attractive proposition to designers) as well as on the analytical problems generated by planning requirements. German architects referred to the pristine, clean, pure, logical or rational aspects of their architecture as 'objective' (*sachlich*), implying its hygienic and utilitarian basis, while the Dutch architects' term *zakelijk* implied that this was the new 'business-like' architecture.

The word 'functional' and the slogan 'form follows function' gained world-wide currency in the nineteenth century. They are to be found in the writings of the American sculptor Horatio Greenhough at mid-century, in Viollet-le-Duc's books, the writings of the Morris circle and the Chicago school. In 1908, Frank Lloyd Wright, in his paper *In the Cause of Architecture*, spoke of the relationship of form and function lying at the root of the architect's practice, in which their connection with the organic aspects of nature were indispensable. Wright's own built work at this time also provided him with an opportunity to consolidate his theories on 'Organic Functionalism'. He later abruptly rejected faceless, continental 'functional' design.

European ideas on Functionalism developed on a broader basis and were marked by at least three different attitudes to building. The first of these, which seems to have come quite logically out of the expressionist phase in the early part of the decade, has been called 'Expressive Functionalism', as it related logical planning and the formal ideas for a new architecture to external and artistic goals. This can be seen in the work and theories of the mature Erich Mendelsohn, in the designs of Behrens and his school, as well as in the ideas of Hugo Häring and Hans Scharoun.

Allied to this, but not essentially part of it, was a rather naïve approach to architectural problems that could be called 'Pragmatic Functionalism'. This attitude insisted that by the manipulation of certain parts of a building – the planned areas and the structural system – a design will be mysteriously generated that will be at once the anonymous result of the problem itself and the logical expression of the building's function. Such an attitude, which produced few important buildings in the 'twenties, was linked to a pretentious body of theoretical knowledge on structures, sociology and economics.

The third attitude to building was the one exemplified by the German Werkbund Exhibition at Stuttgart in 1927 and the writings and buildings of Le Corbusier, and popularized by Hitchcock and Johnson as 'International Functionalism'.

The pivotal year in this development was 1927. The three years that followed were the most important in the dissemination of cubic, white-finished, flat-roofed, concrete architecture. At Stuttgart, the Werkbund, following a consistently polemical approach to design, financed the building of an estate of houses, the Weissenhofsiedlung, under the direction of Mies van der Rohe. Model villas, workers' apartments and terrace-houses were erected and furnished with the express intention of indicating the maturity of the new architecture. Significantly, it brought together the older generation of German architects, such as Behrens and Poelzig, the hard-line Functionalists from abroad, Le Corbusier and his cousin and partner, Pierre Jeanneret, the Dutchmen J. J. P. Oud and Mart Stam, the Belgian Victor Bourgeois as well as the younger German architects, Gropius, Scharoun, Mies, Hilberseimer, Taut and Rading whose work had reached maturity about 1925.

Above: Expressionist designs by the Luckhardt brothers and Hermann Finsterlin
Hannes Meyer's entry for the League of Nations hq competition

A portrait sketch of Ernst May (1886–1970), the influential city architect and planner, Frankfurt am Main, 1925–30, who was responsible for Das neue Frankfurt

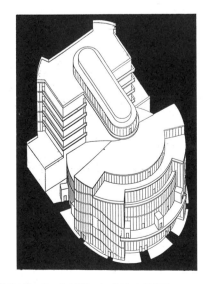

Walter Gropius, *Total Theatre Project*, 1926–7

The exhibition had been decided on in 1926 by the Württemberg Chapter of the Werkbund in conjunction with the City Council of Stuttgart. The new settlement was presented to the general public in the form of an exhibition called 'Die Wohnung', but unlike previous model exhibitions the estate itself was to be permanent and can still be seen today, only slightly altered during the course of four more decades.

Mies van der Rohe, appointed a Vice-President of the Werkbund in 1926, had become convinced that planning problems could only be solved by the fusion of creative minds, and he was instrumental in carrying out the Werkbund's call, of 1926, for a united front among the 'new' architects to enable a consistent aesthetic to emerge for popular housing. This was successfully achieved, although site work proved immensely difficult and numerous interpretative problems emerged during the course of construction, as few of the workmen employed had any experience of the new materials and constructional techniques employed.

While Mies assumed overall planning responsibility for the layout, the supervision of the construction of individual buildings was carried out by Richard Döcker. In all, there were thirty-one buildings in the exhibition, providing sixty units of accommodation – small, perhaps, by today's standards, but a remarkable sight to most of the 20,000 visitors daily during the period it was open in 1927. The estate had the stylistic unity that Mies and his colleagues had searched for, without recourse to uniformity. The units may have looked similar externally but technically they were vastly different. Mies himself produced the long workers' apartment block with a composite structure of steel columns and block walls. Gropius designed a prefabricated house and Le Corbusier and Jeanneret developed a design based on the earlier Citrohan House, fully embodying the five principles referred to on page 60. Le Corbusier claimed that he was not dealing with fashionable whims but with 'an absolutely new method of building'. His built statement was equally clear and his principles applied; none of the other Weissenhof buildings exhibited the same clarity of thinking.

Each, in its own way, was a product which conformed in spirit to the tenets of so-called 'International Functionalism'. As such, it was all condemned outright by the National Socialist Party, which began to purge the 'radical elements' in German building soon after the Weissenhof was built. Later, after the Nazis had come to power, the estate was caricatured as an *Araberdorf* (Moorish village) and scorned for its flat-roofed display of cultural decadence.

Internal hostility could hardly stem the influence of the estate on contemporary architecture throughout the world. It had fulfilled the Werkbund's aim, identified the new architecture with housing and gone far beyond it in creating an architectural vocabulary – if not a grammar – for the next quarter of a century.

Unification of the radical elements within the German architectural scene had occurred earlier, in 1925, with the formation of a group known as 'The Ring' – originally consisting of ten members but soon absorbing other acceptable newcomers – but it was not fulfilling the international role looked for by its participants. It was not until a year after the Stuttgart exhibition that a truly international group appeared, and then in somewhat unorthodox surroundings. Accepting the hospitality of a Madame de Mandrot, the Swiss historian Sigfried Giedion and Le Corbusier convened a two-day meeting from 26 to 28 June 1928, at her château, La Sarraz, in Switzerland, ostensibly to establish a programme of action 'to drag architecture from the academic impasse'. Delegates from a number of countries were invited to the meeting, at the end of which a declaration was signed forming an organization entitled CIAM (Congrès Internationaux d'Architecture Moderne).

The following year the well-organized Germans took the initiative in setting up the first major congress of the new organization at Frankfurt-am-Main which, under the direction of the City's Architect Ernst May, concentrated on the burning issue of low-cost housing.

Although they may not have made as immediate an impact on public opinion as the Stuttgart estate and the founding of CIAM, other equally important developments at the levels of both theory and practice, such as Gropius's housing estates and the Dessau Bauhaus buildings, provided an impetus to the spread of machine-age consciousness that penetrated art and architecture everywhere.

Hannes Meyer's and Le Corbusier's competition designs of 1927 for the League of Nations Headquarters at Geneva were among the first attempts to create a striking modern building complex within the new idiom and, incidentally, to overcome the obsessive interest in monumentalism upheld by the old guard. Gropius had attempted to do this earlier with his Chicago Tribune Tower competition submission in 1922. However, these projects were not successful and never built, though today the designs are the only reminders of the competitions. Who actually remembers who designed the League of Nations building or the Chicago Tribune Tower?

In New York a 'Machine Age Exposition' was held in 1927. Simple machine

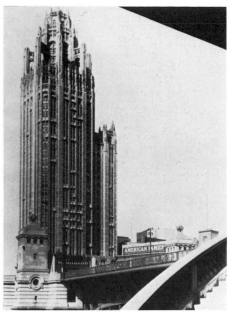

Top: the *Chicago Tribune* offices competition, 1922. Entries by Loos (left) and Gropius and Meyer (centre), with the winning design by Hood and Howells, as built, 1925 (right)

parts and products were ranged side by side with Russian constructivist art and photographs of contemporary European buildings. Referred to as the first 'major event in the modern movement in America', this may be true for the eastern seaboard, but hardly so of the situation developing on the sunnier west coast. As early as 1916, an indigenous kind of modernism, bereft of superficial ornament but still spatially static, had emerged in Irving Gill's work.

By the date of the New York Exposition, the 'new' architecture had taken firm root on the west coast under the capable hands of two Austrian *émigré* architects, Richard Neutra and R. M. Schindler, both of whom had spent some time in Frank Lloyd Wright's studio. Neither was typical of the camp-followers Wright's office seemed to produce. Neutra gained a world-wide reputation, but the recent rediscovery of R. M. Schindler – who for generations has only been recognized in Europe through the excellence of his Lovell Beach House at Newport Beach, California of 1926 – has revised many people's views on the extension of modern functionalist architecture into the US.

Neutra's Health House at Griffiths Park, Los Angeles, also for Dr Lovell, was probably the most important modern design to be built in the US during the decade. Its initial design goes back to the significant year 1927, and to the time Neutra published his book *Wie Baut Amerika?* in Germany, in which his influential proposals for a futuristic planning scheme, 'Rush City Reformed', appeared. Modern architecture made little, if any, impact on the great commercial skyscrapers of urban America but there is clear evidence that Neutra's scheme was to influence the high buildings of the next decade, particularly the Philadelphia Fund Savings Building of 1930–32.

The final years of the decade were among the most productive for architects of this century. The old battle of styles had been won, the new architecture was established and the radicals had become successful contemporary practitioners. But all was not so happy in other areas. The foolish 'twenties came abruptly to a halt with the collapse of Wall Street in 1929. Despair filled the minds of many who had previously only dreamt of greenbacks and building monuments (modern or otherwise) to their own glory. The political atmosphere in Soviet Russia, and in Germany too, was rapidly hardening on anti-cultural lines.

Within three years of the opening of the next decade, the internationalism that had been observed by so many enthusiastic commentators during the 'twenties became a bitter reality as artists, architects and designers were forced to leave their countries of origin and, thereby, themselves to reinforce the modern movement in countries which they had originally hoped would produce their own radical groups. Le Corbusier, however, was to retain through all these years an almost infallible position. His building work increased – largely for wealthy clients, but including important social experiments like the houses at Pessac – while his pen was never still. His vision of a synthesis in the arts and a new architecture of form, structure and space had materialized in an absurdly short period of time.

Above:
'La Maîtrise' Pavilion, Paris Exposition, 1925, by Hiriart, Tribout and Beau

Robert Maillart, *Schwarnendorf Bridge*, Switzerland, 1929

Right: Albert van Huffel's grandiose Church of the Sacred Heart, Brussels, took National Romantic aspirations to new heights in 1922. It was not completed until the 1950s

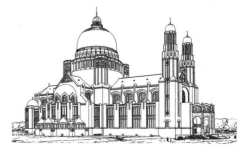

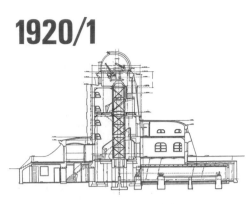

Erich Mendelsohn. *Einstein Tower*, Potsdam, Germany.
1921 (1919–21)
Top right: external view of the Einstein Tower
Above: section of the building and a detail of the main
entrance

J. J. P. Oud. *Workers' Houses*, 'Tussendijken', Rotterdam,
Netherlands. 1920
Centre above: general view of the exterior
Centre left: internal view of the 'Tussendijken' housing
Above: ground-floor plan

Michiel Brinkman. *Spangen Housing*, Rotterdam,
Netherlands. 1920
Left: circulation routes of the Spangen flats

Michel De Klerk. *'Eigen Haard' Housing*, Zaanstraat,
Amsterdam, Netherlands. 1921 (1913–21)
Right: the indented group of smaller houses at the base
of the triangular site, with a central tower feature
Bottom: detail of the fenestration to the Zaanstraat
block

Erich Mendelsohn's small, but powerfully
modelled, tower, built to symbolize the
greatness of the Einsteinian concepts, was
also a quite functional house. It was designed to hold Einstein's own astronomical
laboratory, and began as a series of sketches
carried out for Einstein's assistant, Dr
Freundlich. One of these became a reality
on a site in Potsdam, presented by the
government. Work began in 1919, the
building was effectively finished in 1921 and
was finally officially opened in 1924. It is a
bit of a cheat, in that it looks like something
that it is not. Mendelsohn was after a completely plastic kind of building, *moulded*
rather than built, without angles and with
smooth, rounded corners. He needed a
malleable material like reinforced concrete,
which could be made to curve and create its
own surface plasticity, but due to post-war
shortages, some parts had to be in brick and
others in concrete. So the total external
effect was obtained by rendering the surface
to make it appear like one continuous
material. Even so, this 'sarcophagus of
architectural Expressionism' is one of the
most brilliantly original buildings of the
twentieth century.

J. J. P. Oud, who became city architect
and director of housing at Rotterdam in
1918, built several schemes of workers' flats,
of which the best-known is probably the
'Tussendijken' block erected in 1920. It is in
marked contrast to the flamboyant, decorative brickwork of the large apartment blocks
designed for the suburbs of Amsterdam by
De Klerk and Kramer, but it fills the site in
the same kind of way, hitting the edge of the
pavement and rearing up three or four
storeys. Although not a prime example of
Oud's later functional mode, it is distinctly
related to Brinkman's apartment block
'Spangen', built in Rotterdam the same
year. This was one of the first major balcony-
access schemes to go up anywhere in the
world – a sort of pre-run of the Le Corbusier
work of the 1920s, in which the street became
an elevated platform joining the entry
points to each flat.

In the year the Einstein Tower was completed, De Klerk's apartment housing in
Amsterdam was completed. The more
traditional, idiosyncratic work of the Amsterdam school differs from the more
obvious Mendelsohn symbolism. This Dutch
block was built less to create a community
(as such a scheme probably would nowadays) than to explore an architecture halfway between Romanticism and Verna-
cularism, while answering the Amsterdam
overspill problem.

1922

Le Corbusier. *Ozenfant House and studio*, Paris, France.
1922 (Altered)
Right: the north light studio and entrance staircase

J. G. Wiebenga, in collaboration with L. C. van der Vlugt.
Technical School, Groningen, Netherlands. 1922
Below: entrance front of the Technical School

The house and studio in Paris for Le Corbusier's friend the painter Ozenfant is an early example of 'minimal' architecture, a prototype of the *Dom-ino* house and a manifestation of some of the principles which Le Corbusier was to set out in his famous 'five points'. It possessed a geometrical clarity inside and out which has since been lost with the elimination of the north-light roof and its replacement by a flat one.

Another clear, rational statement of architectural aims is to be found in the Technical School at Groningen, but one which still relied on a central axis. A certain ambivalence exists in the design that could perhaps be explained by Wiebenga's Amsterdam background and Van der Vlugt's commitment to the Rotterdam school.

Frank Lloyd Wright endured a lot of ridicule after he had claimed that his design for the Imperial Hotel would withstand the severest earthquake. In April 1922, when nearing completion, it was put to the test in the worst earthquake for 50 years. It stood up. It did not, however, survive the demolisher's ball and chain and in 1967 this noble building was eliminated to make way for a new hotel.

The original plan for the building was in an elongated H-shape, the two 500-foot long wings containing the guest rooms. The structure was unique: resting on short piles which held the building in a soggy sub-soil like the expert fingers of a waiter supporting a dish of food, the structural slab could move and take up subsidence. The outer walls were made of specially notched blocks with an inside layer of hollow blocks, the cavity filled with steel rods and concrete.

Frank Lloyd Wright. *Imperial Hotel,* Tokyo, Japan. 1922
(1916–22) (Demolished in 1967)
Above: general view
Below: exterior detail
Left: detail of the dining room

1922

Auguste Perret. *Notre Dame du Raincy*, Raincy, France. 1922
Right: interior of the church
Below: the centrally-placed tower in reinforced concrete
Below right: ground floor plan

Michel de Klerk. *Apartment blocks*, Henriette Ronnerplein,
Amsterdam, Netherlands. 1922 (1921–2)
Bottom: the Henriette Ronnerplein flats across the
forecourt

Probably the best-known of all modern
churches, Perret's Notre Dame du Raincy
is a remarkable essay in reinforced concrete;
the new material has literally replaced traditional masonry and brought with it the
'intimation of ineffable space' which the
great Gothic builders referred to. Tall, slim
columns rising to a height of 35 feet are no
thicker than 14 inches around their girths;
large windows (also in concrete) encompass
the space of the church itself like filligree
grills. Rationalism in the design of this
building has replaced 'mysticism', and the
whiff of Gothicism is subordinated to Perret's
mastery of his material and its structural
potential.

The De Klerk flats are also a flight from
convention. Set against an open courtyard,
they look remotely like a row of inflated
semi-detached houses. They are, however,
an attempt at creating an articulate layout
for a series of linked blocks and at reducing
the bulk and lack of identity to be found in

Arthur Korn and Sigfried Weitzmann. *Garden layout to a house,* Grunewald, Berlin. c.1922
Left: fountain court with water machine sculpture designed by Rudolf Belling

Albert Kahn. *Glass Plant,* Ford Motor Company, Dearborn (River Rouge), Michigan, USA. 1922
Below: general view
Bottom: interior of Glass Plant

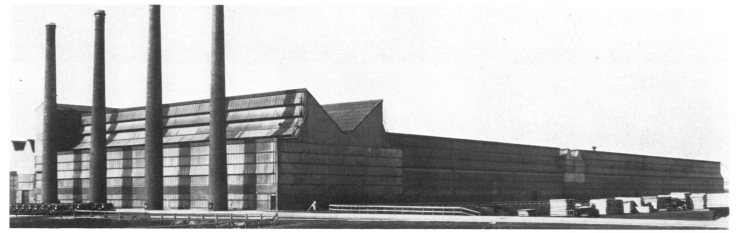

more conventional tenement housing.

The areas surrounding a building are often neglected or left to chance, but Korn and Weitzmann, in their house at Grunewald, were commissioned to provide a layout for the garden. It was a significant opportunity in a period of post-war austerity met with confidence and originality. The sculptor Belling created the abstract water machine, and the swimming bath (under construction in the picture) was clearly as contemporary as anything from the Bauhaus.

The Ford Glass Plant at Dearborn was the work of the largely underrated architect and engineer Albert Kahn who led the US out from the cottage-industry approach to engineering into the modern world of industrial process planning. His first factory at Buffalo for Pierce was innovatory and employed design principles that led, somewhat falteringly, to its form. The Glass Plant shows its full maturity.

1923

Piet Kramer. *'De Dageraad' Housing*, Amsterdam, Netherlands. 1923 (1918–23)
Below: the emphatic corner of the 'De Dageraad' complex
Right: detail of an internal corner

Erich Mendelsohn. *Herrmann Hat Factory*, Luckenwalde, Germany. 1923 (1921–23) (Destroyed)
Centre: general view of the factory with the dye-vat in the background.
Bottom: detail of the brick dye-vat

The search for an identifiable mode of expression in modern architecture was linked to a curious overlaying of symbolism, not least during a period when new types of buildings were being built in the early 1920s. In the Netherlands, many architects were involved in the vast programme of rehousing to take Amsterdammers out of the crowded city centre. Of the architects commissioned to carry out this work, Michel De Klerk and Piet Kramer produced the most novel designs for apartment blocks. In the units designed for the 'De Dageraad' housing association, Kramer showed himself to be, as one historian has put it, 'even more of a virtuoso in the handling of curved wall elements of brick . . . than De Klerk'. Undulating surfaces of brick, keypoint features and an almost rustic use of brick are characteristic of this 'humane' housing.

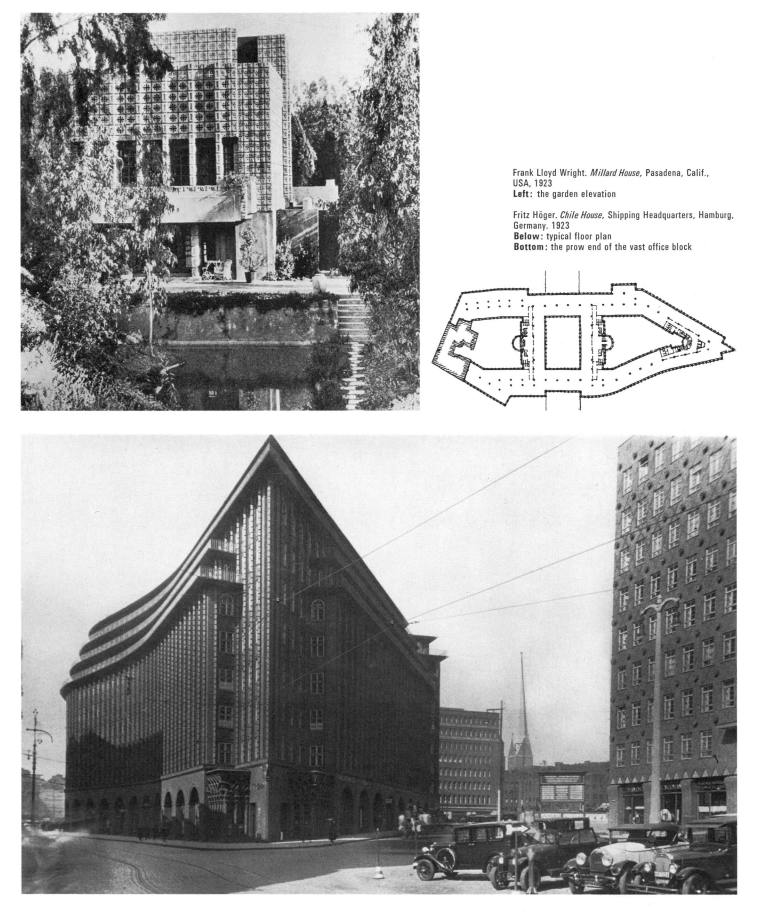

Frank Lloyd Wright. *Millard House,* Pasadena, Calif.,
USA, 1923
Left: the garden elevation

Fritz Höger. *Chile House,* Shipping Headquarters, Hamburg,
Germany. 1923
Below: typical floor plan
Bottom: the prow end of the vast office block

An absorption in the potentialities of
brickwork, but this time in terms of vertical
patterning, can be seen in the huge shipping
offices by Höger at Hamburg. Here the
symbolism is clearly apparent and everything in the design leads up to its climactic
expression. Mendelsohn's hat factory is more
subtle. A kind of chimney-pot hatblock

motif is expressed in the dye-vat building,
but it is dictated by the innovatory use of
concrete portals to create the basic building
shape. Mendelsohn was never naïve.

The background symbolism of Wright's
beautiful house for Mrs G. M. Millard is
obviously Mayan, but here again innovation is the key to an understanding of the

building. This is Wright's first use of a
hollow, precast concrete block (some perforated, some plain, others patterned) which,
when combined with steel rods and filled
with concrete, could act equally well in
compression or tension. A grid-like appearance resulted from this advanced design.
Its main living-rooms are on the first floor.

1923

Ragnar Östberg. *Town Hall,* Stockholm, Sweden. 1923
(1911–23)
Below: a general view of the Town Hall on its island
site

Gunnar Asplund. *Skandia Cinema,* Stockholm, Sweden.
1923
Right: interior of auditorium

Le Corbusier. *La Roche-Jeanneret Houses,* Paris, France.
1923
Above: the La Roche House garden elevation

The Stockholm Town Hall has been called
the 'first really important piece of architecture in Sweden in two hundred years'. It
did in fact take almost a quarter of a century
to materialize. As early as 1902 the idea of a
new Town Hall was mooted, a two-stage
competition was held in 1903–04, basic
revisions were made to Östberg's plan in
1909, work began in 1911 and the new
hall opened in 1923 to worldwide acclaim.
It is a frankly romantic design, a beautiful bit
of eclecticism carried out with confidence
and consumate design skill, situated on what
the guide-books would call a 'heavenly'
site. Östberg was a 'modern traditionalist'
and, like Gunnar Asplund, a designer who
could cope as confidently and romantically
with a new type of building – the Skandia
cinema opened in the same year as the
Town Hall – as he could with a building
in the great European public building mode.

At this early stage of modernism, it was
the French architect Le Corbusier who was
setting out practically the whole vocabulary

of the new architecture. In the double house for his brother Albert Jeanneret and M. La Roche, he introduced his now famous ground-floor, free-standing columns (*pilotis*), a roof garden, a small explosion of high double-storey internal space, and even attempted to modulate the proportions of window and wall spaces.

But if what Corbusier was attempting to do in his houses was of great significance to modern architecture, what Dr Matté-Trucco achieved at Turin was of equal significance. Here for the first time was an example of twentieth-century thinking imbued with the dynamism of the Futurist theory of speed and modern life, lessened in total effect, perhaps, by the Perretesque reinforced concrete structure, but evoking through the rooftop test track a multi-dimensional architecture.

The first major example of reinforced concrete parabolic buildings were the Orly hangars, designed to house enormous dirigibles. The lighting for the interior was provided by strips placed horizontally between the vaults.

Giaccomo Matté-Trucco. *Fiat works,* Turin, Italy. 1923 (1920–23)
Top: detail of the parabolic roof testing track in use in the 1920s
Middle: artist's impression of the Fiat Lingotto complex

Eugène Freyssinet. *Airship hangars*, Orly, near Paris, France. 1923 (1916–23) (Destroyed)
Right: aerial view of the hangars

1924

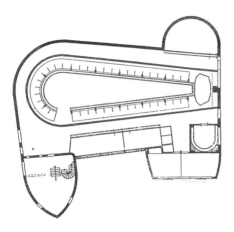

Hugo Häring. *Gut Garkau Farm Buildings,* near Lübeck, Germany. 1924 (1923–24)
Above: plan of cowshed
Right: a recent photograph of the exterior
Below: interior of the cowshed, taken in the 1920s

Walter Gropius and Adolf Meyer. *Municipal Theatre,* Jena, Germany. 1924 (1923–24)
Bottom: the remodelled exterior of the Jena theatre

The oddly extravagant complex of farm buildings near Lübeck has been called one of the masterpieces of modern architecture. It is indeed an accomplished and boldly sculptured example of modern building. Its designer has referred to it as being both organic and functional and through the years it has clearly worked exceedingly well for its purpose. It incorporates traditional materials used in an exceptionally new way. The curves of the wild period of Berlin Expressionism and the technology of the modern engineer are root factors in the design. The interior of the horseshoe-planned cowshed consists of a series of exposed concrete portal frames.

One of Gropius's early theatre projects was the remodelling of the Municipal Theatre, Jena. The well-known, unbuilt projects followed: the Total Theatre for Piscator and the great auditorium for the Palace of the Soviets.

If one needed one building to demonstrate what twentieth-century architecture meant, one would probably choose Rietveld's Schröder House. Here invention is total. It is also deceptive, as this is not a geometrical, modular kind of building set out with spaces relating mathematically to each other, but one designed by eye in order to materialize the two-dimensional qualities of the *De Stijl* aesthetic. Rietveld roughly sketched out the design and produced a model of it and Mrs Schröder, the owner and occupier of the house, collaborated on the final design of the interior. Theodore Brown has referred to the visual independence of the various parts throughout the building. These overlap and separate and are made more obvious by the application of colour; the total mass of the building is minimized and exterior space becomes an extension of the interior spaces. Even Le Corbusier in his most inventive phase produced nothing quite so comprehensive.

Gerrit Rietveld (with Mrs Schröder). *The Schröder House,*
Utrecht, Netherlands. 1924 (1923–24)
Above: a recent photograph of the Schröder House
Right: a photograph taken at the time of completion
Below: ground-floor and first-floor plans

1925

H. P. Berlage. *Church of Christ Scientist*, The Hague, Netherlands. 1925
Right: general view of the exterior

Peter Behrens. *Administrative Building*, IG Farben AG (now Hoechst Werke), Dye Works, Hoechst, Frankfurt on Main, Germany. 1925 (1920–25)
Below: interior of the entrance hall, finished in coloured brickwork
Right: a general view of the offices

The internal organization of Berlage's most famous church building has been likened to the treatment of the internal spaces of Wright's Oak Park Unitarian Church, Chicago. Berlage had visited Oak Park earlier in his career. There is also an obvious link with the work of the brickwork fanatics of the Amsterdam school, although this is a considerably more influential building than most of their structures.

Behrens' large industrial complex for IG Farben bears the stamp of his original approach to this type of building. His earlier work for AEG in Berlin had indicated his interest in monumentalism as well as in technical innovation and efficient planning. In the Frankfurt building, he displays his virtuosity in the use of brick. The amazing, colourful entrance hall to the office block is not so far removed from the decoration of Poelzig's Grosses Schauspielhaus, but it is more fundamentally truthful in its use of materials. In Poelzig's scheme, the decoration was applied to an existing structure; at Frankfurt the great oversailing triangular brick columns rise through four storeys. The bridge in the photograph of the exterior links an older administrative block with the new.

Pessac was Le Corbusier's largest and most comprehensive development up to 1925. This estate, built for the developer Frugès, was not completed until well into 1926, although a number of the house units were erected in 1925. The estate was an opportunity for Le Corbusier to realize his 'theories in practice' – a laboratory for industrialized housing. Almost all the prototypes for his later villas and row houses can be found on this estate. It immediately fell foul of the bureaucrats, who refused occupancy certificates; more recently it has been surveyed by sociologists and architects, who have found little of Le Corbusier's

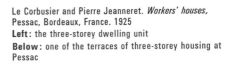

Le Corbusier and Pierre Jeanneret. *Workers' houses,*
Pessac, Bordeaux, France. 1925
Left: the three-storey dwelling unit
Below: one of the terraces of three-storey housing at
Pessac

Henri Sauvage. *Flats*, Rue des Amiraux, Paris, France.
c. 1925 (1923–25)
Above: the cascading terraces of the flats to the side street
Left: main entrance façade

design left. It has been transformed into
more acceptable 'conventional' architecture
by generations of inhabitants.

Sauvage's cliff-hanger of a building is,
with the Fiat factory at Turin, a futurist
type of building, clearly in the tradition of
Sant'Elia's *casa a gradinati*, if not influenced
by it. In section, the stepped-back fronts are
balanced by overhanging floors to the rear,
supported by arches which in turn span a
swimming-pool and garages.

1925

Victor Bourgeois. *La Cité Moderne*, Bercham-Sainte-Agathe, Brussels, Belgium. 1925 (1922–25)
Right: a row of workers' houses under construction in 1924
Below: the architect's drawing of a group of six houses for La Cité Moderne
Middle: a general view of the suburb

Konstantin Melnikov. *USSR Pavilion, Paris Exposition,* Paris, France. 1925 (Demolished)
Below: the architect's drawings (isometric and plan) of the Pavilion
Right: the Pavilion at the Paris Expo of 1925

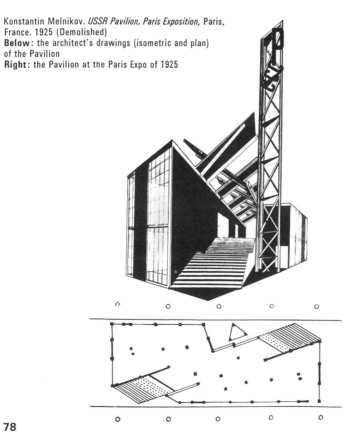

Le Corbusier. *Pavillion de l'esprit nouveau, Paris Exposition,* Paris, France 1925 (Demolished)
Top left: exterior of the Pavilion

J. F. Staal. *Netherlands Pavilion, Paris Exposition,* Paris France. 1925 (Demolished)
Above: the exterior of the Dutch Pavilion

Jiří Kroha. *Technical School,* Mladá Boleslav, Czechoslovakia. 1925 (1923–25)
Left: the end wall of the Technical College

J. J. P. Oud. *Café 'De Unie',* Rotterdam, Netherlands. 1925 (1924–25) (Destroyed in 1940)
Below: the entrance front to the Café

Begun in 1922, Bourgeois' tentatively modern housing estate in a suburb of Brussels owes something to Tony Garnier's *Cité Industrielle* project, as well as to the workers' estates that had been going up in Europe since the end of the previous century. Brick-built with flat roofs, the development was one of the first to incorporate 'mixed' types of dwellings at two and three storeys with communal garden areas.

As the Paris Exposition of 1900 can be viewed as the high-point of Art Nouveau, so the Exposition of Decorative and Industrial Arts of 1925 was in its way a similar high-water-mark for the 'new architecture'.

It was, however, dominated by the style which takes its name from the exhibition, Art Déco. The Pavilions designed by Le Corbusier, Melnikov, Staal and Behrens cannot be identified with that aspect of the Exposition. The USSR Pavilion was the first major Russian Constructivist building

built; that it should have appeared in the West is in itself significant. Corbusier's pavilion represents, as its names implies, the new spirit and was based on a cell designed for his villa-apartment scheme of 1922, which proposed a new formula for urban dwelling. It was designed also as a kick in the face of the so-called *arts décoratifs* – in fact it was itself screened off from public view by an exhibition committee, only to be later nominated for the highest award at the exhibition. Staal's Pavilion owed much to the Amsterdam School tradition but was a richly detailed Indonesian-inspired exhibit.

Kroha's Tech. and Oud's Café have one thing at least in common: they are obviously rooted in the same geometrical and painterly conventions. Oud's façade – highly coloured in Mondrianesque primaries – is a two-dimensional composition, Kroha's a highly organized cubistic work in three dimensions.

1926

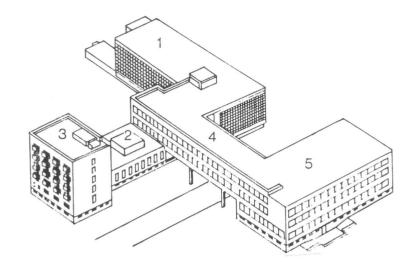

Walter Gropius, *Bauhaus*, Dessau, Germany, 1926 (1925–6);
restored 1976
Right: block view of Bauhaus building. Key: 1, workshop;
2, dining hall; 3, studio workshops; 4, administrative offices;
5, trade school
Below: general external view
Bottom left: the renovated studio workshops façade
Bottom right: original ground-floor and first-floor plans

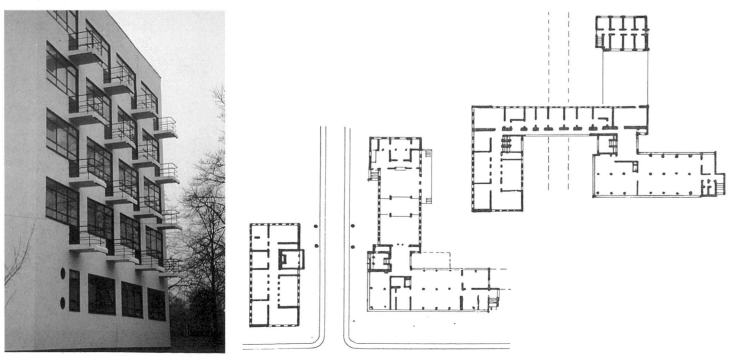

Antoine Pompe. *House*, Uccle, Brussels, Belgium. 1926
(Destroyed)
Right: the front elevation
Below: architect's original pen drawing

Mies van der Rohe. *Monument to Karl Liebknecht and Rosa
Luxemburg*, Berlin, Germany. 1926 (Destroyed)
Bottom: the brick-fronted monument

After the Bauhaus at Weimar had hit political troubles, an offer to move to Dessau was accepted by its Director Walter Gropius. Life began again for the Bauhaus students and staff in a new building and spacious surroundings. This key building was designed by Gropius and his partner Meyer (site architect: Ernst Neufert,) and a certain amount of participation was allowed from students, particularly on decoration and furnishings. The complex which spanned a planned, but never completed, road, consisted of five main elements: a fully glazed, three-storey workshop block, a teaching block, social areas, a five-storey study-bedroom block, and an administration wing spanning the roadway. The forms of the parts of the complex were derived from their separate functions but all contributed to a general consistency. Aesthetically, the Bauhaus was an advanced building but technologically – probably because of limited funds – it was some way behind the contemporary work of the successful Berlin practitioner, Erich Mendelsohn.

In other places, particularly in the Low Countries, the romantic element in architecture was still at work. Some of this work, like Pompe's decorative house at Uccle, has to be admired for its sheer self-confidence and attention to detailing. It was a part of a brickwork tradition held in high regard by many 'modern' designers. Mies van der Rohe's houses of this period, too, owe much to this tradition; his monument to the Communist revolutionaries was its best expression. This chunky piece of wall can hardly be referred to as a building. It is, however, clearly architectonic, and one critic has suggested that it 'foreshadows some of Wright's later houses'. It was destroyed by the Nazis.

1926

Peter Behrens. *House*, 'New Ways', Northampton, England. 1926.
Right: the garden elevation

R. M. Schindler. *Beach House for Dr P. Lovell,* Newport Beach, Calif., USA. 1926 (1925–26) (Altered)
Below: a recent view of the Lovell Beach House, with alterations

The private house played an important part in the dissemination of modern movement ideas. Many were extremely expensive 'one-off' structures built for wealthy patrons, others were simpler and more economic, providing family accommodation on a relatively modest scale. A variety of such projects is shown on these two pages.

Schindler's inexpensive Beach House for Dr Lovell (also the client for the luxurious Health House in Los Angeles by Neutra, see 1929) is arguably his best work. Indeed, leaving aside the question why it has rested in relative obscurity for so many years, it is one of the few buildings in the USA in the 1920s that matches the best-known European modern-movement buildings of the same period. It is an exercise in space and structure, somewhat crude perhaps, but one which epitomizes the central architectural problems of the first half of the century.

Not so Peter Behrens' house at Northampton. This, the first 'modern' house built by an original pioneer Continental architect in Britain (Waugh's Professor Silenius?), was remarkable and influential (see Tait's work at Silver End), but, although built for the inventor Basset-Lowke, somewhat short on inspiration.

Another under-estimated house architect is the Belgian Louis H. de Koninck. His house and studio for the painter Lenglet was built in the same street as his own house, a modest but competent work by an architect who helped to consolidate modern-movement ideas in Belgium.

When Walter Gropius and the teaching staff moved from Weimar to the new Bauhaus at Dessau, an opportunity was presented for a number of important housing commissions both from the City Council and from the new Bauhaus itself. Gropius built himself a new detached house, and the Masters and other faculty members were provided with houses of their own. These contained some salient features for 'advanced designers', among them labour-saving devices in the kitchens and totally rationalised methods of construction. This was taken further in the workers' houses in Dessau-Törten which were early – and somewhat primitive – attempts at industrialization or method building.

L. H. de Koninck. *House and Studio*, Uccle, Brussels,
Belgium. 1926 (Altered)
Above: the dining room corner
Right: the studio house elevation to Avenue Fond'Roy

Walter Gropius. *Housing,* Dessau, Germany. 1925–26
Right: a pair of houses for the staff of the Bauhaus
Below left: the architect's own house at Dessau
Below right: Bauhaus Masters' house
Bottom: part of the Dessau-Törten estate

1927

J. J. P. Oud. *Workers' Housing*, Hook of Holland.
Netherlands 1927 (1924–27)
Right and Below: general views of the housing at the Hook
Middle right: ground floor plans showing the layout of individual living units.

Bonatz and Scholer. *Railway Station*, Stuttgart, Germany.
1927 (1911–27)
Bottom: the entrance façade of rock-faced ashlar blocks

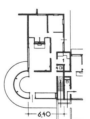

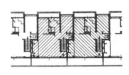

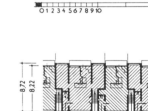

The workers' terrace houses by the then city architect of Rotterdam, J. J. P. Oud, (see page 64) are, with Le Corbusier's and Gropius's houses of the same period, probably the best-known of all the so-called 'functionalist' buildings. They seem to breathe the very essence of a humanized modernity that is far removed from the boxed-in concrete houses that have got modern architecture a bad name.

The Stuttgart Railway Station went through a long building period but finally opened in 1927. It has been described as one of the finest stations in the world. Obviously inspired by the Munich architect and theorist Theodor Fischer, it also owes much to the traditional German approach to monumentality and to Eliel Saarinen's great terminus at Helsinki. It can hardly be called a *modern* building.

Loos, the irritant in the flesh of Viennese modernism, moved to Paris in the mid-1920s and enjoyed a vogue in Corbusian circles. The Tzara house was built during this period, a stark but locally-inspired addition to the range of artists' studios in Montmartre which has suffered somewhat from recent alterations. On a restricted and awkward

Adolf Loos. *House for Tristan Tzara,* Paris, France. 1927
(1925–27) (Altered)
Above: street façade to Avenue Junot

J. A. Brinckmann and L. C. van der Vlugt. *Van Nelle
Shop*, Leiden, Netherlands. 1927 (1925–27)
Top right: the Van Nelle shop on the Aalmarkt

Robert Mallet-Stevens. *Apartments,* rue Mallet-Stevens,
Passy, Paris, France. 1927
Right: one of the semi-detached blocks in the
fashionable sixteenth Arrondissement

site, Loos placed this vertical six-storey box,
cutting a large balcony space into the two-
storey recess on the fourth and fifth levels.

The small Van Nelle shop at Leiden was
another unified box, forming a strange
contrast to its vernacular neighbours, but
nevertheless a clear definition of modern
movement aims from the architects who
(with Mart Stam) also designed that masterpiece of modern architecture, the Van
Nelle factory at Rotterdam.

Mallet-Stevens was not a forerunner in
the modern movement, but he did manage to
create a distinctive, almost 'moderne',
French line in design which displayed
overtones of the Cubism that had gripped
the Czech school. The Paris apartments
consisted of three semi-detached blocks each
of four storeys constructed in monolithic
concrete.

1927

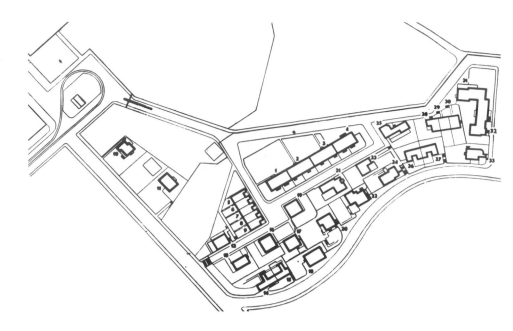

Mies van der Rohe (planning director), Richard Döcker (site architect). *Werkbund Exhibition,* Weissenhofsiedlung, Stuttgart, Germany. 1927 (1926–27) (Some houses since altered or demolished)
Right: key plan of the exhibition

1–4	Mies van der Rohe	20	Hans Poelzig
5–9	J. J. P. Oud	21–22	Richard Döcker
10	Victor Bourgeois	23–24	Max Taut
11–12	Adolf G. Schneck	25	Adolf Rading
13–15	Le Corbusier, with	26–27	Josef Frank
	Pierre Jeanneret	28–30	Mart Stam
16–17	Walter Gropius	31–32	Peter Behrens
18	Ludwig Hilberseimer	33	Hans Scharoun
19	Bruno Taut		

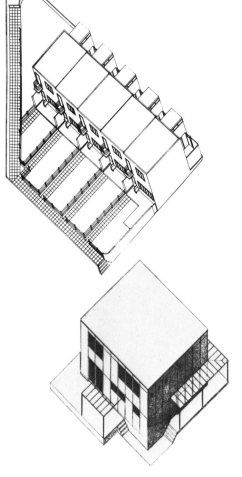

J. J. P. Oud. *Terrace Housing,* Weissenhofsiedlung 1927
Centre left: road entrance to terrace-houses
Centre right: axonometric

Walter Gropius. *Prefabricated House,* Weissenhofsiedlung. 1927
Above: general view showing the front entrance and glazed canopy
Bottom right: axonometric

The spectacular success of the Weissenhof-siedlung exhibition and its lasting prominence as a key event in modern movement history was undoubtedly due to its 'newness' and consistent appearance. Under Mies van der Rohe's direction, a representative group of European architects had been brought together to design a model estate of 'modern' houses for people with moderate means, as well as for the client with aspirations towards villa life. The larger, more luxurious houses took a back seat to the display of houses that would be appropriate to the new urban density problem facing many city councils at the time. The architects had not

Weissenhofsiedlung. 1927
Mies van der Rohe. *Apartment Block*
Above: a recent view of the block, with plan below
Le Corbusier and Pierre Jeanneret. *Villa and apartment block*
Below: general view and plans of the apartment block
Mart Stam. *Terrace Housing*
Bottom right: front elevation

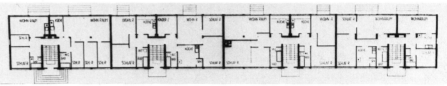

worked closely together (Mies' own design for an apartment block had been worked up in a few days in the office of the Brothers Rasch), but, amazingly, the results suggested a uniformity of approach if not a conspicuous conformity. It did, however, to many a layman look almost all the same even though it could be easily demonstrated that each architect had added to his own work – for example, Le Corbusier's villa is clearly an exhibit based on his earlier Citrohan house, a further significant building.

1928

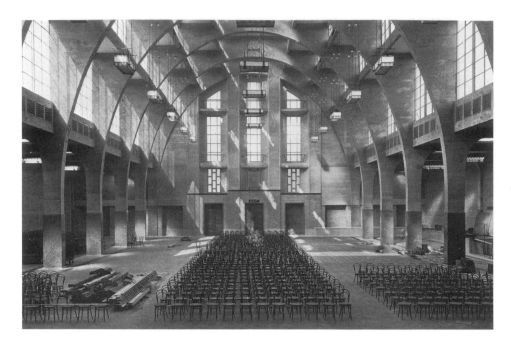

Easton and Robertson. *Royal Horticultural Hall,* Westminster, England. 1928
Right: interior of the then 'New Horticultural Hall'

Mies van der Rohe. *Hermann Lange House,* Krefeld, Germany. 1928 (Badly damaged)
Below: garden elevation

I. P. Golosov. *Zuyev Club,* Moscow, USSR. 1928
Left: general street view of the Zuyev Club; present condition
Above: ground and first-floor plans
Below: an earlier photograph of the circular staircase tower and corner

The stone and brickwork exterior of the New Horticultural Hall by Easton and Robertson was uninspiring, but internally the vast 150-foot long by 72-foot wide hall, constructed from elliptical reinforced concrete arches edged with vertical glazing, was a significant step towards modernism in British architecture at a time when a 'high peak' of mediocrity had been reached by most designers.

Mies's Lange House, and the Wolf House at Guben built two years earlier, were both related to a brick country-house De Stijl mode with an interpenetrating project of 1923 very much in the Dutch plan and purist façades.

The Lange House is deceptively simple, with the crisp outline of its windows cutting into plain wall surfaces which, on the garden front, act as a foil to vegetation which at one time clambered over the open balconies and the terrace.

Gunnar Asplund. *City Library,* Stockholm, Sweden. 1928
(1920–28)
Left: aerial view of the City Library

Erich Mendelsohn. *Schocken Department Store,* Stuttgart,
Germany. 1928 (1926–28)
Middle left: the main street elevation
Below: side elevation leading to the corner staircase
tower

Ludvík Kysela. *Bata Store,* Prague, Czechoslovakia. 1928
Bottom: day and night views of the Bata Store façades

Few buildings were actually erected by
the Soviet constructivist architects; nothing, in fact, of any significance before the
1925 Paris Exhibition. In Russia itself, the
workers' clubs and experimental communes,
which began to appear about the time of the
tenth anniversary of the October Revolution, are of chief interest. Golosov's
Zuyev Club is one of the best buildings of
the period. It uses simple volumes (parallele-
piped, cube and cylinder) and glazed surfaces and is flexible in layout.

The City Library at Stockholm is also a
simple geometric solution, but one steeped
in Classicism – a cylinder rising from an
enclosing cube (in actual fact, a three-
winged square block). The entrance is
placed on a main axis. Mendelsohn's work
continued the current fashion in geometrical
organization but in a way that is at once
more eye-catching and emphatically connected to the detailing of the building. His
horizontal use of striated glass corners and
brickwork were to catch on as a design
motif throughout the world. At Stuttgart
he incorporated in his design enormous
advertising letters for the name 'Schocken,'
a feature that was also to be seen in the
contemporary Bata Store in Czechoslovakia
by Kysela. In this design the eight-storey
glass infill façade is particularly noteworthy.

1928

Le Corbusier. *Les Terrasses* (*Villa Stein*), Garches, France. 1928 (1927–28)
Right: the interior with staircase
Below: view from the drive
Middle: rear elevation of the house showing the concrete veranda and the staircase leading to the garden

'Les Terrasses', and the earlier La Roche and Savoye houses, are Le Corbusier's most important generic works. Each in its way is a mature design but all are interrelated; his principles for a 'new architecture' are to be found expressed in all three examples. The three-storey house at Garches, with its roof garden and veranda on the first floor leading down into a fine garden, is less severe than the earlier examples – less a monumental object and more a generous place of human habitation. The side walls were left almost blank, as the unit itself was designed as a prototype for a repetitive block. Internally, columns are free from planning restrictions but gridded in such a way that they relate to the design of the façades. A proportional system was used to create the façade sub-divisions but it should

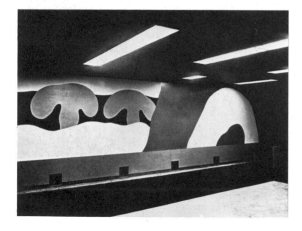

Theo van Doesburg (with Hans Arp and Sophie Tauber-Arp). *'L'Aubette' Cabaret, Cinema and Café*, Strasbourg, France. 1928 (1926–28) (Demolished)
Above: the 'dancing cave' of the 'Aubette' with a mural by Arp
Right: interior of the restaurant/nightclub/cinema

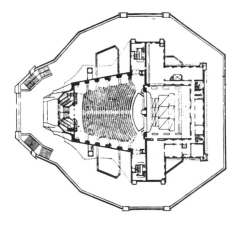

Rudolf Steiner (Architect: Hermann Ranzenberger; Engineers: Leuprecht and Ebbel). *Goetheanum II,* Dornach, near Basel, Switzerland. 1928 (1924–28)
Above: ground floor plan
Right: a detail of the exterior concrete work of the Goetheanum II
Below: the main entrance frontage

be noted that the architect did not allow his main elevations to touch the ground – they are suspended from a cantilevered first floor. The double-height garden terrace explodes through the whole of the house at one end but is unified by the roof garden itself which runs the full width of the building.

The 'Aubette' café/cabaret and Steiner's massive concrete Goetheanum are both highly idiosyncratic buildings which, when placed in context with the Corbusian house, indicate the diversity of thinking and design

commitment in this period. The Aubette has often been dismissed as simply an 'art work' or an interior décor scheme of some substance but little significance. Yet it involved a substantial remodelling of part of a historic building: a ground floor area with bar and club facilities, a mezzanine and a cabaret and banqueting rooms on the first floor. The interiors were decorated on 'elementarist' principles, except for the purely abstract surfaces by the Arps.

The expressionist work of Steiner defies

normal critical evaluation. His personal style of 'soul architecture' transcends functional requirements or structural efficiences. The Goetheanum II, replacing the earlier timber Goetheanum I (see page 47), was the world's largest raw concrete building and was erected with the aid of sectional profile drawings. It remains one of the most amazing technical achievements of the twentieth century as well as one of its aesthetic curiosities.

J. W. E. Buys and J. B. Lürsen. *Co-operative Store 'De Volharding',* The Hague, Netherlands. 1928
Right: general view

Gerrit Rietveld. *Garage and chauffeur's quarters,* Utrecht, Netherlands. 1928 (1927–28)
Below: the garage with the chauffeur's flat over it

Erich Mendelsohn. *Universum Cinema,* Berlin, Germany.
1928 (1926–28)
Above: the sweeping curve of the auditorium of the
Universum

Below: exterior of the development of which the
Universum formed a part

The co-operative store 'De Volharding' has been described as one of the most confident Constructivist building of the Dutch school, yet Buys can hardly be called a true Constructivist. He knew, as did many Dutch architects of his generation, about the Soviet work, but this store is really an extension of the interest in planes and surfaces exhibited in many previous buildings by the Dutch, principally in Dudok's stores. The five-storey 'De Volharding' is a cross between imported Constructivism and the controlled aesthetic of the native *De Stijl.* All the more so, when one realizes that this flat and rather plain building by day livened up

at night as an extremely bright example of illuminated architecture.

Still with the Dutch – Rietveld's small garage and quarters was an exceptional example of prefabricated concrete construction, integrated within a framework of steel sections. The concrete planks were painted with black enamel before installation, and when they were dry a perforated metal sheet was laid over them and then painted white, giving a black surface with white dots. Materials and construction are here more important than space and planes, in remarkable contrast to Rietveld's earlier Schröder House (see page 75).

The Universum cinema near Berlin's fashionable Kurfürstendamm was designed to celebrate the twentieth-century invention of commercial cinematography. Designing for the government-sponsored UFA company, Mendelsohn devised his now famous horseshoe cinema plan, surrounding it with cloakrooms and wide entrances. The plan was obviously influenced by earlier opera houses and national theatres, but the Universum set the highest possible standards in a period when films had just changed to sound, and the flamboyance of earlier movie houses was yielding to the controlled, plain, efficient acoustic box.

1928

Thomas Tait. *Crittall Housing Estate,* Silver End, near Chelmsford, Essex, England. 1928 (1927–28)
Right: reinforced concrete Welfare Club building
Below right: oriel window feature on terrace
Below: general view of brick-built terrace

J. J. P. Oud. *Kiefhoek Housing Estate,* Rotterdam, Netherlands. 1928 (1925–28)
Bottom left: one of the two curved corner blocks: the canopy covers the 'corner shop'
Bottom right: one of the side streets of the Kiefhoek Estate

The Continental modern architectural idiom had been imported into Britain with Behrens's Northampton house (page 82), and soon after then, a number of British architects began to experiment in the modern mode, chief among them Joseph Emberton and Thomas Tait. The steel window manufacturers Crittall's, under pressure from designers, began to produce their standard-sized steel windows based on Continental patterns. They also commissioned one of the most forward-looking young British architects, Thomas Tait, a partner of the famous Scottish architect Sir John Burnet, to design an estate of houses for their workers and staff. The estate is superficially modern, in the sense that it incorporates the flat roofs and plain surfaces associated with the European Masters' work, but on closer examination it can be seen that in fact the houses are in conventional brickwork with a painted finish and sprout incongruous chimney stacks. The motifs are distinctly Behrensian.

The difference between the real and the imitation modern can be seen by comparing Tait's houses with those completed by Oud

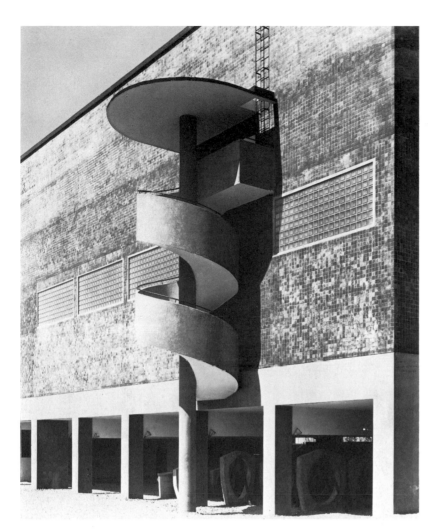

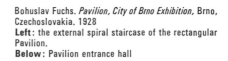

Bohuslav Fuchs. *Pavilion, City of Brno Exhibition,* Brno, Czechoslovakia. 1928
Left: the external spiral staircase of the rectangular Pavilion.
Below: Pavilion entrance hall

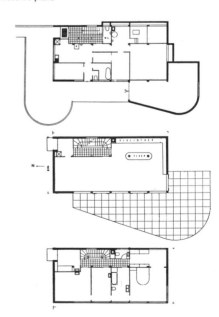

Hans and Wassili Luckhardt (with Alfons Anker). *House* (one of three), Am Rupenhorn, Berlin, Germany. 1928
Left: the road elevation of the first of the Berlin detached houses
Below: plans

in the same year. They follow on the pioneering work started at the Hook of Holland in 1924.

Fuchs's Pavilion is a typically good example of his work in Czechoslovakia in the late 1920s. He was the country's best modern architect. However, the light openness of the interior of the Pavilion is not carried through to the outside, and the spiral staircase, an

effective decorative item, was little more than a useful appendage to relieve a stark façade.

The Luckhardt houses were consummate pieces of domestic architecture, thought through to the last detail and combining the free-shapes of the Expressionists with the efficient planning of the Functionalists. This, the first of three houses, was construc-

ted with a steel frame with concrete cavity walls; the whole exterior was then rendered on a wire mesh backing. The steel frame offered flexibility, the concrete surface the right kind of appearance.

1928

Jan Wils. *Olympic Stadium,* Amsterdam, Netherlands.
1928 (1926–28)
Right: exterior of the stadium with the tower feature

Otto Bartning. *The Steel Church,* Press Exhibition,
Cologne, Germany. 1928
Above: the church as part of the exhibition, with the
Ernst Barlach statue beside the entrance
Right: the rounded and glazed apse

Jan Wils was one of the few Dutch architects who, during the early period of the Romantic/Rationalist controversy from about 1917, had a foot in both camps. Wils's work was in line with the Amsterdam school's attitude, was obviously influenced by Wright (probably via Van 't Hoff and Berlage) and was part and parcel of the 'De Stijl' achievement. The Olympic Stadium, his largest single work, was very much a synthesis of these various influences: a sort of picturesque Wrightian elementarism, mixed with Constructivist inventions. Metal structure was mixed with large areas of brickwork and a fanciful tower was included.

Bartning's German church work is of major significance within the modern liturgical developments in Protestantism in the first half of the twentieth century. His buildings were always very original and houses and churches are among the many building types he worked on. The steel church for the Press Exhibition at Cologne had a simple plan which gradually curved round at the altar end. Compared with the early Bartning star-shaped church, produced as a model for discussion on church organization in 1924, it had a fairly conventional layout. But whereas the Star Church had only limited influence among designers, the Cologne one was actually built and received wide publicity.

With his 'Zonnestraal', Duiker (of the partnership Bijvoet and Duiker) created a total twentieth-century architectural ambience. It is indeed one of the most competent of the International Functional buildings. Early in relation to other European examples, it is among the most neglected. Hidden in a wooded site outside Hilversum, the group of buildings is symmetrically arranged around a central

services block. A service road goes across the site and, at one point, under the building (à la Bauhaus). The aesthetic treatment is admirably consistent and white straight and curved wall surfaces wrap around the various one and two-storey elements.

Johannes Duiker. *'Zonnestraal' Sanatorium*, Hilversum, Netherlands. 1928 (1926–28)
Top: general view of the Sanatorium
Centre: the connection between a single-storey and a two-storey section
Above: the predominance of glass and concrete evokes a thoroughly modern feeling
Right: the connecting block spanning the roadway within the site

1929

Mies van der Rohe. *German Pavilion,* International
Exposition, Barcelona, Spain. 1929 (Demolished)
Right: the main entrance to the Pavilion
Below: ground-floor plan
Middle: the larger Pavilion from the outside pool
Bottom: interior, looking towards the half-covered
Internal pool

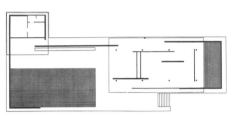

The Barcelona Pavilion has become a kind
of symbol of modern architecture, in the
same way that the Eiffel Tower symbolizes
Paris. It, too, was an exhibition set-piece, an
object for visitors to admire, to walk through
– a structure, more than a building with a
defined function. However, whereas Eiffel's
object was concerned with an exploration
of technical possibilities, Mies's exhibit
clearly was concerned with spatial problems,
heightened by the use of rich reflective
materials. Its conscious simplicity was
deceptive, the result of deduction, not of
naivety. Take two planes, he seems to have
been saying, horizontal and vertical and
then juxtapose them in such a way that they
overlap and extend the limits of defined
space; isolate the support elements and
introduce space-extending, opaque and
transparent materials and what emerges
is a totally controlled project. 'Along this
path, industry and technology,' wrote Mies
in a prefatory statement in 1928, 'will join
with the forces of thought and culture.'

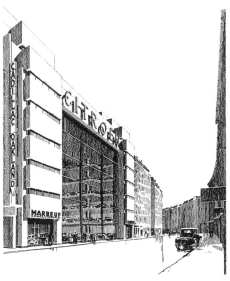

Albert Laprade and L. E. Bazin. *Le Marbeuf Garage,*
Paris, France. 1929
Left: interior of the grand automobile hall
Below: the original façade drawing by L. E. Bazin

Eileen Gray and Jean Badovici. *Sea-side house,*
Roquebrune-Cap-Martin, France. 1929 (1926–29)
Below: general view of the balconied front

Majestic building materials were used in
the Pavilion to underline its message:
Roman travertine for the base and light
coloured walls, green Tinian marble for the
walls to the sculpture pool, bottle-green and
grey glass for partitions and onyx for the
free-standing wall in the main hall.

Le Marbeuf, the Citroën Sales building in
the Rue Marbeuf, Paris, has been called 'a
shop window six storeys high and 68 feet
wide'. Another enterprising building from
the highly productive period at the end of
the 1920s, it was designed round customer
requirements. Side portals to the vast
central plate-glass window allowed customers to drive their old vehicle in and leave
in a new model. An older building at the
rear of the cantilevered showroom served as
a storage garage.

The other French building on these
pages, by Gray and Badovici, is another
well-known international style two-storey
house, but one which also reflects the more
local Mediterranean seaside villa tradition.

1929

Theo van Doesburg. *Studio House,* Meudon-val-Fleury, Paris, France. 1929
Right: the studio end of the house
Below: plan

Konstantin Melnikov. *The architect's own house,* Moscow, USSR. 1929
Above: a recent photograph of Melnikov in his own house
Right: exterior of house

Theo van Doesburg's studio house, built between Paris and Versailles for his own occupation, was his last architectural work. It is a mature building in the International Style, owing little to such excesses of the De Stijl aesthetic as are to be found in the earlier Strasbourg Aubette night-club. Again, it is the extended cube which forms the basis of the design. On the first floor, a large studio space takes up a square area at the northern end of the plan; living accommodation backs on to this space and kitchen and garage space is provided below. Except for the north studio wall, solid concrete walls predominate, relieved by an external stair at the south end.

The differences between the European-inspired modern movement buildings and those of the modern movement in Soviet Russia can be clearly seen here. Melnikov is still essentially an individualist, searching for unique design solutions. His circular house with its hexagonal windows and plain concrete surface is far removed from the cubic expression of the studio house in France. His Workers' Club is a complex structure in concrete whose shape is dictated by a main, flexible, 1400-seat auditorium. Its outer contours are dictated by smaller halls. Khrushchev called it, in 1963, 'an ugly building . . . as ugly as sin'!

By the end of the 1920s commercial architecture in the 'moderne' style had really broken through: glittering hotel interiors by Bernard and others could be found in many capital cities. Mendelsohn's supreme commercial solution was his curved Schocken Department Store at Chemnitz. Technically adventurous, confidently styled and commercially viable, it is a master-work of the decade.

Konstantin Melnikov. *Rusakov Workers' Club,* Stranynka, Moscow, USSR. 1929 (1927–29)
Top: view of the main entrance

Oliver P. Bernard. *Strand Palace Hotel Foyer,* London, England. 1929 (Removed)
Right: the foyer *c.* 1930

Erich Mendelsohn. *Schocken Department Store.* Chemnitz, (now Karl-Marx-Stadt), Germany. 1929 (1928–29)
Left: the main frontage of the Schocken, Chemnitz
Above: night view

1929

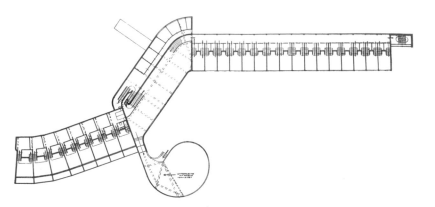

Hans Scharoun. *Rest Home,* (Hostel building, 1929
Werkbund Exhibition ''Wohnung und Werkraum''),
Breslau, Germany (now Poland). 1929 (1928–29)
Top right: ground-floor plan
Below: section through the living accommodation
Middle right: the 'middle building' from the terrace
Bottom: general view of the Rest Home

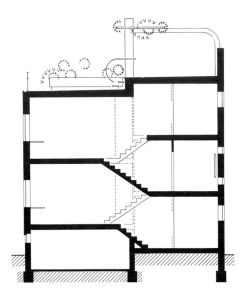

Scharoun, it has been observed, is concerned with architecture as a moral, political, act: the architect exerts his influence in creating the spaces in which people live, work, relax and move. In the 1920s, he was also associated with a side-movement of Expressionism concerned with what was termed 'organic building'. This was not the Wrightian concept of 'organic architecture', although it obviously is related to it, but a peculiarly German idea of wholeness, of appropriateness of materials and forms, spaces and

structure. The Rest Home at Breslau – the city that housed the influential Breslau Academy, where Scharoun came into contact with Poelzig – is clearly not 'ascetically' modern. On its own terms, within German modern architecture, it could probably be described as a rich, humane building, rationally organized but one degree deeper in content than most of the other buildings going up at the time.

Asecticism – or Geometric Purism – can be seen in a contemporary building in

Brno. Kranz's Café Era was like a white, solid cube out of which carefully balanced voids were cut. The main storey elevation was so precise as to suggest a two-dimensional canvas. The subtle changes of texture (glass bricks let light into the staircase well) and the concealing of the sevices within this strict façade (some of the small slots were ventilators) indicate a thoroughly worked-out design.

By the end of the 1920s, a number of remarkable new building types existed in

Michael Barsch with Michael Sinyavsky. *Planetarium,* Moscow, USSR. 1929 (1927–29)
Below: the main entrance to the Planetarium
Left: the emergency staircase and projection wing

Josef Kranz. *Café Era,* Brno, Czechoslovakia. 1929 (Destroyed?)
Above: the main flat façade of the Café Era

Soviet Russia. The Planetarium, referred to by Gan as a 'theatre without actors', had a double role to play: it was designed for scientific purposes but was also an educational and entertainment building for the workers.

1929

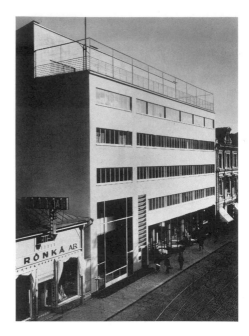

Alvar Aalto, *Turun Sanomat Building*, Turku, Finland, 1929 (1928–29)

Le Corbusier and Pierre Jeanneret. *Villa annexe*, Ville d'Avray, Seine-et-Oise, France. 1929 (1927–29)
Right: view from the living-room towards the bedroom wing of the annexe
Below right: the roof garden
Below: the pavilion, a renovated building

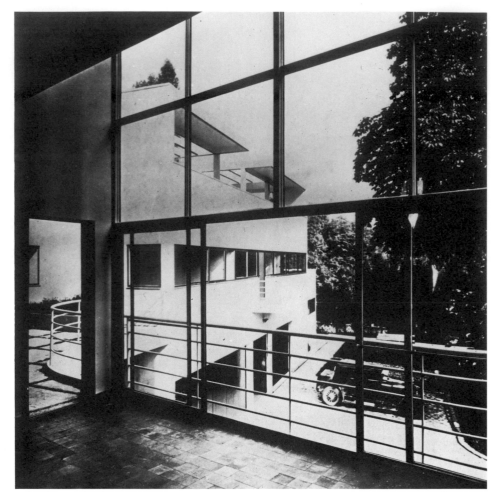

At Ville d'Avray, Le Corbusier worked on the remodelling of the old villa, built an annexe based on a hockey-stick-shaped plan, and refurbished the existing *Pavillon* which stood in the middle of the extensive grounds. The annexe is one of his finest projects, embodying most, if not all, of his principles for a new aesthetic. The furniture, in tubular steel, was also designed especially for the client by Le Corbusier, Pierre Jeanneret and Charlotte Perriand.

The Luckhardt Brothers' concern with the freely curving building had not been abandoned with their dismissal of their earlier exuberant Expressionism. The Telschow House was a dynamically curving building situated on the Potsdamer Platz in Berlin;

the horizontal strips, unlike those used in Mendelsohn's designs, are controlled within the overall framework of the façade and do not continue through to the edges or around the block.

The late Ernst May's name is synonymous with interwar Frankfurt. He was City Architect from 1925 to 1930. He was responsible for the general planning of the city and its suburbs, for the design and layout of a number of these suburbs and for the employment of eminent modern designers within his teams. His work included the establishment of new standards for house layouts as well as for small items like standard kitchen details. The work covers a period of some five to six years, but by 1929 most of the

suburban developments were either completed or nearing completion. The illustrations shown indicate just a fragment of this important work.

The Turun Sanomat building in Turku brought Aalto into the international limelight. It is a fully fledged modern building in the sense that it met CIAM criteria and reflected many of the current international trends, including the plain façades and long windows advocated by Le Corbusier, full concrete column construction and asymmetrical composition. The interior, with shaped concrete supports and pertinent designed fixtures, achieved a high standard.

Wassili and Hans Luckhardt (with Alfons Anker).
Telschow House, Berlin, Germany. 1929
Above: the curved exterior of the Telschow House

Ernst May (City Architect). *Suburban development*,
Frankfurt-am-Main, Germany. 1929 (1925–29)
Right: part of the low-rent housing scheme
completed in 1928
Bottom right: a house on the Frankfurt housing estate
Top right: a construction photograph
Below: plan of the development on the Rotenbusch
sector (Riederwaldkolonie), east of Frankfurt

1929

Richard Neutra. *Demonstration Health House* (*Lovell House*),
Los Angeles, Calif., USA. 1929 (1927–29)
Right: the south (garden) elevation
Below: the main entrance which gives access to the top
floor of the house
Bottom: general view

This three-storey house, together with
Schindler's Beach House for the same client
at Newport Beach, has been described as
'the greatest monument of the International
Style in Southern California'. It is comparable in its architectural clarity to the
important exhibition buildings that went
up in Europe prior to 1927. It was, in fact,
a demonstration house in its own right,
incorporating family accommodation as
well as an experimental open-air school.
The house was constructed in steelwork
(erected, it is said, in 40 hours!) with a
concrete finish. The internal divisions
accord with standard-size windows. Access
to the house is on the top floor.

This was Richard Neutra's first large
building after the Jardinette Apartments,
and through it he became widely known in
Europe. Its position on a site overlooking
the Pacific near the mountainous park
reserve makes it one of the most desirable
properties in the world.

Decade 1930

Connell, Ward and Lucas. *House*, Hayling Island, Hants, England. About 1936

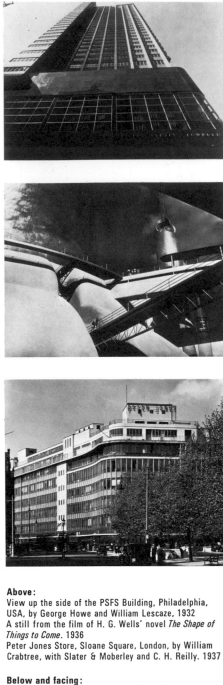

In the nineteen-thirties, the new architecture gained a firm foothold throughout the world. The long-sought-after unity of effort among the élite 'modern' architects had occurred, and the old issues of academicism and eclecticism which had caused so much dissension earlier were virtually swept aside. By the middle of the decade, many countries had at least one or two buildings which had clearly been influenced by Le Corbusier or other CIAM members.

With the wide dissemination of the tenets of the new architecture, a crop of derivative modern buildings was built, bearing the unmistakable stamp of what was known as the 'new style'. Flat roofs, white and plain surfaces, 'liberated' interiors, concrete structures, long narrow horizontal windows and cubic exteriors were its hall-marks. Juxtaposed with more conventional and traditional structures in locations in various parts of the world, the new buildings looked somewhat self-conscious and vulnerable to disparaging criticism.

But soon their very newness created its own tradition, and architectural journals throughout the world were recording each new example on glossy pages, thereby perpetuating the new white aesthetic through the magic of the black and white photograph. The picture itself was somewhat misleading as it over-simplified the new architecture, but there is no doubt that where the original building could not be visited and seen at first hand it provided the necessary substitute.

Examples of the new building were to be found in London, Brighton, Los Angeles, Johannesburg, Tokyo, Athens, Helsinki, Belgrade and Barcelona, as well as in the towns and cities of those European countries from which the original impetus had come. Picture-books on 'modern' houses, flats, industrial buildings, schools and hospitals proliferated. The appropriateness of the new architecture, the pedigree of its leaders and its popular success were assured. There was to be no looking back, but there was strong reaction. Opponents of the new architecture were vocal in their criticism of the 'inhuman' nature and 'plainness' of what was derisively called *Modernismus*. Le Corbusier's analogy of the house as a machine for living in (an idea derived from earlier German sources) became the subject of satire. In Britain, in particular, local authority officials and representatives became obstructive and in some cases were unwilling to provide the necessary permits to build 'modern' buildings.

Almost simultaneously with its world-wide expansion, a systematic suppression of modern movement ideas took place in the Soviet Union and in Germany and a kind of grotesquely monumental, nationalistic architecture replaced the radical work that had been going on in these countries. A positive flirtation with modern art and architecture occurred in Fascist Italy and it was brought, for a time, into the political arena.

In the United States, continental European modern architecture was not received with open arms, but there was at the beginning of the 'thirties a growing sympathy on the east coast for the work of the pioneers and that of the succeeding generation. In 1931, an exhibition devoted to the 'International Style: Architecture since 1922' was held in the newly opened Museum of Modern Art building in New York, including work from fifteen countries.

The specific and all-embracing term 'International Style' was itself significant and was re-used by Henry-Russell Hitchcock and Philip Johnson as the title for the

Above:
View up the side of the PSFS Building, Philadelphia, USA, by George Howe and William Lescaze, 1932
A still from the film of H. G. Wells' novel *The Shape of Things to Come*. 1936
Peter Jones Store, Sloane Square, London, by William Crabtree, with Slater & Moberley and C. H. Reilly. 1937

Below and facing:
Three English super-cinemas from the 1930s – Odeon, Leicester Square, London, by Harry W. Weedon and Andrew Mather, 1937; Dreamland, Margate, Kent, by Iles, Leathart and Granger (original perspective), 1935; Odeon, Chingford, Essex, by Andrew Mather, 1935

book they wrote concurrently with the New York exhibition and published the following year. What had existed ten years earlier as an intimation of a new spirit of restless originality had crystallized by 1932 as something that could be described by Alfred Barr in his introduction to this book as a 'modern style as original, as consistent, as logical and as widely distributed as any in the past'.

That some sort of modern 'style' as such existed is beyond dispute. What is disputable is whether it was as truly international and consistent as Barr claimed. Both the exhibition and the book had underlined the fact that a number of architects had been producing work with certain common characteristics and aims and these new men – the second-generation pioneers who included Le Corbusier, Mies van der Rohe, Walter Gropius and J. J. P. Oud – were intent on creating an architecture with a 'universal' validity. The book misconstrued some of these aims by over-emphasizing stylistic similarities and undervaluing the anti-aestheticism and social concern of the architects themselves. Indeed, one critic has gone as far as to say that Hitchcock and Johnson took a 'disdainful stance *against*, not for, Functionalism'.

Paradoxically, it was at this moment of maximum influence and acceptability that the first few nails were innocently driven into the coffin of the 'new style' by those very enthusiasts who had seen it as the manifestation of their own hopes: as the longed-for new aesthetic viewpoint and as the desired challenge to accepted life-styles. During the critical years from 1934 up to the war, it was being undermined at the same time as it achieved world-wide dissemination. During the burgeoning that took place in the late 'twenties, universality and uniformity had come to be seen by some as a basic requirement of the new architecture, without regard for national tendencies and preferences. This was asking too much. The white, 'Mediterranean' box had been rather overdone by the small group of pioneers who made the new architecture possible, and their polemics about function defining form in the derivation of plan shapes and structural systems had remained somewhat hazy.

Basic limitations were recognized shortly after the next generation began to interpret the work of the pioneers. The plain white concrete walls did not work at all well in some countries, and flat roofs – concrete or otherwise – were clearly a hazard in places with heavy rainfall and recurring frosts. In England, some attempts were made in the 'thirties to overcome the technical limitations of reinforced concrete solid walls by resorting to conventional brickwork and either painting it white or rendering it to simulate the appearance of continental modern architecture. This was not a success.

In Finland the work of Alvar Aalto indicated a much more mature attitude to the new architecture. Here was an originator in his own right, although one committed whole-heartedly to CIAM principles. His flirtation with 'white' concrete architecture began in the 'twenties and by 1935 he had produced in his own country two of the most important buildings of the modern movement, the Library at Viipuri (1927–35), and the extraordinarily confident Piamio Sanatorium (1929–33). But somehow in producing his new-style buildings he had not abandoned the timeless quality of the traditional architecture of his own country. In scale and in relationship to the landscape, his buildings – as they do to the present day – made a positive contribution to the environment.

Below: Iakov Chernikov (1889–1951) published his architectural fantasies in the early 1930s in Leningrad, influencing buildings as far apart as the Tower and Restaurant at the Glasgow Empire Exhibition, 1938

Below:
Scheme for the Milton Shep House, Los Angeles, by R. M. Schindler, 1935
Housing exhibition at Tel Aviv, Palestine (now Israel) by Arieh Sharon, 1937

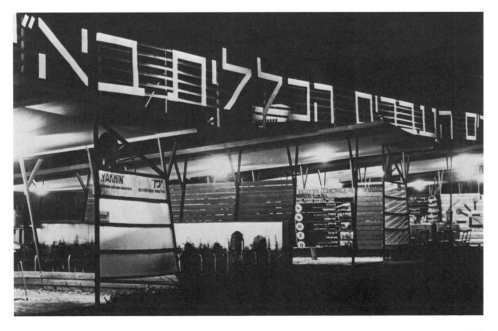

E. Persico, M. Nizzoli, *the Gold Medal Hall of the Italian Aeronautical Exhibition*, Milan, 1934

Walter Burley Griffin (1876–1937). One of a number of incinerators designed by Griffin (former Wright assistant and city planner of Canberra) situated in Willoughby, Sydney, NSW, *c.*1936

Edwin Lutyens (1869–1944) *Rashtrapati Bhavan* (formerly Viceroy's House), New Delhi, India. Not completed until 1929–30, the Viceroy's residence was larger than Versailles and an amalgam of eastern and western stylistic ideas. Enormous garden also designed by Lutyens

Below:
Czechoslovak Pavilion at New York World's Fair, 1939, by Josef Gočár (architect's model)

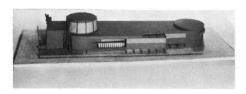

It could be argued that it was relatively easy for an architect of Aalto's talents to exert a powerful influence in a small country. Elsewhere it was more a question of conditioning an already suspicious public to accepting new ideas on architectural design. For a period, the vocal minority took on the role of propagandists in assembling exhibitions, writing pamphlets and building exemplars for those clients who were willing to back the new style. In Germany, a number of manufacturers and municipalities had commissioned new buildings from the radical architects in the late 'twenties and continued to do so until the National Socialist take-over. In Holland, J. J. P. Oud, the City Architect of Rotterdam, was able to exert an effective influence on his own and other municipalities.

But on the whole it was left to the more wealthy and enlightened clients to commission new work. This was, in a sense, a contradiction of CIAM aims. The furtherance of an architecture of universal validity depended on its acceptance at all social levels – in truth, perhaps, on an ardent left-wing idealism as well as on an area of freedom for individual expression. The first was not possible without the active co-operation of governments, the second became possible, but only through competitions and exhibitions. Throughout Europe, therefore, the new architecture in the 'thirties operated from a pragmatic base and instead of large estates of impeccably designed workers' houses or community buildings, the new style is best seen for the most part in villa designs, expensive apartments, zoo buildings, shops and stores, newspaper and other commercial and industrial buildings.

Another brand of modernism had also grown up parallel with the work of the avant-garde architects, deriving from the Paris Exposition of Decorative Arts held in Paris in 1925. It had little connection with the work of the radical architects but it did reflect certain characteristics of the work of the hard-core modernists. Nowadays, this parallel style is referred to under the terms 'Art Déco' or 'Moderne' or 'Jazz Age Modern', and its superficial resemblances to international functional architecture are both puzzling and informative. Although it has been virtually ignored by architectural historians because it lacked a consistent programme as a design style, it gained a world-wide currency and a measure of popular success. It incorporated many decorative features that would have been anathema to the Functionalists, including zigzag surface patterns, rounded arches and curved corner details, elaborate 'ship-prow' embellishments and the employment of materials with mirror surfaces, quite often black-finished. This ambivalent kind of modernism, often to be seen at seaside resorts and in popular entertainment buildings and garages, is as clearly a part of twentieth-century architecture as the modern movement buildings, but its cumulative effect was negligible. For most 'serious' architects and critics of the 'thirties it was considered 'not quite' architecture.

What was real to the architects associated with CIAM was the continuation of the principles that had been established in the late 'twenties, the furtherance of the international acceptance of these principles as a point of view wholly in keeping with the times, and a consistent development in the areas of technical innovations and aesthetics. Indeed, in the minds of a few architects within CIAM, including Gropius, Le Corbusier and Alfred Roth, there was a need to revive interest in the idea of a synthesis of the arts which had occupied the post-war revolutionary groups in Berlin. It was felt that a closer association with artists in all fields would provide a larger platform for modern movement views. The CIAM call in 1933 for a 'collaboration of all productive forces' was also aimed at a unification of aims across national boundaries and the enhancement of joint effort in overcoming the problems created by the increased scale of urban environments.

Within a few years, the national groups that had been founded were making an effective contribution to CIAM congresses and working groups. Groups in Spain (largely centred in Catalonia and headed by J. L. Sert), Britain, Switzerland, Greece, Belgium and the Netherlands were all effectively contributing to the local scene as well as to the parent body. Each group dealt with problems from the scale of the single building through to the problem of the city and the region. In Britain, the Modern Architectural Research Group (MARS) became, although primarily London-based, a powerful national force for the new architecture. Its importance was considerably enhanced by the influx of refugee architects to England during the 'thirties and at one time it could claim to have provided a short stop-over home for many of the second-generation pioneers of the new architecture.

Much of the building produced by modern architects associated with the MARS Group, including the work of the most successful and original British firm, Connell, Ward and Lucas, was of a very high architectural standard. But before any real progress could be made in influencing the general run of the mill architectural standards, the war put a stop to the promising start made by British architects. In Europe, those countries that escaped the totalitarian régimes had also virtually come to a standstill and the most fruitful decade for the new architecture came to an abrupt and unfulfilled end.

1930

Hans Scharoun. *Apartments and shops,* Siemensstadt,
Berlin, Germany. 1930 (1929–30)
Right: a corner shop in the Siemensstadt development
Below: a general view of one of the long apartment
blocks

L. H. de Koninck. *Canneel Cottage,* Auderghem, Brussels,
Belgium. 1930 (Demolished)
Bottom: a contemporary photograph of the cottage

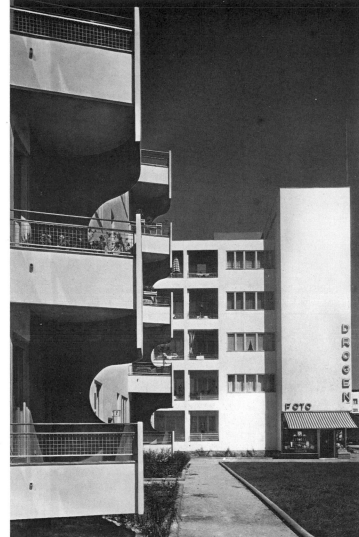

The spread of the modern movement in the
early 1930s was aided by private patronage
as well as by municipal and commercial
bodies. The German industrial concern
Siemens was noted for its enlightened
attitude to social problems and had for a
decade or so provided housing and recreational facilities for the workers employed
in its factories. In 1922, a rather picturesque
estate had been built for the employees at
the Berlin factory. By 1929, the firm was
prepared to commission a newer, more

adventurous scheme in the modern style
by Gropius and a group of colleagues in
the Berlin 'Ring' of architects. Among his
collaborators were Hans Scharoun, Otto
Bartning, Hugo Häring and Fred Forbat.
The Grosssiedlung at Siemensstadt was
one of the most important modern-movement estates to appear after the Stuttgart
Exhibition. It was completed in 1931.
Since that time, a further extension of
Charlottenburg North has been completed
by one of the original architects working for
Siemens, Hans Scharoun.

Scharoun had earlier designed the
development shown on this page, a scheme
which incorporated apartments and shops
set out informally round a cul-de-sac.
These buildings, together with Gropius's
well-known long rectangular blocks across
the road (illustrated on page 112), were constructed in load-bearing brickwork finished
with white rendering. But there was a great
deal of difference in the actual planning
of the blocks and in their appearance.
Scharoun's consistent and original approach
to architecture makes a sharp contrast to
the more common vocabulary of rectangular forms.

De Koninck's isolated house of the same
date exhibits an experimental approach,
but although the 'trade-mark' of modernism
is apparent it lacks the power of the German
work.

1930

Karl Ehn (City Architect). *Karl-Marx-Hof,* Vienna, Austria. 1930
Right: detail of the main façade which faces the large open public space
Centre right: general view of the main façade of a block of flats at Karl-Marx-Hof

Walter Gropius. *Housing estate,* Siemensstadt, Berlin, Germany. 1930 (1929–30)
Bottom: the south elevation of the five-storey block by Gropius
Below: detail of the south-fronting balconies and stair tower of the four-storey block

With housing as a chief concern of the architect in the 1920s and 1930s, some remarkably interesting schemes emerged. The out-and-out modernism of Siemensstadt built for the municipality but backed by the industrial concern can be usefully contrasted with the work of no less adventurous, but more conservative, councils in Britain (for example, Leeds, Liverpool, London and Manchester), the Netherlands and Austria. Of all those schemes perhaps the best-known and most widely featured housing scheme was the Karl-Marx-Hof in Vienna, designed by the then City Architect. Based on high-density planning principles developed by the London County Council's Housing Department, it is grandiose but well laid out. As a settlement it is defective in its detailed planning of the flats, many of which are back-to-back and do not benefit from sunlight.

Mies van der Rohe. *Tugendhat House,* Brno, Czechoslovakia.
1930 (Damaged and altered)
Right: road elevation
Below: the living-room and study divided by a marble
slab partition

Amyas Connell. *High and Over,* Amersham, Bucks, England.
1930 (1929–30)
Bottom: view of the entrance side of High and Over

Arne Korsmo, *Villa Dammann,* Oslo, Norway, 1930
Above: garden elevation

A way out of this problem of orientation
was put forward by German architects whose
coolly planned rows of north-south blocks
at least overcame the sunlight problem, if
they did not add a great deal to layout. At
Siemensstadt, Gropius's long low block has,
with a low density, the advantage of facing
large green swards. This estate, and May's
layouts at Frankfurt, were to become
prototypes for innumerable estates built
throughout the world in the 1930s and
again after 1945.

Mies's Tugendhat house follows a theme
within his own work, beginning with the
unbuilt country-house project of 1923 and
culminating in the Barcelona Pavilion.
What he demonstrated at Barcelona as a
total design theme is here adapted and
modified for domestic use. The freely
flowing space is largely confined to the
lower living-room floor. Above this, a more
conventional room layout occurs. Connell's
High and Over is the first major house in
England to reflect the values of the continental Modernists. It is of key importance in the
history of English domestic architecture,
providing double value as virtually the
last of the great country villas (built for the
Director of the British School in Rome) and
the first fully-worked-out example of the
new wave of modern architecture which
was to gain a firm hold by 1933. The Y-
shaped winged plan generated from an
hexagonal hub is unlike anything else
planned at the time in England or abroad
and creates a sense of interest that is missing
from much of the 'boxy' functional building
then in vogue.

The Norwegian architect Arne Korsmo
designed this pioneer Modern Movement
house for an art collector; hence the blank
walls to the living room on the garden
façade. This vast room is lit by clerestory
slot windows. The house is finished in brick
and concrete.

1930

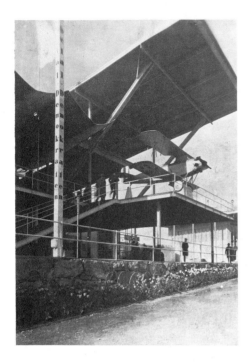

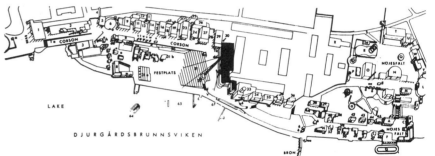

Gunnar Asplund. *Stockholm Exhibition,* Stockholm,
Sweden. 1930
Above and top right: two of the pavilions designed by
Asplund
Middle right: layout of the Exhibition

W. M. Dudok. *Town Hall,* Hilversum, Netherlands. 1930
Right: the Town Hall entrance façade

The Stockholm Exhibition was a notable
triumph for Gunnar Asplund and the
Exhibition Director, Dr Paullson: it brought
together for the first time in Sweden a
group of modern buildings, including an
extensive section of housing, where before
only isolated examples of modern-movement buildings were to be found. It also
underlined the social and economic basis
of the architecture designed, revealing the
architect as 'a worker in the service of the
broad masses of the community'. The best
individual building was without doubt
Asplund's own Paradiset Restaurant, but
other pavilions indicated a real grasp of
exhibition display problems.

Dudok's Hilversum Town Hall is his
best-known building. In its way it is
one of the great milestones of twentieth-
century architecture, not perhaps of the
exciting innovatory type, but one which
displays a completedness of concept and
execution of the kind which suggest a
masterwork.

Stam's Home for the Aged was won in
competition in 1928 when he was working
with the Swiss architect Moser. It was a
well-thought-out solution which in actual use
proved immensely satisfactory. The plan,

a simple H-shape, provided privacy for the
old people without isolating them from the
communal activities.

Meyer's major building, the Federal
School of the General German Trade
Union Federation at Bernau, was the result
of a limited competition in which Mendelsohn, Berg and Max Taut also competed.
Meyer's scheme consisted of a central square
building with two staggered wings of linked

rectangular blocks. It was built on a 12-acre
clearing in the Bernau State Forest.

The chief interest in Gropius's Werkbund
exhibit at Paris was the introduction of
rectangular metal framing with glass and
metal panels for a design for an hotel-
apartment project. Comparison with Taut's
much earlier Glass House at Cologne (1914)
is telling, but the exhibit has a more obvious
connection with Chareau's Maison de Verre.

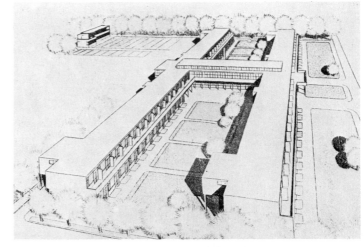

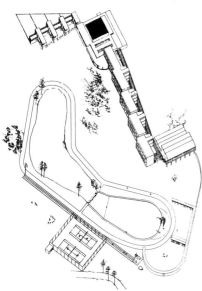

Mart Stam and W. Moser (with F. Kramer).
Budge Home for the Aged, Frankfurt-am-Main, Germany.
1930 (1928–30)
Top left: part of the façade of one of the living-room wings
Top right: the original perspective submitted by Stam and Moser for the competition of 1928

Hannes Meyer. *German Trade Unions School,* Bernau, near Berlin, Germany. 1930 (1928–30)
Above: the architect's drawing for the scheme
Middle right: general exterior view

Walter Gropius and Marcel Breuer. *Werkbund Exhibition,* Paris, France. 1930
Right: part of the exhibit devoted to the design of a coffee-bar for an hotel. The furniture was designed by Breuer
Below: staircase detail from the stand, displaying a glass and metal design for an apartment

1930

Arthur Korn and Siegfried Weitzmann. *Fromm Rubber Factory*, Friedrichshagen, near Berlin, Germany. 1930 (1928–30)
Right: aerial view of the factory layout, with the boiler plant in the distance
Below: rear elevation of the office block

Johannes Duiker. *Open-air School*, Cliostraat, Amsterdam, Netherlands. 1930 (1928–30)
Bottom right: general view of the four-storey cuboid building
Bottom left: floor plan of the open-air school

One of the most highly sophisticated rubber-goods factories for its time, the Fromm works consisted of an office block, production halls and heating and power plant. It was the second project by Korn and Weitzmann for Fromm. The layout was based on a precise diagram of the functional operations performed in the buildings, and the finishes and details were dealt with in an expertly clinical way. Part of the building was air-conditioned. The four-storey administrative building was L-shaped on plan and constructed from exposed steel frames infilled with glazed brickwork.

Duiker's four-storey open-air school can be viewed architecturally as either a basic cube shape, cut up and subdivided into internal and external sections, or as a vertical slab of ground-floor open units etc, and educationally as a school which, in its architect's words, 'should be built so that it does not produce sick children'. He diagnosed two basic types of school, 'normal' ones which produce patients and open-air ones which attempt to heal them. The reinforced concrete-framed structure was filled in at strategic points with folding windows or left open as the edges of the extended roof terraces.

Another key Dutch building was the Van Nelle factory at Rotterdam, designed mainly by Mart Stam when he was working for the architects whose names are more usually associated with it. This enormous complex was greatly admired by German and British architects as well as by industrial concerns which viewed its straightforward functional design as an asset for a building type which was usually cluttered up with additions and awkward connections. The curved building contained administration, café and library.

Dutch architecture was represented at the Austrian Werkbund's model settlement in 1930 by a housing block by Gerrit Rietveld. The principle of the exhibition was similar to that of the German Werkbund show at Stuttgart in 1927 (see pages 86–7), and among the architects who designed housing units were Lurçat and Loos (both of theirs are shown here in their more recent states), Neutra, Häring, Hoffmann and Frank. Le Corbusier was not represented.

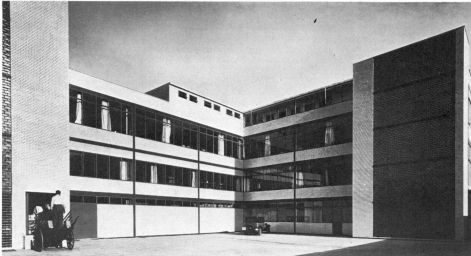

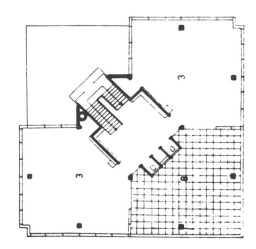

Key to layout (Vienna architects unless stated otherwise):
Veitingergasse 71, 73 Hugo Häring (Berlin); 75, 77 R. Bauer; 79, 81, 83, 85 J. Hoffmann; 87, 89, 91, 93 André Lurçat (Paris); 95, 97 W. Sobotka; 99, 101 O. Wlach; 103, 105 J. Jirasek; 107, 109 E. Plischke; 111, 113 J. Wenzel; 115, 117 O. Haerdtl
Jagdschlossgasse 68, 70 Wagner-Freynsheim; 72, 74 O. Breuer; 76, 78 J. F. Dex; 80, 82 A. Grünberger (Hollywood); 88, 90 E. Lichtblau
Woinovichgasse 2, 4 M. Schütte-Lihotzky (Moscow); 6, 8 M. Fellerer; 1, 3 H. Gorge; 5, 7 J. Groag (Paris); 9 Richard Neutra (Los Angeles); 11 H. A. Vetter; 13, 15, 17, 19 Adolf Loos; 10, 12 G. Guevrekian (Paris); 14, 16, 18, 20 Gerrit Rietveld (Utrecht); 22 E. Wachberger; 24, 26 W. Loos; 28, 30 A. Bieber & O. Niedermoser; 32 J. Frank; 34 Hugo Häring (Berlin)
Jagicgasse 8, 10 C. Holzmeister; 12 E. Wachberger
Engelbrechtweg 4, 6 Hugo Häring (Berlin); 5, 7 O. Strnad; 9, 11 A. Brenner

J. A. Brinkman and L. C. van der Vlugt (Project architect: Mart Stam). *Van Nelle Factory*, Schiedam, Rotterdam, Netherlands. 1930 (1927–30)
Above: general view

Werkbund Exhibition, Vienna, Austria. 1930
Gerrit Rietveld. *Apartments*,
Bottom right.

André Lurçat. *Apartments*
Bottom left.

Adolf Loos. *Two-storey housing*.
Below: the houses are now hemmed in by trees

1931

Le Corbusier. *Villa Savoye,* Poissy, France. 1931 (1929–31)
Right: entrance hall staircase
Centre right and bottom: original sketch of roof garden and a contemporary view of the Villa Savoye
Below: first-floor plan and section

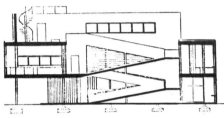

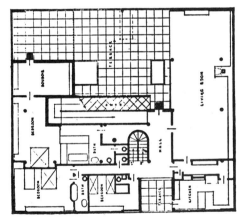

Peter Behrens. *House in the Taunus Hills,* Cronberg, Germany. 1931
Right: the garden elevation

Joseph Emberton. *Royal Corinthian Yacht Club,* Burnham-on-Crouch, England. 1931 (1929–31)
Left: side elevation showing the terrassing and cranked

staircase windows
Bottom: the elevation overlooking the River Crouch

The Villa Savoye needs little introduction to architects. It was a pivotal building in Le Corbusier's development and an alien object in a tradition-bound country. Now a *monument,* it suffered from the neglect of years, and cows once grazed within its rigid framework. Le Corbusier's five principles can be seen embodied in this two-storey building.

The main living-room is on the first floor, a solarium above is approached by a long, slightly inclined ramp – the whole box of spatial tricks balanced on legs as thin as a ballet dancer's, poised and alert.

Le Corbusier wrote of his villa and explained the idea behind its conception as a design: 'The house must not have a façade . . . it must open on to all four directions. The living area with its hanging garden will be raised above the columns so as to give views right to the horizon.'

Behrens's attitude to architecture constantly changed with the times and each commission was treated on its own merits. This two-storey house, finished with thin slabs of white limestone on a brick backing, is a kind of classicized modern movement building set in parks and gardens laid out by Schneider. The luxurious interior included a wall to the living-room covered in real animal parchment.

Emberton's Royal Corinthian Yacht Club at Burnham was the first modern movement building in Britain to receive an award by the official architects' body, the RIBA. This award for design quality was a recognition of its maritime character rather than an indication that English architects had accepted 'modern' design. It is a deceptive building, constructed in steel and brickwork and not as it appears in reinforced concrete. The steelwork was used skilfully to provide the cantilevered stepped balconies on the south side, and ample spaces for communal use are provided internally.

1931

Erich Mendelsohn. *Columbushaus,* Berlin, Germany. 1931
(1921–31) (damaged)
Right: the main façade of the Columbushaus during
construction in 1930
Below right: part of the completed façade
Below: plans and section

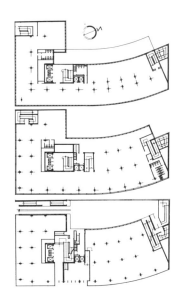

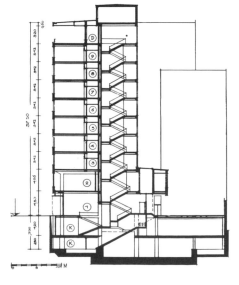

The Columbushaus, an office and shops building on the Potsdamerplatz in Berlin, was Mendelsohn's last great German building. Other projects were started before he began his extensive travels and before he finally left Germany in 1933. The depression put a stop to his work and National Socialism drove him from his land.

Like the earlier Schocken stores, the appearance of the Columbushaus had a profound effect on the design of commercial buildings throughout Europe. The curved front in particular became a popular cliché and the thin, narrowly spaced stanchions a feature used *ad infinitum* by builders and architects ever since. The best-known example in Britain based on Mendelsohn's design is the Peter Jones store in Sloane Square, London, built in the mid-1930s. The Columbushaus, however, had much more to it than a change in façade treatment and constructional techniques. It incorporated, at the time, some of the most advanced ideas on building servicing and lighting.

Dudok's De Bijenkorf store no longer exists, finally removed, after extensive bomb damage in 1940, by the development planning for Rotterdam which got under way after the war. The original design was based on Dudok's conviction that a store building could be virtually all glass and that this would provide a high level of daylight within the building during day-time and a light-emitting source at night. It had a market 'feel' about it, set out on horizontal layers, which were themselves stressed on the elevations. Later on, Dudok confessed that his idea had been wrong and his revised scheme of 1942 depended on artificial light sources.

Taut's highly controlled Trade Union House also relied on the extensive use of glass, but in this case the concrete structure provided a grid into which the pattern of glass and solid fitted.

W. M. Dudok. *Bijenkorf Store,* Rotterdam, Netherlands. 1931 (1929–31) (demolished)
Above: a contemporary general view

Max Taut. *Trade Union House,* Frankfurt-am-Main, Germany. 1931 (1929–31)
Below: the main street frontage
Left below: internal detail of corner staircase

1932

Charles Holden of Adams, Holden and Pearson.
Arnos Grove Underground Station, London, England. 1932
Right: the entrance side to the station

Le Corbusier. *Pavillon Suisse* (Swiss Students' Hostel),
Cité Universitaire, Paris, France. 1932 (1930–32)
Below: ground-floor plan
Right: the south wall of the Hostel showing the
original glazing which has more recently been altered to
incorporate sun-blinds
Bottom: the entrance to the Hostel with the dormitory
block behind

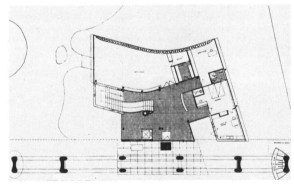

Under the direction of Frank Pick, the London Passenger Transport Board were one of the first major British public bodies to commission contemporary designers and openly to support their work. Called by one critic 'the most satisfactory series of modern buildings in England', the stations themselves were but one part of an over-all policy towards design. Holden's Arnos Grove is probably his best-known design and untypical of his later, rather ponderous buildings for other bodies. The circular brick exterior is topped by a concrete roof. One mushroom column in the middle of the foyer is used to support this roof. The influence to be traced in the design is obviously Dudokian.

Le Corbusier's Swiss Pavilion was a prototype of the 'vertical slab' method of building. Resting on a heavy and centrally placed supporting concrete structure, the five-storey dormitory block appears to ride free of its base. In fact, it is cleverly linked

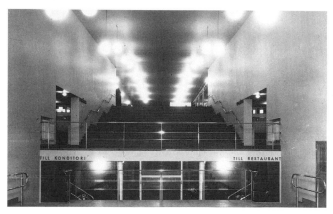

Sven Markelius, *Hälsingborg Concert Hall*, Sweden, 1932
(1925–32).
Top: A contemporary night-time shot.
Above: The grand staircase

Herbert Ellis and W. L. Clarke with Owen Williams
(Engineer). *Daily Express Building,* Fleet Street, London,
England. 1932 (1930–32)
Left: a picture of the main Fleet Street façade under
construction

P. L. Nervi. *Giovanni Berta Stadium,* Florence, Italy. 1932
(1930–32)
Left: the main covered grandstand

back to a single-storey communal building and to the main entrance hall. It is one of Le Corbusier's most important buildings, human in scale, rich in materials and spatially alive.

The Daily Express Building is the very opposite of the Hostel, a period piece which magnificently accentuates the preoccupa-tions of its designers with new materials (the exterior is a skin of black glass) and advanced forms of heavy concrete engineer-ing. There is nothing quite like it anywhere in the world – except for the sister-offices of the Daily Express at Glasgow and Man-chester, also by Williams.

Nervi's Muncipal Stadium for Florence was won in competition. It is basically oval in shape with a covered concrete-shell grandstand on one long side. Five 10-foot-wide helicoidal spiral stairs lead the specta-tors up from the ground to the top of the uncovered part of the stadium. In all, before more recent extensions, it could hold 35,000 people.

Markelius's Concert Hall in Hälsingborg was the first major international-style build-ing in Sweden. Earlier versions were in a stripped-down Nordic classicism. Func-tionalism triumphed at the Stockholm Exhibition, 1930, and heavily influenced Markelius.

1932

Amyas Connell and Basil Ward. *'New Farm'*, Grayswood, near Haslemere, Surrey, England. 1932
Right: the entrance side with the glazed staircase tower

Pierre Chareau and Bernard Bijvoet. *Maison Dalsace* (Maison de Verre), Paris, France. 1932 (1927–32)
Below: exterior of the Dalsace House
Below right: the internal staircase to the main room

One of the most revolutionary houses built in Britain, Connell and Ward's 'New Farm' had all the cubic qualities of the mainstream modern movement, yet had about it as well a unique quality of originality of both form and structure. The concrete walls were 4 inches thick and the staircase was cantilevered from a central column.

The remarkable Maison de Verre was inserted into an existing building and is one of the unique buildings of the twentieth century. It is like a complete mechanized scenario, a set clinically constructed for the performance of modern medicine. The earlier Scheerbartian 'glass architecture' notion finds its full interpretation in the hands of Chareau and Bijvoet, whose attention to detail in this building is breathtaking. The dissolving of views through semi-transparent materials, the juxtaposing of metal and glass, 'free' space and solid add a dynamic dimension to this house which almost takes it into the realms of Surrealism.

Haesler's Old People's Home consisted of two long, rectangular, parallel blocks, linked near one end by a two-storey com-

Otto Haesler. *Old People's Home*, Kassel, Germany. 1932
(1930–32)
Above: the two parallel residential blocks

Owen Williams. *Boots' Factory*, Beeston, Notts., England.
1932 (1930–32)
Left: the external loading bays and glass pavilions
Below: interior of the manufacturing space
Bottom: the upper part of the factory area and glazed
roof lights

munal wing. It was a fine example of the glass-and-steel 'factory aesthetic' translated into the context of building for social purposes. The south-facing rooms were light and airy, but somewhat over-exposed.

Qualities not unsimilar to those of the two preceding buildings can be found in Owen Williams's Boot's Factory and what could easily have become a dead-pan factory is transformed into a virtuoso piece of engineering. The key to the understanding of this building is to be found in the integration of structure and glazing on a functionally organized planning grid. One of the world's largest reinforced concrete buildings, its four storeys were almost entirely enveloped in glass. The main working areas are four storeys in height and galleries on mushroom-headed columns define these parts. The external result is architecturally somewhat confused but the total effect is confidently stunning.

1933

Alvar Aalto. *Tuberculosis Sanatorium*, Paimio,
Finland. 1933 (1929–33)
Right: a sharp view of the south-facing front
Below: layout plan
Bottom: the main entrance and long wing

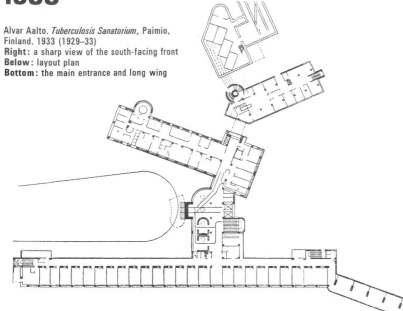

According to the late Sigfried Giedeon, whose *Space, Time and Architecture* was itself a landmark, two buildings were inseparably linked with the 'rise' of contemporary architecture: Gropius's Dessau Bauhaus and Aalto's Piamio sanatorium. He links these two built structures with Le Corbusier's project for the League of Nations competition of 1927. That kind of assessment is no longer valid, perhaps as a number of other buildings and projects have since emerged from obscurity; even so, the sanatorium remains a principal front-runner. Aalto's achievement is all the more amazing considering his lack of links with the European avant-garde. The building was designed and laid out with the closest liaison between architect and physicians. It is interesting to note that at the time (and probably because of the winter climate), rooms were separated from balconies. The roof space was used as a sun hall and patients were wheeled there from lifts. The construction was in reinforced concrete; the finish a white paint.

Lucas's early 'cube' house in Kent was built for his own use. It was an early British example of reinforced concrete used for house construction incorporating an external (Corbusian) staircase to the upper floor. In its way – before the surge of modernism in Britain – it is a masterpiece.

This day school by Lurçat ignored all the preconceived ideas on educational buildings current at the time. Like Aalto he too, consulted the experts. An 'ideal solution', according to Lurçat, resulted with a three-storey linear block of classrooms, segregated sexes and a kindergarten with east-facing classrooms. Services were at the centre.

Colin Lucas. *'The Hopfield'*, St Mary's Platt, Kent, England. 1933
Top and above: general views

André Lurçat. *School*, Villejuif, France. 1933
Below: aerial view

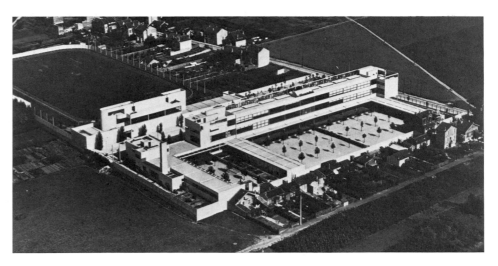

Hans Scharoun. *Schminke House,* Lobau, Germany.
1933 (1932–33)
Below: the interlocking balconies on the south-east
corner of the house
Right: living-room and conservatory
Bottom left: the independent staircase entry to the
upper-floor balcony
Bottom right: first- and second-floor plans

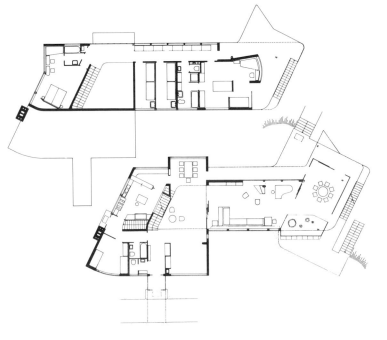

J. A. Brinkman and L. C. van der Vlugt. *Sonneveld House,*
Rotterdam, Netherlands. 1933 (1932–33)
Left: the garden façade
Centre left: the road façade

Le Corbusier and Pierre Jeanneret. *Cité de Refuge,*
Paris, France. 1933 (1929–33) (Altered)
Below: general view
Bottom: the main entrance canopy

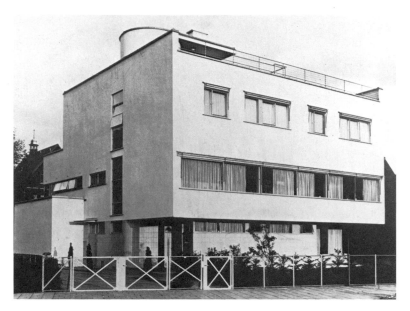

One of Scharoun's most exciting houses, the
Schminke House is two-storeyed and steel
framed. Out of the wedge-shaped plan an
elaborate system of balconies thrusts out
from the main living and bedroom areas on
free-standing columns. The house demonstrated what could be done with a relatively
simple basic plan shape; curves replace
corners and moveable vertical screens and
curtains replace the more conventional
fixed partition walls.

The Sonneveld House, another important
steel-framed house of the 1930s, is entirely
controlled by its rectangular envelope.
Even so, the interior was also flexible, with
living rooms situated on the first floor and
the flat roof used for open-air living. The
projecting wing at the side of the house contains an upper-floor kitchen with a garage
below. As Arnold Whittick has written:
'the whole effect is one of lightness and simplicity'. It was also representative of the very

best in Dutch architecture at the time.

Le Corbusier's Salvation Army Hostel for
down-and-outs was probably his best building. Claimed as 'the first building for human
habitation entirely hermetically sealed'
when it was built, it later suffered from
neglect and vandalism. Corbusier claimed
after the German evacuation of Paris that
'the building can no longer be thought of as
architecture'. Not so the original scheme,
which was in a sense 'total architecture',
controlled and confident. The design relied
on the juxtapositioning of geometrical
solids: a cubic entrance hall led to a circular reception point and to the rectangular
restaurant. Above this the great rectangular
bedroom cliff reared up six storeys.

1934

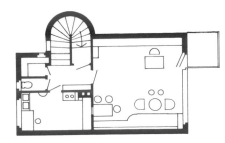

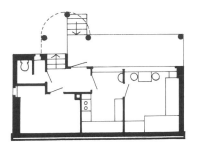

Josef Fischer. *Villa Hoffmann*, Budapest, Hungary. 1934
Below: the rear elevation of Villa Hoffmann with the semi-circular concrete staircase
Left: ground and first floor plans

Alfred and Emil Roth (with Marcel Breuer). *Flats*, Doldertal, Zürich, Switzerland. 1934 (1933–34)
Above: general view of the Doldertal Flats

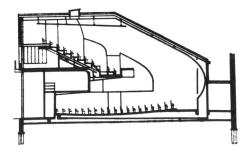

Johannes Duiker. *Handelsblad-Cineac Cinema,* Amsterdam, Netherlands. 1934
Above: the Cineac exterior with publicity tower, with section below

Commissioned in 1933 by Dr Giedion, the Secretary of CIAM, the two four-storey blocks of flats at Doldertal were placed diagonally on a long, narrow, sloping site. They were designed as rather superior private houses and their disposition on site obviated the problem of overlooking. Constructed with steel frames, the curtain walls are supported by the floors. Sun protection is provided by awnings and wooden roller-blinds.

The Fischer villa also housed office space for its businessman-owner. The whole building was constructed in reinforced concrete, punched on the sides facing the sloping gardens by rectangular window openings. It is a typically modern, 1930s design, cohesive but cold.

Fundamentally, Duiker's Cineac was a stark rectangular box, housing an egg-shaped cinema with exposed projection-room round the lower part of the building. But what a box! The squat corner building hemmed in by narrow streets, and situated opposite one of Amsterdam's most ornate movie-houses, seems to explode three-dimensionally into a super-sign system – an effect that has to be experienced after dark. With the Zonnestraal Sanatorium, the Schröder House and the Van Nelle Factory, the Cineac forms one of the four cornerstones of Dutch modern architecture.

With the old Curzon in London's Mayfair, the Cineac was one of the best cinemas to come out of the movie boom years. The Curzon has, alas, gone, but been replaced

130

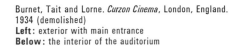

Burnet, Tait and Lorne. *Curzon Cinema*, London, England. 1934 (demolished)
Left: exterior with main entrance
Below: the interior of the auditorium

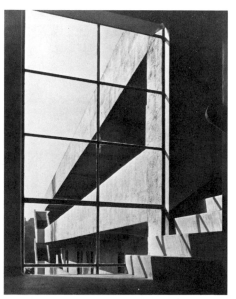

Wells Coates. *Lawn Road Flats,* Hampstead, London, England. 1934 (1933–34)
Left: the galleried exterior
Below: looking back at the galleried front from the staircase window
Bottom: ground-floor plan

by an unsympathetic substitute by the same architects in the bowels of a new office block. The Curzon seated 500 in luxurious but somewhat spartan-looking surroundings. The original owed much to the Dutch work of Dudok with its lack of decoration and red and dark grey brick exterior.

Wells Coates's best-known scheme is the Lawn Road Flats, a home, as well as point of pilgrimage for many of the progressive architects of Europe in the late 1930s. An interesting aspect of the client's (Jack Pritchard's) brief was that the building should not be out of date in 1950. The original flat design was exhibited in London in 1933 and Coates's first major commission was complete early in 1934. It had repercussions throughout the country.

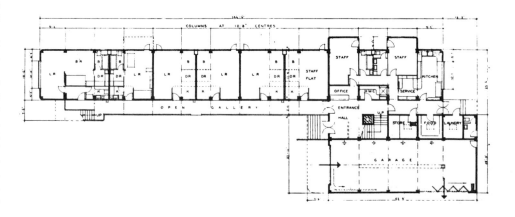

1934

H. P. Berlage. *Gemeentemuseum (Municipal Museum),* The Hague, Netherlands. 1934 (1919–34)
Right: view from the garden court
Below: an interior view of the museum

Wells Coates and Pleydell-Bouverie. *Sunspan Exhibition House*, Olympia, London, England. 1934 (Demolished)
Centre: the garden side of the Sunspan house
Bottom: general view

The Gemeentemuseum or Municipal Museum at The Hague has a long building history and was only completed in 1934, the year of Berlage's death. The building was first projected in 1912 when a museum committee was formed, a second and final scheme was designed in 1928, agreed in 1929 and work started in 1930. The building relies for its external effect on the articulation of two-storey box-like shapes arranged around an internal garden court, and internally on the fusion of the spaces formed by these boxes and a bold exhibition of structural elements.

The English Sunspan house was one of those prophetic buildings which soon after disclosure at a fashionable exhibition seem to pop up in the most unexpected places; in this case at Ditton Hill, Welwyn and elsewhere. It was adaptable as a week-end house or a five-bedroomed house. A compromise between 'modern' and 'modernistic', its popularity at the time is understandable, even though its slickness is disturbing.

Ironically enough, one of the first modern movement buildings in London was a pool for penguins. Tecton's analysis of the penguin's habits led to the design of an elliptical plan structure with two interweaving cantilevered concrete ramps. All was designed to give the spectator maximum viewing space and the birds an exciting environment. This witty piece of architecture is also partially covered to provide protection from the sun and its walls are shaped in such a way as to provide a sounding-board for the penguins' cries.

Sir Owen Williams's Empire Pool was a spectacular design for its time. Then the

largest covered swimming-bath in the world, it had a main bath 200 feet long by 60 feet wide and fixed seating for 4500 spectators. The roof consists of three-hinged arches spanning over 236 feet, with heavy buttresses on the outside.

Lubetkin, Drake and Tecton. *Penguin Pool,* Zoological Gardens, Regent's Park, London, England. 1934
Top: the Penguin Pool in use

Owen Williams. *Empire Swimming Pool,* Wembley, London, England. 1934 (1933–34)
Above: the main entrance façade
Right: the giant concrete stiffening fins on the side elevation

1935

Embassy Court is one of the best modern seaside apartment blocks in Britain, a confident essay in reinforced concrete construction which sweeps round its corner site uncluttered by frills and fussiness usually associated with this kind of building. The plan is L-shaped and gallery access to all the upper flats is to the rear. The local authority refused permission for it to be built in an advanced diagonal beam method of construction, and a more conventional beam and solid wall construction was employed.

The two-storey rectangular house at Warsaw by the Syrkus was one of the more interesting 'white' buildings (with the almost inevitable horizontal strip windows) to be built in Poland in the 1930s.

The heavy-handed monumentalism of Russian building at this time is related to the demise of Constructivism in or about 1932. The Kharkov complex, however, contained a bit of the originality of the Constructivists overlaid with the monumental. Le Corbusier's Centrosoyus project, on which studies began in 1928, is a travesty of the original design solution, although what is there remains essentially faithful to his concept for a large ministerial building.

Torroja's Hippodrome, completed in 1935, was constructed in concrete, and a series of shell vaults (shaped as hyperboloidal sectors, cantilevered 40 feet over the terraces) were arranged round the stadium.

Helena and Szymon Syrkus. *Skolimow House,* Warsaw. 1935 (1931–35)
Above: the north façade

Wells Coates. *Embassy Court,* Brighton, England. 1935 (1934–35)
Top right: rear of the block from back balcony
Right: the sea-front elevation

S. Serafimov and K. Kravetz. *Department of Industry and Planning,* Kharkov, USSR. 1935 (1925–35) (destroyed, but rebuilt)
Top: general view of the various buildings which make up the Department
Above: a recent view of the dominating central block

Le Corbusier and others. *Centrosoyus Building* (now Central Statistical Board of the USSR Council of Ministers), Moscow, USSR.
Centre left: the main entrance facade

Eduardo Torroja, (Engineer), Arniches and Dominguez (Architects). *Zarzuela Hippodrome*, Madrid, Spain. 1935
Left: one of the racecourse stands

1935

Alvar Aalto. *Municipal Library*, Viipuri, Karelia, Finland (now USSR). 1935 (1927–35) (damaged 1940; restored 1958)
Below: the staircase and main entrance to the Library
Right: the auditorium interior
Centre: general external view

The Viipuri Library is now within Soviet boundaries, part of the area of Finland ceded after the abrupt war between the countries. It was Alvar and Aino Aalto's first major public building. Won in competition in 1927, it is one of the keystones of modern Finnish architecture and as competent a building as any in the world at that time. The functional planning is noteworthy: the library block, with its controlled lighting and use of half-levels, worked extremely well and was essentially inward-looking; the auditorium and committee spaces, in a separate two-storey block are glazed and outward-looking.

The Health Centre at Peckham was a pioneer building, erected to a brief prepared by Dr Scott Williamson for dealing with health problems of families in a particular social milieu. 'The Peckham Experiment' was a bold social venture, based on an earlier experiment in 1926. At Peckham, however, an entirely flexible building materialized which embodied the principles behind the health-centre philosophy. The simple rectangular plan centred on a large swimming-pool with other accommodation ranged round it on three floors.

The De La Warr Pavilion was Mendelsohn's first major British building. Won in competition, with Chermayeff, in 1933–34, it is typical of the great German architect's work, precisely detailed, spacious and direct in its aesthetic expression. The whole three-storey building was constructed from welded-steel frames. Large Germanic *Garderoben* and long horizontal balconies with sea views make this a rather special British building. The architects – both with foreign names – were criticized in the Press by British architects for having the audacity to win the competition – in fact, a first prize of £150!

The Tecton Group, under Lubetkin's leadership, was one of the first teams of architects set up in Britain with a commitment to modern design. The eight-storey Highpoint I apartment block was one of their most successful buildings.

Owen Williams (Engineer). *Peckham Health Centre*, Peckham, London, England. 1935 (1933–35)
Right: the symmetrical façade of the Health Centre

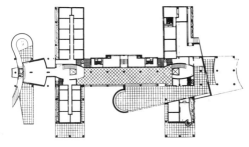

Tecton and Lubetkin. *Highpoint 1*, Highgate, London, England. 1935
Top: general view of the completed flats
Above: the double cruciform ground-floor plan

Erich Mendelsohn and Serge Chermayeff. *De La Warr Pavilion*, Bexhill-on-Sea, England. 1935 (1933–35)
Above left: general view of the elevation to the sea
Above: the curved staircase in the round-nosed entrance hall
Left: detail of the south elevation from the old grandstand

Stamo Papadakis. *House*, Glyfadha, near Athens, Greece.
About 1936
Right: garden elevation

Maxwell Fry. *Sunhouse*, Hampstead, London, England.
1936
Left: road elevation

Erich Mendelsohn and Serge Chermayeff. *House*, Chelsea,
London, England. 1936
Bottom left: road elevation
Bottom right: the circular sun-bay to the living-room

Maxwell Fry and Walter Gropius. *House*, Chelsea, London, England. 1936
Left: road elevation

Giuseppe Terragni. *Casa del Fascio* (Renamed: Casa del Popolo), Como, Italy. 1936 (1932–36)
Below: general external view

The variation on the theme of a detached house in the International Style was end-less. The ideas seem to have been inter-changeable from country to country, architect to architect. On these pages, a typical Greek example is isolated, and a number of English ones included which though home-grown were produced in collaboration with well-known émigré architects.

Fry's Sunhouse, built near Wells Coates's pioneering Lawn Road Flats (see page 131) was a large-scale town-house three storeys in height and constructed in reinforced con-crete. On the south side of the house, a continuous terrace runs along the first floor. All the living-rooms are on this floor.

There is in the Mendelsohn and Cherma-yeff house in Church Street, Chelsea, something of the spirit of the Bexhill Pavilion: the rectangular treatment of the two-storey building is similarly elongated and a single-storey semicircular projecting window in a predominantly flat façade echoes the large staircase window in the Pavilion. Again, the structure is steelwork with a cement-rendered finish, giving the aesthetically acceptable white appearance.

Less successful, perhaps, than the Mendel-sohn and Chermayeff collaboration was the partnership entered into by Fry and Gropius, at least in terms of the other house, designed by them, in Church Street. It has its importance within British archi-

tecture, but its construction was unresolved, partly brick, partly steel, with reinforced concrete appendages. The planning, how-ever, was efficient.

Completed the same year as these houses was Terragni's aesthetically pure Casa del Fascio, which had been justly described as 'one of the canonical works of Italian Rational architecture'. Originally designed as a building surrounding three sides of a square court, the structure erected is a simple half-cube, 33 metres square by 16·5 metres high. The court became a large central double-height meeting-hall. Stand-ing just opposite the Renaissance Cathedral, the Casa was very much a radical thumb-to-nose building.

1937

L. H. de Koninck. *Cottage Berteaux,* Uccle, Brussels,
Belgium. 1937
Right: garden façade
Below: the main front with separated garage block

Alvar Aalto. *Finnish Pavilion,* World Exposition, Paris,
France. 1937 (1935–37) (Demolished)
Right: exterior and entrance to the Pavilion

Frank Lloyd Wright. *Falling Water,* Bear Run, Penn., USA.
1937 (1935–37)
Right: the south side of the house cantilevered out over
Rock Ravine and Bear Run
Below: a view of the upper part of the house
Bottom: cross-section

Nothing evokes the spirit of twentieth-century architecture in quite the same way as Wright's splendidly confident country-lodge for Edgar Kaufmann at Bear Run. Without twentieth-century engineering skills, methods and materials it would have been impossible to produce this house. But it is timeless in spirit, a design dependent on its magnificent site, on its intelligent (and rich) client, and on Mr Wright's sense of space, materials and structure. It was, he once said, his first 'streamline' building, claiming the currency of a term that somehow does not quite fit this building, except in a humorously topographical sense. Masonry materials were used throughout, except for the redwood lining, steel and glass sashes and asphalt protection layers. The section is said to have been derived from a Mayan pyramid, and is the key to the whole design. Poised on a steeply sloping wooded site, its cantilevered trays overhang a waterfall, access to which is provided through a hatch from the enormous living-room. The solid core of the house on the upper part of the slope acts as the counter-weight to the cantilevers.

To juxtapose Falling Water with Cottage Berteaux may be going from the sublime to the ridiculous, but by doing so the extension of doctrinaire 'Functionalism' in Europe can be seen. Whereas Wright's architecture was imbued with an exciting space concept and fully articulated surfaces, the Belgians (and the Dutch) were interested in the careful placing of voids in blank surfaces. This house by De Koninck actually has an endless surface which wraps itself round the square plan.

Aalto's native pine architecture lay close to his heart and at the Paris World Exposition, and later at New York, he developed his exciting use of timber for exhibition pavilions. The upper part of the Pavilion was in steelwork.

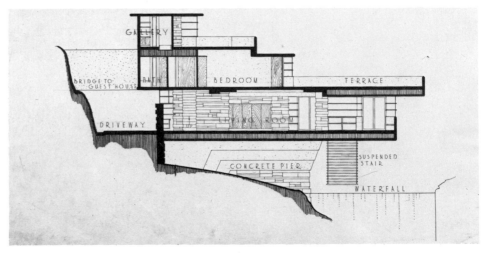

1937

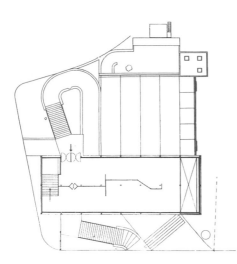

José Luis Sert. *Spanish Pavilion,* International Exposition, Paris, France. 1937
Top right: interior view, showing the position of Picasso's *Guernica* on the end wall under the upper-floor level
Above: ground-floor plan of the Spanish pavilion

Bruce Goff. *Colmorgan House,* Glenview, Ill., USA. 1937
Right: garden side
Below: street frontage

The Spanish pavilion at Paris by Sert is of marginal importance in the international architecture of the 1930s, but of major significance to the Catalonian-inspired modern movement. As the first display cabinet, so to speak, of Picasso's masterpiece *Guernica*, it has retrospectively taken on a new significance.

Typical of Goff's work during the period he was in Chicago, up to the war years, the Colmorgan House is ·in a sense a kind of American 'House Beautiful' and fits into its epoch fairly comfortably. But it has about it, too, an elasticity of approach which suggests that Goff was using commissions such as this as a kind of limbering up before the more adventurous houses built during the 1940s (see pages 159, 169) and the so-called 'regional houses'. Wright's influence had pervaded the domestic architecture of the prairie lands. Goff from this early example on was to become the architect of the 'country regions', inspired by 'found' materials and complex forms. The Colmorgan House is two-storeyed and conventionally organized with living-rooms on the ground floor and bedrooms above. It is virtually pinned to the ground by the great masonry (obviously Wright-inspired) chimney.

McGrath was responsible for a remarkable circular house built in Chertsey in 1936–37. The kind of design most architects toy with at some time or another in their careers, the concentric plan is notoriously difficult to deal with. It crops up a number of times in twentieth-century architecture as a plan form but few examples are as successful as this one. Constructed in reinforced concrete (Hennebique system), the north side of the building was shaped like a drum. The south side opened up to reveal layers of terraces pivoting above a luxurious and enormous living-room.

Highpoint Two extended the estate begun in Highgate by the Tecton Group in the early 1930s (see page 137) by the addition of a further thirteen luxury dwelling units. These flats were published throughout the world because of the fine finishes, their modern appearance and the odd pair of caryatids which supported a Le Corbusier-inspired porte cochère.

Raymond McGrath. *House,* Chertsey, Surrey, England. 1937
Top: garden side of the circular house

Tecton. *Highpoint II*, Highgate, London, England. 1938 (1937–38)
Right: south front of Highpoint II
Below: layout plan showing the relationship of the two Highpoint buildings (see page 137)

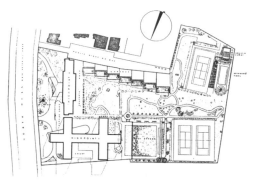

1938

Frank Lloyd Wright. *Taliesin West,* near Phoenix, Arizona,
USA. 1938 (1934–38)
Above: the impressive entrance and pool
Left: interior of the living area
Bottom: Taliesin West in its fertile setting

Frank Lloyd Wright fell in love with the Arizona landscape and began work on his winter residence, office and foundation there in 1934. By 1938 it was substantially complete, although many additions and changes have been made since. With his uncanny instinct for the rightness of his decisions, he developed a piece of the desert which his critics claimed was infertile: he found water. Built over the years by his apprentices, Taliesin West is an exceptional place constructed in canvas, glass and timber, with a heavy stone base. Wide roof-overhangs provide protection against the searing sun; water is a visual relief to the arid desert. The use of natural materials, the rough finish to the timbers and the way the group of buildings sits on the stepped site offer physical evidence of Wright's mature 'organic' architecture, at once at peace with its surroundings and a creative gesture of the highest order.

The entrance to Taliesin West is marked by a stone pylon and the American flag. In the grounds are many minor structures erected by generations of apprentices for their own occupation.

Thomas Tait's Empire Tower was the first major constructivist building to be erected in the United Kingdom. Based on the work of the Russian Jacob Chernikov, it formed the centre-piece of the 1938 Glasgow Exhibition. It stood on a hill and could be seen on a clear day from as far as eighty miles away. The central lifts took people up to viewing platforms on all four sides of the square building and thus afforded panoramic views across the whole Exhibition. The Tower was erected in nine weeks and constructed out of special steel angles riveted and covered with corrugated-steel sheeting. At night the Tower shone out like a beacon from its elevated position.

Thomas Tait with Launcelot Ross. *Empire Tower and Restaurant,* Empire Exhibition, Glasgow, Scotland. 1938 (Demolished)
Right: the 250-foot-high Empire Tower
Above: night view of the Tower

1938

Serge Chermayeff. *Own House,* near Halland, Sussex, England. 1938 (1935–38)
Below: general view of the garden side
Right: the living-room opened up to the terrace
Bottom: ground floor plan of Chermayeff's house

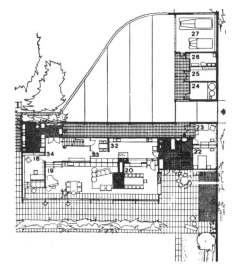

This two-storey house, the architect's own when he lived in England, was built after a planning inquiry had granted permission in his favour. It was one of a number of houses in England that had been refused permission by lay committees. It was constructed entirely in timber except for the east wall and basement, which were in brick. Timber was used like structural steelwork and faced with clap-boarding. Large openings were formed in the framing for the windows and the whole effect of the house was of airiness and lightness. The main living accommodation was planned to run along the whole of the south façade and to extend into the open terrace. Service accommodation was situated in a single-storey section adjacent to the kitchen. A sense of privacy was accentuated by the single access point for both pedestrians and vehicles on the east side.

Gropius's house in Lincoln, Mass., finished in the same year, was also of timber box construction, except that this time steel instead of brick was used as a secondary stabilizing material. The timber cladding was hung vertically and a somewhat inconsistent use of feature elements (for example, spiral stairs to a roof terrace and sun lounge) was incorporated into the scheme. The plan was without corridors and essentially a compact functional solution to the requirements of modern house-planning.

The TB clinic was also an enlarged rectangular box, but constructed in reinforced concrete. An uncompromising building, which used a modern version of traditional ventilated walls to provide air to the solarium, the texture of its main south façade forms a strong contrast to a plain concrete-surfaced north elevation.

Ignazio Gardella. *Anti-tuberculosis Clinic,* Alessandria,
Italy. 1938 (1937–38)
Below: the main entrance frontage

Walter Gropius and Marcel Breuer. *Gropius House,*
Lincoln, Mass., USA. 1938 (1937–38)
Above left: the garden elevation
Above right: the sun lounge

O. Bang, *Workers' Union building*, Oslo, Norway, 1938 (1937–8). Main elevation.

Philip Goodwin and Edward Stone. *Museum of Modern Art*, New York, USA. 1939
Right: main elevation

The New York Museum of Modern Art was the first major international-style public building on the east coast. Stone and his partner, the late Philip Goodwin, had become known through their domestic work in the United States and this important public building opened up a new phase in his career. He later retracted his interest in what he called the 'cold, arid and sparse' aesthetic of Functionalism.

The six-storey building has now been extended but much still remains of the original design. Activities were arranged on the layer-cake principle, with each floor acting as a functional zone: the lecture theatre was in the basement, the entrance and gallery on the ground floor, the first and second floor were exhibition spaces, the library was on the third floor, the offices on the fourth floor and club-rooms with terraces under the 'hat' on the top.

Robert Maillart, the master bridge-builder of the twentieth century, also built an exhibition of some importance in 1939. Not a functional structure of the kind usually associated with this engineer, it was another of those ambitious exercises in symbolic expression to be found as centre-pieces to exhibitions, which are neither quite architecture nor practical engineering. Inspired by Freyssinet's constructions, this thin shell roof was an advertisement for Portland cement.

Wells Coates's last major building before the war was this apartment block in London, faced in Portland stone and beautifully crisp in detail.

The large-scale eight-storey Workers' Union building in Oslo by Bang is one of the most impressive buildings in Norway. It makes a positive contribution to the urban scene.

Robert Maillart. *Cement Hall*, Swiss National Exhibition, Zürich, Switzerland. 1939
Left: general view

Wells Coates. *Flats*, 10 Palace Gate, London, England. 1939
Bottom left: general view
Bottom right: a detail of the garden façade

1939

Alvar and Aino Aalto. *Finnish Pavilion*, World's Fair, New York, USA. 1939 (1937–39)
Right: the curved interior wall of the pavilion

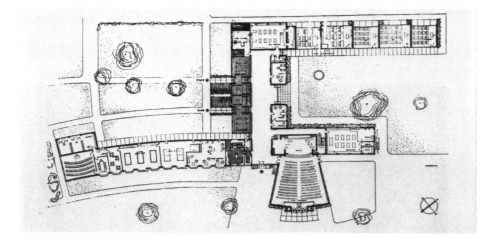

Walter Gropius and Maxwell Fry. *Village College*,
Impington, Cambridge, England. 1939 (1936–39)
Above: main assembly hall and entrance to the college
Left: ground-floor plan

In 1937, the Aaltos submitted two projects, and Aino Aalto herself submitted a third, for the competition for the New York pavilion. Between them, they won all three prizes. The final exhibition building was arranged on two levels within a rectangular room and almost entirely constructed in wood or its by-products. The strongly curved 'free wall' of timber ran up the whole side of the 52-foot-high pavilion. The sloping wall was divided vertically into four sections devoted (from the top) to the country, its people, its work and its products.

Alvar and Aino Aalto. *'Mairea'*, Norrmark (Noormarkku), near Björneborg (Pori), Finland. 1939 (1937–39)
Above: garden elevation

Arieh Sharon. *Co-operative Housing*, Tel Aviv, Palestine (now Israel). 1939 (1934–39)
Right and below: main façade of the terrace housing

The fourth village college to be erected in England was a co-operative effort between the German architect Gropius, the young English modernist Fry and the Cambridge Education Secretary, Henry Morris. It embodied many of Morris's educational ideas and was a considerable advance architecturally on the earlier ones at Sawston (1928) and Bottisham and Linton (both 1937). Set in a park at Impington, the College is single-storeyed except for a double-storey block in front of the large assembly hall. Each classroom was connected to an outside patio. One wing was devoted to Senior School, the other to adult recreational activities.

Aalto's two-storey house for Gullichsen, the paper manufacturer, is another of the Finnish landmarks in modern architecture. The curved wall on the first floor enclosed a large studio. Another interesting feature of the house was the grass-grown roofs to the sauna and terrace.

Sharon's co-operative housing scheme in Palestine is a good example of this Bauhaus-trained architect's work. The series of grouped apartments in terrace blocks went through a number of developments, and the final version is illustrated here.

1939

Otto Salvisberg, *Hoffmann La Roche Factory*, Welwyn Garden City, Hertfordshire, UK, 1939 (1936–39)
Below: contemporary general view of the building

Norman Bel Geddes. *General Motors' 'Highways and Horizons' Pavilion*, World's Fair, New York, USA. 1939
Above: general view of the exhibit, with the street intersection

The Bel Geddes Pavilion, devoted to 'Highways and Horizons' and built for General Motors at the New York World's Fair of 1939, covered an area of some seven acres. The exhibit included mock-ups of a full-size street intersection with segregated pedestrian routeways, as well as moving walkways (which had been first introduced at the Paris Exposition of 1900) and escalators. A vast 'Futurama' exhibit was devoted to depicting the America of 1959. Visitors toured this exhibit in moving chairs.

Situated in the 'new town' of Welwyn, the second of the Howard-inspired garden cities of Hertfordshire, the Salvisberg design brought not only modern architecture design to an otherwise mainly Georgian-revival settlement but also Swiss precision of finish and detail. Stucco-faced and concrete-framed, the original buildings, including some fine stores, still stand but are somewhat overwhelmed by recent developments.

Decade 1940

Wartime forts in the Thames Estuary.
An anonymous contribution to twentieth-century architecture

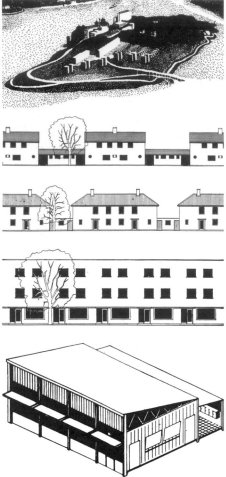

Above:
Housing scheme for Kvarnholmen, Sweden, with projected point blocks in front of the earlier terraces
Selection of elevations for Local Authority model housing, published by the British Ministry of Health (*Housing Manual 1949*), showing 'rural semi-detached', 'urban semi-detached' and 'three-storey terrace' types
Isometric view of a prefabricated classroom unit by Arcon, about 1948

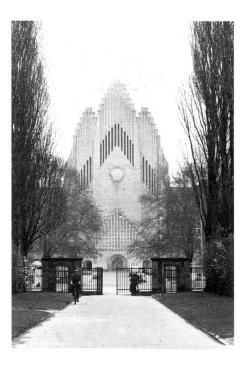

P. V. Klint and Kaave Klint's *Gruntvig's Church* in Copenhagen, with its estate of almshouses, was completed in 1940 (1913–40)

'The frugal 'forties', 'the utility years', 'the war-torn period' – these epithets emphasize the problems of a period near enough for most of us to recall them with a shudder of fear.

European architecture during the years 1939–45 virtually came to a standstill. Money was scarce, commissions few and far between and what work was carried out was largely concerned with the war effort. It was a period of austerity but not entirely devoid of innovation. In Scandinavia, a kind of decorative, neo-traditional, 'modern' architecture came to the forefront during the period as a sharp reaction to the functional architecture of the previous decade. This 'new empiricism' was brought about by a feeling of isolation, particularly in Sweden, and a deep-rooted concern to regain national identity. Swiss architects made some headway on housing and planning issues and built a number of important new buildings.

But it was North American and Latin American countries that took over the lead from Europe in modern architecture. After passing through Britain in the late 'thirties, many of the best-known continental architects settled in the United States and during the interregnum in European architecture commenced work on a number of large-scale projects in North and South America.

The war created many new opportunities for industry. In America, especially, an acceleration of productivity, unprecedented since 1929, occurred and led to what has been referred to as a *qualitative* change in consumer demands in the post-war period. Housing was particularly affected and the practical breakthroughs in building technology which had existed in the minds of designers and manufacturers before the war – for example, prefabricated panelling, air-conditioning, automatic service units for kitchens and bathrooms – became a practical possibility in the late 'forties, as did curtain-walling for office buildings. Buckminster Fuller, who had been agitating for prefabrication since his 'Dymaxion' house was published in 1927, had a vision of a technologically based building industry which provided an impetus to other creative thinkers to establish new priorities quite outside the mainstream modern movement attitude.

When building activity commenced again in Europe after 1945 it was fitful and slow. It was a traumatic period of stocktaking and reconstruction. It took Germany a full ten years to re-establish the principles forcibly surrendered to National Socialism in the early 'thirties. There was no outburst of the confident Utopianism that had filled the air after the First World War. Few groups were formed and hardly any were effective. Morale was low for those architects and artists who had remained in Germany throughout the war years. In a German magazine produced in 1947, men like Bartning, Baumeister, Döcker, Pechstein, Schwarz and Max Taut complained of the total collapse that had 'destroyed the visible world that constituted our life and our work'. 'We realize,' they and others wrote, 'how much the visible breakdown is but the expression of a spiritual devastation, and we are tempted to sink into despair.'

The challenge of post-war reconstruction was immense. The responsibilities for its success, daunting. Cities and villages had to be rebuilt, new homes for returning heroes and for refugees had to be erected efficiently and quickly and a positive policy to planning based on individual nations' needs and financial and technical resources had to be worked out.

But what of the 'new architecture', CIAM and men like Le Corbusier? Had the war killed the idealism of the 'thirties? In a way, it had, as the architects who had created the forum of opinion out of which the new architecture had emerged were widely dispersed. Those of them who had built according to the CIAM and Corbusian principles had in most cases closed their practices. But whereas there had been an extensive dissemination of views and international collaboration in a somewhat restricted sense before the war, in the post-war period a new kind of eclecticism emerged. The so-called 'modern functional style' became the acceptable mode in which to work and new, exciting and original solutions to design problems were searched for and in many cases discovered. The technical excellence, functional organization and aesthetic idealism that had been latent in the new architecture since its inception became a reality. So did a new kind of freedom in expression, derived from the projects of older-generation architects like Frank Lloyd Wright, Frederick Kiesler and Le Corbusier. A younger generation of Latin American architects led by Lucio Costa and Oscar Niemeyer, all disciples of Le Corbusier, pushed forward the boundaries of twentieth-century architectural expression much further than most European designers. In his Pampulha buildings of the early 'forties, Niemeyer hints at an integration of painting and architecture and effectively introduces a much wilder (and gayer?) interplay of forms and levels into his buildings. Even so, the *éminence grise* behind this work was still very obviously Le Corbusier.

Le Corbusier spent the period 1940–44 away from Paris, devoting most of his time to painting and to the furtherance of his ideas on planning and the proportional system he called 'The Modulor'. He produced a number of important publications, including *La Maison des Hommes*, *Les Etablissements Humains* and the *Charte d'Athènes*, the last based on the 111 propositions on town-planning problems established by CIAM during the 1933 Congress held on board SS *Patris*. The document was a pivotal one and was probably Le Corbusier's greatest contribution to the pre-war CIAM deliberations. It established a method of defining the problems inherent in town design and related a hierarchical arrangement of problem-categories (Dwellings, Recreation, Work, Transportation and Historic Buildings) to an optimistic belief in universal solutions. In the hands of Le Corbusier, however, it was a master tool that aided the creation of his Algiers Project and the 1945 town-planning scheme for the historic core of Saint-Dié in eastern France.

The fifty-storey skyscraper block designed by Le Corbusier in 1938–39 for Algiers was based on what he called Cartesian principles – as opposed to the 'irrational skyscrapers of New York or Chicago' – and represented another radical departure in his thinking. He gave up the use of a regular geometrical envelope which had become a characteristic of his built work up to 1938, because he had quite suddenly discovered a proportional system and a method of breaking up the huge façades of a massive structure. Based on some observations Le Corbusier had made on one of his own paintings in 1931, it eventually led to the delineation of his proportional system – a system which could encompass all design contingencies ('Modulor partout!') – and to the mathematics behind the vast Unité d'Habitation at Marseille which occupied him from the end of the war until 1952.

While Le Corbusier was engaged in fostering his new human-scale monumentality, architects and planners elsewhere were also confidently pursuing large-scale opportunities.

Few planning schemes that came out during the war period could match the comprehensive approach to renewal and reconstruction contained in the MARS Group Planning Committee's 'master plan for London'. It summed up, as no other plan did anywhere in the world at that time, the whole nature of the CIAM approach to a hierarchical structure for a city. Published in the English *Architectural Review* in 1942, it had been tentatively drawn up in 1938 but only gained credence after the extensive war damage in central London. The plan, resembling the bone structure of a kipper, took in the whole of the Greater London Area and linked the various zones, for housing, industrial, recreational and historic use, by service and distributor roads to a central linear routeway which was capable of extension along an east–west axis.

It was meant to be taken as a conceptual plan, capable of free interpretation by planners and designers. But, as in so many cases, the value of the overall approach was minimized by its being interpreted literally. The more conventional planners, brought up as they were on the notions of Ebenezer Howard and the Garden City movement, were horrified by this radical and audacious 'continental' approach. But, together with Le Corbusier's books and schemes for Algiers and Saint-Dié, it was eventually to exert far more influence on the younger generation than the more cautious garden city approach. However, the work carried out by Abercrombie on London, Sir Alker Tripp's advocacy of 'precinct' planning, and the new ideas that were gaining popularity in planning circles for Stein's American 'Radburn' layouts, were to provide the staple diet for those responsible for planning the British New Towns from 1947 onwards.

Unfortunately, the advocates of green pastures and traffic-free precincts had not fully recognized how big the threat of the automobile was to become to urban living. In the United States, it had been taken far more seriously and by the middle 'thirties the first urban expressway had been opened in St Louis. By 1940, a number of turnpikes had been constructed and a new linear urban pattern was gradually overlaying itself on the American continent. Car-ownership increased rapidly in the USA after the war. The motels and drive-in movie theatres, diners, stores and restaurants specifically designed for car-encased customers, which are now so characteristic of the American scene, sprouted up as a necessary adjunct to the new roads.

The automobile and other economic factors brought about another significant change in urban life in the USA at the end of the 'forties. The beginning of what has been described as the 'third skyscraper age' saw the erection of the great post-war apartment and office blocks with their lightweight glass and metal walls and regular shapes. Mies van der Rohe's Lake Shore Drive Apartments in Chicago and Pietro Belluschi's Equitable Savings Building at Portland, Oregon, set entirely new standards for this kind of problem.

In Europe, standards of new houses, apartments and offices were much lower, even though for a time many new methods of prefabrication were introduced. But Europe was caught up in an emergency, while America was enjoying prosperity.

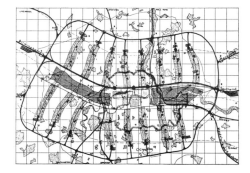

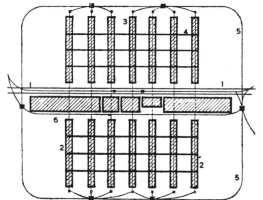

1940

Reinhard and Hofmeister *et al. Rockefeller Center,* New York, USA. 1940 (1930–40)
Above: an aerial view of the Rockefeller Center
Top right: one of the sculptures on the Plaza of the Rockefeller Center
Below: section and ground floor plan of Radio City music hall
Bottom right: interior of the Radio City auditorium, with concrete panels

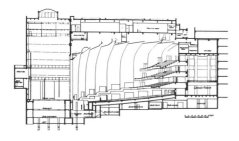

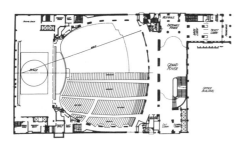

Gunnar Asplund. *Forest Crematorium,* Emskede, Stockholm, Sweden. 1940 (1935–40)
Above: the entrance to the Forest Crematorium

Construction of the Rockefeller Center – America's largest privately-owned business and amusement complex of the pre-war period – began in 1931. In total, ten different units were constructed on the twelve-acre site, the last of which (the National Cash Register Company's offices) was completed in 1940. Situated on a block that lies between New York's busy 5th and 6th Avenues and 48th and 51st Streets, the development represents the culmination of pre-war skyscraper design and comprehensive planning. Public and private activities are brought together in the scheme and the whole design creates an atmosphere that is a direct and positive contribution to urban life. The great RKO motion picture theatre was the first building completed (designed by the main architects with Corbett, Harrison and MacMurray, Hood and Fouilhoux) and opened in 1932. It seats over 3,500 patrons and has a full stage.

Asplund's Crematorium accommodates 300 mourners. It was his last and probably his best architectural work, and can justly be claimed to be the finest *memento mori* in Europe. Cremation is standard funerary procedure in Sweden. The Chapel and the outstanding cross rest on the top of a gently sloping hill, creating a suitable yet simple symbolism which is carried through into the actual ceremony of commital in which gas lamps in the courtyard are extinguished as the urn is lowered into the crypt.

The Hangar at Orbetello is one of about a dozen designs prepared by Nervi for the Italian Government between 1937 and 1943 on various sites. There were two main types, of which this is the most exciting from an engineering point of view. The vast 336 feet by 120 feet concrete roof is supported by six buttresses. Stiffening beams run along the edges to resist thrust and winds (see construction picture) and the roof is covered with asbestos-cement sheets.

The outcome of a competition held in 1937, the Richmond School is of considerable importance to educational architecture in Britain. It was a premonition of the prefabricated schools that were to become a hallmark of the postwar period. It also pioneered open planning.

Pier Luigi Nervi. *Hangar,* Orbetello, Tuscany, Italy. 1940 (1937–40)
Above: the precast concrete latticework of the hangar roof
Left: the completed hangar

Denis Clarke-Hall. *Secondary School,* Richmond, Yorks., England. 1940 (1937–40)
Below: the classroom blocks and connecting corridors of the Richmond School seen from roof level

1941

Werner Moser. *Protestant Church*, Altstetten, Zürich, Switzerland. 1941 (1938–41)
Right: general view of the church with the clergy house in the foreground
Below: side view and ground-floor plan

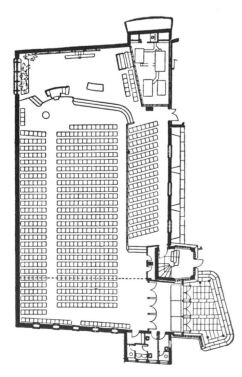

Werner Moser's Reformed Church at Zürich-Altstetten is one in a line of important landmarks in Protestant architecture. Together with Karl Moser's St Antony, Basel (1927) and Rudolf Schwarz's Corpus Christi at Aachen (1930), it represents the culmination of the new liturgical and community thinking on the Continent at the beginning of the 1940s and established a mode of design for many American and later British examples. But whereas Karl Moser had seen his design as an extension of Perret's neo-Classicism, the younger Werner discovered a more informal architectural vocabulary.

The Altstetten church relies on a simple monopitch covering of a trapezium-shaped plan for its effect; on plain brick walls internally and externally and on a perpetual assymetry. The assymetrical aspect of Protestant architecture is interesting and so far not much studied. It is a useful device for breaking away from the formality and axiality of the classical tradition and, by implication, the Roman Catholic tradition too. It is also an essential ingredient in the symbology of the reformed tradition which requires emphasis to be laid, not on sacramental space, but on man, book, table and font.

The Cemetery chapel is also Protestant and assymetrical – one of the finest buildings of Bryggman and of pre-war Finland. Although this single-storey chapel was started in 1939, its completion was held up by the Winter War. The mortuary lies in line with the chapel but is separated from it by an open portico.

Goff's 'Triaero' house marks another distinct phase in this architects' development. The house has a triangular plan and the roof cantilevers from a central services core. Finished in copper and redwood, its importance within the American domestic architectural tradition is only now being realized.

Erik Bryggman. *Cemetery Chapel*, Turku (Åbo), Finland.
1941 (1939–41)
Right: interior of the chapel

Bruce Goff. *'Triaero' Vacation House*, Fern Creek,
Louisville, Kentucky, USA. 1941 (1940–41)
Below: roof detail
Bottom: side view

Bruce Goff. *'Triaero' Vacation House*, Fern Creek,
Louisville, Kentucky, USA. 1941 (1940–41)

1942

Walter Gropius and Marcel Breuer. *Defense Housing,* New
Kensington, Pennsylvania, USA. 1942 (1941–42)
Top: group of terraced dwellings on the New Kensington
estate
Right: original layout plan prepared in 1941

Oscar Niemeyer and Lucio Costa. *'Casino Pampulha' and
Yacht Club,* Pampulha, Brazil. 1942
Below: the Yacht Club at Pampulha
Bottom: the entrance to the 'Casino Pampulha'

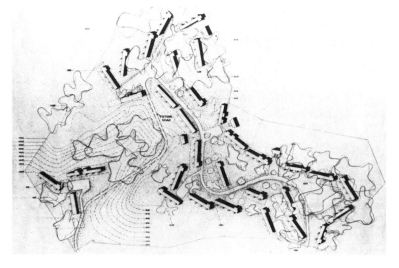

The New Kensington Estate of 250 Defense
dwellings, built near Pittsburgh by Gropius
and Breuer, was especially constructed for
workers in the Alcoa aluminium plant. The
spacious layout followed the contours of the
site and all the dwelling units have south-
facing living rooms. Externally, the timber-
framed units were finished in brick veneer
with vertical cedar sidings. Internally, a
significant advance was made in American
domestic public housing whereby partitions
were eliminated from the ground-floor
rooms to create open-planned living/dining
and kitchen areas. A number of house types
was incorporated into the layout, including
one and two-storey, one—three bedroom,
terraced groups, the most common being the
two-bedroom type. Most of the dwellings
had small private terraces adjacent to the
open spaces that penetrated between blocks,
yet even so they were disliked by the resi-
dents, who considered them little better
than 'chicken coops'!

It is a long jump from the serious attempt
of Gropius and Breuer to provide well-
situated war-time housing for workers to the
recreational and amusement architecture
of Brazil of the same period. Pampulha was
established as a rich man's play resort –
outside Belo Horizonte, north of Rio. Its
architecture was exciting, exploratory

1943

and confident if, for its time, structurally somewhat over-ambitious. The Pampulha Casino, the Yacht Club, the church of St Francis and a circular dance hall, established Niemeyer as a world-class architect. However, Niemeyer's best known individual building is the Ministry of Education at Rio; he had succeeded Costa as head of the Design Group in 1939. The

original inspiration for the building was Le Corbusier's, whose first project was drawn up in 1936, followed by a second one in 1937. The young Niemeyer worked with Le Corbusier during his short stay in Brazil and was decisively influenced by the elder architect's work. In the final building in Rio, there is still much that can be described as essentially Corbusian.

Oscar Niemeyer (with Lucio Costa, Alfonso Reidy and others; Consultant: Le Corbusier). *Ministry of Education and Health*, Rio de Janiero, Brazil. 1943 (1936–43)
Above: the building that represents the birth of modern architecture in Brazil, first projected in 1936

Mies van der Rohe. *Alumni Memorial Hall,* IIT, Chicago,
III., USA. 1946 (1944–46)
Right: detail of the steel mask at the base of the
concrete frame columns
Below: general view of the entrance façade

Soon after Mies arrived in the USA in 1938, he took up the appointment of Director at the Armour Institute, later to become the Architecture Department in IIT. In the same year he was commissioned to plan the new campus for the Institute. It was probably the largest project of its kind anywhere in the world at the time. By 1940 a plan had been finalized and in 1943 the first building was completed. Building after building – related to the simple geometry of the plan – followed. One of the early examples, and one which received world-wide publicity, was the Alumni Memorial Hall, situated adjacent to the Metallurgy and Chemical Engineering Building completed about the same time. The Alumni Memorial Hall was admired most of all for its cunning prowess: finished in steel that covers a concrete frame, the details are so articulated as to suggest a completely steel and brick building. The concrete was necessitated by fire regulations. This steel mask reveals itself at the base of the columns.

The shaping of the church by Niemeyer and his engineer Cardozo is not so playful as it at first appears. This controversial church was built up through a series of mathematically determined parabolic arches, the main chapel arch itself covering a further platform for the choir. The campanile and entrance porch are free-standing elements. Light penetrates the vaulted building through the vertical louvres at the entrance and above the altar. The spaces inside remain relatively subdued. Overlaying the structure, the architect invited artists to cover the concrete walls with mosaics which, when seen with the whites, blues and browns of the uncovered parts, create a polychromatic effect.

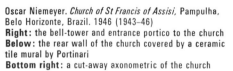
Oscar Niemeyer. *Church of St Francis of Assisi,* Pampulha, Belo Horizonte, Brazil. 1946 (1943–46)
Right: the bell-tower and entrance portico to the church
Below: the rear wall of the church covered by a ceramic tile mural by Portinari
Bottom right: a cut-away axonometric of the church

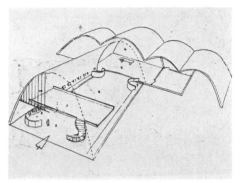

1947/48

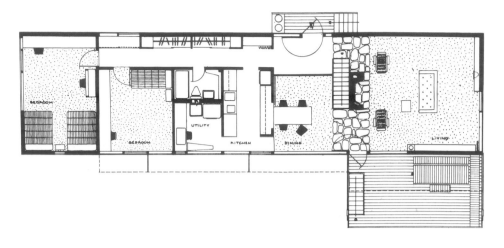

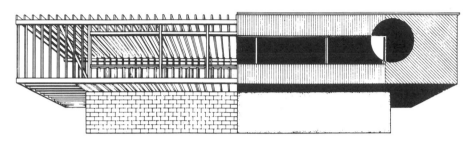

Marcel Breuer. *Breuer House I*, New Canaan, Conn., USA.
1947
Top right: main floor plan
Right: drawing showing the structure of the house
Below: entrance side

Richard Neutra. *Kaufmann Desert House*, Palm Springs, Calif., USA. 1947 (1945–47)
Above: the Kaufmann House in its desert setting – a well-known, much-used, but evocative, photographic image of this famous house
Right: main floor plan

Richard Neutra. *Tremaine House*, Montecito, Santa Barbara, Calif., USA. 1948
Bottom right: general view

Marcel Breuer's own house – Breuer House I – was built on a hillside. It was a small yet very open house, based on a rectangular plan, with the main living accommodation on an upper floor. A workshop was situated beneath it, together with other ancillary domestic accommodation. An unusual feature of the design was the way traditional timber-frame construction was used: cantilevers spanning to a width of ten feet are not normally found in timber frames.

A winter house for Edgar Kaufmann – the same client who in the 1930s had commissioned Falling Water from Frank Lloyd Wright (page 141) – was designed for a desert site at Palm Springs by Richard Neutra. A luxurious house with large servants' quarters, it is by anyone's definition a magnificent design. Glass is everywhere, yet the plan is so arranged that the space flows from interior to exterior with complete freedom. Walls can be pulled back to allow the physically confined interior to become part of the much wider external courtyard spaces. The environmental control systems used in the house were highly sophisticated.

Although the Desert House seems isolated, it is not so far removed from civilization as the picture would suggest. It makes a fitting contrast to the Tremaine House at Santa Barbara, which merges into the lush greenery of that region. This very well-planned house is also clearly joined to nature in a completely Californian and capitalist celebration of ownership.

1947

Hertfordshire County Architect's Department.
Cheshunt Burleigh Junior Mixed and Infants School, Cheshunt,
Herts., England. 1947
Right: interior of classroom in use
Below: ground-floor plan
Bottom: main entrance to the school

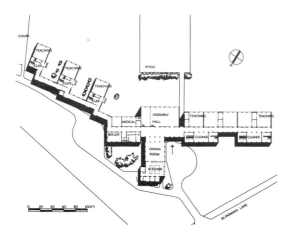

The school building programme embarked on in Britain immediately after the war gradually brought to the fore the need for rationalization, standardization and 'industrialized' building methods. With some architects industrialization became a new catchword and a philosophy of system building (as opposed to a systems philosophy, which was to come later) grew up, nurtured by County Architect's departments such as Hertfordshire and Nottinghamshire. These departments became for a time flash-points of progressive attitudes in architecture. Cheshunt School was one of the earliest of the Herts CC prototypes based on a proprietory concrete system, with a steel frame. It set an important precedent, and variations on a similar theme have constantly appeared.

1948

Pietro Belluschi. *Equitable Savings and Loan Association Building*, Portland, Oregon, USA. 1948
Right: general view of the twelve-storey offices
Below: detail of the precise glazing and the main entrance

There is another kind of approach to standard units and industrialized manufacture of building components which is best exemplified in the North American large-scale office block. Here the repetitive detail is of considerable importance, and the façade of Belluschi's building is pulled taut like the skin on a drum – the maximum projection is no more than seven-eighths of an inch from the building face. The building is double-glazed, air-conditioned and has windows of blue-green heat-absorbing glass. The planning layout is more conventional, with the first two floors occupying the area of the site and the rest set back at the rear to a depth of some sixty feet.

1949

Saarinen, Saarinen and Associates (Associated Architects: Hills, Gilbertson and Hayes). *Christ Church,* Minneapolis, Minn., USA. 1949
Below: the Lutheran Church of Christ on its narrow corner site
Right: interior of the church, showing the angled, brickwork clerestory wall

The Lutheran Church at Minneapolis was the elder Saarinen's last completed work. A simply planned, steel-framed building, it was built for a congregation of about 750 to a very tight budget. It has influenced church design throughout the world and in turn can itself be seen as part of the new kind of Protestant church building which began in Switzerland in the 1930s.

Aalto's serpentine Dormitory is the Finnish architect's major American work. Built in red brick with a reinforced concrete frame, it provides accommodation for 350 Seniors on six floors. Most of the study-bedrooms overlook the Charles River on the south side, while the sheltered northern side is dominated by two projecting staircases. Goff, a Wright apprentice at one time, has a distinctive style. This 166 feet in circumference, dome house is one of his finest works. Built in red-painted steel 'Quonset' hut framing, butt-welded to bent steel beams at the base, it is covered in shingles and provides some most exciting interiors.

Alvar Aalto. *Student dormitory block,* Massachusetts
Institute of Technology, Cambridge, Mass., USA. 1949
(1947-49)
Left: the projecting staircases on the north side of the
Dormitory
Middle: the curved south façade which overlooks Charles
River

Bruce Goff. *Samuel Ford Residence,* Aurora, Ill., USA. 1949
Below: general exterior view of the house of domes
Right: dining and kitchen area below the upper studio,
seen from the living room

Charles and Ray Eames. *Case Study House* (Eames House),
Santa Monica, Calif., USA. 1949 (1947–49)
Right: photograph taken during the construction stage
Middle right: ground floor plan and roof plan
Below: interior living space
Bottom: a view from the courtyard between house and
studio, looking towards the house

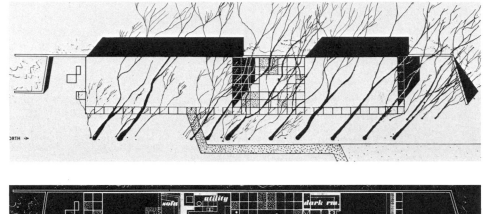

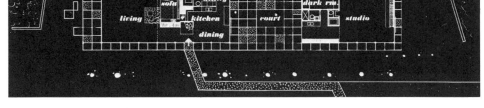

Here are two of the finest American houses
of the late 1940s. Both in their separate
ways were experimental structures; both
hold unusurped places in modern architectural history.

Charles Eames' own house was one of a
number of Case Study Houses sponsored by
the West Coast journal *Arts and Architecture*.
The aim of the magazine was to seek out
new design ideas – particularly in the use
of new materials and techniques – and to
propagate good design. Eames' house was
certainly unconventional, a package of
standard, off-the-peg components which,
when assembled, made up an art-work as
unique as a Duchamp *ready-made*. Basically
it is a double-storey unit divided into house
and studio areas by an open court. The
house itself has a full-height living room at
the south end and takes up eight of the
seventeen standard 7 foot 6 inch bays.
The house and studio were built against a
200-foot long concrete retaining wall and
constructed as steel skeletons designed to
receive standard industrial sashes and panels.

Twitchell and Rudolph. *Healy Guest House,* Siesta Key, Sarasota, Florida, USA. 1949 (1948–49)
Left: the living/dining end of the house
Middle left: floor plan
Below: the landing stage-cum-terrace to the Guest House
Bottom: interior of living space

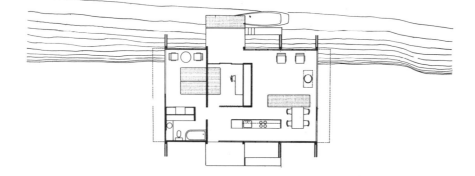

The Healy Guest House is small in comparison; only 735 square feet in area. The plan is rectangular, with a porch and a balcony on the river side. The roof is interesting: a simple catenary roof spanning 22 feet was developed, using flat steel bars at 12 inch centres, spanning between the more normal post and beam construction of the flanking sides. A sprayed plastic finish was used to complete the roof and steel tension straps employed to tie it in. The architect claims that it should have been designed as a single volume. He is right, but it was not – four separate spaces are provided under the concave ceiling.

1949

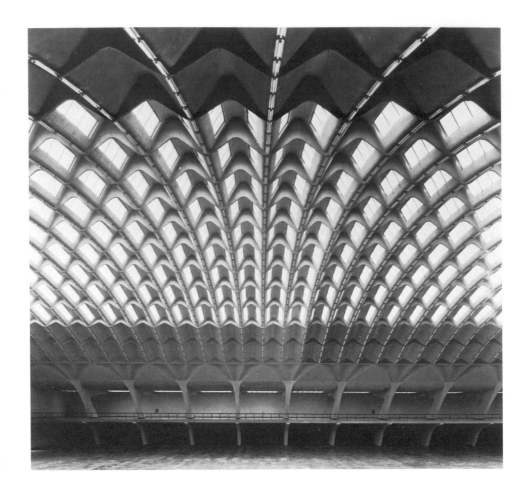

Pier Luigi Nervi (Nervi and Bartoli). *Exhibition Halls,*
Turin, Italy. 1949 (1947–49)
Right: the great glass and concrete vault of the
Salone Principale, 312 feet wide by 250 feet long
Below: exhibition hall C, completed in 1950
Bottom: a detail of the concrete work of the great roof

Philip Johnson. *Glass House,* New Canaan, Conn., USA.
1949
Above: a night view of the Glass House. The circular
brick element which pierces the roof off-centre contains
the bathroom and hearth
Right: the 'kitchen' end; note the full-height door
Below right: the living area furnished with chairs
designed by Mies van der Rohe

All his life Nervi has condemned the kind
of thinking, common to many engineers,
that relies on conventional techniques to
solve new structural problems. He has
written that the Turin halls would 'have
been impossible without a simultaneous
invention of the structural method'. The
Salone Principale is one of his finest design
achievements. Although innovatory in the
use of structural methods, it relates consistently to a series of designs prepared in the
1940s for wide-span prefabricated concrete
structures. The prefabricated sections of the
vault each weighed 1½ tons and measured
15 feet in length, 8 feet 2 inches in width
and 5 feet 4 inches in height. Each section
was joined *in situ* and the enormous vault
built up in a short period of time, with 30
sections placed in position per working day.

The vault and the box are two recurring
themes in the history of architecture.
Few boxes have ever reached the degree of
sophistication to be found in Johnson's
steel-framed Glass House. Inside the transparent box, objects and fittings (for example
the free-standing 'buffet bar') take on the
significance of chess pieces – checkmate
produces a perfect ambience! The *éminence
grise* behind the design is Mies, and so is
also (as a number of critics have playfully
suggested) an eclectic pot-pourri ranging
from Choisy's Acropolis plan, Schinkel's
Casino, Mies's own Farnsworth House
sketches and IIT plan, Ledoux's rationalism
and possibly even Malevitch's 1913 'Circle'
painting.

1949

Frank Lloyd Wright's small compact shop is one of his more important experimental projects and is insufficiently known. He had experimented since the mid-1920s with the idea of a snail spiral. In 1925 he had produced a circular planetarium project for Gordon Strong based on a circling ramp principle. It was developed in a number of later projects but finally emerged as a built idea in the face-lifting scheme for the V. C. Morris Gift Shop. The final, fully blown-up version culminated in the construction of the New York Guggenheim Museum (page 227) where ramp and structure return to the unification they had in the earlier planetarium project. The external wall of the Morris Shop is not without precedents (mostly from turn of the century architecture in the US and Britain), but it remains one of the most audaciously conceived blank walls in twentieth-century architecture. It is penetrated only by a bold, semi-circular arch.

Craig Ellwood's elegant West Coast manner was established with his Hale House at the end of the 1940s. Since then, many other equally interesting and well-detailed buildings have emerged from his office which echo the European International Style of the 1920s and 1930s, to complement the American Mies and Johnson buildings on the East Coast and surprise even the most rationally-minded Californian architect. His work is to be admired mostly for its slenderness and articulation. The Hale House exemplifies this approach with its narrow 'H' steel columns and wooden beams. Although it was to be completely steel framed – and the structure completely exposed inside the dwelling – it proved an uneconomical proposition at the time.

Frank Lloyd Wright. *V. C. Morris Gift Shop*, San Francisco, Calif., USA. 1949 (1948–49)
Top: interior view of the circling ramp in the Morris Gift Shop
Left: the street frontage, with its blank brick wall
Above: the cut-off round arch of the entrance

Craig Ellwood. *Hale House*, Beverly Hills, Calif., USA. 1949
Right: general external view of the Hale House on its steeply sloping site
Above: interior view of the open-plan dining area, with screened-off cooking area beyond

Decade 1950

Skidmore, Owings and Merrill. *Lever House*, New York,
USA. 1952

Amyas Connell *et al*, *Crown Law Court Building*, Nairobi, Kenya, 1955

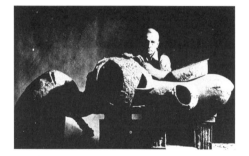

Frederick Kiesler's studies for an 'endless' spatial architecture began early in his career but received a fillip in the 1950s. Study for the Endless House, unbuilt

Below:
Master plan for Brasilia, the new capital of Brazil, by Lúcio Costa and others. 1960 onwards
Bottom right:
Cumbernauld Town Centre Project, near Glasgow, Scotland, by Hugh Wilson and others

The architects and planners who had returned from the war and resumed their training in various institutions throughout the world, accepted implicitly that post-war recovery would go hand in hand with the continuation of the ideas for a modern architecture that had taken root so firmly in the pre-war period. For the most part they were right, and by the beginning of the 1950s, what had been essentially an *avant-garde* movement became a 'forefront' convention. Initially this led to a general uncritical acceptance of CIAM and so-called 'international functionalist' tenets, as well as to the growth of a more popular 'contemporary' mode of interior, furniture and domestic design. Although clearly part and parcel of the new architecture, such design owed much too to the continuance of the 'art déco' and 'moderne' ideas derived from successive exhibitions held in Paris after 1925. Indeed, this rash of 'contemporary' architecture (a term promoted mainly by glossy American and British consumer-goodies journals) led to some odd and quirky detailing and to the popularization of clichés from well-known architectural examples. (In Britain and the USA, Breuer's and Le Corbusier's use of rubble walling was repeated as a fashionable 'feature' in a number of post-war house designs.)

In the 1950s, the 'new architecture' was in the hands of the third generation of designers, whose work, at least until the end of the decade, appears less competent, less original and less experimental than that of the previous generations. It is not surprising, therefore, to find that the 'old guard' were given almost reverential treatment, and that they were themselves largely responsible for the innovations and trends that ruled the day. The work of Le Corbusier, Mies van der Rohe and Alvar Aalto in particular was widely published and visited by architects and planners, resulting inevitably in a proliferation of Corbusian tenements, Miesian office blocks and Aaltoic brick and timber detailing.

In Britain, it was a national exhibition, held to commemorate the centenary of the Great Exhibition of 1851 as well as to demonstrate 'the contribution Britain had made to world civilization through the initiative of the people and the resources of their land', that created the climate of opinion for the acceptance of modern architecture, clichés and all. The idea for a 'Festival of Britain' had been first mooted as early as 1945 and by the time it actually materialized on London's South Bank in 1951, the invective of the Press had subsided into acquiescence, then amazement and praise for the thirty-odd pavilions which had been erected. The central building was Ralph Tubb's Dome of Discovery, the largest aluminium domed structure in the world. Powell and Moya's impressive cigar-shaped Skylon acted as a symbol for the whole show. The exhibition was designed to show the way forward, and in Lansbury and Poplar, London, model estates were laid out which were meant to demonstrate the quality of environment that could be attained at the time. These estates underlined an important fact of post-war Britain: building was being canalized into national schemes for new work and rehabilitation for the first time. Indeed, by the commencement of the decade, the first New Towns were well under way, and the programme for new school building had begun in 1946. There was little private building of any significance until 1954, when at last the wartime restrictions were finally lifted.

By that time, too, the vast rebuilding programme in Europe was well under way and much time and money was being spent on retraining craftsmen to reconstruct facsimiles of the great historical European cities and villages which had been

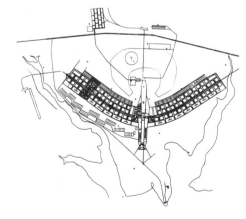

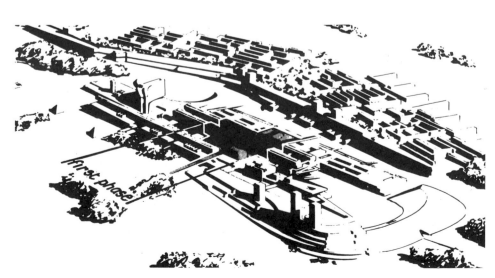

Facing page, top:
Main public entrance to Crown Hall, Illinois Institute of Technology, by Mies van der Rohe
Facing page, bottom:
Angelo Mangiarotti and Bruno Morassutti, *Church*, Baranzate, Milan, 1957

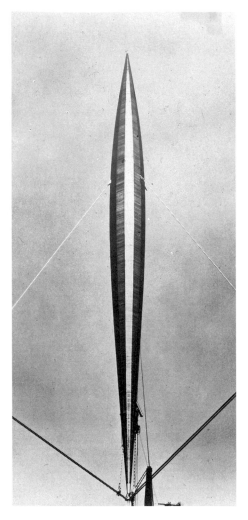

The advertising feature of the Festival of Britain was a spectacular Skylon designed by Powell and Moya, 1951

Below:
Interior of Le Corbusier's Maisons Jaoul, France
Bottom right:
Patio and pavilion by Peter and Alison Smithson, Eduardo Paolozzi and Nigel Henderson, an exhibit 'presenting the fundamental necessities of the human habitat'. *This is Tomorrow* exhibition, Whitechapel Art Gallery, London. 1956

ravaged during the war. Prague and Warsaw, as well as picturesque medieval towns in Germany and France, were tenderly nurtured back to life and the morale of their inhabitants was strengthened when old and familiar street scenes were successfully recaptured through the use of modern materials and constructional methods. This kind of conservation came in for a good deal of criticism from those who wished to see modern cities replace the old, but on the whole it seems to have been psychologically the right thing to do, while the experience gained by the exercise has been of inestimable value since in the many schemes for the redevelopment of historic cities that have been undertaken in the Western world. Another by-product of reconstruction was the interest that developed among architects, critics and scholars for a deeper and contextual knowledge of the history of architecture.

This too had its effect on practice and critics who felt that this reappraisal went too far dubbed it a 'return to Historicism'. It was nothing of the sort. Each age reconditions its thinking about architecture and the arts, firstly, in relation to current values (both aesthetic and technical), and secondly, to the sources which inspire originality. In many cases these sources are historical. The earlier generation of pioneer modern architects had successfully managed to obscure their historical sources – creating the illusion (and proclaiming) that their work was free from historical precedent. What happened in the mid-1950s, I believe, was a much more open-minded acceptance of modern architecture, seen in relation to the whole tradition of architecture.

The chronicling of the history of the modern movement and the work of individual architects was well advanced by this time, and serious studies appeared which supplemented the polemical books and magazines of the 1930s and 1940s. Although the bedrock for this approach had been laid, for English-language readers, in Pevsner's *Pioneers of Modern Design* (first published in 1936), in Giedion's *Space, Time and Architecture* (first edition, 1941) and in Richards's *Introduction to Modern Architecture* (a Pelican Original which first appeared in 1940), the new material that was built on it aided its dissemination. New published material was of three kinds: individual monographs; surveys of work in various countries, incorporating photographic records (for example, the books by G. E. Kidder Smith); and the on-going, and influential, publication of current projects by the international magazines, all of which were, by the 1950s, firmly committed to a mainstream modern line.

If, however, the modern movement was now good box-office, the situation of an *avant-garde* attitude having become a universal panacea had its drawbacks. A false situation was created that was a direct result of the misappropriation of so-called 'functionalist' ideas that I mentioned in the decade opener for the 1930s. The divisions that existed then were never adequately healed over, social problems somehow got haphazardly mixed with aesthetic ideals and an architecture emerged in the early 1950s that was painfully inadequate to meet the needs of the time. The 'new' town-planners were probably the worst culprits. Never having understood, even partially, the basis on which the new architecture had attained its pre-eminent

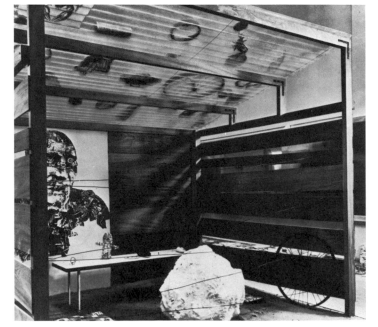

position before the war, they now accepted a facile kind of modernism in conjunction with a pedestrian and almost mindless acceptance of a *beaux-arts* kind of civic design. Many examples of this approach exist in England, much of it fortunately bound up in published reports for town centres and never carried out. The City of Plymouth, and the central-area developments of a number of European and American cities and the early British New Towns, are, however, still with us as reminders of the appallingly facile approach to both architecture and planning in the 1950s.

Municipal bodies, New Town commissions, commercial firms and private clients were all prepared to pay lip-service to an architectural vocabulary they did not, or were unwilling, to understand. Young designers were caught in a cleft stick, during a period of fast-expanding building activity: either copying the best features of the master works, and designing within the idiom of an established innovator (the Chicagoans's allegiance to Mies is a case in point) or establishing some kind of originality of their own. Something of the current attitude was expressed in Tom Lehrer's popular song lyric of the mid 1950s, 'Lobachevsky': 'plagiarize, plagiarize, don't let anyone else's work evade your eyes'. It was left to the self-appointed new *avant-garde* to break the authoritarian hold of the older generation architects in CIAM. The confusion that had set in, the Formalism and, indeed, the cribbing was brought to a head by Team X (Ten), a group of young radicals which included the British architects Peter and Alison Smithson, John Voelcker and William Howell, the Dutchmen Bakema and Van Eyck and the Greek-born French architect Georges Candilis. The final break occurred at Dubrovnik in 1956 when CIAM was almost wound up. Its life was prolonged for a further three years, and the final débâcle took place at the CIAM 1959 Congress at Otterlo in the Netherlands, a Congress dominated by Team X.

The demise of CIAM was brought about by a growing dissatisfaction among the younger generation of architects who felt, justifiably it seems, that the older members of the Congress were fossilizing into an establishment group, becoming too autocratic, academic and generalized. The younger men reacted strongly against the impersonal concepts of order that CIAM applied willy-nilly to the problems of urban living, which they felt were more tangibly personal. In 1955, the Smithsons wrote: 'each generation feels a new dissatisfaction and conceives of a new order. This is architecture. Young architects today feel a monumental dissatisfaction with the buildings they see going up around them.' With their terse, direct vocabulary, the Smithsons were speaking for their colleagues in Britain and Europe with whom they were engaged in establishing the components of a new scene.

The term 'New Brutalism' was actually coined by Alison Smithson in 1954, but it has since been used as an extensible word to cover a multitude of architectural variations. Its meaning was never very precise. It describes, I would suggest, an attitude to design – grounded in the structural logic of Mies's work and in the clarity of form to be found in Le Corbusier's post-war projects – which had an ethical and empirical basis, which saw modern architecture as a slow evolutionary process, was 'honest' in intention and execution and was direct in its aesthetic vocabulary. In its initial phases, Brutalism was intrinsically linked with the beginning of the Pop Art movement; as a term it was a 'throwaway' or, conversely, an *objet trouvé*. It was, therefore, as much a descriptive term of a disruptive period in architecture and art as it was a metaphor for the concrete finishes (the *béton brut*) to be found in the work of Le Corbusier.

Other currents, too, were at work in the English scene in the late 1950s which were attracting critical comment throughout the architectural world. Significant advances were made in industrialization and prefabrication in the public sector, and the school-building programme and the competition-based public authority housing in particular received a wide Press coverage. This in turn led to an over-emphasis on industrialization and method-building which seduced a number of highly imaginative designers into jobs where they were to become stultified by repetition work.

Just at this very moment of anonymous industrialization in Britain, of a new kind of Formalism in the USA (for example, the Lincoln Center), and an awakening of interest in Functionalism in Japan, Le Corbusier dropped a bombshell into the international architectural arena: in 1955 he completed his incredible Chapel at Ronchamp. Nothing was quite the same again in twentieth-century architecture. Symbolism, plasticity, function and form, construction and technique – subjects that were being freely discussed in the international journals at the time – all took on a new meaning. The 'box', it appeared, had exploded. Other projects followed from Le Corbusier in a similar vein; one, the Philips Pavilion at the World Fair at Brussels, could be viewed dispassionately alongside what was considered to be the most advanced architectural thinking from other nations. Like Taut's Glass House at Cologne in 1914, Ronchamp was a design that represented a newly-lit flame.

Above:
Frank Lloyd Wright (1869–1959)
Below:
Frank Lloyd Wright's design for Price Tower,
Bartlesville, Oklahoma, USA. 1953

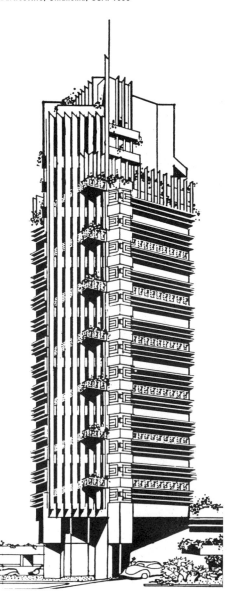

Mies van der Rohe. *Farnsworth House,* Fox River, Plano, Ill., USA. 1950 (1945–50)
Right: the kitchen galley
Below: the entrance platform leading into the house on the right
Bottom: ground-floor plan

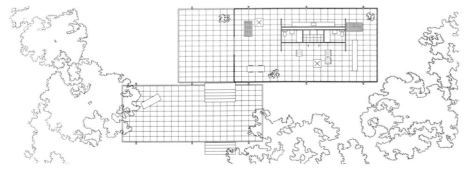

The house for Dr Edith Farnsworth was Mies's first domestic commission in the USA. It took five years to design and build. Essentially this 'pure' design consists of one glass-enclosed room – 77 feet long by 28 feet wide – but the resultant space is flexible and divided by a centralized service core.

The design is as sensitive as a harp string – tension is everywhere to be found in the building; it is held by taut steel columns that sensitively perform their supportive function at roof and floor levels. It does not actually touch the ground and long-legged columns transfer its loads emphatically down to land which is liable to flooding. A terrace platform connects ground and living levels by means of wide flights of steps.

Wright's second major scheme for the Johnson Wax Company incorporated a spectacularly beautiful glass and brickwork tower in which 40-foot-square floors alternate with circular mezzanine floors. All floors are cantilevered from a hollow reinforced concrete core. New offices connect with the 1936 administration building and materials were matched. Pyrex glass tubing was used extensively (21 miles of it!) as a light-source.

The Health Centre by Mendelsohn was his first completed American building. It is one of his few post-German buildings that match his earlier brilliant concepts of the 1920s and 1930s. It has been altered and spoilt. The project was large, the plan E-shaped but constricted by a limited site.

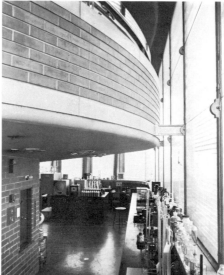

Frank Lloyd Wright. *Helio-Laboratory and Research Tower,*
S. C. Johnson and Son Inc., Racine, Wisc., USA.
1950, Second Phase, (1947–50)
Left: interior showing mushroom columns
Below: a detail of one of the circular brickwork
balconies at mezzanine level within the squarish tower
Bottom: the fifteen-storey Research Tower above the
new offices

Erich Mendelsohn. *Maimonides Health Centre,* San Francisco.,
Calif., USA. 1950 (1946–50) (Altered)
Left: the freely-flowing balconies on the south-facing
rooms of the Maimonides Health Centre

1950

Walter Gropius (The Architects' Collaborative).
Harvard Graduate Center, Cambridge, Mass., USA. 1950
Right: the connecting canopies between blocks
Below: the Graduate Center lounge and meeting-room
building

Arne Jacobsen. *Soholm Housing Estate,* Klampenborg, Gentofte, Denmark. 1950 (1946–50; further houses built 1955)
Left: the two-storey chain houses

Bruce Goff. *Wilson House,* Perdido Bay, Pensacola, Florida, USA. 1950
Right: the rear of the house
Bottom: the entrance porch

Not one of Gropius's best buildings by any means, the Harvard Graduate Center was the product of the early years of the team organization TAC. However, the group of eight buildings arranged round small and large courtyards on the Oxbridge pattern has a good community feel about it and is humanly scaled. The various buildings house dormitories, common-rooms, refectory and a lounge convertible into a meeting-hall for 250 people. The dormitory blocks are constructed in reinforced concrete and the community buildings in steelwork. The planning of the dormitories is of the conventional central-corridor type with single and double rooms off either side.

Jacobsen's estate of seaside houses at Klampenborg has had considerable repercussions on domestic design throughout Europe. The chain of houses, arranged in terraces, was planned in 1946 to conform to the maximum floor area then permitted – 110 square metres. The first part of the estate was completed in 1950, the second part in 1955. The houses are planned in such a way that the courtyard garden space becomes an important adjunct to the interior, and a degree of flexibility was allowed for in the design, as the courtyard itself can be covered to provide an additional room. The living-rooms are on the first floor with a narrow dining-room below. The exteriors of the houses were finished in yellow brick with asbestos cement roofs.

'Look at that crazy house' is a remark that Bruce Goff knows only too well, but this original, unclassifiable architect has done much in the United States to make people look afresh at the intimate problems of domestic design. His Wilson House, unlike the Ford House (see page 169) and the Bavinger House (see page 203) was built entirely of timber and is a thoroughly harmonious construction.

183

1951

Eugenio Montuori with Catini, Castellazzi, Fadigati, Pintonello and Vitalozzi. *Rail Terminus,* Rome, Italy. 1951 (1947–51)
Right: the main concourse
Below: external view of the main concourse building

John Lloyd Wright. *Wayfarer's Chapel,* Palos Verdes, Calif., USA. 1951 (1949–51)
Left below: interior of Chapel
Below: exterior view of the Chapel with its extensive use of glass

In Europe, the start of a new era of post-war architecture began in Italy: one of the more impressive public buildings to go up at the time was the new rail terminus at Rome. In America, the rational style of the European Mies van der Rohe took a firm grip on the Chicago school.

A building which seems to combine the 'organic' architecture of the United States (a direct result of Frank Lloyd Wright's philosophy) and the European obsession with 'glass architecture' is that by Wright's son John Lloyd Wright at Palos Verdes.

The terminus, a large, long, low vaulted structure has had a tremendous effect on railway-station design. Its efficient plan is based on a simple interpretation of station functions. In the nineteenth century a hotel often provided the frontage to the station – an idea derived from the notion of the train as an 'iron horse' whose stable was a vast glass and iron shed. This modern station symbolizes the modern view of rail travel: the flowing concrete roof which covers the ticket-offices extends to provide a protective canopy for cars and travellers; a concourse behind this vast hall brings passengers to each railhead and connects, by stairs and escalators, a restaurant and offices above.

The two lakeshore apartment blocks of Mies are the best-known 'monuments' of post-war American architecture. To catalogue their influence, both in the United States and abroad, would take a whole volume. Set at right angles to each other, the twenty-six-storey blocks are steel framed with windows from floor to ceiling. The two blocks are connected by a minimal canopy. Built as a co-operative housing venture, the tenants share facilities such as laundries, deep-freeze rooms and basement car space.

The Wayfarer's Chapel, built for the adherents of the eighteenth-century theologian Emanuel Swedenborg, was opened in May 1951, but designed some years earlier. It is a place of beauty, quiet and comfort situated in a breathtaking natural setting. The design is simple: rigid redwood frames branch out at their haunches into Y-shapes. The resultant roof triangles are filled alternatively with glass and tile panels. Nature has invaded the building and today it is almost enclosed by shubbery. The lay-out, and the elements of the building itself, relate to angles of 30 and 60 degrees – a symbol of the Trinity.

Mies van der Rohe. (Associated Architects: Pace Associates; Holsman, Holsman, Klekamp and Taylor).
Apartments, 860 and 880 Lake Shore Drive, Chicago, Illinois, USA. 1951 (1948–51)
Below: the pair of twenty-six-storey blocks on Lake Shore Drive
Right: detail of free-standing external column at ground level
Bottom: site plan
Bottom right: construction photograph showing the steelwork

Ralph Tubbs. *The Dome of Discovery*, Festival of Britain, London, England. 1951 (1949–50)
Below: interior of the *Dome of Discovery*
Bottom: aerial view of the Festival of Britain South Bank site showing the relationship between the *Dome of Discovery* and the *Royal Festival Hall*

Key to axonometric:
1 roof garden   6 grand tier   11 terrace
2 choir   7 entrance staircase   restaurant
3 boxes   8 side promenade   12 escape stairs
4 orchestra   9 main foyer   13 terrace
5 stalls   10 restaurant

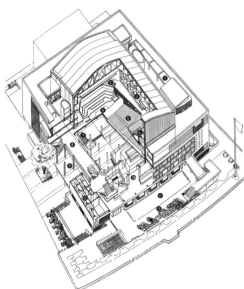

Ralph Tubbs' Dome of Discovery was the largest domed building in the world when it was built in 1951. It was 93 feet high to the central point and 45 feet high to the surrounding caves. Inside it was divided by three platforms, 12 feet, 22 feet and 35 feet from the ground-floor level, reached either by staircases or by the 35-foot long escalator.

The 1951 exhibition came in for much adverse criticism from the national and technical Press, but the Dome of Discovery received only appreciative comments. One critic at the time referred to it as being 'a construction as brave and as adventurous as anything seen in Britain' up to that time. The scale was colossal and gave a sense of almost Wellsian unreality.

The Royal Festival Hall has never looked entirely satisfactory, although internally as a festival concert-hall, it aroused high hopes for acoustical perfection. In it the 'black science' of acoustics was taken to what were then considered to be its logical conclusion. The auditorium was 'tuned up' by adjustment of sections of the acoustic material with which its internal walls and other surfaces were lined. Technically it was a great success. The main rectangular concert hall has 2,740 seats on two levels. As steel was rationed in 1951 the Hall was constructed in reinforced concrete.

By 1951, Felix Candela had formulated his new philosophy of structures in which, as one writer has put it, he 'cut himself loose from all conventional methods of calculation.' One of the most spectacular buildings of this period was the Cosmic Ray Pavilion constructed on the spot where Valarta and LeMaitre made discoveries concerning cosmic rays. Two small laboratories for the measurement of cosmic rays and the phenomenon of nuclear disintegration were erected on this site. The thin concrete shells were the thinnest ever cast, $\frac{5}{8}$ inch thick at the roof edge. The roof shapes themselves were two hyperbolic paraboloids coupled along a principal parabola.

LCC Architect's Department. Robert Matthew (Architect to the Council), J. L. Martin (Deputy Architect), Edwin Williams (Senior Architect), Peter Moro (Associated Architect). *Royal Festival Hall*, London, England. 1951 (1949–51)
Above: the Hall adjacent to the old shot tower (demolished)
Right: axonometric drawing of the Festival Hall
Below: auditorium interior of the Festival Hall

Felix Candela, Engineer (J. G. Reyna, Architect).
Cosmic Ray Pavilion, University City, Mexico. 1951
Right: oblique view of the Pavilion

1952

The Olympic Stadium, Helsinki, was won in competition as early as 1933 and most of it built during the period 1934 to 1940. It was intended for the 1940 Olympiad, which did not take place, and was not completed until 1952, for use by the second post-war Olympic Games in Helsinki. The stadium started as an important manifestation of the 'white architecture' of the 1930s, but a later wooden addition (including cladding) for the 1952 Games somewhat spoiled the concept. As with most stadia of this type, there is a tower feature, this one being very high, at the southern end of the main arena.

Caesar Cottage is one of the more 'precious' works of Marcel Breuer. It is simply a one-room week-end cottage with a porch constructed in timber and situated on a narrow beach line site. Structural screen walls which are suspended outwards to carry the porch also act as blinkers against overlooking from neighbouring properties.

The living space of the Desert House by Soleri and Mills is covered with a moveable glass-domed roof, which reacts immediately to temperature changes; the living space is carved into the hillside and enclosed by masonry walls. This incredible house by Soleri is an expressive example of a cave-like structure aligned to modern technology. Everything about it is responsive to the needs of the site, the structure and the occupants.

Yrjö Lindegren and Toivo Jäntti. *Olympic Stadium*, Helsinki, Finland. 1952 (1933–52) (Extended and altered)
Right: general aerial view of the stadium in 1952

Marcel Breuer. *Harry A. Caesar Cottage*, Lakeville, Conn., USA. 1952
Below left: entrance view of the cottage, with lake in the background
Below right: view from the living-room across the lake

Paolo Soleri and Mark Mills. *Desert House*, Cave Creek,
Arizona, USA. 1952 (1951–52)
Top: the Desert House in its setting
Centre left: the glass roof retracted

Above: interior of the Desert House

1952

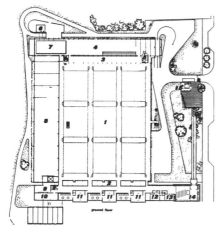

Architects' Co-Partnership. *Factory* for Brynmawr Rubber
Ltd, Brynmawr, South Wales. 1952 (1946–52)
Top: the south side of the *Factory*
Above: ground-floor plan and section
Right: interior of one of the large domed production
areas

Alvar Aalto. *Civic Centre,* Säynätsalo, Finland. 1952
(1950–52)
Above: general view, with the library block in the
foreground
Right: view through into the upper courtyard with
library on right

ACP's research for the Brynmawr factory
began in 1945. The largest Government-
owned factory in the South Wales Development Area, it was specifically designed for
the production of rubber articles. Constructed in reinforced concrete during a period
of acute steel shortage, it proved difficult to
erect but revolutionized factory design in
Britain. The factory is divided into a main
production area and the raw-material
processing area. The functional plan
follows the lines of production processes.
The 77,000 square feet of production area
is covered by nine shell domes, each 85 × 62
feet, allowing freedom from the clutter of
structural supports. The domed spaces were
then the largest of their kind in the world,
lit by clerestory windows on all four sides,
supplemented by circular roof-lights in the
domes themselves.

The Säynätsalo Civic Centre is also
basically a building of the 'forties, won in
competition by Aalto in 1949 and erected
1950-52. It represents the opposite end
of the design spectrum to the ACP factory:
built of red brick, wood and copper, it is a
gem situated in a town which is virtually
devoid of other permanent buildings.
It is centrally organized around an elevated
courtyard, and nature pours through into
the design from all sides. Beside the well-
finished timber and brick Council chamber,
the scheme incorporates a bank, stores, a
post office, offices and a public library.

The Palace Hotel scheme won a competition for offices for several industrial
organizations and a sixty-bedroom hotel
in 1948. Splendidly situated on the water's
edge in Helsinki, the hotel was a major
contribution to the new urban architecture of immediate post-war Finland.
Originally, the scheme incorporated a
parking level at second floor but this was
later enclosed.

Viljo Revell with Keijo Petäjä. The *Teollisuuskeskus*
building (Palace Hotel), Helsinki, Finland. 1952
(1949–52)
Right: street façade overlooking Helsinki harbour

1952

Le Corbusier. *Unité d'Habitation,* Marseille, France. 1952
(1946–52)
Top right: a typical floor plan and section of the
Unité
Middle: a main elevation
Bottom left: the giant *pilotis* at ground-floor level
Bottom right: detail of external concrete finishing

The culmination of Le Corbusier's quiet
wartime thinking was seen in the massive
'Housing Units' (*Unité d'Habitation*) at
Marseille, a residential complex designed
principally for workers. Many design problems are solved in this scheme, including
those of the dwelling unit itself, and of the
circulation and planning of community
residences within an 'urban-scale' block.
The seventeen-storey block, resting on
giant supports (*pilotis*) and containing 337
flats of twenty-three types, also incorporates
'internal streets'. The living units are based
on earlier concepts with living-rooms two
storeys high interlocked round the 'street'
entrances and running the full width of the
block. Community facilities are provided on

Wallace K. Harrison (Director of Planning) and Max Abramovitz (Deputy Director). *UN Headquarters,* New York, USA. 1952 (1947–52)
Left: the *Secretariat,* 1950.
Below: the complex completed in 1952

the roof and a central service area midway up the building. *Unités* were also built at Nantes and Berlin.

In 1947 Le Corbusier went to the USA as one of ten architects selected to design the UN Headquarters. After the failure of his League of Nations scheme, he felt the project was his by right. Although the finished building reflects Corbusier's basic concept, he can hardly be called its architect; it was designed by a committee!

The result was an important building, but hardly great architecture. The complex consists of three separate buildings, the Secretariat tower, a conference area and the Assembly. The Secretariat contains thirty-nine storeys of offices. The Assembly, in Corbusier's original sketch, was to have included two auditoria head to head. Now reduced to one, its shape is his, retained for political expediency.

In the early 'fifties, blocks were 'in' but

Juan O'Gorman. *University Library,* National Autonomous University of Mexico. 1952 (1950–52)
Above: the mosaic-covered book-stack tower of the Library

few received the overall treatment like the Mexico Library. Originally designed to resemble a Meso-American pyramid, O'Gorman's final solution is more conventionally a box with highly coloured mosaics.

1953

Van den Broek and Bakema. *The Lijnbaan Shopping Centre,* Rotterdam, The Netherlands. 1953 (1951–53)
Below: aerial view of the *Lijnbaan*
Right: the pedestrian precinct

Ralph Erskine. *Cardboard Factory,* Fors, Sweden.
1953 (1950–53)
Below: the curved brick centre portion of the factory, with the air ducts on the right

The Lijnbaan lies between a scheme of high buildings which includes department stores, apartments and offices. It was one of the first exclusively pedestrian shopping precincts to be erected in post-war Europe; the main walkway is crossed in places by vehicular streets which connect with the service roads behind the shops. A continuous canopy penetrates the shops at display level and these cross over at intervals along the main walkway. All shops in the scheme are of two and three storeys.

Ralph Erskine's cardboard factory was completed in the same year as the Lijnbaan. It is brick-faced but has a reinforced concrete frame on 15-foot bay widths. This building is the product of industrial designing for weather demands; straight-line machinery, here 426 feet long, has to be protected from the danger of condensation. Large amounts of moisture are,

therefore, removed by hot air and the air-intakes form a feature on the central part of the building; placed on the double curve of the external wall, they are turned down for protection against snow. The double roof also forms an air-duct to prevent condensation falling on to the machinery.

The aluminium-faced, thirty-storey, steel-framed office block in Pittsburg was, with the Equitable Life Building in Pittsburg, one of the first metal-faced curtain-walled buildings to be erected in the United States. The technique of cladding in metal took several years to develop and, for this building, a particularly good example of a preformed metal panel exterior was devised. The 12-foot storey-height aluminium panels are 6 feet wide and ⅛ inch thick, stamped out 8 inches deep in an inverted pyramid. The windows also form part of the panel and are reversible through 180

degrees. The main entrance lobby, a separate birdcage structure, was suspended from the main tower by two cantilevered girders. The total site area covered by the building was nearly 18,000 square feet and no car parking facilities were provided.

Soleri's Ceramica Artistica Solimene was erected to accommodate a traditional one-family business. Conceptually, the building is similar to Frank Lloyd Wright's Guggenheim Museum. Internally, five floors are connected by a continuous ramp which runs round a large open sky-lit hall, as a response 'to the lineal sequential functions of the ceramic process'. The building is situated on a tiny site hanging on a cliff over the Mediterranean. Externally, it is covered with glazed forms based on pot shapes which do not entirely marry with the angular shapes of the windows to the factory itself.

Harrison and Abramovitz. (Associated Architects: Altenhof, Bowen, Mitchell and Ritchey.) *Alcoa Headquarters,* Pittsburg, Penn., USA. 1953 (1951–53)
Left: general exterior view, with the lower entrance porch in the foreground

Paolo Soleri and Mark Mills. *Solimene Ceramics Factory,* Vietri-sul-Mare, near Salerno, Italy. 1953
Below: interior showing the five-storey reinforced concrete structure
Bottom: general external view

1953/54

Affonso Eduardo Reidy. *Apartments*, Pedregulho Estate,
Rio de Janeiro, Brazil. 1953 (1947–53)
Right: one of the blocks
Below: general plan of the estate

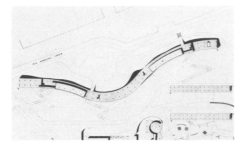

R. Buckminster Fuller. *Ford 'Rotunda' Dome*, Dearborn,
Mich, USA. 1953
Above and left: the 'rotunda' fixed in place inside the
earlier structure designed by Albert Kahn Associates

Alvar Aalto. *Rautatalo (Steel Federation) Office Building
and Coffee Bar*, Helsinki, Finland. 1953 (1952–53)
Left: main street façade
Above: the internal covered courtyard

The long, curved Pedregulho block must be one of the longest housing units in the world – 826 feet long and seven storeys high, containing in total some 272 apartments. This dominating, curved block – which is one of a number of blocks that form the whole neighbourhood scheme – follows the line of the hillside around the craggy site. Included in the scheme are many communal buildings and all the blocks have cross-ventilation and external-access corridors.

The geodesic dome, designed by Buckminster Fuller for the Ford Rotunda, was the first major large-scale use of this type of dome structure for industry. It spanned the 93 feet of the existing building and was constructed from plastic and aluminium sections. It indicated the advantage of using these materials and this geometric method – it was erected in thirty working days and weighed less than 9 tons, compared to a more conventional covering which would probably have worked out nearer 160 tons. It was erected from the top downwards and is held up by twenty supports around its rim. The plastic skin was added when the structure was completed.

Aalto's Rautatalo offices are a highly successful addition to an old central area street in Helsinki. Clad in bronze, the simple façade is effective as a complement to the existing buildings. The façade conceals, however, an exciting internal arrangement: shops run along the main street at ground level, but inserted between them is a short staircase which leads to an internal, marble-faced courtyard containing a coffee bar. The upper-floor offices are approached from this court via the balconies which run around it.

One of Le Corbusier's finest buildings in India is undoubtedly the Ahmedabad mill-owners' building. It is a simple box with two open sides and two almost blind sides. The open front end is like a deep egg-crate with slim concrete louvres angled to protect the public rooms from the searing sun. A ramp leads the visitor out from the car-park into the shaded recesses of the belly of the building, where access can be obtained to the upper floors. The building was orientated according to prevailing winds and the hall is indirectly lit by reflected light from the curved ceiling, which is kept cool by a water pool on the roof.

Le Corbusier. *Millowners' Association Building*, Ahmedabad, India. 1954
Top: the entrance front
Above: rear view
Bottom right: the freestanding staircase
Bottom left: interior with bar

1954

Alison and Peter Smithson. *Secondary Modern School,*
Hunstanton, Norfolk, England. 1954 (1950–54)
Right: the link between the single-storey block and the
main block, with the water-tower behind
Centre: the detached gymnasium to the right of the
main block
Bottom: ground floor plan and interior of hall

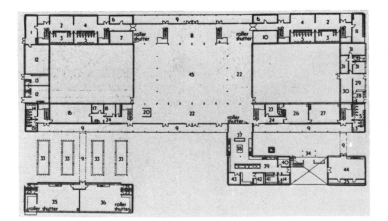

Above: Luis Baragan, *Casa Antonio Galvez*, San Angel, Mexico, 1954

Felix Candela. *Church of the Miraculous Virgin*, Mexico City, Mexico. 1954
Left: interior of church during construction

Louis Kahn with Douglas Orr. *University Art Gallery and Design Center,* Yale University, New Haven, Conn., USA. 1954
Below: interior of one of the ground-floor galleries

The design for the best-known and most influential post-war British secondary school was prepared in 1949 and awarded first place in competition in 1950. It was not completed until 1954. It thus represents an attitude of mind of the late 1940s and early 1950s when strong admiration was felt throughout the world for the work of Mies van der Rohe. Significantly, it was Mies's disciple Johnson who referred to it as an 'extraordinary group of buildings'. Technically, it was almost perfect. Aesthetically, the most distinguished of buildings of the time. The main two-storey block encloses two open courtyards and contains within its precise steel and brick envelope the main teaching-rooms. The gymnasium is in a separate box to one side of the main building. The whole building has exposed services and all the steelwork was site-welded, giving a precise, mechanical feeling to the scheme.

The opposite approach is Candela's church, his first commission as architect *and* engineer. It consists of a series of double-curved surfaces in concrete, and bears some resemblance to the architecture of Antonio Gaudi. The surfaces are generated from a rectangular plan, as is Baragan's Modernist Galvez House.

Kahn's extension to the Yale Art Gallery, a fine four-storey concrete box, was the first modern building to go up at that University. Today, it faces the Art and Architecture building by Paul Rudolph. The maximum use is made of open spaces for exhibition purposes and the simple wall treatment and heavy ceiling coffers offer a neutral background for display.

Le Corbusier. *Pilgrimage Chapel of Notre-Dame-du-Haut*,
Ronchamp, Vosges. 1955 (1950–55)
Right: exterior of the Chapel from the south-east
Centre left: part of the northern façade with the open-
air pulpit in the centre of the picture
Centre right: the northern façade
Bottom: axonometric

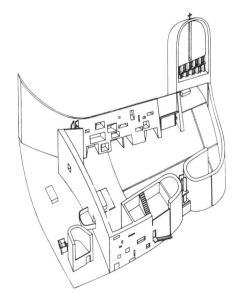

In building the Chapel at Ronchamp, Le Corbusier claimed he 'wished to create a place of silence, of prayer, of peace, of spiritual joy'. His commitment to the project was almost medieval: he referred to his 'sacred task' and to the 'drama of Christianity' that had taken possession of the Chapel.

The Chapel has been attacked for being too theatrical, 'irrational' and neo-Baroque, and praised for its spatial organization, its originality and the way, as a design, it enriched rational architecture. Theatre is an aspect of the Church's history that is revived in the planning and execution of this shrine, which has a dual function. Inside the womb-like interior, the believer finds peace, while the outside can be transformed into a focal point for a congregation of up to 10,000 pilgrims.

The design was received by the architectural world with amazement when it was first published. It represented a radical departure from Le Corbusier's previous projects, even though still controlled by his 'Modulor' laws. Its influence had been world-wide.

Situated on a hilltop near Besançon, it relies for its effect on the interplay of curvilinear surfaces, a plain whiteness, thick walls and splashes of colour in door and window openings. The vast roof over-sails the battered walls; the curved towers funnel light into the dark interior.

There is no mystery about GM's dynamic Technical Center. It is one of the prime examples of the clean-limbed aesthetic – crisp, industrialized and well detailed against the foil of a silver lake. It includes twenty-five separate buildings completed between 1949 and 1955. It was opened in 1956. The scheme shares its one-square-mile site with other GM concerns. The shiny surfaces and the forms of the Styling Center auditorium and the water-tower (a true ellipse in elevation) counterbalance the aluminium trim, the black vertical steelwork columns and the reflective, glare-absorbing glass of the other buildings.

Eero Saarinen and Associates. *Technical Center,*
General Motors, Warren, Mich., USA. 1955 (1949–55)
Right: the Styling Staff building and the aluminium domed
auditorium at the south end of the Technical Center Lake
Below: the auditorium
Bottom left: the water-tower
Bottom right: bird's-eye view of the 330-acre
Technical Center

1955

Max Bill. *Hochschule für Gestaltung* (College of Design),
Ulm, Germany. 1955 (1950–55)
Below: general view of the Hochschule
Right: the prefabricated blocks

André Studer. *Low-Cost Apartments*, Casablanca, Morocco.
1955 (1954–55)
Right: detail of balconies
Bottom: general view

The Hochschule at Ulm was referred to,
when it was set up, as the second European
Bauhaus. Max Bill, its designer and first
Rektor, was a Bauhaus student. It suffered a
similar fate to the earlier Bauhaus and was
closed by the authorities a few years ago. The
first stage of the design for the buildings was
completed in 1955, some five years after the
preliminary project. The scheme was substantially completed in the early 1960s,
although lack of funds proved a drawback.
The group of buildings rises to a crest on
a hill-top overlooking the Danube. The
blocks, which were mostly made up of simple
industrialized units, varied from a five-storey
student dormitory to two-storey workshop
blocks.

A low-cost housing programme was introduced in Morocco soon after the end of the
Second World War. Government policy
favoured the erection of what became known
as '8 × 8' houses (a single-storey dwelling
8 metres by 8 metres), which included
usually two rooms, a W.C. and a courtyard.
Later, the French ATBAT Afrique Group
(Candilis, Woods and Bodiansky) developed
a characteristic modern version of this tra-

ditionally based plan, using white finished reinforced concrete construction with staggered plans and continuous balconies. A year or so later, André Studer produced a further variation on this theme.

The Olivetti head offices in Milan are situated near the Piazza del Duomo. They are air-conditioned and constructed in reinforced concrete which was designed to be strong enough to take an additional top deck for helicopters. The ground floor of the eight-storey block (which has two further four-storey wings) is completely glazed, giving a view into the showrooms and through to the gardens beyond.

Bruce Goff's 'snail house' is one of the most famous architectural oddities of the postwar era built in the USA. Its oddness should not be allowed to belie its serious intent in dealing with the continuity of a spiral for spatial reasons. The house is described as 'for a lover of plants' and its organisation is clearly based on natural forms. The parts, or subdivisions, of the building do not grow up conventionally from the ground, but hang between – or span – successive rises in the spiral form. The house is surfaced in rough stone and the whole interior, except for the central service core, is open.

G. A. Bernasconi with A. Fiocchi and Marcello Nizzoli. *Olivetti Offices*, Milan, Italy. 1955 (1954–55)
Above: main façade

Bruce Goff. *Bavinger House*, Norman, Oklahoma, USA. 1955 (1950–55)
Left: section
Below left: view from downstream
Below: the building includes several suspended areas. The skylight follows the line of the stairs

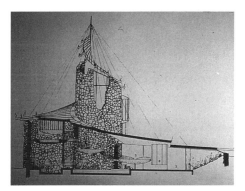

Mies van der Rohe. Associated architects: Pace
Associates. *The S.R. Crown Hall*, Illinois Institute of
Technology, Chicago, Illinois, USA. 1956 (1952–56)
Below: the main entrance to *Crown Hall*

Peter Smithson. *House of the Future*, Ideal Home
Exhibition, Olympia, London, England. 1956
Left: bird's eye view of the interior, and section below

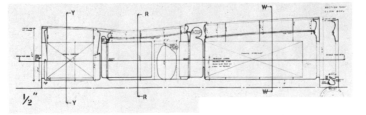

½"

Crown Hall houses the School of
Architecture and Design at IIT and was
built during the period when Mies was in
charge. The massive single space provided
by the building measures 220 × 120 feet. It is
nearly 20 feet high and walled with panels of
obscure and clear glass, framed in steel.
The great open space has been harshly
criticized by those weak-minded theorists
who have been scared by Mies's confident
use of 'big' areas. The students who have
lived with it are more enthusiastic. The
whole building is massively in scale with
its frame hung from four exposed plate
girders, shop-fabricated, and each delivered
to the site in two 60-foot sections. The
basement houses ancillary accommodation.

The House of the Future was intended to
show a probable design for living in the
1980s. Basically, it was a town-house with
a patio garden inside a rectangular plan.
The unit itself was capable of grouping
with other similar units to form a compact
community. The house was constructed
from large moulds of plastic-impregnated
plaster. It was a skin structure built up in
parts with flexible joints. Electrically heated
and air conditioned throughout, the rooms

flowed into each other, each defined by curved walls. Doors folded away into the walls themselves and the roof, which was highest in the living-room on the patio side (facing south), was lower on the bedroom side of the unit. The front door was operated electrically from the hall and the kitchen, and a warm-air screen came on when the front door opened. There was also a system of removing dust from shoes! The furniture and fittings were integral with the house itself.

Aalto's National Pensions Institute, Helsinki, was won in competition in 1948. It was not completed until 1956. It is one of Aalto's largest buildings and occupies a triangular site in the northern part of the city. Externally, it is finished in Aalto's characteristic red brick. This is contrasted with the clear lines of the copper trimming that run along the top and bottom of all window openings and round the blank areas of brickwork. At the apex of the triangular site, a copper-clad water-tower rears up and creates a significant feature in a dull part of the city.

It is a confident building and its multi-level blocks wrap around a large raised courtyard planted with mature trees. Internally, the detailing is superb and Aalto has created some of his finest public spaces in this building.

The Maisons Jaoul by Le Corbusier, projected in 1952, were an important departure in domestic design and had their most important influence on the British-inspired 'Brutalist' faction. The two houses have a common entrance and are placed at right angles to each other. Gardens and courts are in the basement and each house has two gardens separated by walls. The plans are rectangular. The innovation occurs in the interior, which incorporates Catalan vaults formed with tiles as permanent shuttering. The 'Modulor' proportional system was used in the design of these houses. The roofs are planted with grass.

Alvar Aalto, *National Pensions Institute*, Helsinki, Finland. 1956 (1948 Comp.; 1952–56)
Top: a long view of the Institute
Above: corner view

Le Corbusier. *Maisons Jaoul*, Neuilly-sur-Seine, Paris, France. 1956 (1954–56)
Below: general external view of one of the Maisons Jaoul

1956

Anshen and Allen. *The Chapel of the Holy Cross,*
Sedona, Arizona, USA. 1956
Above and right: general views

Anshen and Allen's Chapel of the Holy
Cross, set in a cleavage in the rocks of
the mountains north of Phoenix, Arizona,
is a votive Roman Catholic chapel.
Symbolism on the impenetrable mountain-
side of the building is, as the picture shows,
direct and simple, a contrast to the complexity of the north side. Here a visitor
leaves his car at a lower level and makes his
way up to the entrance of the reinforced
concrete church by means of a winding
pedestrian ramp. Once inside, the visitor
is trapped in a confined but splendid space
and caught like a television camera looking
out on a wild natural scene with the
Christian Cross as the foreground motif.

The Peace Centre in Hiroshima was
Kenzo Tange's first large-scale building. In
1946, a competition was organized for this
Peace Centre to be erected on the spot
above which the first atomic bomb had
detonated. It was intended to be a community
centre as well as a memorial to be built
within the fifteen-year plan for the construction of the city. Although Tange's plan
had won the competition, a large number
of changes were made before construction
work got under way in 1950. In the finally
executed plan, the museum building was
placed centrally and was thus made to
dominate the whole complex, which

Johnson's clean-limbed Synagogue is a
clear Modernist statement with the kind of
neo-classical references to be found in the
work of his mentor, Mies van der Rohe. It
consists of two connected geometrical
elements externally with an oval-shaped
vestibule placed symmetrically against the
steel-framed but precast concrete-panelled
rectangular hall.

Philip Johnson, *Kneses Tifereth Israel Synagogue,* Port
Chester. New York, N.Y. USA 1956 (1954–6).
Right: a simple external statement that enriches the
Miesian vocabulary

Kenzo Tange, in association with Takashi Asada and Yukio Otani, *Peace Centre,* Hiroshima, Japan. 1956 (1949–56)
Above: the Peace Centre lined up on the Atom Bomb memorial

Le Corbusier. *The Shodhan House,* Ahmedabad, India. 1956 (1951–56)
Left and below: the garden elevation and a general side view

included a community building as well as an auditorium. In front of the museum was a large open area to accommodate up to 50,000 people, and beyond that the peace memorial itself, designed by Tange and completed in 1953. The museum is a deceptively simple building. A long, low, rectangular structure in which one storey is raised above columns, it is penetrated by an open staircase from the ground. Exhibits are simply laid out and in themselves provide a further memorial to the destruction of the city of Hiroshima.

The Maison Shodhan by Le Corbusier was originally commissioned by the Secretary of the Mill Owners' Association, but before building had begun on the site, it was sold to Mr Shodhan who built the house on another site. As a design, it recalls the ingenuity of the earlier Villa Savoye by Le Corbusier, although it is far more complex in its external arrangements. However, this complexity was to a certain extent dictated by the climatic conditions, and the outer fretwork is in fact a series of *brise-soleil* behind which the building is organized on seven levels. Similar to the Villa Savoye it has a long internal ramp which leads to the mezzanine and the main level. Above the main level are situated three apartments separated but made to contact. The building also incorporates a hanging garden and, overlooked by the main living areas, is a free-shape swimming-pool.

Le Corbusier. *The Courts of Justice,* Chandigarh, India.
1956 (1951–56)
Below: the *Courts of Justice* with the *Palace of Assembly*
(Parliament Buildings in foreground)
Below left: part of the main façade of the *Courts of Justice* building

The Courts of Justice at Chandigarh, together with the Palace of Assembly, the Secretariat, the Governor's Residence and the Monument of the Open Hand, form the city Capitol. The Courts Building was conceived like a giant umbrella, under which space was made available for the general public and for the functions of the court. The section is a simple, longitudinal one and the plan is subdivided into a series of courtrooms with attendant waiting areas. The effect is stunning. Sigfried Giedion has written that 'in this building, modern, articulated processes, functionally planned, are adapted to climatic conditions, to the country and to its customs'. In the building an attempt was made by Le Corbusier to meet the conditions of building in India. Giant *brise-soleil* break up the façade of this powerful structure and air circulates through it. But inevitably it still appears as a rather ponderous Western kind of building in an alien culture. The polychromatic effect of Le Corbusier's palette is an alien element at variance with the vernacular tradition. However, the building is spatial, even authoritarian, and a monument to the achievements of the great architect/planner.

Jacobsen's open-courtyard school at Gentofte has been referred to as 'the finest secondary school in Europe'. Clinically laid out in the Jacobsen manner, each courtyard provides additional teaching space for the classroom which opens on to it. Each one is different in treatment, though the main characteristics of all the courtyards are common. Four rows of classrooms run east and west and give south orientation to all the rooms. The planning is rigid yet there is a tremendous variety within this building. Built at the time when the English schools programme was well under way, it offers a significant contrast to the technologically minded British architects, absorbed with their industrial systems. Jacobsen was able to produce at Gentofte a series of units using standard components and lightweight materials which in fact added up to a remarkable example of national architecture.

Precision of a different kind is found in Candela's Celestino's Warehouse of the same year. Here, we see again the great Mexican engineer at work using this time not thin shells but umbrella concrete construction. The building is engineer's architecture in which structure, material, space, colour are all related: the walls, the roof and the floor of the building are all of the same material and coloured the same neutral grey. But, played off against this neutrality, the columns appear, as one critic has put it, as 'white masts' to delineate space. It did not require a large amount of natural light and the light it does receive enters indirectly, creating a static, almost theatrical, effect.

Arne Jacobsen. *Munkegaards School,* Gentofte, Copenhagen, Denmark. 1956 (1952–56)
Right: an interior of one of the courtyards of the school
Below: plan
Middle: a general view of the courtyard arrangement

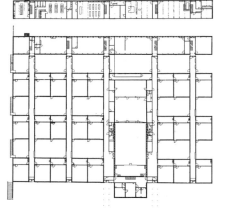

Felix Candela. *Celestino's Warehouse,* Vallejo, Mexico City, Mexico. 1956
Left: constructional photograph showing the interior of the *Warehouse* with the folded plate roof

209

1956/57

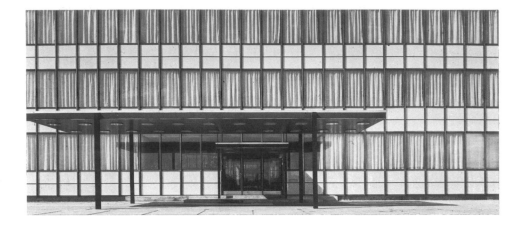

Arne Jacobsen. *Town Hall*, Rødovre, near Copenhagen,
Denmark. 1956 (1954–56)
Right: entrance to the municipal offices
Below: elevation drawing of the office block and ground-
floor plan of the whole building
Below right: the steel and glass staircase

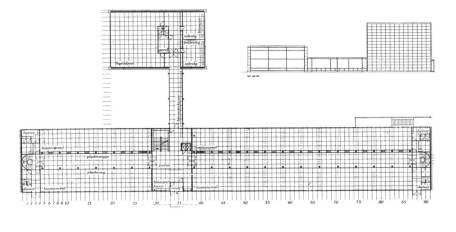

Carlo Scarpa, *Castelvecchio Museum*, Verona, 1956. View
of the ground floor spaces

Jacobsen's Rødovre town hall consists of two separate buildings: the three-storey municipal offices connected by a corridor to a single-storey block of conference and committee rooms. It is an industrialized building with a precise, almost machine-like appearance. The divisions of the vertical spaces are based on a planning module of one metre. The meticulous steel and glass staircase is as famous for twentieth-century architecture as the stairs of the Biblioteca Laurenziana at Florence are for the sixteenth.

By no means so polished as the Rødovre town hall, Jacobsen's motor factory was finished in brickwork facings and concrete columns. It is a well-controlled scheme, providing an environmental standard probably· undreamt of by factory owners in other countries. The dirty-work areas (for cylinder boring and motor renovation) are separated from the clean areas on an east-west axis.

St Louis Airport terminus did not, it must be admitted, come up to the standard required by its designer Yamasaki, and he has put on record four major reservations, about its shape (it should have been based on parabolas rather than arcs of circles), its windows, its supports (they should have been expressed) and its canopies (which should have been curved). Even so, it was of considerable local significance as built. Its failings apart, its vast concourse, providing over 42,000 square feet of space under three intersecting barrel-vaulted sections, further intersected by six dormer arches, was a jump in the direction of the later structural expressionism of Saarinen's Dulles Airport building. The three-level plan overcomes difficult site problems.

Carlo Scarpa's sensitive alterations to the Castelvecchio in Verona was a pioneering example of conservation and creative modern design.

Arne Jacobsen. *Carl Christensen Motor Works*, Aalborg, Denmark. 1957 (1956–57)
Above: general view

Hellmuth, Leinweber and Yamasaki (Architect in charge: Minoru Yamasaki). *Terminal Building*, Lambert-St Louis Airport, Miss., USA. 1956
Below: interior of the concourse

1957

Heikki and Kaija Siren. *University Chapel,* Otaniemi, Finland. 1957 (1952–57)
Right: outside the small timber chapel, a white metal cross stands against snow-covered trees in winter
Below: the chapel with the entrance courtyard in the foreground

This charming small chapel by a husband and wife team was built on a shoestring. A competition for a chapel was held in 1949 and won by Aalto. However, the Sirens' competition entry was purchased and it was realized in 1956-57.

Set in dense pine woods, adjacent to the on-going development at Otaniemi 'Tech' town, the building consists of three simple elements: an entrance courtyard, protected from snow-drifts by an open screen made of pine branches and old railway track, a vestibule and the chapel itself, which slopes sharply towards the altar and the external white cross. The building is constructed in red brick and creosoted timber and has an asbestos roof above timber lattice-beams.

The small brother of the Palazzo dello Sport (designed and constructed by Nervi, and built between 1958 and 1960 – see 1960), the Palazzetto was also erected for the 1960 Olympiad. It is the more structurally explicit of the two buildings.

Designed to hold between 4,000 and 5,000 spectators, it is covered by a hemispherical shell roof of precast concrete units, nearly 200 feet in diameter. The Y-shaped supports transfer the loads to a concrete foundation ring.

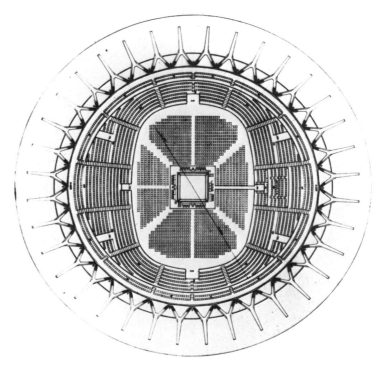

A. Vitelozzi and P. L. Nervi. *Palazzetto dello Sport* (the smaller sports hall), Rome. 1957
Top: the sports hall exterior
Centre: interior of the dome
Right: ground-floor plan

1957

BPR (Lodovico B. Belgiojoso, Enrico Peresutti and
Ernesto Rogers). *Velasca Tower,* Milan, Italy. 1957
(1956–57)
Right: a view of the *Velasca Tower* in its street situation
Below: detail of the corner of the upper part of the
Tower

The Torre Velasca is a strange building
erected during the high point of the
'neo-Liberty' movement in Italy. Externally,
its castellated top section is reminiscent of a
medieval stronghold. Twenty-six storeys
high – the enlarged tower section is above
the eighteenth floor – it is situated close to
Milan Cathedral. The architects for this
building exploited the use of structure in an
idiosyncratic way, using the external
columns like strands of string pulled taut
round two rectangular boxes.

Another interesting feature of the exterior
is the way the windows are placed within
the main panel sections between the
columns. Here, haphazard blank spaces are
left, and the normal repetition of windows
that one usually finds in high office blocks
is lost – or made fun of?

A more conventional approach to office
buildings is to be found in the large complex built over a long period of time
by Figini and Pollini at Ivrea for Olivetti.
The offices which form part of phase
two consist of a three-storey box with a
flat roof and are themselves only a small
part of the industrial centre. But they
indicate the high design standards set.
Other buildings include a staff housing
scheme, a nursery school, a social services
building and the ICO building. The
more recent ICO building on the left of
the photograph is a five-storey square

Luigi Figini and Gino Pollini. *Olivetti Administrative and Industrial Centre,* Ivrea, Italy. 1957 (Built in four phases: 1934–35, 1939–40, 1947–49, 1956–57)
Above: the complex as it appears today

Kenzo Tange with Nagashima and Okamura. *Sogetsu Art Centre,* Tokyo, Japan. 1957 (1955–57)
Right: the lateral façade seen from the sculpture court

building with protruding triangular service areas and five ceramic-tile-faced lift towers. For the rest of the building, a steel frame is used with an infill of glass panels. Its plain walls facing south present a contrast to the earlier building which incorporates a protective *brise-soleil* façade to the south.

The Sogetsu Art Centre is devoted to the traditional art of flower arrangement. It is very small although it has an impressive, almost monumental, quality. Situated on a sloping site near the administrative district of Tokyo, it is a two-storey structure containing at first-floor level administrative offices and a salon and on the second floor individual classrooms. The roof of the auditorium has been developed as a sculpture court and as an extension of the ground-floor foyer. The sculpture garden also serves as an open-air theatre. The main lateral façade of the building overlooks this sculpture court and · the two ends of the building are virtually blank, finished in a blue ceramic tile, bordered by drawn-on white lines.

1958

R. Buckminster Fuller (Synergetics Inc.).
Dome, Union Tank Car Company, Baton Rouge, LA., USA.
1958
Top: the Dome during erection, with section
Above: air view of Dome (384 feet diameter) at Baton Rouge

At the time of building, Fuller's Union Dome was the largest circular structure in the world (see Dome of Discovery, page 186). As high as a ten-storey office block, and big enough to house a football-field, the dome accommodates the regional tank car repair and maintenance facilities. When built, it was the first major industrial application of the geodesic structural principles developed over many years by Fuller.

Inside the dome, a smaller 80-foot diameter open dome-shaped structure forms the node of service operations; the major repair unit is located at this centre. From the domed space a 200-foot-long connecting tunnel, finished in similar hexagonal steel as the main dome, serves as a painting-shop.

A further dome for the same company was erected at Wood River, Illinois in 1961, and was built from the top down over a huge pneumatic nylon bag.

The dome has been revived by the modern architect; the Y-shape, another traditional plan form, also often recurs in the modern age. The two best-known European examples in the post-war period are both by the naturalized American architect Marcel Breuer: Unesco HQ in Paris and the IBM administration building at La Gaude (1960).

The Unesco HQ's building history can be compared with the UN. Inevitably there was a large panel of distinguished consultants, including Le Corbusier, Gropius, Costa and Rogers. A compromise was also inevitable.

The eight-storey, Y-shaped block, with large windows, *brise-soleil* and tapered concrete columns, houses the Secretariat, and is a contrast to Nervi's concrete conference-hall structure.

Aalto's building houses Finnish left-wing organizations. The auditorium is a freely curved element connected – not too happily – by a two-storey link to a rectangular five-storey office block. The auditorium is finished in wedge-shaped hollow bricks, designed by Aalto to produce the curved surface.

Marcel Breuer, P. L. Nervi, Bernard Zehrfuss.
UNESCO Headquarters, Place de Fontenoy, Paris, France.
1958 (1953–58)
Right: entrance façade of the Y-shaped building
Middle right: interior of the Conference Hall

Alvar Aalto. *House of Culture,* Helsinki, Finland. 1958
(1955–58)
Below: exterior and detail of the auditorium block
Bottom: interior of auditorium

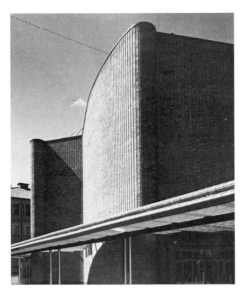

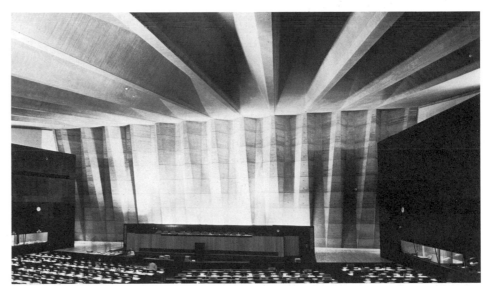

1958

The American-born Minoru Yamasaki has been referred to as an 'architectural Humanist' with a considerable technical knowledge and a delight in the serenity of Japanese design. He came to the fore in the early 1950s, but his somewhat later McGregor Center embodies much of the maturity of his later thinking, after he had travelled widely and cooled his decorative eclecticism. The building stands as a kind of focal point within the campus as a link between town and gown. The folded concrete slab structure creates a rhythm both internally and externally, and the Center is placed next to a decorative and Japanese-inspired pool garden. Adjacent to the Center stands the College of Education building, also by Yamasaki and completed in 1960.

The Secretariat at Chandigarh forms the northern-most side of the new Capitol. The Ministerial offices are all grouped in the centre of the 800-foot long slab block. The whole of the building is constructed in raw concrete. Public access and movement within the building is based on a ramp system which echos some of the ideas Corbusier was exploring in his early villas.

Minoru Yamasaki. *The McGregor Memorial Conference Center*, Wayne State University, Detroit, Mich. 1958
Right: interior view
Below: exterior, with pool garden

Le Corbusier. *Secretariat*, Chandigarh, India. 1958 (1951–58)
Above: a long view of the Secretariat building with
the Palace of Assembly (1953–60) to the right
Right: the Secretariat from the Palace of Assembly
Bottom: details of part of the *brise-soleil*, behind which are
situated the ministerial rooms

1958

Candela's delightful octagonal shell restaurant replaced an earlier timber structure destroyed by fire. Called *Los Manantiales* (literally, 'The Springs'), it is virtually surrounded by water. The setting is beautiful, the building revolutionary. Its distinctive circular wave-like form is derived from four hyperbolic paraboloids intersecting at the groins of the vaults. The support for the building comes from these groins, which leave a plain white-painted interior free from encumbrances.

Another simple, confident and economical shell structure designed by Candela was the 'Jacaranda' night-club at Acapulco. It is essentially a visual metaphor for what he calls his 'sixth or seventh sense', the one which somehow, creatively, combines structural intuition with the visual rightness of a design. Theory, he once wrote, 'must be accompanied by progressive realization'. It is displayed in these two buildings.

Felix Candela and Joaquín Alvarez Ordóñez (Architect). *Restaurant Floating Gardens,* Xochimilco, Mexico City, Mexico. 1958
Right: the 1000-seat restaurant at Xochimilco

Felix Candela (Engineer), with Juan Sordo Madaleno (Architect). *La Jacaranda Night-club*, El Presidente Hotel, Acapulco, Mexico. 1958
Below: the simple shell of La Jacaranda

Anders Tengbom. *Pedagogical Institute*, Miljö, Sweden.
1958 (1955–58)
Right: aerial view
Below: layout plan of the Institute
Bottom: view of the 'pleated' façade of the hostel

Anders Tengbom, son of the famous
Swedish architect Ivar Tengbom, designed
the teaching institute at Skogshem on a flat
but fairly heavily wooded site. The 'pleated'
façade of the hostel building is a strong
feature in the design, and it also provides
privacy for each of the study-bedrooms.
The 2-storey restaurant building and the
main lecture room complex are both sited
separately, away from the residential
accommodation.

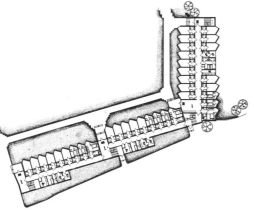

1958

Mies van der Rohe, with Philip Johnson (Associated architects: Kahn and Jacobs). *House of Seagram* (Seagram Building), 375 Park Avenue, New York, USA. 1958
Right: general view of the Seagram Building
Below: ground-floor plan

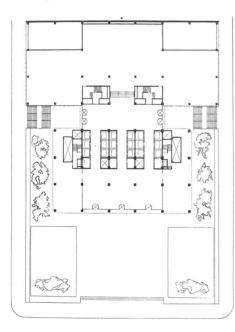

Egon Eiermann, with Sep Ruf. *West German Pavilion*,
World's Fair, Brussels, Belgium. 1958
Right: bird's eye view of a model of the scheme

Le Corbusier (with Janis Xenakis). *Le Poème Electronique*
(*Philips Pavilion*), World Exposition, Brussels, Belgium.
1958 (Demolished)
Below: general external view of the pavilion at the
World Fair with section and axonometric

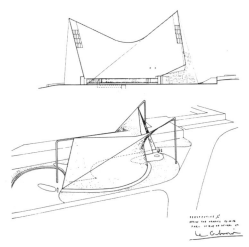

The Seagram is, without doubt, the world's finest and most expensive 'gin palace'. Built by Mies and Johnson for the gin manufacturers, Seagram, it is one of the postwar masterpieces of world architecture. No self-respecting architect or student anywhere in the world can, I imagine, have failed to hear of it and use it as an example to condemn or admire. One architect has even claimed that he knelt in front of it! It is finished in bronze-gold-coloured mullions and rivers of glass run upwards for thirty-eight storeys. It was Mies's first New York building, the largest of its type in the world at the time it was completed, expensive to build but in turn freeing some of the most highly-priced urban land to the city. Locally, it started a whole new phase of high building based on the crisp, vertically accentuated rectangle.

The chain of fully-glazed, rectangular pavilions composing the West German exhibit at Brussels was linked by a continuous walkway. Constructed in welded steel, the pavilions were of two types: five two-storeyed groups and three three-storeyed ones. Each façade had electrically-operated white venetian blinds to help offset the glare. The scheme was designed so that it could be re-erected in Germany after the fair and used as a secondary school.

The Philips Pavilion by Le Corbusier was a brilliant 'one-off' essay in conoids, designed to provide a total light-and-sound experience. The sound zipped up the sides of the tented form through concealed and electronically controlled speakers and the light flashed from numerous sources.

223

1958

The President's Palace is sited three miles east of the Capitol at Brasilia, on a promontory near the golf-course and lakes. It is a huge rectangular building of two storeys plus a basement, shielded from the sun by a continuous open veranda. Adjacent to the building is the small, curved Presidential Chapel. The President's Palace is raised 4 feet above ground-level and approached by a ramp. The surrounding veranda is connected to the main building by a diamond-shaped cantilevered structure. The chain of connected diamond-shaped supports is structurally important but they have obviously been developed to a high degree as aesthetic elements in the design and form part of Niemeyer's bold concept for a building for a capital city which itself incorporates a degree of symbolic exaggeration that is to be found echoed in the Parliament Buildings.

Aalto's Vuoksenniska Church lies in

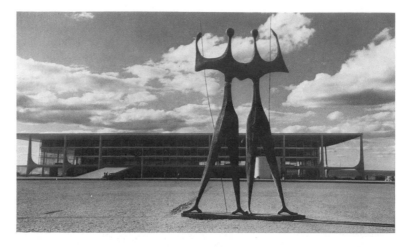

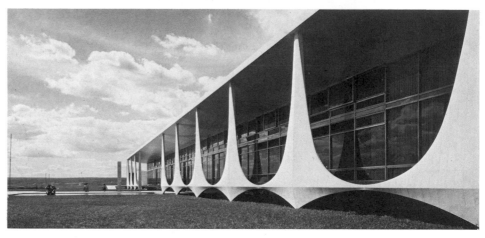

Oscar Niemeyer. *President's Palace of the Dawn,* Brasilia, Brazil. 1958 (1956–58)
Top: general view. Sculpture in the foreground by Bruno Georgi
Right: the beaded reinforced concrete external supports of the Palace

Alvar Aalto. *Vuoksenniska Church,* Imatra, Finland. 1958 (1956–58)
Below: the church sitting among the pines
Below right: interior of the main church

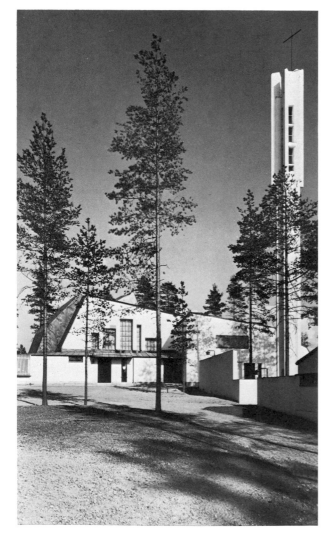

eastern Finland near the Soviet border and serves a group of industrial communities in the town of Imatra. Although mannered, the church is a highly functional structure, built not simply to house the normal functions associated with a church but also to act as a social and community centre. The church consists of three rooms separated by movable sound-proof concrete walls. Each section has its own entrance; one section, containing the altar, is reserved for religious functions. The church can seat approximately 800 people.

The characteristic Aalto curved ceiling – to be seen in early buildings such as the Viipuri Library of 1935 and the House of Culture, Helsinki, in the 'fifties – is designed to meet acoustical requirements, although it quite obviously has given the building its distinctive shape.

It was originally intended that the building should stand in a small grove of slender pine trees but unfortunately most of these were uprooted in a freak tornado when the building was being built. New pines have now grown up and provide the foil to the white bell-tower.

Eero Saarinen thought that his ice hockey rink was one of the best buildings he and his associates had designed. He states that 'the concept of the building was arrived at as a completely logical consequence of the problem. There was the site, an open location . . . it seemed a place where one could express the special nature of this absolutely independent building and could express its structure freely.' Situated on the Yale campus, the rink is of standard size and seating is arranged round it for 2,800 people. When the rink is used for other purposes the accommodation can be in-

Eero Saarinen and Associates (Associated Architect: Douglas W. Orr) *David S. Ingalls Skating Rink,* Yale, New Haven, USA. 1958
Top: the dramatic entrance to the ice rink
Above: the fish-form back
Right: layout plan

creased to 5,000. The building's plan is elliptical and cast-concrete walls run round the two long edges of the ellipse. These walls slant upwards and outwards at an angle of 15 degrees; above them the drama of the roof occurs. A central arch spans the major axis of the ellipse and from this great spine-like arch, cables take out two catenary curves in both directions. The concave and the convex forms create a mutual tension and through this a dynamic building emerges.

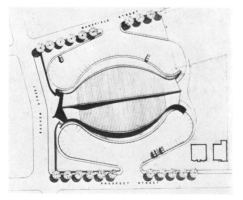

1959

Gio Ponti, Antonio Fornaroli and Alberto Rosselli, (Architects); P. L. Nervi and A. Danusso, (Consulting engineers). *Pirelli Centre,* Milan, Italy. 1959 (1955–59)
Below: the tapering corner of the thirty-four storey block, with section through the tower and a lower ground plan of the whole site
Right: the lateral façade

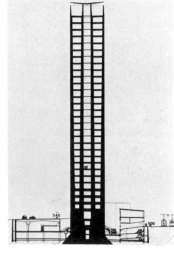

The Pirelli building was the result of close collaboration between architects and engineers. Situated in a prominent position near Milan Central Station, it is in a class of office blocks far removed from the square-faced monsters that despoil city centres from Moscow to Manchester. It is unfortunate (though this may be considered professional carping) that the dynamic double-vertebrate structure indicated in Nervi's section does not get expressed in the elevational treatment. But Ponti was after something different: a 'finite' or 'closed' form. The lenticular plan of the thirty-four-storey office tower (407 feet high) rises from a lower portion of irregular shape which runs round the boundary of the actual site. The tower plan covers about $\frac{1}{7}$th of the site.

The Guggenheim Museum, with a much

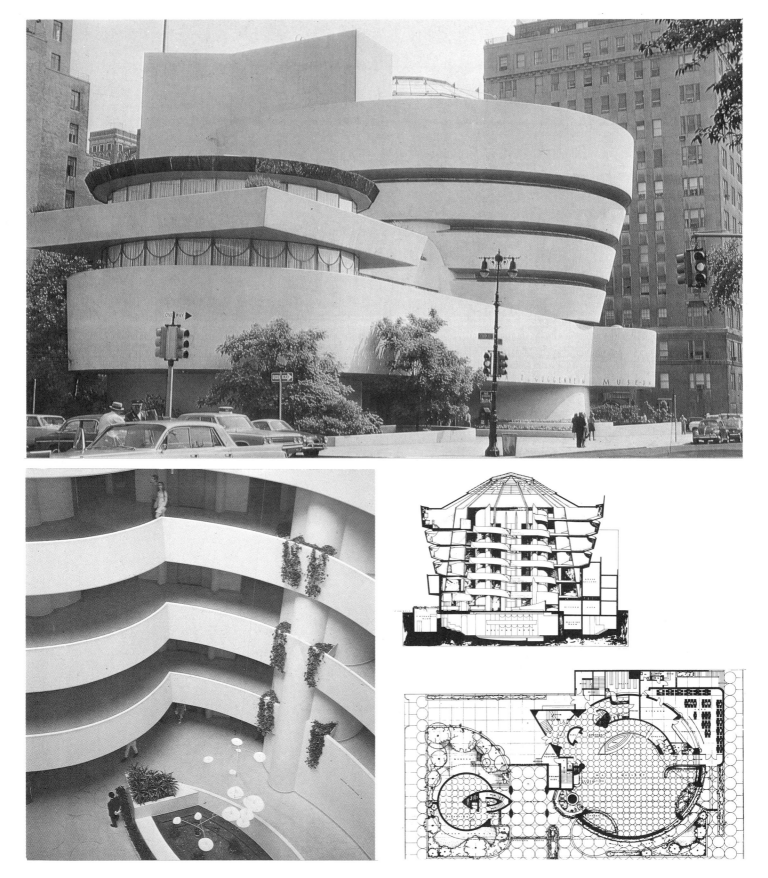

longer building history than the Pirelli tower, is also a finite piece of architecture. Wright's first studies for the Museum based on a spiral form (see page 174) go back to the early 1940s. The design that emerged for the site (which was acquired by Guggenheim in 1947) was ridiculed and considered by 'experts' to be subject to fire hazards. As ever, Wright defended the uniqueness of his 'organic' idea and began work on the most important building of his last period

in May 1957. It opened in October 1959 to a blaze of publicity and controversy, five months after Wright's death. Peter Blake, an American critic, calls it 'important as Wright's last slap at the city'. The Museum may sit uncomfortably among the high towers of New York, but the brilliance of Wright's vision is in its civilizing influence; a man-made oasis based on natural form, powerful, rhetorical and free from commercialized clap-trap.

Frank Lloyd Wright. *Solomon R. Guggenheim Museum,* New York, USA. 1959 (1943–59)
Top: the 5th Avenue façade from Central Park
Above left: the interior of the main hall, round which the spiral ramp of the exhibition gradually ascends to the full height of the building
Above: section with ground-floor plan beneath

1959

Hans Scharoun. Associated architect Wilhelm Frank.
Apartment blocks *Julia*: 1959; *Romeo*: 1957. Stuttgart-
Zuffenhausen, Germany. 1959 (1954–59)
Below: plan and general view of the *Julia* flats

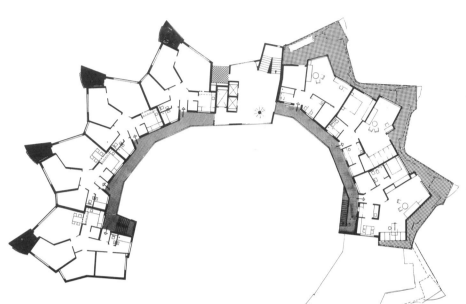

Above: south-east side of the *Romeo* flats
Below: typical floor plan of the *Romeo* flats

The overt symbolism of Scharoun's flats is obvious. *Romeo*, the earlier of the two apartments blocks is an erect nineteen-storey point-block with six dwelling units per floor all entered from central landings. *Julia* is a complex horseshoe block with balcony access varying in height from five to twelve storeys. Both buildings sit somewhat uncomfortably in a new housing estate on a hilltop outside Stuttgart. Since they were

built, a group of architects in the city – principally led by Rolf Gutbrod – have continued to design buildings in the 'free-form' Scharoun style.

The English architects of the 'fifties were obsessed with Le Corbusier's work and far less interested in a latter-day revival of expressionist tendencies. The Alton East point and slab blocks, designed by Lucas, Howell and Killick, were an attempt to

translate the Corbusian Ville Radieuse ideas into reality in public authority housing. The strong external treatment and the landscape setting caught the imagination of the architectural world and many countries now have third-hand schemes based on Roehampton. More recently, the social problems engendered in the estate the size of Alton East – 2,600 dwellings at a density of 100 per acre – has given cause for concern.

GLC Architect's Department. *Alton West Estate,*
Roehampton Lane, London. 1959 (1955–59)
Above: view of point blocks and old people's homes

Top: *Alton West* slab block
Right: detail of a corner

x

GLC Architect's Department. *Alton West Estate,*
Roehampton Lane, London. 1959 (1955–59)
Above: view of point blocks and old people's homes

Top: *Alton West* slab block
Right: detail of a corner

Oswald Mathias Ungers. *Own House,* Cologne, Germany.
1959 (1958–59)
Right: road elevation
Below: side elevation with ground floor and second
floor plans beneath

There is much in Ungers's own house at Cologne that suggests an allegiance to the ideas of the British 'Brutalists', or even perhaps to the much earlier English red brickwork tradition. The house is extremely well organized and situated in an undistinguished neighbourhood. It does not overpower adjacent properties and the eaves-line of the adjoining house is continued as a sort of respectful datum on Ungers's house. It is arranged on three floors, with the architect's office on the ground floor and living accommodation above. Privacy for the internal courtyard space and small garden areas is obtained by a network of high walls that cut the house off from the road.

The 'push and pull' external aesthetic treatment of modern buildings, like for example, the Ungers's house, owes much to the Corbusian ideas of interrelated spaces which are themselves expressed on the façade (or, better, through the three-dimensional form of the building) through an element jutting out here and another part being recessed there. It is by no means as haphazard as it sounds but to keep such a design under control demands a mastery over form and materials that few architects

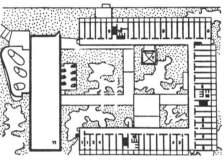

possess. When it results in a building of the
overwhelming majesty of La Tourette then
one is really talking about great architecture.
This important religious building is based
on traditional monastic precedents re-
arranged in a typical Corbusian scheme for
the modern age. It is a rectangular building
with a central court, a church forming its
northern side and a cloister and refectory
creating a symbolic cross in the centre
of the court. Cells are provided, coolly,
repetitively and emphatically, above the
communal spaces. The external treatment
of these cells and all the other parts of the
building is in a spartan concrete finish, a
foil to sunlight and to the grass which
appears even on the inner roofs.

Vittoriano Vigano. *Marchiondi Spagliardi Institute for difficult children,* Baggio, Milan, Italy. 1959 (1953–59)
Right: part of the main façade of the dormitory block
Below: staircase detail showing the open-treads
Bottom right: section and site plan

This building, designed to house children who are difficult to educate, has been criticized for providing a 'difficult' and harsh environment. It was, in fact, designed for a specific programme of reform in the teaching and care of the children it houses. The harshness is to be found in the use of materials – fairfaced reinforced concrete, inside and out – and in the way the programme has generated a rigid authoritarian plan. It is a self-contained community, and includes a school unit and dormitory set in open countryside. The long seven-storey dormitory block dominates with its 'brutalist' external concrete frames and projecting concrete cubes. In the dormitory block, double-height sleeping spaces are provided and twelve boys are accommodated in each bay width. The authoritarian attitude of the programme is best seen in the division of circulation space within the building which isolates boys from staff.

In formal architectural terms, it would be difficult to criticize the building and its influence on a number of more recent structures in various parts of the world is noticeable.

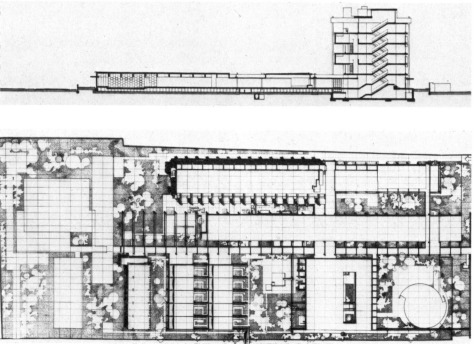

Decade 1960

Louis Kahn. *Richards Medical Research Building*, University
of Pennsylvania, Philadelphia, Pennsylvania, USA.
1960 (1958–60)
Above: general view

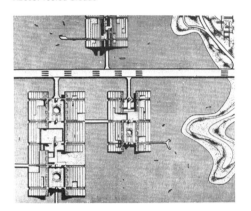

Sigurd Lewerentz, *St. Mark's Church*, Björkhagen, Stockholm, Sweden 1960
Above: roofed arcade

Above: plan of Kenzo Tange's Tokyo Bay scheme, 1960

Below:
Night views of Reno, Nevada, USA

The problems of dealing with the immediate past are legion: only the most intellectually suicidal historian would attempt to draw too many conclusions from a period so close at hand. The dust of history, once settled, has a habit of obscuring many of the episodes and trends that seemed significant at the time. I am therefore avoiding the temptation of making presumptuous judgements and classifying the unclassifiable. At best I can search for connections in recent architecture along the strands of continuity that I have isolated in earlier decades, deduce new trends, innovations and fashions and indicate the nature of the changes that began in the 1960s.

As this book is concerned with buildings in their chronological context, it seems only sensible to continue this kind of presentation up to date. There was no let-up in building work in the 1960s, but there was, however, a shift in emphasis in architectural thinking throughout the world that had far less to do with actual building than in previous decades. Architectural theory came in from the cold and warmed itself up at the fires of discontent among the Functionalists and the Methodologists. Many of the buildings of the decade represent a sort of swan song of modern architecture; in the paper projects and exhibition schemes the nature of the new architecture can be seen. The 1960s appear to have been used as stocktaking years by the theorists and as periods of experiment by the practitioners. Certainly the division between practice and theory in a period of prosperous building activity has never been wider. Some theorists sought to transform architecture by paper designs, sketching out exciting Utopias and banging the drum of rhetoric on behalf of a type of design appropriate to the new Space Age; other theorists actively examined the well-springs of creativity and the fundamental methodologies of design. Borrowing techniques from the American Space Programme, other architects became absorbed with their colleagues in management, engineering and the social sciences, in methods of prediction which began to show an influence on large-scale planning schemes, if less often on individual buildings. Both Doxiadis's *Ecumenopolis* and Fuller's World Game are products of this era.

Whereas architecture had been in a relatively steady state from the beginnings of its functionalist phase in the late 1920s until the end of the 1950s, deviations now crept in which suggested that fundamental changes in the *nature* of architecture had begun. This time it had little relevance to the previously acceptable framework of modern movement design. It was an odd situation in which the old battle between Classicism and Romanticism was revived in architecture, as well as in the other arts, under the guise of a dichotomy between formal and informal principles. The word 'informal' is helpful in defining the looser, inexact parameters within which designers were prepared to work.

In an area of complexity such as city-planning informality was seen as an *ad hoc* ingredient, indefinable perhaps in elemental terms, but essential as part of the approach to the growth of complicated organisms like cities. Some critics, fully aware of the need to create order, polarized their arguments in terms of the rational and the irrational. Theo Crosby, for example, writing in *Architects' Year Book 12* in 1968, on what he called the 'newer rationality', criticized Christopher Alexander's well-known essay 'The City is not a Tree' for its academic Formalism and practical uselessness in actually designing cities: 'In a situation so complex, because of the scale and the numbers of people involved, I would suggest that the ultimately rational, orderly solution is to deliberately introduce into the equation an entirely irrational element: the gesture, gratuitous, ambitious and extravagant.' The use of the word 'gesture' is peculiar but significant among architectural critics in the 1960s, whose own 'gesticulating' at sources, innovations and revivals caused something of a cultural furore. If generalizations may be made, it was a time for the critics and historians, culminating at the end of the decade with the critics and historians receiving the gold medals and awards for the 'furtherance of architecture' and not the practitioners.

In both theory and practice the biggest change that occurred in the 1960s was a conceptual one, one which relates to the problem of informality I mentioned earlier. It could be argued that on the whole architecture up to about the mid 1950s was deterministic, that is to say, the planning of a building was determined by its function, by the way people were expected to use it, and its appearance determined by the acceptable aesthetics of the modern movement tradition as well as by variables brought in by the employment of certain structural systems and new materials. The main concern of the architect, therefore, was still with the building *per se*, and not necessarily with its social, planning or even national context. 'Determinist' was interchangeable as a term with 'functional' and 'rational'.

There were, however, other practitioners whose view of architecture, and its place in society, was less regimented, more complex and clearly integrative, whose ambitions for man's habitat were intricately tied up with a total view of the physical environment in which the divisions between planning, landscape and building were erased. These people were galloping towards a definition of architecture that would be all-embracing. No better word could have been found than the in-word of the late 1960s, 'environment', a term which, so far as I can infer, means that when architects use it for 'physical' design they include among their problems everything everywhere. From desert island to moon landscape through the ocean systems, all is defined as environment. The architect, it seems, can come up with solutions to all of these problems. All was looking well for the ambitious designer, whose design

Below:
Frederick Gibberd & Partners. *Metropolitan Cathedral of Christ the King*, Liverpool, England. 1962–67

Right:
Model of a tower for the Pilkington 'Glass Age' project

Top right: *British Telecom Post Office Tower*

Clorindo Testá, *Bank of London and South America*, Buenos Aires, Argentina.
Bottom right: street elevation

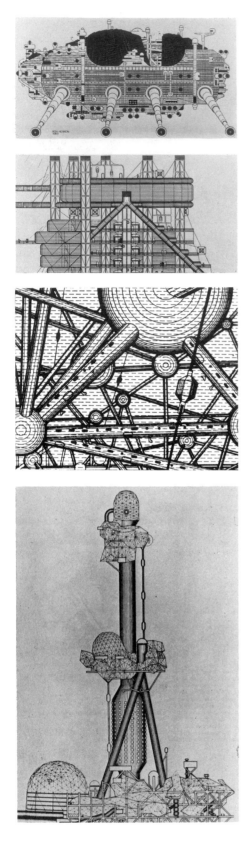

brief could cover hardware and software systems (the hardware of building fabric and elements and the software thrown up in the consumer society by electronics, computer and other advanced technologies), until the explosion of popular interest in ecology, pollution, new life-styles, the politics of revolution and democratic participation swept virtually every other specialisation into a field extended under the new and definitive label 'environment'.

As Simon and Garfunkel were singing their good-bye lament to Frank Lloyd Wright – 'I can't believe your song is gone so soon, I barely learned the tune' – it was gradually dawning on the more historically minded architects the world over that an epoch had ended. Wright had died in 1959, Le Corbusier in 1965, Mies and Gropius in 1969, Neutra in 1970. The inexorable laws of change had overlapped their life-spans and while their own fortunes had been in turn in and out of favour, they contributed to new sensibilities, had seen their colleagues of earlier days discarded by their own generation but revived by succeeding ones, and their own students and apprentices become established.

So much for the old generation. What of the new? The younger generations of designers emerging from schools of architecture throughout the world at the beginning of the 1960s – some progressive, others still held down by conventions – began establishing a network for the exchange of ideas and the promotion of particular points of view. This loose-knit arrangement which depended on informality and personal contact grew into an almost world-wide movement by the end of the decade, bolstered by the Buckminster Fuller World Design Decade programme, by highly successful magazines and road-shows like the English 'Archigram' Group, by existing journals such as *Architectural Design* and by the mutual exchange of heroes of the decade. The importance of all this was to loosen the architectural scene up to new ideas, ideas expressed in theoretical terms rather than as practical solutions to particular building problems. The whole train of events was, therefore, running counter to the aims of many more traditional schools whose role was envisaged as more directly concerned with the production of protégé architectural practitioners than that of precocious evolutionaries. With a few architectural faculties reduced to ashes, some broken-hearted prima-donna academics losing their sense of purpose and self-esteem, and a healthy alienation of students and staff in establishments which were prepared to democratize (heightened by the events in Paris in May 1968), the revolution in architectural education, and by implication, in architectural attitudes, had started.

The architectural world turned its eyes towards the technologically and scientifically respectable game of 'futuristics' in an attempt to divine by speculative means, prognostic if not prophetic, what the next moves would be. As environment is by definition everywhere, 'ecology' soon came to mean everything. The temporary, the 'throw-away', the extensible, the flexible and multi-dimensional structure, the blow up, the 'controlled environment' and the miniaturized city were all predicted, and some were already there to stay. All of these, it will be seen, are part of the technology race and responses to consumer requirements. They do not necessarily provide an environment more conducive to human contentment – perhaps the studies in vernacular settlements, also a feature of architectural interest over the last five or so years, might provide more useful results here – but are rather one part of a search for a new identity for architecture and for a new role for the designer.

In the late 1950s, architects were bombarded with talk about 'anonymous' architecture – an architecture that found its expression through the carefulness of its detailing and the purity of its structure. It looked then as if, in the sheer desperation of trying to find ideas during the last years of Le Corbusier, the creative designers had opted out. If architecture was to serve the needs of people and also play a significant part in people's lives, then the society being designed for would have to become anonymous too. But that was hardly the case: quite suddenly, the medium for designers – the built object – became the message once again. And although environmental design has become (to use an American phrase) 'technologically

Above:
Ron Herron's Walking City, 1964
Peter Cook and 'Archigram'. Drawings for Plug-In City. 1964
Peter Cook's tower project for Expo 67, Montreal
Right: Pier Luigi Nervi, *Paper Mill*, Mantua, Italy

complex social hardware design' for an initiated few, the imagery it has produced is exciting and stimulating. The word 'performance' can now be substituted for 'anonymity'. The work of the more advanced groups stands somewhere between the technically possible and the actually realizable. Its main validity is in the way in which it implies that the physical environment could be organized. It will never be carried out in its purity as a Utopian concept, for we know that change, adaptation, renewal, conservation and obsolescence also influence physical planning and design.

Side by side with the work of 'architectural visionaries', the writings of the space-fiction experts began to take on a new meaning for environmentalists. Writers whose predictions had in some cases fitted hand in glove with the findings of the space scientists and technologists seemed to many of the younger generation of designers to be spelling out the variety of life-styles they had been searching for and to be defining a future world which would require a complete shift in attitude towards architecture. Optimistically, the predictors were saying that the biggest change that will occur will be in man himself. Electronics have already speeded up simple mental operations. Eventually there will be new types of intelligent beings – the humanoid is not too far away. Man's relationship with machines will change and consequently man's relationship with fellow man will change also. We shall work without using our muscles, see without sight, hear without our ears and feel without our hands. The earth itself will be like a village. We have heard the predictions.

At the personal level, electronic information and news services will replace newspapers and telephones, clothes will become additional body skins, transport will be rationalized and food will be chemically processed. Industrially there will undoubtedly be a programme for the conservation of energy (both inside and outside buildings) and the wholesale re-use of materials. Society will become junkless (but not perhaps in the way Charles Platt suggests in his science-fiction story *The Garbage World* where all the scrap and waste of the pleasure worlds of the solar system was dumped on a distant asteroid). Sea-water will be de-salinated, sewerage and liquid waste will be chemically treated and redistributed for industrial use. Conveyor belts, underground arteries, tunnels and service pipe-lines will gradually replace road and rail connections within industrial and commercial areas. Full-scale area heating will be the rule.

Those are just a few of the large-scale predictions, but it is the changes at the other end of the scale that will probably affect mankind earlier than we now assume: the multiple application of lasers and masers for cutting, welding and illumination; the use of extremely high-strength and high-temperature structural materials; the widespread introduction of new and improved mass-produced building materials, including plastics, glasses, alloys, ceramics, and inter-metallics reinforced by fibres for alloys, the building of underground structures on a large scale with completely controlled environments; an increase in the number of short-life multi-purpose light-weight buildings; the development of support structures for 'choice and change' housing; extensive use of earth-moving and heavy construction machinery; and also the extensive use of computer services for educational, informational, personal and design purposes.

Clifford Simak, an old and trusted science-fiction writer who is at heart a back-to-the-soil American sentimentalist, destroys the whole concept of cities in his novels. His hero in *Ring Around the Sun* returns from space to an earthly rural paradise, while in *City*, mankind forsakes the teeming cities, which he calls the ancient huddling places of the human race, and finds a new home in the 'psychological campfire' of the human mind. Mankind is, of course, soon superseded by a new race of more intelligent and harder-working beings!

Be that as it may. It all contributes to a universal conviction that the architectural profession as it has existed over the last two centuries – largely as a super-service profession – will be extinct within a decade or so. Architecture is already becoming such a broadly general name for a complex of subjects and sub-studies connected with the physical environment that it will in the future be utterly meaningless to describe a man simply as an architect. He will, like the modern biologist, become a specialized cog on a wheel of specializations related to man and his habitat. Thus the 1960s seem to have been years of fundamental change in architectural thinking and practice. The changes that have begun are changes of kind and definition. The theory has yet to follow: a few provocative pointers already exist, not the least of which is a suggestion that the suburban house might be viewed as a temporary element within the planning situation and that architectural projects on the large scale should be considered as public monuments. Such revolutionary suggestions indicate the continuing vitality of thought that has been fostered on the architectural scene over the past seventy years.

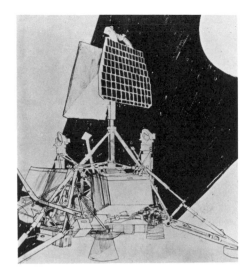

Above:
Space-vehicle designs from a NASA handout
Below:
Yona Friedman. Infrastructure over Paris
Nicolas Schöffer. 'Suspended cap' city

Above:
Exterior and interior views of the Krupp pressurized air-bubble in use in Schleswig-Holstein

1960

Helmut Hentrich and Hubert Petschnigg. *Phoenix-Rheinrohr Company. Office Tower,* Düsseldorf, Germany. 1960 (1957–60)
Below: a general view of the 310-foot towers
Bottom: side view of the slab blocks by night

Alfred Roth. *Own House,* Zürich, Switzerland. 1960
Above: west front

Lucio Costa (Planner) and Oscar Niemeyer (Architect).
Plaza of the Three Powers, Brasilia, Brazil. 1960 (1956–60)
Below right: the cleft tower containing Senate and Assembly offices, the Assembly 'saucer' and the Senate 'dome' about the plaza

Alfred Roth, one of the more important CIAM architects in Switzerland, remained faithful to the white architecture of the 'twenties in his own house built in 1960. He continued his thoughtfully controlled attitude to white concrete design. The house also has accommodation for six students.

The innovatory Brazilian, Niemeyer, returned to an almost classically inspired formalism with his design for the Plaza of the Three Powers, the focal point in the new capital city of Brasilia. This is no ordinary monument. Niemeyer was concerned with unity and creates his effect of monumentality from the shapes of the buildings themselves, thus lifting the scale of monuments to a new plane. The Plaza is positioned on top of a building, with the bifurcated multi-storey blocks of offices, the Assembly Chamber and Senate House, at the apexes of an equilateral triangle.

The Rheinrohr tower is made up of three vertical slabs serviced by a central core. The taller middle block goes up to 310 feet, and has twenty-six storeys, while the shorter side blocks have twenty-three floors. The staggered layout of this administration building was an important development in

Atelier 5 (Fritz, Gerber, Hesterberg, Hostettler,
Morganthaler, Pini and Thormann). *Siedlung Halen*,
Kirchindach, near Berne, Switzerland. 1960
Left: three of the Halen units.
Left below: a general view in winter

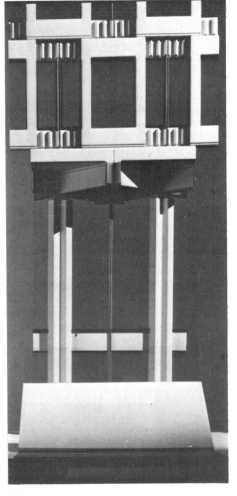

Eero Saarinen and Associates. British Associated
Architects: Yorke, Rosenberg, Mardall. *United States
Embassy*, Grosvenor Square, London, England. 1960
(1956–60)
Left above: the elevation to Grosvenor Square
Above: detail of a model showing construction of the
external panels

European tall office design. It was built
with a steel frame, completely air conditioned with sealed glazing, and finished
in stainless steel and aluminium.

The Halen neighbourhood unit is an
estate of privately owned, concrete-finished,
terrace-houses with its own community
facilities, including a restaurant, shop,
service station and swimming-pool. Each
house is narrow and deep and enclosed by a
walled garden. Two main types of four-
room and six-room houses are provided,
all of which are two storeys high on the
entrance side and three storeys high on the
garden side. This ambitious example of
private-enterprise housing overcomes many
of the problems of privacy and shelter.

Won in competition in 1955, the US
Embassy is frankly one of Saarinen's more
disappointing buildings, although not without its imitators. The architect, sympathetic
to the Georgian town-house tradition in
central London, attempted a compromise
in scale and treatment. While the technical
aspects of the composite construction are of
interest, and the interior spaces are fairly
successful, this pioneer 'American' building
in England is something of a failure.

1960

The Union Carbide Corporation building on its island site between Park and Madison Avenues and the Chase Manhattan Bank building in the Wall Street area (completed in 1960 and opened in 1961), both by SOM, are further refinements of the Miesian 'skin and bones' aesthetic begun with their Lever House in 1952. The architecture of the older Master took on a new brilliance with the construction of his Seagram building in Park Avenue, creating a forthright precedent for the tall New York skyscrapers at the end of the 'fifties.

These two office blocks, both designed under Gordon Bunshaft's direction have a common identity but are radically different in detail and in their treatment of the all-important New York groundscape. The fifty storey United Carbide building released space on its Park Avenue sidewalk for public use, following the Seagram example. The Chase Manhattan Bank – a single shaft of sixty storeys – incorporates a generous public concourse. The United Carbide building is a shaft of steel offset by a black curtain of glass; the Chase Manhattan Bank is an essay in aluminium.

From the office warren to the shrine is but a short step in modern life and Philip Johnson, Mies van der Rohe's collaborator on the Seagram building, provided in 1960 a simple rhetorical statement of 'pure form' for the Robert Lee Blaffer Trust. The ground plan of the New Harmony Shrine consists of six interlocking circles round an inner one; the hooded roof is a series of parabolic curves in timber. Wood arches rise in the valleys of the roof as columns, and curved ribs arch outward between

Skidmore, Owings and Merrill. *Union Carbide Corporation building*, New York, USA. 1960 (1957–60)
Bottom: the Union Carbide's Manhattan profile at dusk
Left: the fifty-storey block

Skidmore, Owings and Merrill, *Chase Manhattan Bank*, New York, USA. 1960 (1957–60)
Above: the sixty-storey block at dusk

columns, giving the internal space an almost medieval quality. But the formal situation in which it stands makes this shrine a really eclectic piece.

A new kind of eclecticism emerged in the post-war world. It was supranational and recognized a Western tradition in modern architecture led by men like Le Corbusier and Mies. Whether in London, Berlin, Sydney or Tokyo, architects reinterpreted Corbusian ideas to suit their own localities. Few have reached the high interpretative standards of Kenzo Tange. The Kurashiki civic complex is a monumental example of his Corbusian leanings.

A cult building in the 1960s, Van Eyck's orphanage brought to the surface an idiosyncratic interpretation of modern architectural ideas enriched by pattern and forms and by balancing repetitive pavilions. Constructed in reinforced concrete panels and glass bricks, it has undoubtedly worn badly. It now houses the Berlage Institute.

Aldo van Eyck, *Children's Home*, Amsterdam, 1960 (1956–60)

Philip Johnson, Shrine, *New Harmony*, Indiana, USA.
1960 (1958–60)
Above: the Lipschitz sculpture sheltered under the
50 foot-high shingle roof

Kenzo Tange. *City Hall,* Kurashiki. Japan. 1960 (1958–60)
Bottom: the rear street façade

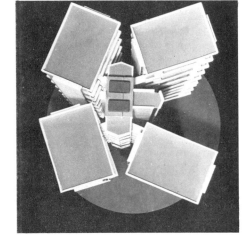

Denys Lasdun and Partners. *Cluster Block*, Bethnal Green, London, England. 1960 (Usk Street, eight-storey blocks, 1954–58); (Claredale Street, fifteen-storey block, 1955–60)
Above and left: general views of the Claredale Street block
Top left: original model of the Claredale scheme

Richard Sheppard, Robson and Partners. *Churchill College*, Cambridge, England. 1960– (1st phase, 1959–60)
Bottom: the graduate flats from the playing-fields

Lasdun's 'cluster blocks' of flats were both an architectural and a social experiment, an attempt to imbue repetitive housing with a sense of community as well as a sense of individual identity. Flats were clustered round a central core, most had direct access from the core to the front door. The core contained the services for the building and also served as a communal activity zone. It would have worked better if the architects had recognized the wind hazard created in this open-core space. Set in a slum district, the design reflected the current architectural interest in the *cluster* 'as a unit of natural aggregation', an idea of Kevin Lynch's, related to the analysis of what he referred to as the *grain* of urban complexes – the size and disposition of ingredients in the urban mix.

Churchill College was won by Sheppard, Robson and Partners in competition in 1959. The first stage (twenty flats for

Van den Broek and Bakema. *Reformed Church,* Nagele,
Netherlands. 1960 (1958–60)
Left: general view of the church and ancillary
accommodation

Picr Luigi Ncrvi. *Palazzo dcllo Sport,* Romc, Italy. 1960
(1058–60)
Right: cross-section
Below: the completely glazed exterior to the Palazzo
Bottom: the apex of the internal hemispherical shell

married Fellows) was opened in 1960 and
the remaining stages completed in 1964.
Basically it follows the traditional Oxbridge
pattern, if in a less nuclear arrangement.
The brick architecture of the first stage was
again a fashionable aesthetic at the time;
later, the dominating hall complex was
finished in concrete.

Brickwork (or rather blockwork) was
used by Van den Broek and Bakema for
their church for the new town of Nagele –
a stark, puritanical exterior in the Reformed
tradition for a community meeting-place
which belies its careful massing and
symbolism.

Nervi's Palazzo, like the earlier
Palazzetto dello Sport (see page 213) was
constructed for the 1960 Olympiad.
Roofed by a huge hemispherical shell dome
328 feet in diameter, it was designed to
accommodate 16,000 people. The circular
outer skin was completely glazed.

1961

Pier Luigi Nervi (Interior design: Gio Ponti).
Palace of Labour (*Palazzo del Lavoro*), 'Italia '61' Exhibition,
Turin, Italy. 1961 (1959–61)
Right: night view of exterior
Below: the ribbed mushroom construction with main
concrete supporting column
Below right: the 'Italia' Pavilion linked to its mono-rail
system in 1961
Bottom right: main elevation of the Palace

The Palace of Labour designed and built by Nervi and his son Antonio for the Turin exhibition of 1961 was the result of a competition held in 1959. The building – containing 85,000 square feet of exhibition space – had to be capable of conversion to a technical school at the end of the exhibition. It was erected in less than eighteen months.

Like Mies van der Rohe's buildings, there is a subtle fusion of structure and space in Nervi's buildings. But whereas Mies searched for free internal space, Nervi's aesthetic is dependent on an energetic exhibition of the structural parts of a building. The Palace of Labour was no exception: the simple 525 feet square shape was divided into sixteen structurally separate steel-roofed compartments each supported on 65-foot-high concrete stems. The external walls, entirely clad in glass, wrapped round the perimeter of the building and incorporated large 70-foot-high vertical mullions.

Nervi's buildings were greatly admired by architects throughout the world in the 1950s, but by the start of the next decade, architects themselves began to explore the sheer architectural possibilities of the remarkable technologies developed by the master-engineer/architects. One of the most self-assured, self-confident – even self-conscious – buildings to emerge as a result of the interplay of the architectonic and the engineer-inspired buildings was Saarinen's TWA Terminal Building at New York. It alarmed the remaining purists of modern architecture. Its bird-like symbolism, exciting forms and cavernous interior were not simply a casual reminder of the changes that had taken place in architectural thinking in the 1950s, but a demonstration of the architect's role as an originator and, in the American scene, as a 'building stylist'. Le Corbusier had loosened the architect's attitude to space and form with his Chapel at Ronchamp; Saarinen confirmed the newfound confidence in the creation of dynamic spaces within a fluid structural framework. Clearly it represented a revival of architectural Expressionism. The architect sought to 'express the excitement of flight'.

The reinforced concrete shell roofs over the building are made up of four intersecting barrel-vaults, all slightly different in shape but all supported on Y-shaped buttresses. Dividing each vault, a ridge of skylights ran along the intersection, lighting the interior by day and at night providing a strip of illumination.

Everything within the building follows the free shapes of the exterior – the staircase is humped, the electronic flight information board is shaped like a SF plant form. A tubular concrete flight walkway extends from the building to the aircraft aprons.

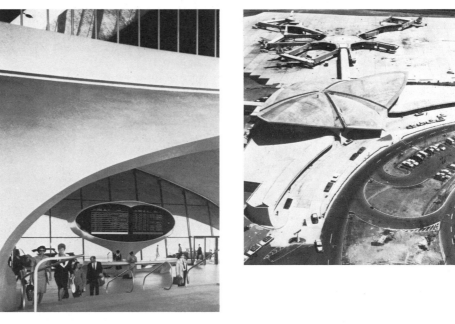

Eero Saarinen and Associates. (Associate in charge: William Gardner). *TWA Terminal Building,* Kennedy (formerly Idlewild) International Airport, New York, USA. 1961
Top: exterior of the main terminal building
Centre left: interior, with the indication board designed as an integral part of the building on the left
Centre right: aerial view showing the original tubular concrete walkway to aircraft
Bottom: section

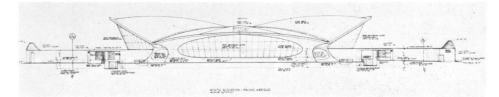

Philip Johnson. *Nuclear Reactor,* Rehovet, Israel. 1961
Right: general external view

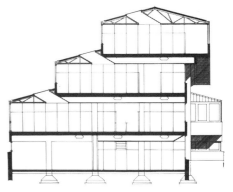

Gino and Nani Valle. *Offices for A. Zanussi Rex factory,*
Pordenone, Italy. 1961 (preliminary studies: 1956;
1959–61)
Centre: the main administrative block
Above: cross-section showing the three floors of
offices and the basement

Marcel Breuer. (Associate: Hamilton Smith). *Lecture Halls
Wing,* Bronx Campus, New York University, USA. 1961
(1957–61)
Left: side elevation seen from dormitory bridge

Johnson's Nuclear Reactor is another example of this architect's 'formalistic' approach, that is to say, creating a building as a sort of monument in its own right, whether or not it accords with what the pioneer generation of architects would have called its functional layout. The symmetrical Reactor has a heavy, almost Egyptian, monolithy with an introverted plan which includes a colonnaded garden court behind the low, enclosed entrance wing. Behind this is situated the faceted, windowless Reactor.

Another kind of formalism is to be found in the offices for the Rex Zanussi domestic appliance factory by the Valles. A dramatic answer to a straightforward problem, it probably over-emphasizes the building's importance but is carried out with a great deal of confidence. Over 300 feet long, the building is planned on a strict horizontal modular grid, the heavy concrete exterior acting as a foil to traffic noise. The section shows the way the building is tiered through its three main floors and the way light penetrates through to the offices on the stepped side. Over these recesses, steel-trussed roofs span back to the main concrete structure. The whole complex is dominated by the overhanging exposed concrete third floor on the south side.

Breuer's buildings for the Bronx Campus at New York University are dominated by the overhanging lecture-theatre block. Here shape follows the function of the building, the tiered seating giving the cut-away appearance. The external concrete is exploited to the full.

The small aluminium building erected on London's South Bank in 1961 served as the HQ for an international conference of architects. Although it leaked like a sieve during the torrential downpours of that summer, it was a temporary structure of some significance. The aluminium egg-crate roof, untreated on the inside, provided clear open areas for the delegates, and a maximum architectural effect was created from the minimum of resources.

The flats at St James's Place by Denys Lasdun, also completed in 1961, are a contrast to the previous buildings mentioned: 'luxury' flats but still very much in the international functionalist tradition, efficiently planned, beautifully detailed and powerfully modelled, they fit comfortably among the grand buildings of Mayfair. They vindicate the architect's concern with real 'luxury' in building: spaciousness, environmental control and attention to the minutiae of detail and finishes. Nothing happens by chance in this building. The reinforced concrete block contains eight flats. The four large flats have 13-foot-high living-rooms which create a split level into which the smaller, one-floor flats are inset. This sectional articulation is reflected in the external balcony arrangement.

Theo Crosby. *Pavilion for the IUA Conference,* South Bank, London. 1961 (demolished)
Top: aerial view of the Pavilion and the adjacent exhibition building with 'super graphics' by Edward Wright
Centre: interior of the Pavilion

Denys Lasdun and Partners. *Flats,* 26 St James's Place, London. 1961 (1959–61)
Above: the Green Park frontage of the flats with Vardy's eighteenth-century Palladian Spencer House to the right
Left: interior of the two-level flats, looking from a stark, unfurnished living-room to the dining-gallery beyond

1961

Herb Greene. *Greene Residence*, Norman, Oklahoma, USA. 1961 (1960–61)
Below: side view of the house
Right: detail of the 'bird's eye' window under the cedar shingle roof
Bottom left: the upper floor and stairs
Bottom right: ground-floor interior, looking up to the stairs illustrated at the left

Herbert Greene's work is to a certain extent like that of his fond hero, Bruce Goff. Both are unclassifiable. Here, someone with an intensely personal vision, employing pertinent metaphors, seeks to create images that evoke a response at many levels. He has recently written about his own house: 'there is the impression of a form that might be a house, made manifest by shingled surfaces, enveloping and roof-like. . . . The creature-like metaphors in the image cannot be easily verbalized, but they include impressions of a large object, thing or creature, rather at home on or accommodating itself to an expanse of natural prairie.' There is also a reference to how a creature shelters itself with its coat or its feathers. Greene's 'Buffalo' house is an intense image but within this image the use of materials and the creation of space are factors which

Kunio Mayekawa and Associates. *Metropolitan Festival Hall*, Tokyo, Japan. 1961
Below: general view
Left: the conference auditorium
Bottom: one of the end elevations of the Festival Hall

harmonize in the final building.

Le Corbusier has inspired many archi-tects of the new Japan. The Metropolitan Festival Hall by Mayekawa is situated next door to Le Corbusier's own Western Art Museum in the residential area of Taiko-ku. A long sprawling building, it is definite in its form. It provides large-scale space at entry level and the careful sculpturing of its individual building masses, which en-close the various spaces used for concerts, opera, ballet, conferences, library, restaurant and exhibitions give a strongly horizontal emphasis. The structure is mainly in reinforced concrete cast on the site, although the interior of the large auditorium is faced with rough-surface, pre-cast units. This enormous building took something like two and a half years to build.

H. T. Cadbury Brown, Casson and Gooden. *Royal College of Art,* London, England. 1962 (1958–62) (Library block, 1963)
Right: general view of the main RCA building from Kensington gardens
Below: the main building behind the RCA Galleries

Situated on an important site in South Kensington, the RCA is not typical of the many college buildings that have gone up in Britain since the war. It is a building with a powerful silhouette, eight storeys in height and constructed in reinforced concrete that rises directly from the pavement's edge. The giant windows on the top of the building let light into large studios; beneath them a more conventional structural bay system is used. Against the large slab, a much freer and lower brick building wraps itself round the building to provide an ingeniously situated courtyard.

Harvey Court is more typical of the college tradition in Cambridge, except that college and courtyard are no longer divorced into physical building and green space but merged into a completely built environment. The courtyard is there all right, but on top of the ground-floor communal rooms, elevated as a first-floor platform to provide breathing-space for the three tiers of stepped-back and inward-looking study-rooms. The rooms arranged in this ziggurat fashion provide additional terraces for the rooms above. In the centre of the court, top-light is provided for an underground breakfast-room. The building has not proved to be as exciting in use as it was on the drawing-board, although it has influenced many subsequent college schemes.

Aalto's Cultural Centre for the Volkswagen town of Wolfsburg follows the basic precepts of architecture in Finland. Irregular shapes (for lecture-halls and seminar-rooms) are played off against the rectangular forms (containing offices, libraries and clubrooms). The main front is connected to the quadrant of lecture-rooms by the 'hinge' of a concealed emergency staircase. The largest auditorium accommodates 200 people.

Leslie Martin and Colin St John Wilson (Principal Assistant: Patrick Hodgkinson). *Harvey Court*, Gonville and Caius College, University of Cambridge, Cambridge, England. 1962 (1959–62)
Below: looking towards the garden court

Alvar Aalto. *Cultural Centre*, Wolfsburg, Germany. 1962 (1958–62)
Bottom: general view of the main front of the Cultural Centre

1962/3

Eero Saarinen and Associates. (Associated Architect and Consultant: Ellery Husted). *Terminal Building,* Dulles International Airport, Chantilly, Virginia, USA. 1962 (1958–62)
Right: a corner of the building with the reinforced concrete pylon carrying the cable on which the roof is supported
Below: cross-section
Bottom: the entrance side, with car park

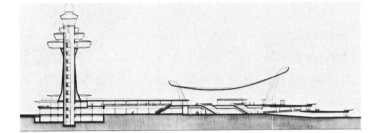

It is clear, when one makes a comparison of the works of Eero Saarinen in the second half of the 1950s, that he was searching for original, even spectacular, solutions to the architectural problems he faced. There is a panache about his American buildings that justifies a claim that he often made in describing his own architecture, that he was in tune with the 'jet age'. Advertising has done much to suggest that the TWA Terminal at New York was the with-it environment for the 1960s jet-set.

At Dulles, Saarinen had a unique series of problems: he was designing a complete new airport, providing a modern gateway to the capital of the nation and building it for the Federal Government. The site was a flat plain. The main terminus is a single, compact structure, not entirely free from formalist tendencies but one which is technically exciting. The final design concept arrived at was a suspended structure, 'high at the front, lower in the middle, slightly higher at the back', generated by a rectangular plan. The building is thus capable of lateral extension. The sixteen pairs of pylons curve outwards and support the hammock-like roof in tension. Passengers are brought into the building at three levels and circulation is made to coincide with the system of mobile lounges which take people to aircraft on the two-mile-long runway.

Paul Rudolph's Art and Architecture Building has come in for much adverse criticism. A *prima-donna* design, it represented a very personal attitude to design as well as to architectural and art education. Its lack of flexibility has proved to be a real problem but its deceptive structure has led a number of critics to suggest that Rudolph was more concerned with the external effects of his building than with its organization. The concrete columns do not pass through and support the floors but go up alongside and are tied in with vast amounts of reinforcement. Indeed, the whole organization of the 'windmill' plan, demanded that vertical elements should support defined rectangular spaces and not 'eat' into them.

Paul Rudolph. *Art and Architecture Building,*
Yale University, New Haven, Conn., USA. 1963 (1959–63)
Top: the main entrance front
Right: detail of window and wall treatment

Ralph Erskine, *architect's own house*, Drottningholm,
Sweden, 1963 (1962–3)

The insertion of a new prefabricated
building into the fabric of the 'Royal Island'
of Stockholm's Drottningholm was a remarkable *coup de grace*. Ralph Erskine also
added a parallel office, again with a characteristic northern roof and a fine garden
court.

James Stirling and James Gowan. *Faculty of Engineering,*
Leicester University, Leicester. England. 1963 (1960–63)
Right: the research laboratory tower and the lecture
theatres of the Engineering building with the workshops
beyond
Below: axonometric
Bottom: the roofs of the teaching workshops

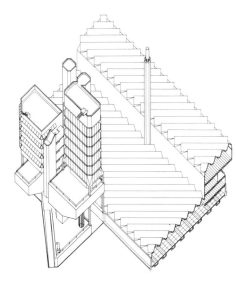

Alfred Roth. *'Riedhof' School,* Zürich, Switzerland. 1963
Left: view from the south

Kenzo Tange. *Cultural Centre,* Nichinan, Japan. 1963
(1961–63)
Below and bottom: the interlocking blocks of the
exterior and an interior view of one of the halls

The Leicester University engineering complex houses a faculty of 250 students and
incorporates teaching workshops, research
laboratories, lecture halls, staff-rooms and
administration offices. The roof-lit workshops cover much of the site and the rest
of the accommodation is arranged in the
tower. This building put British architecture
once again on the world map. It is a powerfully original building, well reasoned,
logically worked out and well detailed. Both
Stirling and Gowan are committed modern
movement designers and although they no
longer practise together, this building
consolidated their reputations. Since the
the early 1960s, Stirling has continued to
design buildings along the same lines.

Roth's School at Zürich is another of his
committed modern movement buildings
but one which, although cubic and crisp
in outline, sits well in its landscaped site
on a hillside. The connections between the
various parts of the school are remarkably
articulate.

A contrast to Roth's School is to be found
in the Cultural Centre by Tange which
depends for its external effect not on a subtle
anonymity but rather on a strident conflict
of interlocking blocks with sloping walls and
roofs. The over-fussy attention to details
is mitigated by the clever way the architect
has harmoniously resolved this problem
into four irregular pyramids (the two central
ones over the main auditorium) and by the
consistent exposed concrete finishing,
both inside and outside the building.

Hans Scharoun. *Philharmonic Concert Hall* Berlin, Germany.
1963 (1960–63)
Top: the west side of the *Philharmonie*
Left: a performance taking place within the main
auditorium
Bottom left: cross-section

The three major buildings on this spread
could not be more varied. All completed
in 1963, they caused controversies that have
hardly settled yet.

The Philharmonie, the home of the
Berlin Philharmonic, is one of those expressionist pieces one immediately hates or
admires. It is so fulsome that there can be
no compromise. Idiosyncratic in the extreme, its massive auditorium is raised up
and 'built in the valley' of the section (left)
while the seats – none of which is more than
115 feet from the stage – are situated in
what Scharoun calls 'vineyards'. The great
roof looks like a vast tent from which are
hung the accoutrements of the modern
acoustics engineer.

The 'PanAm' sits uncomfortably above
Grand Central Station. A powerful, conspicuous office building even for New York,
it sucks up its daily occupants from Grand
Central Terminal and can truthfully be said
to have changed the character of the whole
of the 45th Street area. From the street,
its ten-storey base aligns with the Terminal cornice, but above it rises the forty-
nine-storey lozenge-shaped tower.

While the controversy over the 'PanAm'
was concerned with scale, the controversy
over the Carpenter Center was over conservation. This small, highly complex
series of external and internal spaces is
surrounded by Georgian-style buildings.
Few, however, would argue that Le
Corbusier's first American building (dis-
counting the UN building) was not a
masterpiece.

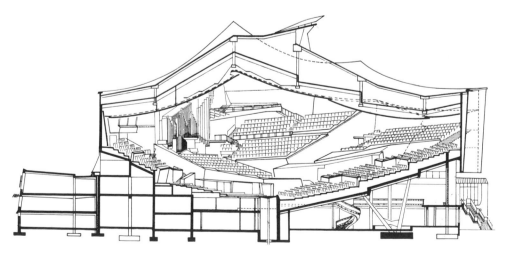

0   5   10   15   20   25

Walter Gropius (The Architects' Collaborative) and Pietro Belluschi. *'PanAm' Building,* New York, USA. 1963
Left: general street views of the 'PanAm' tower

Le Corbusier. Supervisory Architects: José Luis Sert and Associates (Jackson and Gourley). *The Carpenter Center for the Visual Arts,* Harvard University, Cambridge, Mass., USA. 1963 (1961–63)
Left: interior of the studio workshop looking towards the glazed wall
Above middle: a pedestrian ramp penetrates the Center from Prescott Street (seen here) to Quincy Street and passes between the glass-wall workshops and terraces
Right: corner detail

1963/64

Max Abramovitz, *Assembly Hall*, University of Illinois, Urbana, 1963

Paul Rudolph. *Parking Garage*, New Haven, Conn., USA. 1963 (1959–63)
Below: a corner of the garage
Bottom right: night view

Paul Rudolph's garage set a precedent for a new kind of building which has been copied in many parts of the world. Examples exist in Paris and in Preston, England, which clearly owe something to this design. Parking levels are staggered at half-floor heights and connected by ramps across the width of the building. The building is completed in exposed reinforced concrete and from each floor dramatic pedestrian access points lead the parker to street level.

In an attempt to create a new geometrical aesthetic, the late Alfred Neumann developed the architectural use of crystallographic forms. Bat Yam city hall is based on a figure like an inverted ziggurat, built up from 'cuboctrahedral' space-packing units.

The faculty at the Technion was, in its original layout, to have been composed of several inter-connected pavilions. Only one has been built. In the city hall as well as the faculty, a kind of self-conditioned building was developed, breaking entirely from the flat-faced curtain walling of sunbreaker systems (with *brise-soleil*) associated with modern movement ideas before the war. Instead, light and its penetration, and space as an enclosing system, are totally integrated.

St Mary's, won in competition by Tange in 1961, is based on a cruciform plan shape from which the stainless-steel-clad external walls (eight separate hyperbolic paraboloids) extend in geometrical fashion. The shimmering light effects of the external walls add to the symbolic overtones.

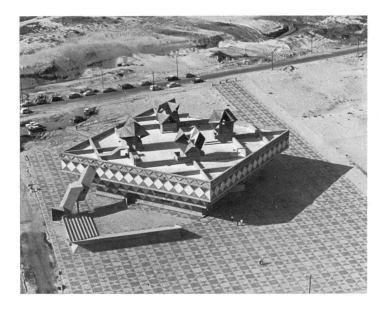

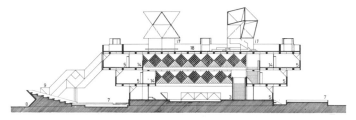

Alfred Neumann, Zvi Hecker and Eldor Sharon.
Municipal Building, Bat Yam, Israel. 1963 (1958–63)
Top and above: aerial view of the town hall on its
extensive plaza, with cross-section

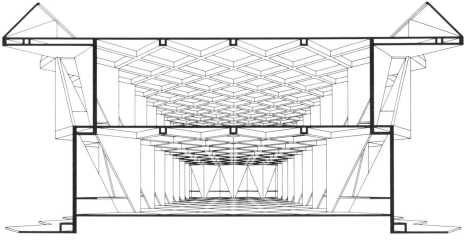

Alfred Neumann and Zvi Hecker. *Faculty of Mechanical
Engineering*, Israel Institute of Technology (Technion),
Haifa, Israel. 1964 (1960–64)

Below: general longitudinal view
Above: a structural cross-section analysis drawing by
Hecker, showing the principles of construction

Kenzo Tange, with Wilhelm Schlombs. *St Mary's
Cathedral.* Tokyo, Japan. 1964 (1961–64)
Above: exterior of the stainless-steel cathedral, with a
cross-section

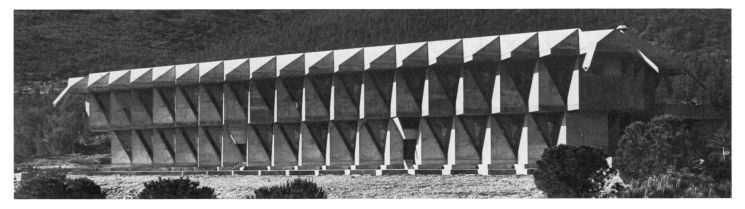

1964

Housing one of the world's richest collections, the 2-storey smooth concrete National Museum of Anthropology in Mexico City is centred on a huge 600-foot court with an enormous umbrella fountain.

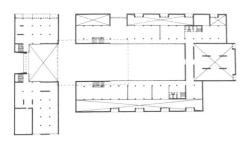

Pedro Ramirez Vazquez, *National Museum of Anthropology*, Mexico City, Mexico 1964 (1963–64)
Above: plan at main gallery level
Right: view of entrance water sculpture

Below: the general layout of the 25,000 square metre factory
Bottom: detail of one of the hollow tubes used for air conditioning as well as for structural purposes and interior view

Kenzo Tange with URTEC. *Olympic Sports Halls,* Yoyogi,
Tokyo, Japan. 1964 (1961–64)
Above: general view of the Olympic pool
Right: interior view of the Olympic pool
Bottom: the two sports halls from the air

Built for the 1964 Tokyo Olympiad, the two
sports halls by Tange are among this
architect's most exciting projects. If the
drama of space is one of the main ingredients
of a really successful piece of architecture,
then here it is, matched by a masterful
technology. Both buildings are developed
from the circle and the ellipse in plan and
section. They are linked by an immense
raked promenade on top of a single-storey
structure. The larger of the two structures is
shown here, but both are generically
similar, with concave suspension roofs.
In the pool, the two main cables of the
roofs are anchored in concrete foundations
and suspended from pylons at either end of
the building, while convex main girders on
either side support the concavely suspended
secondary cables which carry the steel-
sheeted roof.

The designer was aware of the problem
of claustrophobia, and the 'open design'
aims to overcome this by the provision of
full-height windows swooping up into the
cleft roof space.

The factory at Buenos Aires is a product
of the 'cool' school: an efficient, controlled
environment with the minimum of architectural fireworks. Erected for light machine
production, the building has services
organically built in, and the whole complex
is capable of expansion on all sides. The
basic geometrical figure is a rectangle and
the factory relates to a residential quarter as
well as a sophisticated production sequence.
Probably the most interesting aspect of this
building is its use of hollow, reinforced concrete lateral structural beams as channels
for air conditioning.

1964

Robert Venturi and John Rausch. *House,* Chestnut Hill,
Philadelphia, USA. 1964 (1962–64)
Right: the entrance façade
Below: the rear elevation
Bottom: interior of living-room

Robert Venturi's appearance on the
architectural scene in the mid-1960s was
sudden and, certainly for European architects, unexpected. In 1966 he published his
important book *Complexity and Contradiction
in Architecture*. In this 'gentle manifesto'
he combined a scholarly attitude to architecture with a complex series of arguments
– nationalistic, yet with wide practical
applications – which to some degree spring
from the renewed interest in 'popular
culture'.

The residence at Chestnut Hill is a
typical product of Venturi's of that period.
It is featured in his book as a project, which,
in his phrase 'recognizes complexities and
contradictions: it is both open and closed,
big and little; some of its elements are good
on one level and bad on another . . . '
This may sound, as much current theorizing
does, like justifying a thesis for personal
purposes (the house was designed for the
architect's mother), but as it represents a
whole body of thought and project-work, it
would be inaccurate to suggest that this is so.

Enrico Castiglione. *Technical High School* (first stage), Busto Aruzio, near Milan, Italy. 1964 (1963–64)
Above: one side of the symmetrical block of teaching-rooms with the higher public spaces behind

J. L. Martin and C. St John Wilson. *St Cross Library*, University of Oxford, England. 1964
Left: entrance steps to the three faculty libraries
Below: interior of one of the faculty libraries

The house is two-storeyed and finished in yellow stucco. The room shapes are irregular and there is, as one critic has put it, a 'violent combat between the staircase and fireplace'. Externally, the precise relationship between window openings and wall surface are apparent.

If Venturi's work represents a new kind of Mannerism, then Castiglione's School must appear as a left-over gesture to the old kind. Its chief interest, even in its present unfinished state, is in its 'image-ability', and in its unambiguous architectural treatment.

The St Cross Library, Oxford, forms part of a complex development out of which a highly satisfactory architectural group emerges. Environmentally, the building is a great success. A brick building, it is approached by a wide, imposing flight of steps which affords entrance into the three separate libraries contained in a building which is defined on the exterior by their bulk.

1964

Denys Lasdun and Partners. *Royal College of Physicians,*
St Andrew's Terrace, Regent's Park, London, England. 1964
Right: view from St Andrew's Place
Below: the general view of the entrance front from the
Outer Circle
Bottom left: general view from Regent's Park
Bottom right: site plan

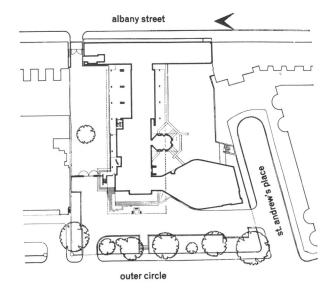

Set at the edge of one of London's great parks, the Physicians' College is conspicuously different from the surrounding buildings by Nash. The architect has not compromised his design in any way to meet governmental requirements that it should conform in its height, scale and colouring with the Nash terraces. It successfully does conform without plagiarism, and even creates its own atmospheric ambience, half-hid behind trees in full summer and arresting the eye like an exclamation mark in the bareness of winter. It is a 'conceptual', élitist modern building which somehow manages to achieve a sense of appropriateness within an important historical place, and might, therefore, be compared to Le Corbusier's Carpenter Center at Harvard. The front part of the building is used for ceremonials. The blue brick-faced portion is capable of extension.

Lasdun's architecture is often successful because of the way he disposes complex spaces around circulation routes and allows these spaces to generate the external form of his buildings. There are other ways of approaching the problem, and from the Smithsons' Economist Buildings a lesson in urban development can be learnt. This immensely important prototype scheme provided three distinct buildings of different heights and bulks on an irregular pedestrian plaza, instead of the more usual kind of vertical ant-hill that passes for offices in the civilized world. The plaza brings the public into the 'private' space, dramatically relates the existing Boodle's Club to the development and, through the three towers, creates an interesting scale to the street. The larger of the towers (the thirteen-storey Economist block) is set behind the smaller Bank building. The residential block for Boodle's is situated to the back.

Alison and Peter Smithson. Associated Architect: Maurice Bebb. *Economist Buildings,* St James's Street, London, England. 1964 (1962–64)
Right: the Economist Tower behind the small bank building from St James's Street
Below right: the original model showing the disposition of the three blocks
Below: ground-floor plan of the development in relation to Boodle's Club

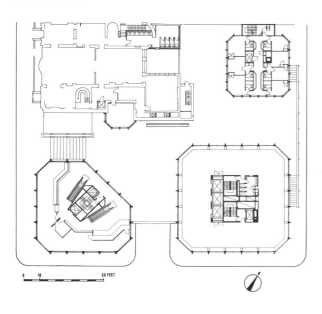

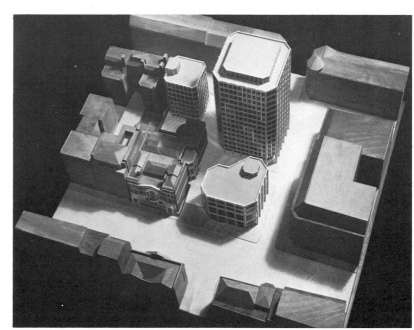

Ahrends, Burton and Koralek. *The Theological College,*
Chichester, Sussex, England. 1965 (1962–65)
Right: the study-bedroom blocks of the College
Middle: one of the internal courtyard spaces

Lyons, Israel and Ellis. *The Wolfson Institute,* London,
England. 1965 (1961–65)
Below: the main front of the Institute

Theological colleges are rare enough
buildings today. To find one designed by a
firm of architects as good as Ahrends
Burton and Koralek is even rarer. A building of domestic scale, the college has had an
influence on many later English courtyard
designs – including speculative housing.
What appeals to the architect about this
building as its appropriateness to a beautiful site, its simplicity of organization and
building is its appropriateness to a beautiful
site, its simplicity of organization and
external finish as well as its controlled
modelling. It is a three and four-storey,
squarish, brick-surfaced block built astride
a pathway between existing buildings and
St Bartholomew's Chapel. The accommodation provided includes thirty-five study-
bedrooms, three staff flats, a library and
lecture-room. These units of accommodation – some large and some small – generated
a design in which the architects 'decided to
build walls of the smaller elements to enclose
the larger elements'. The study-bedrooms
are arranged in groups of seven and are lit
on the outside wall by narrow high windows.
The whole emphasis of the design is on the
internal courtyard, which acts as a core to
the circulation and the building.

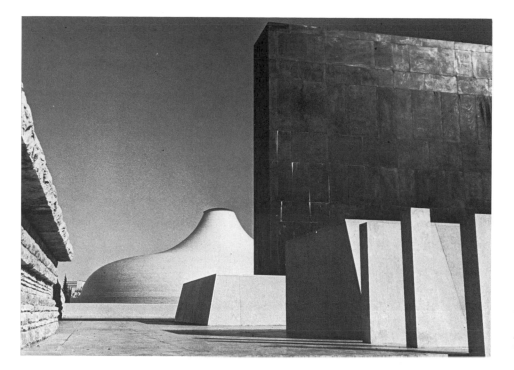

Frederick Kiesler with Armand P. Bartos. *The Shrine of the Book* (D. S. and R. M. Gottesman Centre for Rare Manuscripts), Jerusalem, Israel. 1965
Above: interior with the Dead Sea Scrolls exhibit
Left: the symbolic wall and dome of the Shrine

Viljo Revell with John B. Parkin Associates. *City Hall,* Toronto, Ontario, Canada. 1965 (1958–65)
Left and below: the two curved towers of the City Hall in their plaza setting

Concrete is used as the main structural material at Chichester but warm English brickwork is allowed to dominate. The Wolfson Institute is finished entirely in concrete and the effect, within its urban situation, is very much in the modern movement tradition of the functional parts of the building expressing their residual shapes as the exterior. Thus, the dominating main lecture hall overrides the lower two-storey accommodation. The result is a powerful single image – an important architectural experiment if not an entirely successful one.

The experimentation and symbolism in Kiesler's Shrine is more obvious. He wrote: 'the wall and dome accent the continuity of life emerging from dormancy'. Most of this building, which houses the Dead Sea Scrolls and other Biblical manuscripts, is underground. The black basalt wall and the wall are determined symbols to highlight the building's purpose. Revell's democratic symbolism for Toronto is far less effective, although it has now become one of the sights of modern Canada. Won in competition in 1958, it consists of two crescent-shaped towers clutching at their bases a UFO-shaped Council Chamber.

1965

Sheffield Architect's Department. (J. L. Womersley, former Chief Architect). *Housing, Park Hill and Hyde Park,* Sheffield. 1965 (1955–65)
Right: the Hyde Park development
Below: a comprehensive view of the two developments from the city with Park Hill in the middle distance
Bottom: site plan

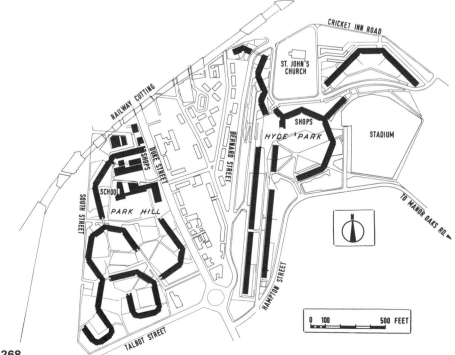

The Sheffield housing scheme is one of the most comprehensive and spectacular developments in post-war Britain, probably in the world. Built by the local authority and designed by a team of architects under the direction of Jack Lynn and Ivor Smith, its importance can only be fully appreciated by having some knowledge of the catastrophic state Sheffield was in after the war. Most provincial cities were quite prepared to rehouse outside the city centre the people who were caught in slum or war-damaged housing; Sheffield revitalized their city centre by retaining the inner ring for housing.

Park Hill, the first part of the development, was completed 1957–60, and Hyde Park 1962–65. The ideas behind the scheme, however, go back to a competition held in 1952 for Golden Lane, in which Lynn and Smith participated. A scheme by the Smithsons for the same competition and another for the University of Sheffield were also of some importance in the formulation of the concept for the Sheffield

Alvar Aalto. *Polytechnic Institute,* Otaniemi, near Helsinki, Finland. 1965 (1963–65)
Right: interior of the main auditorium
Below: the lecture hall and ancillary buildings

housing with its interconnected blocks, streets-in-the-air access decks, bridges and ramps.

All these projects in turn owed a debt to Le Corbusier and in particular to the Unité at Marseille with its interior streets and closely packed living units. This concept was anglicized and an old slum street, with individual front doors to each house unit, was ranged along the access platforms. The rough, rugged, northern atmosphere of the busy communal street was thus elevated at a density and intensity required by the housing programme. A real attempt was made in the scheme to mitigate the effects of the high block by cranking parts of the design to form large open spaces and to obviate the traffic problem by virtually eliminating vehicular access. The result may to the lay person appear harsh and uninviting, but this scheme represented a sincere attempt to break away from conventional local authority housing solutions.

Aalto's Polytechnic buildings have a characteristic warmth, finished in red brick and set in the wooded rural area of Espoo. They form part of a larger plan for the new Polytechnic prepared by Aalto's office in 1949. The complex houses several faculties, the administration and the public auditorium which provides the focus for the whole design.

1965

Casson, Conder and Partners. *Elephant and Rhinoceros Pavilion,* Zoological Gardens, Regent's Park, London, England. 1965 (1959–65)
Right: detail of one denizen against the ribbed finish to the external walling
Far right: cross-section and plan of the Pavilion
Below: the interior public space
Bottom: a general external view

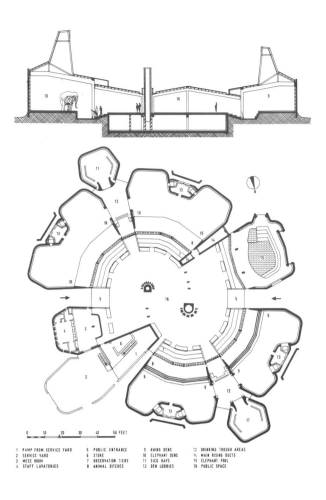

1 RAMP FROM SERVICE YARD   5 PUBLIC ENTRANCE   9 RHINO DENS   13 DRINKING TROUGH AREAS
2 SERVICE YARD   6 STORE   10 ELEPHANT DENS   14 MAIN RISING DUCTS
3 MESS ROOM   7 OBSERVATION TIERS   11 SICK BAYS   15 ELEPHANT POOL
4 STAFF LAVATORIES   8 ANIMAL DITCHES   12 DEN LOBBIES   16 PUBLIC SPACE

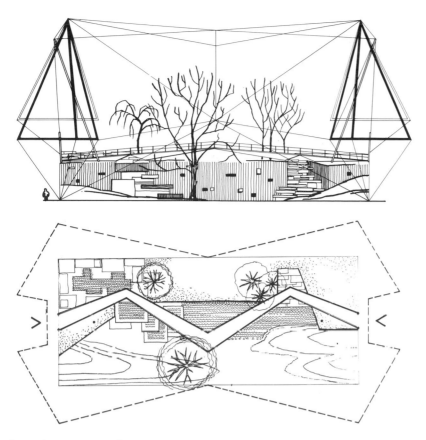

Lord Snowdon, Cedric Price and Frank Newby.
Northern Aviary, Zoological Gardens, Regent's Park,
London, England. 1964 (1961–64)
Left: the original sketch elevation and plan for the
Aviary
Below: interior

After pioneering many modern movement buildings in the 1930s, the London Zoological Society was not slow in commissioning a number of important structures for Regent's Park in the post-war years. Beside the Aviary by Snowdon and others and the Elephant and Rhinoceros Pavilion, a number of other successful buildings have been erected as part of the 1956 Redevelopment Plan prepared by Casson and Stengelhofen. But these two are, in their very different ways, probably the two most architecturally interesting structures. One a not altogether satisfactory 'non-building' (satisfactory, that is, for the birds rather than the building-watcher), the other an overt attempt at 'animal architecture', or perhaps even an 'architectural animal'! The main source of the design, according to the architect of the Pavilion, 'was the arrangement of the pens' – a basic pen unit (two pairs of animals and one sick-bay grouped round an interchange lobby).

Internal observation space is central to the pen groups, while the animals can also perambulate around an outside enclosure. The building has wit: the external concrete ribbing and the curved form are somewhat analogous to the hides of the animals the building houses. But, of course, the architects claim a functional origin, for ease of cleaning and to obviate animal vandalism.

What a romantic image a bird-cage the size of the one in Regent's Park conjures up – Baudelaire would have loved it. Based on a rectangular plan, 150 feet by 63 feet, it is clad in black anodized aluminium mesh and supported by tension cables anchored to four aluminium tetrahedral frames. It is traversed by an elevated public walkway constructed from precast concrete slabs. Inside the cage, men and birds meet face to face and nests are to be found tucked in odd corners of the building.

1965

Sachio Otani. *International Conference Hall,* Kyoto, Japan.
1965 (1963–65)
Right and below: the Conference Hall in its parkland
setting

Otani's building was selected by Robin Boyd in his book *New Directions in Japanese Architectore* (1968) as the building that in its imagery best exemplifies what he calls 'the development of the new Japan Style'. Won in a national competition, this large horizontal complex of conference halls incorporates an indigenous structural device – the diagonal column. All the building elements slant at an angle of 22 degrees to the vertical. When connected up at various points in the design they form a basic trapezoidal shape. The sloping column itself – commonly found in Western timber and A-frame buildings – is also an adaptation of an historical Japanese form of construction, as is the piling of one form upon another up to a 'flying' roof. The resolution of a native tradition with the kind of modern architecture for which Tange is so famous is apparent. (Otani had been a member of Tange's Research Unit.)

The Reliance factory at Swindon was designed and erected in less than a year. It is a good – and probably one of Britain's best – examples of the speedy, efficient and economical approach to factory design. Built on a site with no natural features, it is notable only for its layout and precise use of materials. The interior is well-lit, if

Norman and Wendy Foster and Richard Rogers.
Electronics Factory, Swindon, Wilts., England. 1965
(1964–65)
Top: general view of the factory
Above: interior of the assembly shop

Robert Matthew, Johnson-Marshall and Partners.
University of York, Heslington, Yorks., England. 1965
(1962–65)
Centre right: Langwith College from the grounds of the
old Heslington Hall. Residential blocks are on the left
and the dining-hall beyond
Right: aerial view from the east in July 1969

somewhat soulless.

There is something disturbing about an environment made up of industrialized buildings. York University, officially opened in 1965, is of prime importance as a new, and wholly system-built, university. It is beautifully landscaped, and the plan (first published in 1962) is ambitious and in many ways successful. But for all the skill, all the creative knowhow, it lacks a vital spark.

1965

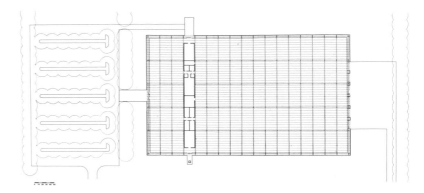

Kevin Roche, John Dinkeloo and Associates. *Cummins Engine Company Factory*, Darlington, England. 1965
Right: factory layout plan
Below: the glazed walling and Cor-ten steel frame of the Cummins factory
Bottom right: a detail of a framework junction

Louis Kahn. *The Salk Institute for Biological Research*, La Jolla, Calif., USA. 1965 (1960–65)
Left: detail of a typical entrance to the laboratories

Although Cor-ten steel had been used in the United States for factory buildings (most notably for the John Deere Company in Moline, Ill., by the late Eero Saarinen, whose firm Roche and Dinkeloo inherited) this was its first application in the United Kingdom. It has had a tremendous impact on factory design since it was built in 1965.

The Miesian influence in this building is obvious: if any building could depict a concept of rationality then this would be it.

Neumann, Hecker and Sharon. *the Dubiner Apartment House,* Ramat Gan, Israel. 1965 (1960–65)
Above and top right: details of the seven-storey block
Right: a general view of the apartment block
Below: section and perspective

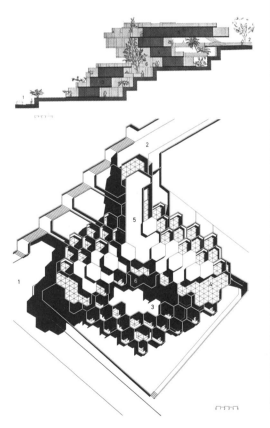

The simply organized, rectangular box encloses all the factory activities as well as the administrative offices. Internally, everything is organized as impeccably as outside; the whole building is air conditioned and artificially lit and the service systems are concealed under the roof behind the beam cornice.

Visually, it is a big jump from the traditional geometry of beam and column and the uncluttered rhetoric of Miesian architecture to the complex use of hexagons.

A hexagonal architecture was developed in expressionist circles in Germany in the 1920s by Hablik and others, and has recurred often in the work of mathematically minded designers since. Few have been able to extend their vision as far as Neumann and Hecker (see also 1963). The apartment block is based on 100-square-foot hexagons. The lower three storeys of the seven-storey block follow the profile of the hill, forming a stepped pyramid inside the block. The prismatic surfaces of the upper floors

overhang, and connect the hilltop to the back of the building.

Dr Jonas Salk's Institute at La Jolla is broken down into three major building groups: research labs and two residential quarters. The labs – two parallel blocks each 245 × 65 feet – were completed in 1965 as the first stage of the scheme, which is well-disciplined, but with lively contrasts between the 'functional' spaces for research and study and the formal treatment of the architectural spaces themselves.

275

1966

Sigurd Lewerentz, *St. Peter's Church*, Klippan, Denmark, 1966
Right: the brick-faced interior

Gillespie, Kidd and Coia. *St Peter's College,* Cardross, Scotland. 1966 (1964–66)
Below: first-floor plan showing the connection between the new and older parts of the college
Bottom: general view of the south front

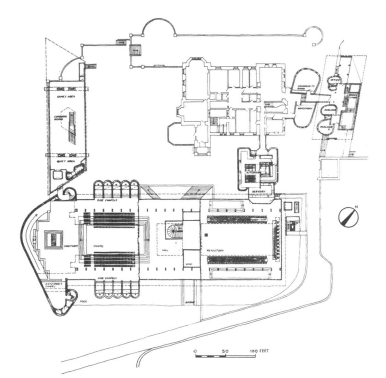

Max Urbahn (Architect-planner), Roberts and Schaefer Co. (Engineers). *Vehicle Assembly Building (VAB),* Cape Kennedy, Florida, USA. 1966 (1962–66)
Right: interior of the VAB
Below right: the largest building in the world stands in splendid isolation on Cape Kennedy

Scotland has few really first-class post-war buildings, and even fewer local architects whose work rises above mundane, conventional solutions for current building problems. The Glasgow firm of Gillespie, Kidd and Coia is an exception. Run by Jack Coia and a group of brilliant younger architects, they have put Scotland back on the map of twentieth-century architecture. One of their best-known and largest projects was the new accommodation for St Peter's College, Cardcross, which allowed them to look again into the traditional problem of seminary design and devise a modern solution to the problem. There is much in the design solution that can be clearly seen to relate to the work of Le Corbusier for the Roman Catholic Church, but on top of this there was also the additional problem involved in relating the new work to existing buildings. The success of Cardross is achieved through integration as well as originality.

The enormous VAB at Cape Kennedy was designed especially for the American space programme, its purpose entirely utilitarian. The high-bay structure can contain four Saturn V rockets on mobile launchers and the low-bay structure can contain eight upper stages of rockets. It has been estimated that the building could easily accommodate four Seagram and six Pepsi-Cola buildings. Its entry doors alone are 500 feet high by 70 feet wide.

The Auditorium at Delft and the Student Union building – Dunelm House – at Durham were both designed as 'status' buildings, as particular solutions to distinct design programmes for public use. As such, they are both memorable buildings.

Following the success of Lewerentz's St. Mark's Church in Stockholm, his last great religious building was in Klippan, also using traditional brickwork. The interior is dramatic, with enormous steel beams supported on a T-section above which ride brick vaults.

Architects' Co-Partnership. *Dunelm House,* University of Durham, Durham, England. 1966 (196—66)
Right: Dunelm House, with the footbridge designed by Ove Arup to the right

Van den Broek and Bakema. *Auditorium,* Technical University, Delft, Netherlands. 1966 (1958–66)
Below: general view of the auditorium; the concrete sculpture is by Carel Visten

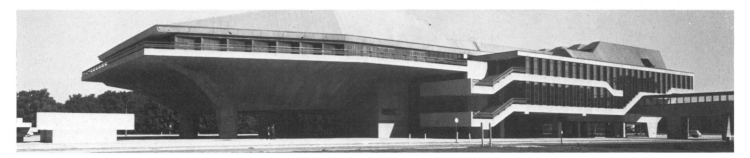

1966

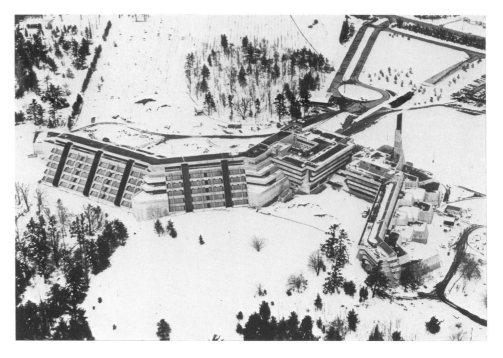

John Andrews, with Page and Steele. (Partner in charge:
Robert Anderson). *Scarborough College,* University of
Toronto, Toronto, Canada. 1966; 1st stage completion.
(1964–66)
Left: rear view of the Science block
Above: aerial view of the College under wintry
conditions
Below: the street in the science wing

Scarborough College is situated on a plateau
20 miles from the centre of Toronto. The
sparsely-developed site is heavily wooded
and the College occupies but one enclave of
the 200-acre site.

Andrews's scheme is an attempt at homo-
geneity: the various elements required to
accommodate Administration, Science and
Humanities departments, are all pulled
together into a two-ringed series of five
to six-storey-height blocks connected and
articulated by 'knuckles' containing lecture
theatres and student lounges. Admin. and
meeting places form the pivot of the scheme,
with the Science wing to the west and the
Humanities wing to the east.

The Lincoln Center represented a spectacular return to architectural formalism. The
origins of its classical layout are obvious and
the attempt to be architecturally pure is
given away by the Michelangelo-type
layout. The Center incorporates a philharmonic hall (opened September 1962),
the New York State Theater (opened April
1964) and the Metropolitan Opera House
(opened September 1966).

What must be the most impressive
'Shantytown' in North America lies approximately 200 miles north of San Francisco. Designed as an integral part of a
14-mile coastal development by Oceanic
Properties, Sea Ranch is a prototype
condominium in which the various living
units aggregate to create an organized
cluster adjacent to a recreation centre
(1965). Each 24-foot cube unit has a view
of the Pacific, but each one plays a part as an
element in the creation of the geometrical
environment in which planes, openings and
traditional materials are played off, each
against the others, to maximum effect.

Max Abramovitz, Wallace K. Harrison, Philip Johnson,
Eero Saarinen. *Lincoln Center for the Performing Arts,*
New York, USA. 1966 (1957–66)
Left: general view of the Michaelangelesque piazza of
the Lincoln Center, with the New York Philharmonic
concert hall on the right

Charles Moore, Donlyn Lyndon, William Turnbull,
Richard Whitaker. (Associate Architect for apartments:
Edward B. Allen). *Sea Ranch*, Gualala, Sanoria County,
Calif., USA. 1966 (1964–66)
Top and above: detail and general views of the
residential resort
Above right: a typical interior

Fuller and Sadao Inc. (Associated designers, Geometrics
Inc.; interior design, Cambridge Seven Associates).
United States Pavilion, Expo '67, Montreal, Canada. 1967
Right: interior of the Pavilion in use, showing the
hexagonal units of the structure
Below: the Pavilion in its Expo setting in 1967

There were many innovatory structures at 'Expo '67' but the three selected here were the most important, and represent three very different approaches to the problem of large-scale exhibition pavilions.

Fuller's 200-foot-high geodesic dome dominated the whole exposition and represents a logical development of his previous ideas on this concept. All systems are integrated to a much higher degree than in any of the earlier models. An enormous volume of visitors passed through the structure by lifts, mini-rail and escalator. The structure as a whole was a prototype of what Fuller calls an 'environmental valve' which encloses sufficient 'space for whole communities to live in a benign physical microcosm'. It had a surface area of 141,000 square feet and was constructed with an outer layer of triangular elements connected to an inner layer of hexagonal elements. The exterior was covered with a transparent skin of plastic.

The Otto and Gutbrod stressed-skin structure was also transparent, covered with a polyester cloth on vinyl chloride sheets, joined to the network of cables by spring plates and spring lines. The area covered was 80,000 square feet. This sophisticated tent was held up by eight tall masts, from which the tension cables were suspended and held taut by a secondary sheet mesh.

Safdie's dwelling complex 'Habitat' was designed to give 'privacy, fresh air, sunlight and suburban amenities in an urban location'. It was designed as a permanent settlement and consists of 158 dwellings, although originally it was intended to provide 1,000 units. The resulting ziggurat was made up of independent prefabricated boxes with fifteen different plan types.

Frei Otto and Rolf Gutbrod. *West German Pavilion, Expo '67* Montreal, Canada. 1967
Above right: details of the cable system and the polyester cloth roof

Moshe Safdie with David, Barrott and Boulva. *Habitat, Expo '67.* Montreal, Canada. 1967 (1966–67)
Below: the complex on Mackay Pier, Cité du Havre, under construction
Right: part of the complex of living units showing the relationship of projecting blocks and roof gardens

1967

Hugh Wilson (Chief Architect), succeeded by
Dudley Leaker; Geoffrey Copcutt (Group Architect).
Town Centre (phase 1), Cumbernauld New Town,
near Glasgow, Scotland. 1967 (1961–67)
Right: interior of shopping mall with section through
mall below
Below: an early aerial view of the Town Centre showing
the first of the five increments of the complex

One of the most ambitious new town proposals to emerge in post-war Britain, Cumbernauld Town Centre is separated from the rest of the New Town and isolated on a hill. It is a precise example of what architects and planners may do if left alone with their zoning diagrams. Its effect on planners and architects throughout the world has been astonishing. Applause for the brilliance of the concept and its great complexity was soon followed, after many critics had visited it, by a conviction that it was wrongly situated, over-dramatic and over-ambitious. This half-mile-long building houses all the main social, commercial and shopping functions of the town and thus deprives other areas of secondary functions. It also contains housing. The complex is constructed in reinforced concrete in a rough 'Scottish' finish. Servicing, garaging and distribution are all integral.

Hubert Bennett (Architect to GLC); E. J. Blyth and N. Englebeck (Group Leaders for project).
Queen Elizabeth Hall and Purcell Room forming with the Hayward Art Gallery (completed 1968) the 'South Bank Arts Centre', London, England. 1967 (1961–67)
Left: interior of the Queen Elizabeth Hall
Below: exterior of the Queen Elizabeth Hall showing walkways
Bottom: the walkway leading to the Hayward Gallery, with the Queen Elizabeth Hall beyond

More or less at the same time that Cumbernauld was acclaimed as a breakthrough in civic design, the new Queen Elizabeth Hall for London's South Bank was voted 'Britain's Ugliest Building' by a group of engineers whose simple, logical minds could see no order in its seeming chaos. The hall and the other parts that make up the South Bank Arts Centre are from the same conceptual mould as Cumbernauld Centre. The guts of each are given over to vehicular functions which do not necessarily require the kind of spaces associated with person-to-building contact. Both complexes – for that is what they are, rather than buildings – are arranged as a series of 'event spaces' connected by irregular circulation routes. A term coined for such architecture in 1968 was 'Adhoc-ism'.

1967

Affleck, Desbarats, Dimakopoulos, Lebensold, Sise.
Place Bonaventure, Montreal, Canada. 1967
Below: detail of the north façade of the multi-use urban complex
Right: interior of the Great Exposition Hall
Bottom: general view of the complex to the south

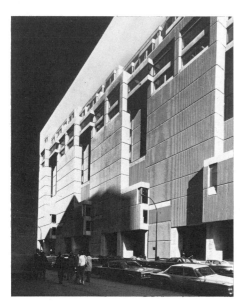

Scale and magnitude became real problems for architects and urban planners towards the end of the 1950s, when city land values escalated to a phenomonal degree and the postwar baby boom became a population reality. There was a need to think through the whole question of multi-uses in cities and to provide solutions – speculative, economic and attractive – for future urban complexes. The days of the restricted site and the one-off concept, it was felt, were numbered.

Both Place Bonaventure and Marina City represent a forward-looking policy of integration of building uses and are attempts at finding a formula for an urban complex. The former solution is more open-ended, the latter finite in architectural terms.

At Montreal, the designers built on air rights above railway tracks, providing a merchandising mart of one million square feet and 100,000 square feet of offices. Marina City is mainly apartments above a vertical tube of car parking spaces.

Bertrand Goldberg Associates, *Marina City,* Chicago, Illinois, USA. 1967 (1964–67)
Below: general view of the two tower blocks
Right and bottom: balcony details

1967

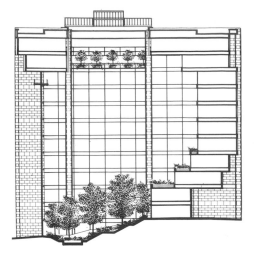

Kevin Roche. John Dinkeloo and Associates.
Ford Foundation Headquarters, New York, USA. 1967
(1966–67)
Top: elevation to 5th Avenue
Above: section

Hara, Hiroshi, *Kindergarten*, Keisho, Japan, 1967.
Above: Interior of hall classroom
Right: general view

The Ford Foundation building is a radical departure from the usual kind of New York office tower. Roche, who was the principal designer of this building, aimed at producing an environment for the prestigious Ford Foundation in which the individual worker or visitor could identify 'with the aims and intentions of the group'. The result is, as far as I know, unique in modern building: within the confines of a twelve-storey block, a vertical conservatory shaft rises to full height and windows open on to this planted space from all floors. The two uppermost floors contain the executive offices and dining areas which, instead of being planned on an L shape, close the square of the building (see section).

Tange's Communications Centre is also innovatory, but is not confined to a real-estate boundary. The Centre provides an open, extensible, spatial structure which develops three-dimensionally, to take into account unpredictable uses that may be imposed on the building in the future. Presently it houses three principal functions: a newspaper printing plant, a broadcasting station and a television studio. Service functions are housed in the sixteen hollow concrete shafts while the structural floors between provide the utilizable work spaces. The design concept that emerges from this building is open-ended and no longer confined by the more traditional architectural approach which relies on finite elevations or a concise image. Indeed, as the illustration indicates, its very uncompletedness is an important aspect of its design.

The Le Corbusier Centre presents another aspect of the flexibility game. This time the building is complete but, within the confines of the spaces provided under the independent umbrella roof, change is possible in the exhibition and meeting room areas. This building was completed after the death of Le Corbusier and was originally planned as a private house – the house area being the detached section under the steel roof.

The Keisho Kindergarten attempts to break down the scale of the constituent parts of the educational process. Its ship-like appearance belies a building that clearly acknowledges its landscaped setting.

Kenzo Tange, with URTEC (Kamiya, Okamura, Yamamoto, Ejiri, Nagashima, Inazuka). *Yamanashi Communications Centre,* Koufu, Japan. 1967
Above: the upper part of the building from the east

Le Corbusier (executed by G. Jullian, J. Oubrerie, A. Taves, R. Rebutato). *Centre Le Corbusier,* Zürich, Switzerland. 1967 (1963–67)
Below: general view of the *Centre*

1968

James Stirling. *History Faculty Library*, University of
Cambridge, England. 1968 (1966–68)
Right: interior of the reading-room, looking towards the
glazed upper corridors
Below: axonometric drawing of scheme
Bottom: view from the south east

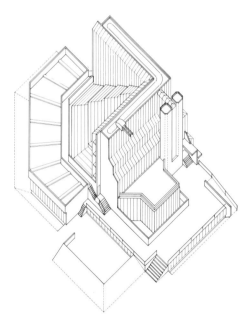

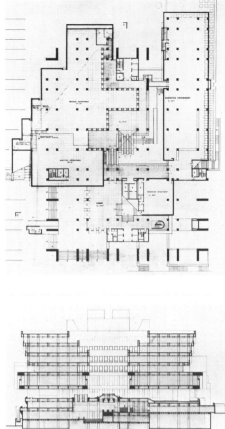

Gerhard Kallmann, Noel McKinnell and Edward Knowles.
City Hall, Boston, Mass., USA. 1969 (1962–69)
Above left: interior of the entrance hall
Above: ground-floor plan with cross-section below
Below: main entrance elevation to piazza

Stirling's best-known building is probably the Cambridge University History Faculty. Since it was built, it has become something of a cult object, visited by earnest architectural students and featured at length in most of the world's leading architectural periodicals. It is a *tour de force*. Set in an open site on the north of the University's Sidgwick Avenue development, it can be approached from all sides. Stirling was commissioned after a limited competition and originally the building was to be sited elsewhere.

The axonometric sketch provides a useful summary of the disposition of the various parts of the complex. The seven-storey L-shaped block houses administrative and study rooms. Within the right angle of the L, the great glazed fan-shaped reading-room roof rises up from the second-floor ceiling to the top of the angle. Glass used on this scale is unusual in a modern building and has led to the serious problem of solar heat gain. Within the tented interior, corridors are glazed and the effect of a second exterior is created within the building. Sealing off the circulation in this manner aids privacy but keeps a sense of visual contact between the reading-room and the other parts of the building.

Boston City Hall was also the result of a competition, the first open competition for a public building in that city since 1909. It was Kallmann McKinnell and Knowles's first major building. (Both Kallmann and McKinnell were trained in Britain.)

The site was provided in a plan drawn

up for the government centre by I. M. Pei Associates. The Hall is a confident, formal concept, not far removed from the dominating town halls of nineteenth-century Britain but tempered to the administrative and functional requirements of

today. The plan is a basic rectangle rising to nine storeys round a courtyard. The building is finished in exposed concrete and the structure, which is clearly expressed on the exterior, is based on modular bays of just under 15 feet and 30 feet.

289

1968

Denys Lasdun and Partners. *University of East Anglia,* Norwich, England. 1969, Phase 1. (1962–69)
Right: University residences and teaching/research accommodation
Below: general view with residences in the background
Bottom: development plan III, 1968

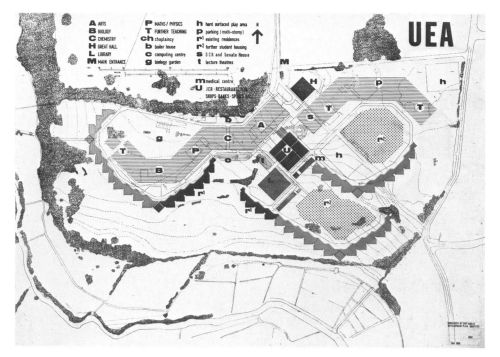

A recurring theme in discussions on architecture in the late 1950s and the 1960s was 'building versus non-building' – whether, in fact, an architect should exert his personality on a problem to the extent of creating a 'monument' to his own ideas or whether, alternatively, a building, or a large complex of buildings, should remain essentially anonymous and not obtrude any more than they have to on a site. These two examples indicate both approaches. Lasdun's University of East Anglia is a powerful statement which creates its own environment, dominates the surrounding countryside and encapsulates the idea of a self-contained 'city-scale' unit. The Oakland Museum is more than a building, it serves as a park for the city as well as a cultural centre. While the Roche and Dinkeloo museum might just as well have been conceived of as a complex of buildings dominating its urban site, the East Anglian University could hardly have been expected to disappear into its rural surroundings.

However, a certain amount of criticism has been levelled at the University's architect for producing such a spread-out and contrived planning solution. But even here appearances are deceptive, as Lasdun and his team were consciously designing for change and growth. Lasdun has written: '[It] is an organism which is architecturally complete and incomplete . . . which does not produce a wilderness of mechanism' – a statement that can be construed as true or – as is the current fashion – true only in relation to what has materialized on the ground. Completedness in terms of single buildings is easy to understand; less so in terms of a University which is based on a traditional element of expansion and change.

Oakland Museum – a complex of three museums – is like a giant flight of steps in reinforced concrete with integral garaging, an auditorium and offices. Here nature is brought in to act as the instigator of change.

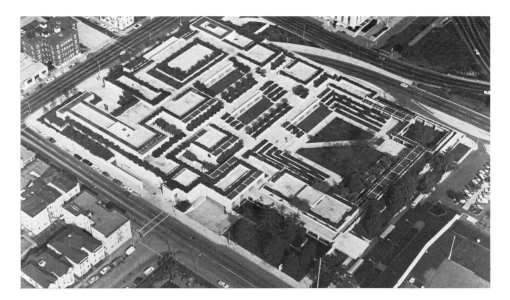

Kevin Roche, John Dinkeloo and Associates. (Landscape Architect: Don Kiley). *Oakland Museum,* Oakland, Calif., USA. 1968 (opened 1969)
Top: aerial view of the museums and park
Middle: the cascading vegetation on the concrete 'rooftop' terrace
Right: the terrace plan

1968

GLC Architect's Department. (J. W. Davidson, Section Leader). *Housing* (*SF 1*), Elgin Estate, Westminster, London. 1968
Right: a tower block on the Elgin Estate finished in rrp panels
Below: the block under construction

Claude and Jean Prouvé. *Palais des Expositions,* Grenoble, France. 1968 (1967–68)
Bottom: general view of the pavilion built for the 1968 Winter Olympic Games

Schipporeit-Heinrich Associates. (Associated Architects: Graham, Anderson, Probst and White). *Apartments, Lake Point Tower,* Chicago, Ill., USA. 1968
Right: the curved façade of the upper part of the Tower
Bottom right: an evening shot taken from Lake Michigan
Below: plan of typical floor and section through the Tower

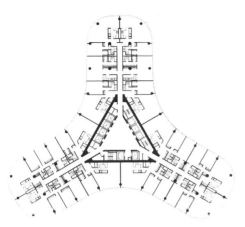

The GLC Elgin Estate development is included not because it makes any major contribution to 'good' architecture; it is neither better nor worse than many similar mixed schemes. However, it does involve a great step forward in building technology. Many architects have dreamt of designing buildings finished in plastic cladding; a few have been built, but no one has used the material before for the external surfaces of a high block. The two twenty-two-storey blocks of flats – SF 1 and SF 2 – are constructed with a composite concrete and steel structure and clad in glass-reinforced panels. The use of plastic offered the designer a number of advantages and once the potential fire-hazard problems were solved the first block went up in ten months. The results are not unattractive but there is a long way to go yet before the industrialized techniques used in buildings such as this create an improvement in architectural standards. Façades are only one element in the mix. 'Well,' the layman might say, 'would it not be more adventurous and pleasing to build industrialized buildings with curved surfaces rather than flat-sided shoe-boxes?'

The Prouvé building was also interesting because of the use of standardized and interchangeable panels. The large hall consisted of 15,000 m² of exhibition space with mobile services. An annexe hall adjoining accommodated reception offices and administration, a thousand-person restaurant and a large conference room.

Lake Point is a clover-leaf-shaped building with a continuous undulating glass wall. While it cannot be compared in any way with the previous example, it indicates the effectiveness of an idea that was current in Germany in the early 1920s. It was then that Mies designed his well-known 'free-form' glass-clad office block. The designers of this building were among his students at IIT as well as staff members in his practice.

Standing in majestic isolation on a finger of land at Navy Pier Park, this modern colossus rises like a gigantic lighthouse to a height of 645 feet. It contains 900 luxury flats, two floors of commercial offices and all the adjuncts of prosperous living.

1969

Charles Moore. *Faculty Club*, University of California,
Santa Barbara, Calif., USA. 1969
Right: general view of the club
Below: the internal courtyard
Below right: bold 'Supergraphics' were incorporated in
the service area of the scheme

Locally, the Faculty Club at Santa Barbara
is looked on as a late reiteration of the
Spanish Colonial Revival style. It does,
indeed, exhibit some of the confusing
characteristics of this style, but more in
terms of its décor than in the building's
formal qualities. These are as contemporary
as the 'Supergraphics' which decorate the
recreation changing-rooms. It is an idiosyncratic piece of design, cleverly integrated
into a unity of disparate parts. It represents
a refreshingly new and different approach
to public architecture and holds in regard a
certain kind of university ambiance. Besides
catering for the club-room and dining
functions of the Faculty Club it also contains a small library and, around a delightful
courtyard, a few guest-rooms.

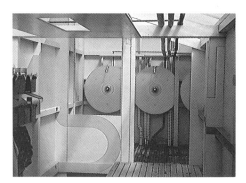

Decade 1970

Pluralism was the name of the game in the 1970s. It was a decade of reintegration and revivals, of intense experimentation and fundamental ideological change. It derived its liveliness in part from a clash of generations as well as from the effects and influences of the changing ideologies that caused the demise of the International Style. It was a decade too which brought the world a little closer together. Buckminster Fuller's and Marshal McLuhan's idea of the instantaneous 'Global Village' came a step closer. Whereas in previous decades of this century the Western nations had exerted an all-pervading influence on the old world and on the developing nations of the 'Third World', these had now begun to exert their own influences. The affluent West at last began to take some architectural lessons from the Third World although the powerful nations still held the purse-strings and continued to seek, through major environmental, international conferences, to exert influence and maintain control.

Much of this left a deeply ingrained, indelible mark on the architecture of the decade. Architect-designed buildings of the period showed a sharp and deeply critical reaction to the previous decade's absorption with large-scale, complicated, amorphous projects. The inner city was rediscovered. *Collage City* (1975, 1978) was an influential text that has to take its place alongside the Venturi's *Learning from Las Vegas* (1972) as a fresh way of looking at existing cities. 'Layering' became a watchword; 'rehabilitation' a byword. Refurbishment of existing historical areas became a preoccupation.

The plural effects of the period often led to acrimonious discussions between the advocates of the continuity of the Modern 'tradition' within architecture and the arts, and those from various quarters who sought to identify with new ideologies such as the neo-vernacular, historicism and, eventually – for want of a better phrase, 'Post-Modernism' – a much abused, philosophical and literary term. Indeed, throughout the 1970s a growing literature had appeared which ranged from enthusiastic Columbus-like claims of the discovery of a new, unmapped, uncharted, and unknown territory within architecture to the garbled misrepresentations of those for whom the salvation of architecture was to be found in the egocentric meanderings of any project which could be labelled 'Post-Modern' something or other. Labels were invented with an enthusiasm more appropriate to Linnaeus and his followers than to architects seeking a successful evolution of their own. But it should be remembered that the labellers (libelers?) were the successful royalty-earning writers of the period. The trumpeting of an entirely new breed of architectural critic and promoter had succeeded in blowing down the walls of

Above: The great pointed symbol of the *Trans-America Headquarters*, San Francisco, USA, 1972 was typical of a number of simple minded structures of that period. Architect: William Pereira

Below: *The Barbican Arts Centre*, London, England took some 25 years to materialise but was widely publicised in the 1970s. This section shows details of the Royal Shakespeare Theatre auditorium and stage tower. Architects: Chamberlin Powell and Bon

restraint and good taste by the end of the 1970s: Post-Modern became the tune; the Modern Movement was declared as dead as the proverbial dodo.

The end of the 1960s had echoed to the words of Fuller, Soleri, the LA harpies and hippies, the advocates of the counter-cultures, as well as to those of Louis Kahn and Le Corbusier. However, it soon became clear that the Post-Modernist phenomenon was essentially an eclectic movement. It soon led to a debasement of forms, a rich but aimless historicizing that encouraged the employment of meaningless combinations of sterile forms.

In theoretical terms the new decade was dominated by individual debates that ranged from the geometrical nature of architecture (derived from sacred geometries and man-environment studies) to the specific organization of modular space and Post-Modernist and Hi-Tech experiments based on the rewarding and caring notions of the advocates of organic architecture and those – like Robert Venturi, Charles Moore and others – who affected an interest in memory and mnemonics.

There were evocative post-Expressionist artefacts by architects such as Piet Blom and Gunther Domenig, whose new Savings Bank building in Vienna caused a sensation but when photographed appeared to have totally lost touch with reality in a frenetic hall of distorting mirrors. It was symptomatic of a whole reappraisal of a certain period of German architectural history that also saw a positive revival of the work of Rudolf Steiner in Scandinavia and Japan as well as in German-speaking countries.

If the pluralities of the period provided an adequate explanation for its lack of direction then the complicated scenario of the ever-widening international architectural circuit needs a special understanding. With British architects working in Luxembourg, France and Libya, Finns and Germans in Riyadh, Italians in Arizona, Kenyans in Mauritius and Danes in Australia, it proved impossible to present a case for a coherent chronological development in architecture, as the following pages show. Since the beginning of the 1970s the previously static frame of reference seems to have warped. It would probably need a special pair of magnetic needles to pick out the interactive groups – teamwork had really taken over on a multi-national scale – and overlapping commitments, which, like iron-filings, appeared to be multi-directional.

A predominant emphasis of the decade was on architectural writing; and reading, and textual study. For the first time, architects were being taught 'literacy' in the design schools. Whereas in previous decades it would seem that detailed coverage of a new scheme in an architectural publication was something of a special event,

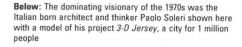

Above and right: The well known group of mushroom shaped *Water Towers*, Kuwait City, received an Aga Khan Award for Architecture as a bold attempt to integrate modern technology, aesthetic values and functional needs in the desert. Designers: VBB, Sweden

Below and right: Another AKAA Award was given to the prototypical structure designed by UNESCO architectural experts for an *agricultural training centre* in Nianing, Senegal

at this time hardly any self-respecting architect could produce a building without having at least one publication dedicated to his project. New architectural magazines, from student publications with a short life to new academic and international journals, proliferated throughout the decade. From Japan, for example, *A&U: Architecture and Urbanism*, was seen as essential reading both in the East and the West. It concentrates on the international buildings outside Japan with a strong Modernist line. It is the most essential pictorial document of the decade.

In 1976 a generous and prestigious new award scheme for buildings in the Islamic World was announced in Pakistan. The Aga Khan Award for Architecture was to be presented to new buildings appropriate to the Islamic World and commendable for their efficacy, sense of innovation and beauty. Some 15 projects were among the Award Winners announced in 1980 from a range of 200 projects. They included the simply vaulted, solid block-faced Agricultural Training Centre, Nianing, Senegal (1977), designed by a group of UNESCO architects and built using local labour and materials, the clay-faced Mopti Medical Centre, Mali (1976) and the Halawa Hase, Egypt by Abdel-Wahed El-Wakil. The Awards created new criteria for judging recent architecture that took into account tradition and local conditions, including materials, climate and town planning. This undoubtedly helped move the emphasis from the tenets of an unfettered international architectural Modernism towards distinct, indigenous, regional cultural values and, by implication, new architectural vocabularies.

The information explosion, which to a large extent had been predicted and promoted, as I have suggested, by popular cultural gurus such as McLuhan and Fuller, opened up like a magical and beautiful new flower garden. Now all planted knowledge was accessible to those designers who began to pick the flowers they liked and bunch them together in never-ending combinations, initially, of course, on the drawing-board. Inevitably it led to eclecticism. But it was not long too before some new species began to emerge with their own special and innovative characteristics. In the United States, for example, Steve Baer's own passive solar cluster house design in New Mexico, (1972), with its living areas heated for 90 per cent of the year by the sun's energy, was an important technological breakthrough, producing hitherto undeveloped ideas for integral urban homes. In the same region another architect and visionary, Paolo Soleri, was engaged on the construction throughout the entire decade of a huge, self-built, ecologically-based city construct (or 'Arcology') which he had begun in 1969. It was called 'Arcosanti' and situated near Prescott in Arizona. Soleri had spent the previous ten years developing the technology and prototypical forms required for such an enterprise at 'Cosanti', close by Frank Lloyd Wright's Taliesin West (where Soleri himself had earlier been an apprentice) down in Scottsdale. Seen very much as a product of the hippy era, it shared anthropological and biomorphic emphases that had left their mark too in other projects, including Ant Farm's 'House of the Century' (1972–73) and Baer's earlier series of Dome houses at Drop City. Much of this work had clearly been influenced by Kiesler's sophisticated 'Endless' projects. They were germane to the whole period, as were the sketches of earlier Expressionists such as Finsterlin whose revival was generated by magazines like *Handmade House* and *Shelter* (both begun in 1973) and the bulky *The Whole Earth Catalogue*. They had a profound effect on the actual self-build process and eventually on the whole worldwide trend towards community architecture and consumer participation.

In contrast, the more esoteric – but equally inspirational – London-based Archigram had a great success, particularly among students, but little practical outcome in the 1970s – notwithstanding the Rogers/Piano design for the Pompidou Centre in Paris.

Most of these counter-culture designers and their projects stood well outside the tradition of the European-based Modern Movement as revised by Team Ten. They belonged to the Alternative Society. Moreover, they did, in expressing individualistic, even at times bizarre, attitudes to the opportunities offered by the new

Below: A revival of interest in the work of Rudolf Steiner was behind the projects for the *Seminary* at Järna, Sweden designed by the Danish architect Erik Asmussen

architectural freedoms remain outside the 'Hi-Tech' ideas also encouraged by Fuller, Prouvé and others. These were more closely linked to the Modernist ideology. To the Post-Modern trends that had produced a new architectural 'get kicks quick' orthodoxy in the late 1970s, the alternative architects had always represented a threat. By the end of the decade a fundamental new interest in an 'organic' architecture had begun in earnest and designers like the American Bruce Goff and the Anglo-Swedish architect Ralph Erskine were sitting on the same conference platform still unclear what the term meant but keen to be seen to be part of it.

The flower analogy referred to earlier – borrowed from those young people associated with the so-called decadent Counter Culture of the hippy-dominated 1960s – was still appropriate to a discussion of the changes that took place in the 1970s. The elusive power of the poppy may have waned but its vibrant colours had taken on a newly-charged symbolism closely associated with the violent and bloody events which throughout the period were shown in all their terrifying and stark cruelty to the world through the impact of colour TV. Society would never be the same again. Nor would architecture, graphics or design. A new age of colour had dawned, preparing the way for a more coloured, ornamented and patterned mainstream architecture. Understandably there was a renewed interest in the ideas of the Bauhaus painters and the Modernist colourists, while the various searches for precedent by some led straight to Gaudi and Baragan. For others the path led more directly to traditional ethnic roots and to exploration involving everything from body painting to sand paintings, painted trucks and tie-dye tee shirts. This aspect Post-Modernist architectural designers exploited in buildings such as Graves's Portland Public Service block.

In a more modest and much more controlled fashion, architects such as Mario Botta in Ticino began employing striated coloured brickwork in their projects for houses although Charles Moore and his colleagues had introduced a kaleidoscope of lurid neon and coloured columns in a controversial cardboard cut-out Post-Modernist jibe for the Piazza D'Italia, New Orleans (1975–80).

In contrast, too, was a wider European interest in re-structuring the existing city – theoretically part and parcel of the Italian New Rationalist thinking of Aldo Rossi and others – and an interest perhaps best referred to as an attempt to fulfil the functional and humanistic architectural ideas associated with the earlier periods of Modernism. This is probably nowhere better seen than in the work of architects such as James Stirling, Richard Rogers and the New York Five although individual contributions, for example those made by Kroll and Segal, were significant at the time, with the architect adopting the role of midwife rather than surgeon.

Yutaka Murata. *Fuji Pavilion*, Expo 70, Osaka, Japan. 1970
Right: general view of the air house

Nippon Telegraph and Telephone Corporation Architects
Department. *Nippon Pavilion*, Expo 70, Osaka, Japan. 1970
Below: the dragon-shaped stretched-skin pavilion

Davis, Brody, Chermayeff, Geismar, De Harrak
Associates. *United States Pavilion*, Expo 70, Osaka,
Japan. 1970
Bottom: no longer a building, more part of the
earth's crust

The theme of Expo 70 at Osaka was 'Progress and harmony for mankind' and was the first Asian event of its kind. Created by the distinguished Japanese architect Kenzo Tange, it covered an area slightly less than Expo 67 in Montreal, but its contribution to world architecture was spectacularly experimental. In a sense it was the first great show-ground of the new architecture of pneumatics, media pavilions and stretched-skin structure. Each pavilion was an isolated piece of environmental design, but many were fragments of a possibly much larger system. Space does not permit a large selection of the many architecturally interesting pavilions, but the three shown on this page were among the most advanced and technically competent. The continuing interest in tented structures can be seen, as well as the potential of space-covering plastics.

The 52-storey world-banking centre for the Bank of America is now the dominant feature in San Francisco. Situated at the foot of a hill, it makes a surprising contrast – brown, shiny and finished – to the predominantly white townscape. Its faceted surfaces catch and reflect the sun and reduce the effects of its overall bulk. In a certain sense, it is still very much a mainstream American 'modern' building, but more sympathetic, perhaps, than its numerous

The Lasdun office always exhibits a concern for people's needs and sometimes it is more successful than at others in interpreting these. This new college at Cambridge is in direct succession to the humanistic-functionalist buildings of an early period. It is, to some degree, based on the forms developed for the less successful University of East Anglia, but it has the concept within perceptual control: you can take in at a glance its chief characteristics, the study-bedrooms themselves providing the rhythmic repetition from the lower court.

Wurster, Bernardi and Emmons; Skidmore, Owings and
Merrill. (Consultant: Pietro Belluschi). *Bank of America*,
San Francisco, USA. 1970
Right: the Bank of America building

Denys Lasdun and Partners, *Extension to Christ's College,
Cambridge*, England, 1970
Above: cross section
Below: general view from the lower court

1970

John Johansson, *Mummers Theater*, Oklahoma, Oklahoma,
USA, 1970 (1969–70)
Right: exterior view of the theatre complex
Bottom left: site plan
Bottom right: plan of stage level
Below: view through the external walkways between the
theatres

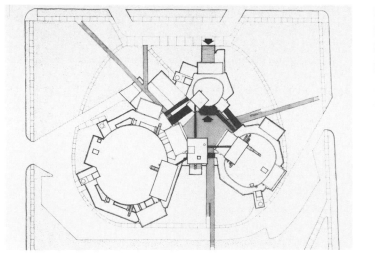

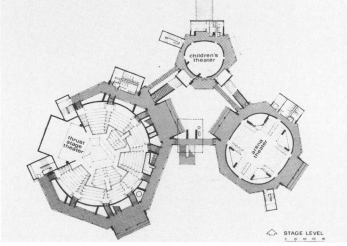

The Mummers Theater by Johansson
and Ashok Bharani has been widely cited as
the pattern for the new theatre of the people.
It was built in reinforced concrete for a local
repertory company with a grant from the
Ford Foundation. It is located in a public
park and incorporated within a much larger
redevelopment scheme. Theatre and acting
school are independent parts of the project.
The design of the Mummers was intended
to be sculptural, expressing the essentials of
public theatre and its open, all-embracing

participatory activities. The large theatre
has a rudimentary backstage area with a
flexible floor stage, while the auditorium
seating can be broken down into group
forms. The *Little Theater* is completely
flexible and exits and entrances can be made
from any point of the auditorium. The
ceiling is an entire grid system which allows
for complete lighting flexibility. The whole
ensemble in its green setting is highlighted
by its rich, theatrical external colouring.

In the 1960s there was a shift towards an

increased complexity in Aalto's architecture. During the decade he produced
libraries at Wolfsberg, Germany and
Seinäjoki, Finland, which incorporated a
fan-shaped plan juxtaposed with rectangular adjoining spaces. At Mount Angel,
largely due to the steeply sloping site, Aalto
returned to earlier ideas developed at
Vipuri, Finland, and combined the interplay of horizontal planes with a fan-shaped
library stack. A two-storey open space is
formed allowing visual security of the entire

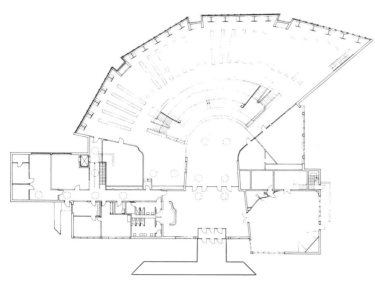

Alvar Aalto, *Mount Angel Benedictine College Library*,
Oregon, Oregon, USA, 1970 (1965–70)
Top left: entrance-level plan
Above: the library building on its craggy site
Above top: interior of library stack

SOM (Skidmore, Owings and Merrill), *John Hancock
Center*, Chicago, Illinois, USA, 1970 (1965–70)
Left: the huge Hancock Center in its street situation

library from one point. The spatial effect is heightened by a dramatic curved skylight which runs between the two connecting stairs.

Entered through the single-storey annexe block situated at one side of the campus courtyard, the nature of the steep sloping site remains hidden by Aalto's Library. It was completed for the Mount Angel Benedictine Order in Oregon a few years before the architect's death in 1976. It is a compact building tucked into the hill at the rear side of a fine open site. Thus, as in many of Aalto's buildings, the irregular shape is contrasted in an abstract manner with the rectangular spine of the administration and the entrance.

Chicago's giant 'Big John' strapped by a dozen pairs of braces was one of the trendiest monoliths to be designed at the end of the 1960s. SOM partner-in-charge was Bruce Graham. It was a monster in anyone's language, probably a symbol of the disenchantment that architects themselves felt over the capitalisation of uses for land in urban centres. It has spawned many imitators. The Hancock houses some seven hundred flats (now 670), five restaurants above the offices, stores and parking floors. It cost just under $100m and it rises just over 1,000 ft from the ground in 100 storeys including roof and antenna farm. Few of the people who use it, or even those who look upon it, may realise that it occupies only 40 per cent of its site of over 104,000 sq ft.

1970

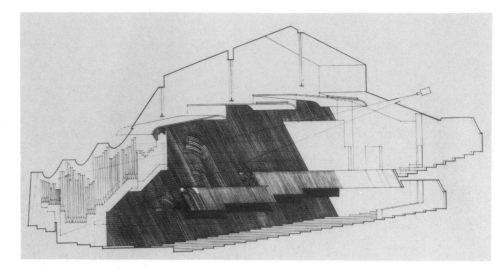

Alvar Aalto, *Finlandia Hall*, Helsinki, Finland, 1971 (196 –71)
Right: section through Finlandia Hall
Below: junction of wall and ceiling in Finlandia Hall
Bottom: the white marble exterior of the concert hall

The Finlandia Hall is one of Alvar Aalto's largest projects. It seats 1,750 people in the main concert-conference hall and has an adjoining 350-seat chamber-music hall. It also includes ancillary conference rooms, offices and restaurants and has a site area of 5,772 sq m.

The new complex was Helsinki's and, indeed, Scandinavia's first and largest tailor-made congress centre. It is situated in the heart of the city, a position that was made possible by the relocation of an existing railway yard. But it stands in splendid isolation, a glittering iceberg of Carrara marble that also exudes architectural excellence. It is constructed from reinforced concrete and faced in limestone and black granite. The music rooms are completely isolated structures.

Offended by the deadpan, repetitive and soulless qualities of a public housing scheme, the local municipal authorities at Alençon in France brought in the Belgian architect Lucien Kroll to work with the tenants in order to relieve the tedium of the repetitive architecture. Kroll and his colleagues introduced traffic-calming schemes

and carried out a number of proto-typical 'add-ons' to the existing blocks to create variety and new harmonious relationships. Tenants were invited to choose from these examples. The courtyards between the blocks were filled with small-scale shops and a school, carried out in practice by another architect but as part of the general plan. The scheme, which was never completed satisfactorily, was meant to be infinitely extensible using the basic framework of the older rectangular blocks as armatures.

Lucien Kroll, *Housing renovation, refurbishment and reorganisation*, Alençon, Normandy, France, 1971 (1968–71)
Above: general view of existing estate
Top right: pilot project under construction
Right: architect's sketches
Below: detail of proposed sun balconies
Below right: overall view of pilot project

1971/72

Richard Meier, *House*, Old Westbury, New York, USA, 1971
(1969–71)
Right: the garden façade
Right middle: the angular entrance front

Meier's house at Old Westbury on Long Island sits in a meadow at the centre of a wooded area where the site slopes down to a pond. The house exerts its presence with a raised-column entrance although the living area, at ground level, is high enough to enjoy the view. The living and family rooms are connected by a complex helical circulation form in steel which disappears into the living-room ceiling and continues to the third floor where it reappears in an enclosed form on the roof terrace. The utilities are situated on the first floor and these adjoin the main dining-room which opens to the 2-storey living-room space. Meier's building is concerned with the interplay of forms and volume, all of which operate within a tightly organised structural framework.

Ontario Place was the by-product of the Toronto Exhibition, an exciting elevated island on the lakeside which now serves as a popular leisure and recreation area. Its unique design presages many of the more adventurous and utopian schemes propounded later in the decade in various parts of the world, including the famous Japanese aqua-cities.

The incorporation of solar energy elements into housing design initially produced few innovations prior to Steve Baer's own solar house. This house has given some iconic significance to solar design but was really assembled using the same kind of junk equipment that was to be found in early and more primitive solar experiments. However, stacks of oil-cans painted black, raised and lowered at dawn and dusk, combine to make a telling piece of architecture. It was largely rebuilt in 1977 with more permanent building materials.

The strange almost bizarre forms of Ludwig Leo's water-processing plant building in central Berlin might well place it in a context outside architecture. It is a brightly coloured machine but one that has had a telling influence on architectural designs elsewhere, particularly among students of architecture. It is bold in its concept and startlingly original in the way its forms are handled, assuming for all its mechanisms the appearance of a humanoid.

Zeidler Roberts Partnership, *Ontario Place*, Toronto, Canada, 1971 (1969–71)
Bottom: the stilted platform with Fuller's dome in the background

Far right:

Steve Baer, *'Zomeworks'*, Solar House, Orrales, New Mexico, USA, 1971 (1971–72)
Right top: external view of the Baer House at the time of construction
Middle and bottom far right: interior of the Baer House

Ludwig Leo, *Circulation Tank*, Institute for Waterways and Shipbuilding, Berlin, Germany, 1972 (1968–72)
Right: the massive external forms of Leo's Water Works

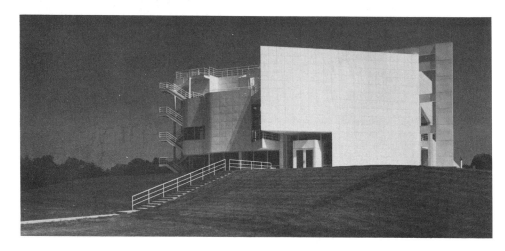

1972

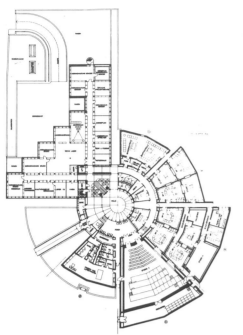

Gustav Peichl, *ORF-Radio and TV Studios*, Innsbruck, Austria, 1972 (1971–72)
Right: aerial view of the ORF Studios
Below: entrance roadway to administrative offices
Below right: the roof area of the studios
Above: ground-floor plan

James Stirling & Partners, *Foley Building*, University of Oxford, UK, 1972 (1970–72)
Far right: the enclosed courtyard that lies on the river's edge

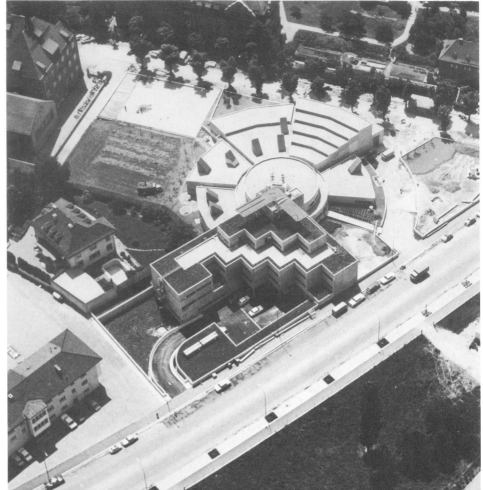

From the late 1960s Austrian architect Prof. Gustav Peichl designed a series of generically similar radio stations for ORF, the Austrian broadcasting company. They are all different but have common design characteristics. Each one has been organically planned with varying size studios, including control rooms and offices often arranged around a central entrance hall. Peichl's buildings give expression to the concept that underlines the modern nature of broadcasting and which is usually emphasised in a forest of gleaming aluminium and steel parts that combine and contrast ducts and antennae, aerials and lattice grids. All these elements seem to have been assembled for their picturesque effect thus emphasising that this is a romantic hi-tech architecture at its heart and is all the more brilliant for that.

James Stirling's Foley Building made a great impact on traditional Oxford. Situated on a sloping site that goes down to the River Cherwell it accommodates graduate students and has been planned in the form of a horseshoe with the structural columns which support the building acting like gigantic stilts.

The building by Kisho Kurokawa has become an important landmark in the downtown Ginza district of Tokyo. It also has, as a 'capsule' building, assumed an important place in modern architectural history. It contains 140 living pods which vary in size and are for use by Japanese workers as overnight accommodation. Each capsule is fully serviced and the prefabricated form of construction facilitated site assembly.

Known as the 'Blue Whale', this mart building and design centre serves the specialised needs of architects and designers involved in contract and residential work. It is a facility that houses a permanent array of top-quality goods by well-known manu-

Kisho Kurokawa, *Nakagin Capsule Tower*, Tokyo, Japan. 1972 (1971–72)
Below and right: elevation, detail and interior

Cesar Pelli, *Pacific Design Center*, Los Angeles, Calif, USA. 1972 (1971–72)
Bottom right: the blue opaque glass end wall of Pelli's Design Center

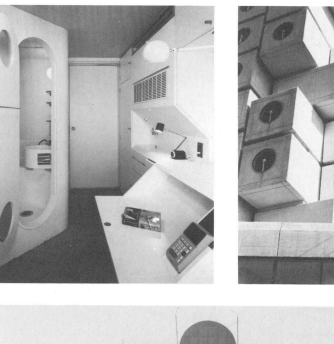

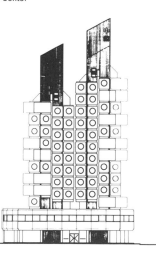

facturers. Thse showrooms are located on levels 2–6. The ground floor is devoted to retail shops and services. There is a net leasable area of 550,000 sq ft, the whole of which is covered by blue opaque glass which reflects and highlights the red bougainvillea in its 350ft-long planter over the south entrance facing the plaza. The frame is in structural steel. The building is designed to withstand earthquakes up to 8.2 on the Richter scale and its air-conditioning is controlled by computer.

1973

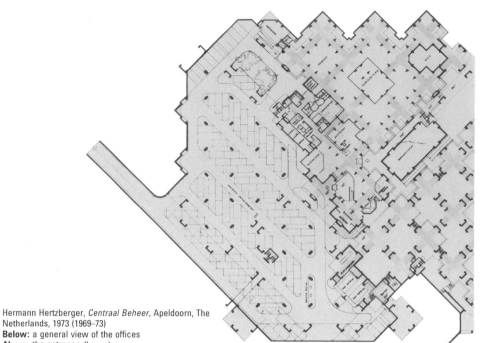

Hertzberger's Centraal Beheer offices house 1,000 people. Located in Apeldoorn, a town like a scattered village on the main railway line from Amsterdam, it was originally meant to be part of a new town centre scheme, a relocation exercise for a large Amsterdam-based insurance company. The building was conceived as a spatial organisation that provided and expressed a varied human environment. People feel at home in a building largely constructed from grey-finished concrete blocks and glass bricks. It is divided into four quadrants with a 'wing-spread' central area and has parking for some 200 cars underneath.

One of the most dramatic of the John Portman 'Hyatt Regency' Hotels is in San Fransisco although the hotel work began in Atlanta. Its celebrated, soaring 17-storey triangular atrium gives a feeling of an overwhelming internal height. It is dominated by the striated balconies and the abundance of trees, flowering plants, sculptures and the busy exposed elevator-cars constantly zipping up and down this space. Externally it is also quite extraordinary, with two sides to the streets but the north face sloping back at an angle of 45 degrees.

Kresge College is situated on the heavily wooded UC Santa Cruz campus overlooking Monterey Bay. It is a residential college accommodating 650 students, of whom half live in. It was built to a tight budget and its architecture attempts to express a 'non-institutional' alternative type of college. All the buildings are 2 storeys and located along a pedestrian street route.

Hermann Hertzberger, *Centraal Beheer*, Apeldoorn, The Netherlands, 1973 (1969–73)
Below: a general view of the offices
Above: the entrance floor plan

John Portman and Associates, *Hyatt Regency Hotel*, San Fransisco, Calif., USA, 1973 (1972–73)
Top right: cross section through the Hyatt Regency Hotel
Top far right: the sweeping lines of the interior atrium

Moore Turnbull & Partners, *Kresge College, UC*, Santa Cruz, Calif., USA, 1973 (1972–73)
Right: residential blocks
Bottom right: a night-time view of the faculty building

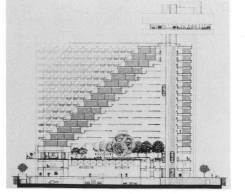

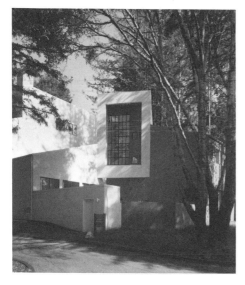

1973

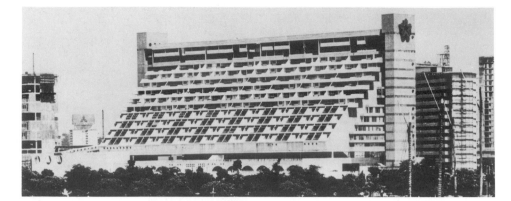

Design Partnership (William Lim *et al*), *Golden Mile Shopping Centre*, Singapore, 1972 (1969–72)
Right: the cascading apartment section of the Golden Mile complex
Below right: the sloping street façade
Below: cross section

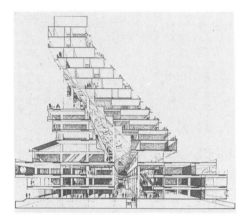

Mario Botta, *Family House*, Riva san Vitale, Ticino, Switzerland, 1973 (1972–73)
Below: the house is approached by a suspended bridge

Mario Botta's house at Riva San Vitale is situated on the shores of Lake Lugano at the foot of St Giorgio's Mountain. It is in the region of the Lombard Pre-Alps and in a flat landscape. A fine house for a local teacher, it was designed to establish a dialectic with this landscape condition. It was conceived as a compact 3-storey tower. Its walls are load-bearing, made from lightweight exposed concrete blocks, which had been whitewashed on the inside. The floors are constructed from hollow flat tiles.

Singapore's Golden Mile Shopping Centre was one of the first attempts to create a new kind of *unité du commerce* on the Island. It reflects the thinking of the time with its emphasis on a vast interrelated superstructure: a giant concrete ziggurat form with offices and showrooms at ground level and apartments cascading down towards the water's edge and located at one end of the Island's busy shop street. It replaced a squatter area. It is finished in the kind of expanded 'Brutalist' concrete construction that was also popular in the late 1960s but today appears somewhat shabby. But it is still one of the most interesting and prominent modern city elements in the whole of Singapore.

The Douglas House is one of Richard Meier's most successful tight geometrical exercises. It is situated on a steep isolated site that slopes down to Lake Michigan. The site is thickly covered by conifers. It is another fine dramatic example of the way this architect uses an articulated, machine-crafted object and drops it on to a welcoming natural site. The 5-storey house is entered at the top level across a bridge and provides about 4,500 sq ft of living space.

Richard Meier, *Douglas House*, Harbor Springs, Mich., USA, 1973 (1971–73)
Top right: the house is set into a well-wooded and steep site
Right: the entrance to the house at the top level

1973/74

Jorn Utzon, *Opera House*, Sydney, Australia, 1973 (1956–73)
Above: architect's original sketch
Right: general view
Below and bottom right: the Opera House from the harbour
Below left: under construction on Bennelong Point, 1968

The construction of the beautiful free-standing, sculptural tripartite Opera House was one of the longest contractual sagas of the century. Sadly, architect Jorn Utzon became the scapegoat of a scandalous political affair and in 1966 withdrew from his project. Sitting on Bennelong Point, virtually in the Harbour and overlooked by the great Sydney Harbour Bridge, the Opera House is completely exposed, as three-dimensional as the orange segments its forms are based on. It is all roofs with an imposing base. These were made possible by Ove Arup. Originally the winner of an international open competition in 1957, it was a scheme that broke most of the rules. It was finally completed in August 1973 by other hands under the direction of Peter Hall. It was officially inaugurated on 20 October 1973, rapidly putting Sydney – even Australia – on the world map for music as well as architecture. The concert hall, with a seating capacity of some 2,800 and now in operation, was achieved by going back to Utzon's original design ideas.

This small RC church by Maltese architect Richard England sits calmly on its craggy hillside site, a curved concrete contrast to the local solid stone and rectangular architecture.

One of the earliest buildings in a group at the Rudolf Steiner Seminary in Järna which will eventually focus on a great hall, it is a charming, small tightly-framed 3-storey wooden music-room with an adjacent house (see 1976). It helped to establish the standard for many later buildings on the site, to evoke strong references to Steiner's own work at Dornach and to gain worldwide publicity for itself. Asmussen, the architect, born and trained in Denmark, has worked extensively in Sweden, living for many years at the site of this building. He has been closely involved with the evolution and design of all the others (see 1977). The use of natural materials, timber, paints and other finishes is an important part of the ensemble, as is the employment of colour both internally and on the exterior.

Richard England, *Church of the Holy Trinity*, Malta, 1974 (1973–74)
Top: the church on the hill and the three holy goats
Centre: detail of entrance

Erik Asmussen, *'Almandinen' (Music Room)*, Rudolf Steinerseminary, Järna, Sweden, 1974 (1973–74)
Below: the copper roof shape of the main first-floor Music Room echoes the local rock formation

1974

Erdgeschoß
Groundfloor

Rolf Gutbrod, Frei Otto *et al, Inter-Continental Hotel and Conference Centre*, Mecca, Saudi Arabia, 1974 (1972–74)
Below: the Inter-Continental Hotel courtyard space
Above: modern structural steel elements are combined with the image of the traditional desert hut
Right: section through conference hall
Above right: the complex layout of hotel, kitchens and conference centre at desert floor level

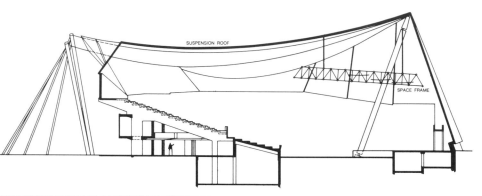

This complex incorporating hotel, conference centre and a mosque is set in the holiest city in Islam. It makes a significant contribution to modern technology in the context of Islamic culture. The Conference Centre avoids existing conventions about architectural expression and draws upon the tradition of tented structures and Arab precedents in a quite sophisticated manner for its 1,400-seat facilities. The suspended steel lattices on their angled steel columns support a hung roof of insulated bronze-ribbed aluminium sheeting under which fly suspended timber sunbreakers. The more compact air-conditioned 170-room hotel is a conventional concrete building but one that lies low and unobtrusively in deference to the surrounding mountains and the nearness of the Holy City itself. The two buildings are both grouped around independent oases between which lies the main public entrance to the complex.

Hertzberger's residential home 'De Drie Hoven' for elderly handicapped people was created to provide a social and caring environment for those of advanced age. It is a modular unit-based scheme within a continuous concrete structural frame, with a basic component size of 92cm. It includes 55 apartments for marrieds, a 171-unit old person's home, a chronic care unit, staff quarters and a 'communal living room'.

Constructed in phases over a long period, in conjunction with Indian architects B. V. Doshi and A. D. Raje, this huge business school is a reminder of Louis I. Kahn's commitment to monumentalism and geometry. Warm red-brick blocks with concrete frames and dressings make up a fine fortress group.

Hermann Hertzberger, *'De drei Hoven', Elderly Persons' Home*, Amsterdam, The Netherlands, 1974 (1965, 1971–74)
Top right: one of the 'outdoor' living areas for old people
Right: a general view of the home

Louis I, Kahn, *Institute of Management*, Ahmedabad, India, 1974 (1962–74)
Below: one of the major lecture-hall blocks

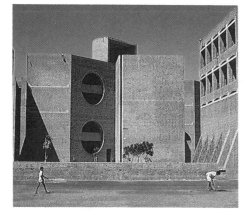

1974

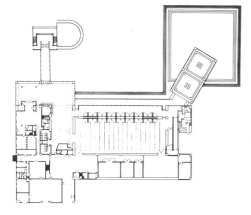

Arata Isozaki, *The Gunma Prefectural Museum of Fine Arts*, Takasaki, Japan, 1974 (1972–74)
Right: general view of main front from hall
Middle: architect's perspective
Above: plan
Below right: detail photograph of the boxed feature window to the main hall

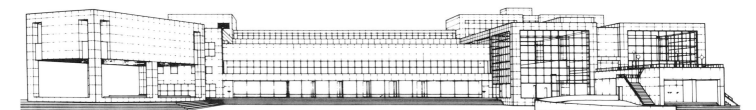

The Gunma Prefectural Museum is a strongly-shaped example of Isozaki's brief Cubist period. Its simple external forms and compositional devices make it a memorable building at the entrance to a public park. The great cubic frames are finished in shiny aluminium panels inset with glazed aluminium sashes. Two of the cubes are joined and angled across a lake to provide a break from the rigidity of the scheme and to give it a dynamic emphasis. An anti-perspective device in the main entrance hall has been introduced to focus attention on the cultural significance and purpose of the building.

The Thau School by MBM, like Isozaki's project of the same year, is organised around a concept of cubic geometry. However, the sloping site has a greater significance, providing an opportunity to develop an interesting sequence of spatial connections. The core elements are joined by a set of externally placed wide steps shaped in the form of a small Greek theatre, which are then echoed in the stairs that are depicted in the cutaway profiles to the elevations of the two rectangular blocks, the main parts of which are faced in metal curtain-walling. The school has 1,440 pupils and is divided into infants, junior and senior departments.

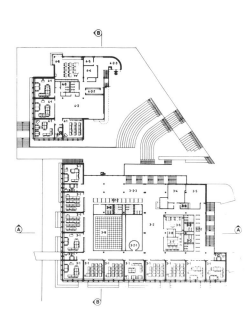

Martorell/Bohigas/Mackay, *The Thau School*, Barcelona,
Spain, 1974 (1972–74)
Top: looking up towards the senior school
Above: ground-floor plans
Right: the internal stair tower with the view out to the
stairs/auditorium

1975

Charles Moore, *Place d'Italia*, New Orleans, La., USA. 1975 (1973–75)
Below and right: concept plan and built version of the Place d'Italia

Kiyonori Kikutaki, *Aquapolis*, Okinawa, Japan, 1975 (1974–75)
Left and below: the visitor centre in place at Okinawa with elevation and section

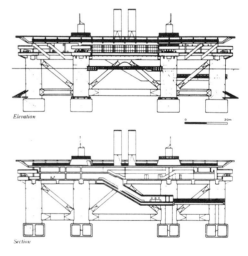

Elevation

Section

Designed for the International Ocean Expo at Okinawa, this remarkable structure called 'Aquapolis' was built for research and information on the sea. It is a totally artificial environment and a semi-submerged system. It is moored and floating on water to provide a research base and serve as a large-volume visitor centre as well. It was built on the island of Honshu and transported when completed to its new anchored position off the Okinawa shore. Built largely in steel tube and sheet it has the appealing appearance of a great, exciting space structure and platform.

The Place d'Italia is one of Charles Moore's exercises in public user-participation as well as large-scale environmental theatre. It is essentially a post-Modernist scheme but transcends the mundanities of that approach in the way it has so successfully related history to place, in order to serve the specificities of the Italian community in New Orleans. It is remarkably rich in metaphors that themselves reveal a deep sensitivity to cultural concerns, as well as a witty, fun-designer place.

All Barcelona's princes of art – Gaudi, Picasso, Chillida, Miro, *et al* – have their own places in the city. Sert's design for the Miro Fondacion at Montjuic was more than a museum piece although it does have that function as well. It was designed (similarly to the same architect's Maeght Foundation and his later Bauhaus Archiv building in Berlin) as a place for cultural study and contemplation and as an archive centre. It is also an international meeting-place. Its clear open spaces, large concrete walls and shaped roofs make up an exciting architectural composition, enriched by paintings, sculptures and wall-hangings. It was created as a space that distinguished itself from its immediate mediocre surroundings in an attempt to provide a community life in the open countryside near Barcelona. It has an austere, monumental, almost fortress-like image with great vertical openings and solid-looking walls. This strong statement kind of design is also to be seen in the fortress like appearance of Bofill's 'Walden 7' also in Barcelona.

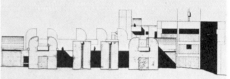

Jose Luis Sert, *Miro Centre*, Montjuic, Barcelona, Spain, 1975 (1973–75)
Top left: main entrance to the Miro Centre
Top right: the glazed staircase connection between levels with section
Above: interior of main gallery

Ricardo Bofill and the Taller d'Arquitectura, *Walden 7*, nr Barcelona, Spain, 1975 (1974–75)
Right: a concrete fortress set in the Catalan countryside

1975

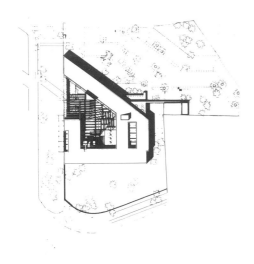

A. Zabludovsky, T. González De León, *Colegio de Mexico*, Mexico City, Mexico, 1975 (1974–75)
Top right: roadside elevation
Top left: site layout plan
Left: inside the well-landscaped open courtyard

The 4 storey concrete faced Mexico College by Abraham Zabludovsky is a much admired complex of educational buildings. Set around an open courtyard that is highly landscaped the building embraces and protects the students and their activities. A bold diagonal classroom block cuts across the site hiving off the extensive car parks.

Legorreta's striking concrete-framed hotel sits on a narrow peninsula of land surrounded by the sea. The sloping west elevation provides a sun-shaded area at the centre of the block, offering cool public rooms with cutaway openings to this central space. A further hotel by the same architect is to be found at Ixtapa, Geurero (1981) where a similar sloping face derives from natural ground contours.

Bofill's own offices were situated in purpose made premises and their industrial shapes soon earned the title 'The Cement Factory'.

Ricardo Legorreta, *Hotel Camino Real*, Cancún, Mexico,
1975 (1973–75)
Above: the slotted and sloping sun protected balconies
facing the bay

Ricardo Bofill and Taller de Arquitectura, *Offices*, (The
Cement Factory), San Justo Desvern, Barcelona, Spain,
1975 (1974–75)
Right: the circular 'Gothick' towers contain the architect's
offices

1975

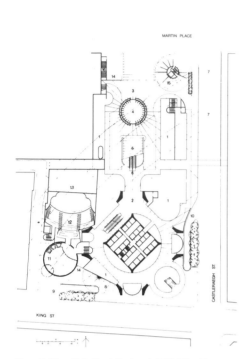

Harry Seidler, (P. L. Nervi, Engineer), *MLC Office Tower and Theatre Royal*, Sydney, Australia, 1975 (1971–75)
Above: site plan of the MLC development
Right: one of the tallest towers in Australia, it dominates the downtown area of Sydney
Below: detail of canopy and the great prefabricated beams
Below right: interior of the Theatre Royal

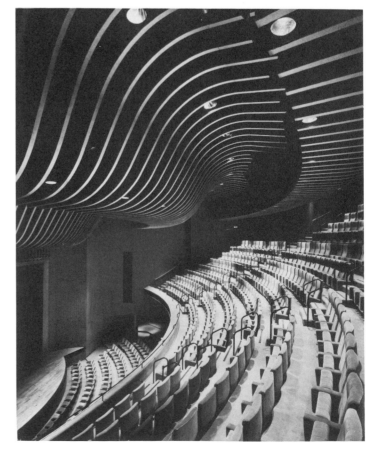

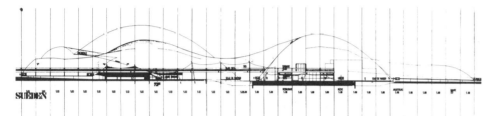

Frei Otto *et al, Garden Pavilion*, Mannheim, Germany, 1975
(1973–75)
Above: northwest view of the Pavilion taken during the
Bundesgartenschau, 1975 with section below
Below: the vast interior space and external views

A tall 67-storey downtown area development, the MLC Tower and Centre with the adjacent Theatre Royal lies at the heart of the trade and entertainment area of Sydney, Australia. Views from its upper floors are sensational. Its careful, repetitive but large-scale precast concrete detailing sets a high standard and provides a pattern for the same architect's work in other parts of Australia and abroad.

The multi-purpose, single-storey, lightweight, low-profile structures at Mannheim were designed for the *Bundes Gartenschau* of 1975. It is one of Frei Otto's most exciting achievements, an amoeba-shaped building which provides a kind of *hommage* in modern technology to Kiesler's ideas for his 'Endless' projects. It acts as a performance and arts space as well as a place of congregation and remained a permanent feature in the city after the garden exhibition was over.

1975

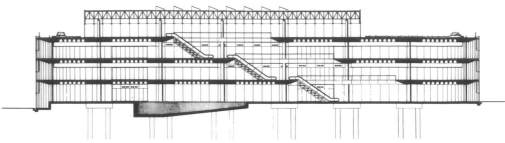

Norman Foster & Associates, *Willis Faber & Dumas Office Building*, Ipswich, Suffolk, UK, 1975 (1973–75)
Top: section through building; swimming pool at basement level
Above and left: transparent night views
Below: site plan

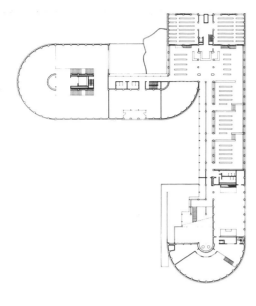

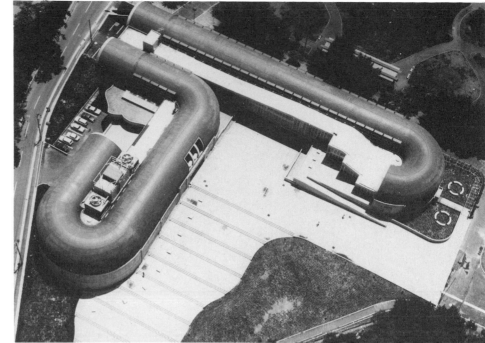

Arata Isozaki, *Central Library*, Kitakyushu City, Japan, 1975 (1973–75)
Above: second-floor plan
Above right: general view showing second-floor recessed windows in curved roof
Right: interior of curved roof

Luigi Snozzi, *Casa Biancetti*, Ticino, Switzerland, 1975 (1974–75)
Bottom: the Casa in its garden setting

An urban design project with a difference in a Suffolk country town. This celebrated, slick, black sheath of offices for Willis Faber & Dumas undulates freely around the perimeter of the site. It is as if Mies van der Rohe's early 1920s free-shaped skyscraper design for Berlin had been bitten off at its lower end. Behind the hung glass façade lies a concrete-framed but free-standing serviced structure. The prefabricated and related management techniques adopted to erect the building saw its completion in two years. As well as a low-profile shape it has a low proportion of glass to floor area. Its high-efficiency lighting and exceptional insulation helped by a landscaped roof garden and swimming-pool results in an effective control of energy consumption throughout. Basically it is an office block with an open plan for 1,300 people.

The Japanese library complex with its bent plan and doughnut-ring core is located in a public park. It was designed, Arata Isozaki claimed, on 'the morphology, syntactics and semantics of the library as a communication device'.

The controlled vocabulary of Snozzi's villa is very different. It depends on its formal geometry to create a telling relationship with nature and site.

1975

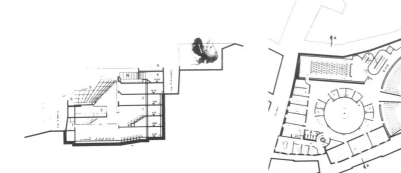

De Carlo has worked for many years knitting together the historic fabric of Urbino to provide new stratas of architecture. His modern configurations draw on metaphors of place, events and discoveries. The Faculty of Education is located within the city's historic core and is cut into a steeply sloping site. Major lecture theatres are grouped around a semi-circular plan, the upper levels of which are fully glazed, south-facing and echo the stratification of the city

Giancarlo De Carlo, *Faculty of Education*, Urbino, Italy, 1975
(1973–75)
Left: garden-level plan and section
Below: view of the enclosed lower level

Michael Graves, *Schulmann House*, Princeton, NJ, USA, 1975 (1974–75)
Bottom left: street façade
Bottom right: garden façade

Denys Lasdun & Partners, *National Theatre*, South Bank, London, England, 1975 (1971–75)
Above: the pedestrian walkway in front of the National Theatre with St. Paul's Cathedral in the background
Right: interior of the Olivier Theatre
Bottom: the spacious foyer area of the Lyttleton Theatre and overall plan

The fragmentary additions to the Schulmann House in Princeton by Michael Graves represents the beginning of a high-profile career for this architect during the Post-Modernist period. Already the historic references show in this design both internally and on a façade that combines traditional architectural features and elements within a modern framework.

The idea of a British National Theatre dates back to the early part of the century. After a number of alternative sites were rejected, the National Theatre designed by Denys Lasdun was finally situated on London's South Bank, adjacent to Waterloo Bridge. This fine, low-profile concrete construction is completely free of contemporary electic mannerisms, an uncompromising modern layered building that allows the internal public spaces to flow out as terraces towards the river. The compact plan houses three theatres in one: the proscenium-arched Lyttelton, the open-stage Olivier and the small studio theatre, the Cottesloe. These splendid auditoria are served by bars, restaurants, bookshops and exhibition spaces.

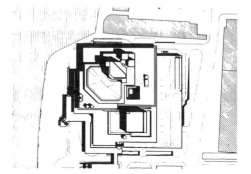

1976

In the 1960s, Kisho Kurokawa emerged as one of the most original members of the 'Metabolists' group of architects. This multi-level showroom for Sony does not betray that original promise. Indeed, it incorporates some of that earlier movement's main tenets, including the tower as 'capsule' and urban tree, bland colouring and mechanistic metaphors. But it is also a building that shows a changing emphasis in Kurokawa's work as it moves towards a wider synthesis of architectural ideas. These new departures bring together Buddhism and elements of western Modernism and post-Modernism. Internally it is still a free and open structure (cf: Piano and Rogers' Pompidou Centre, Paris) with a cubic external composition combining lifts, escalators, steel-clad toilet capsules and an external servicing system for the 72m tower. The showrooms themselves serve as 'stage sets' for Sony products.

Kisho Kurokawa, *Sony Tower*, Osaka, Japan, 1976 (19 – 76)
Right: capsule units are fixed to the tower itself
Bottom right: a cinema/video room
Below: elevation and typical floor plan

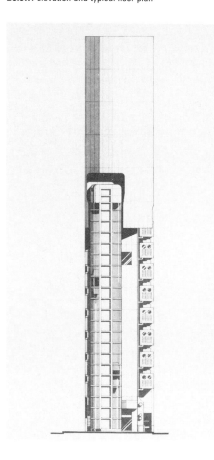

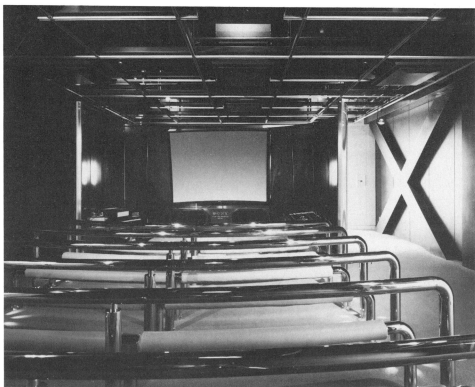

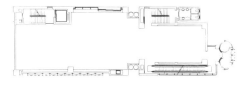

Giovanni Michelucci, *Church of Langarone*, Italy, 1978
(1966–78)
Top left: the entrance to the church
Middle: interior view towards side chapel

Luigi Snozzi, *The Kalman House*, Ticino, Switzerland, 1975
(1973–75)
Bottom: general view of the house and a view along the
bridge that connects to a pavilion with a view

The neo Expressionism of Michelucci was
nowhere better displayed than in his 1964
Chieso dell Autostrada a much criticised and
controversial work. At about the same time
he began work on this much more successful
and much better integrated scheme. Indeed,
it has been referred to as the masterpiece of
the architect's later work. It is unalloyed by
the structural deformations of the motorway
example. Here structure clearly creates the
form, the expression of which the architect
handles in reinforced concrete in masterly
manner.

Snozzi seeks after a simplicity of concrete
forms with bare surfaces in his numerous
emphatic villas. Never crude or simple
minded, this kind of architecture is truly
sculptural, as finely worked as a painting
by Max Bill or, even, Mondrian. Slim,
economic and quite obvious in the external
expression of its inner organisation, the
Kalman House needs little additional explanation.

1976

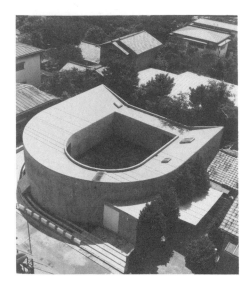

Tooyoo Ito, *'White U' House*, Nakano, Tokyo, Japan, 1976
(1975–76)
Above and left: the dramatic minimalist interiors
Left top: exterior view of house

Levitt Bernstein & Associates. *The Royal Exchange
Theatre*, Manchester, UK, 1976 (1975–76)
Below left: the theatre resides within the older structure
Below: interior of auditorium
Right: section

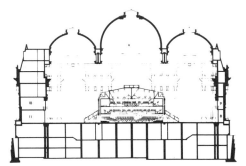

Jorn Utzon, *Lutheran Church*, Bagsveard, nr Copenhagen, Denmark, 1976 (1974–76)
Above: general view of the simple shaped church exterior
Above right: the interior of the church

Lucien Kroll, *Medical Faculty Housing*, University of Louvain, Belgium, 1976 (1970–76)
Right: elevation of the student accommodation
Bottom: detail of the façade of the medical faculty building

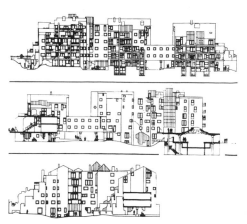

Japanese minimalist architect Toyoo Ito calls his single-storey house *White U* because it is shaped like a U-loop and is white. He conceived the design in these simple terms, which prevented a powerful axial symmetry from invading the design. The loop allowed for a gently curving, enclosing wall surface thereby creating a continuous architectural space with a length of 45m and a ceiling height from 2.2m to 3.9m. The walls are constructed of poured concrete on plywood shuttering, and the roof is plastic paint on a waterproof backing. It has a total floor area of 150 m.sq. Only the front door is white on the exterior, although the architect has argued that the magical power of the ascetic white interior is related to the classical external finishes of certain modern movement masterpieces like the Villa Savoye and the Schröder House.

A smallish, but significant development in theatre design, the Manchester Royal Exchange is a kernel in a much larger shell. Erected within the spaces of the Royal Cotton Exchange, it looks more like a standard alien space-module than a conventional auditorium. However, it serves as a

sealed theatre holding a maximum audience of 750 on three levels that form part of a square around the centralized stage area, planned largely for theatre-in-the-round performances. Constructed mainly of steel, it has limited facilities for flying scenery.

The Bagsveard Church outside Copenhagen, by Utzon, is deceptive. Its cool mechanist external forms give it almost the appearance of a small, well-detailed group of grain silos, concealing from sight one of the most exciting interiors of the decade. This ambiguity is deliberate, with the external finishes of grey concrete panels and galvanised metal roof a fitting economical contrast to the undulating ceiling of the interiors onto which light is reflected into the sanctuary from a single clerestorey. The soft natural light is in turn contrasted with linear, horizontal and sparkling artificial light sources, all of which create a calm but dramatic setting for the liturgy.

1976

Benjamin Thompson and Associations, *Quincy Building and Faneuil Hall Marketplace*, Boston, USA, 1976 (1971–76)
Above: architect's sketch of completed scheme
Right and below: overhead night views and the renewed pavilion
Bottom: measured drawing of the Quincy Building

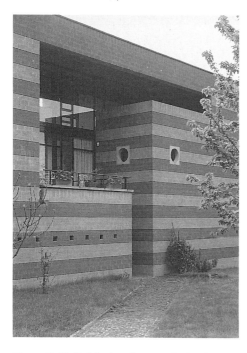

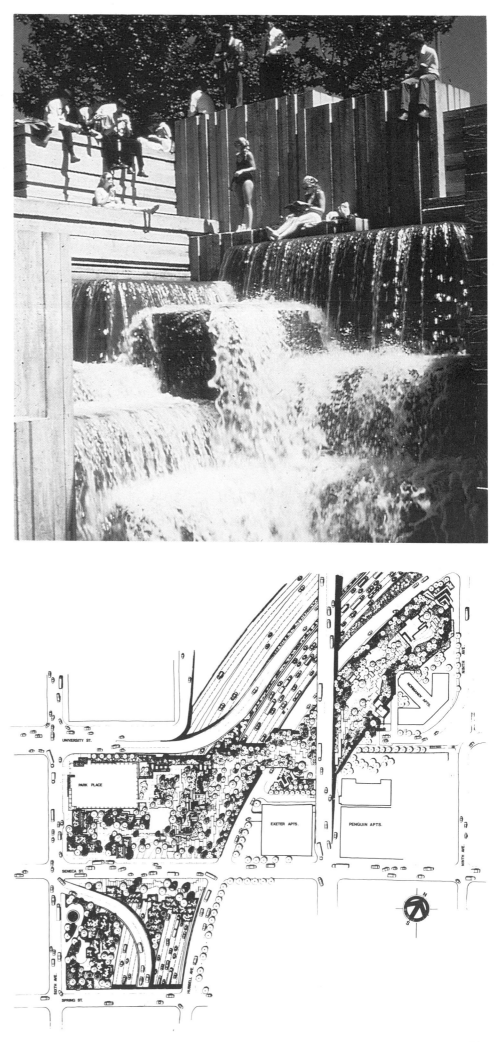

Faneuil Hall Marketplace and the famous Quincy Building have been part of Boston's history for nearly two centuries. They provide a key core element in the existing city pattern and have, as part of a comprehensive redevelopment for a new generation and new uses, been most sensitively revived. They provide the historical backcloth for modern commercial, leisure and recreational facilities on the grand scale. Masonry dominates, lending credence to the architects' desire for what they called authetic *genuineness* as a goal, in which the validity of a live and continuous tradition was carefully considered.

Larry Halprin's extensive public urban park provides a dramatic environment of lawns, gardens, plazas, play-spaces, escarpments, waterfalls and a precipitous canyon descending into the Freeway. This downtown pedestrian area provides the facilities for a multitude of city-type places. It uses the 'free' airspace over the Interstate Road No 5 which bisects the city and reconnects the major residential neighbourhoods of Seattle with the central business district. Its impact as a design has been worldwide.

This house by Botta is located in the Ligornetto Commune in the Swiss Canton of Ticino. It is orientated towards the garden but its 'architectural treatment' focuses on the façade. Here the design aspect is in contrast to surrounding nature. It is divided into two volumes of space and the windows are in the centre of the house and focused on the garden. The external wall consists of a covering layer with internal load-bearing structural bricks. The exterior wall is striated by alternating grey- and reddish-finish cement bricks. The whitewashed internal walls are in reinforced concrete.

1977

Erik Asmussen, *Rudolf Steiner Seminariet*, Järna, Sweden, 1977 (1972–77)
Right and middle: the Library and Eurhythmy Rooms
Below: Library interior and refectory

Imre Makovecz, *Mortuary Chapel*, Farkasrét, Budapest, Hungary, 1977 (1975–77)
Bottom: interior of the chapel

One of the earliest buildings in a group at the Rudolf Steiner Seminary in Järna which will eventually focus on a great hall, it is a charming, small tightly-framed 3-storey wooden music-room with an adjacent house (see 1974). It helped to establish the standard for many later buildings on the site, to evoke strong references to Steiner's own work at Dornach and to gain worldwide publicity for itself. Asmussen, the architect, born and trained in Denmark, has worked extensively in Sweden, living for many years at the site of this building. He has been closely involved with the evolution and design of all the others. The use of natural materials, timber, paints and other finishes is an important part of the ensemble, as is the employment of colour both internally and on the exterior.

Makovecz's small Mortuary Chapel near Budapest was one of his first independent design commissions after he left the state architectural office. It lies in the Farkasrét Cemetery, set into the ruins of the old cemetery chapel. Internally its wooden anthropomorphic ribbed structure resembles the inside of a whale, although it more directly echoes the human rib-cage. The design is a subtle one that brings together the work of interior space design and artisan craftsmanship. The whole building changes its shape throughout its

Paolo Soleri, 'Arcosanti', Cordes Junction, Az, USA, 1977 (1969–77)
Above and below: various views of the Arcosanti site at the time of the 1977 Festival which saw the inauguration of some of the buildings; concept model to right

length, curving from one end to the other at different heights and widths. It gives the impression of a building having an organic and sensual life of its own and in constant movement. It seeks to engage in the kind of artistic metamorphosis advocated by Rudolf Steiner, whom Makovecz greatly admired.

Arcosanti, an arcology (a term for a new city made up from architecture and ecology) was an exciting experiment set up by the Italian-trained architect Paolo Soleri in 1969. That year he purchased a large tract of land near Prescott, Arizona and commenced work on this compact prototype city, aided by apprentices and students à la Frank Lloyd Wright's Taliesin Foundation. By the end of the 1970s a number of the structures on the mesa had opened, and a huge celebratory festival was held, marred only by a tragic fire that spread rapidly through the car park. Using earth-formed concrete structures and introducing on a large scale open apsidal sun-protected buildings based on early designs at his Scottsdale studio, the shape of Soleri's Utopia gradually began to take shape. Now a national landmark, it has been beset by so many problems both personal and material that only slow progress has been made.

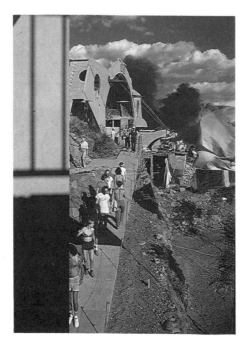

1977

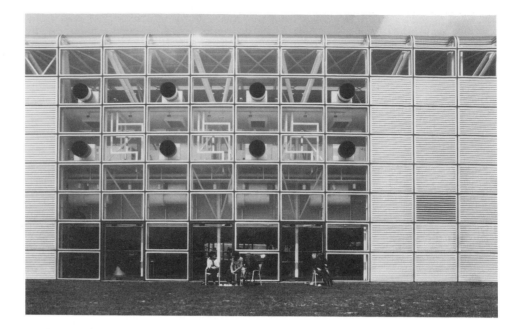

Foster Associates, *Sainsbury Centre*, University of East Anglia, Norwich, UK, 1977
Top: detail of external window wall cladding
Middle: general external view on greenfield site
Left: the flexible interior gallery space
Above: section

The Sainsbury Art Centre at the University of East Anglia, Norwich is described as a well-serviced metal-clad barn. Analogies have been drawn with the simplicity of expression and utility of purpose of Inigo Jones's St Pauls Church, Covent Garden, London. It is a highly tuned and well-engineered shed for art of considerable sophistication, serving as a research institute with public access gallery. It was sponsored by private funds. The white walls and roofs take the form of continuous trusses and all services are housed within the 'outer wall zone'.

Using the Eiffel Tower as a backdrop and responding to the very special conditions of its riverside setting, the concrete Australian Embassy by Harry Seidler (associated with Marcel Breuer (Paris)) is a fine addition to the Parisian urban building scene. It derives its plan geometries from sources as varied as abstract art, the contextual conditions of the site and the structural strategies adopted to exploit economic slip form, in-site construction. It is in two separate parts with a Chancellery building and a 34-unit apartment block for diplomats and their families. Both parts are joined at ground level. Garaging, a swimming-pool, and leisure facilities are in the basement.

Harry Seidler and Associates, *The Australian Embassy*, Quai Branly, Paris, France, 1977 (1975–77)
Above: the Embassy dramatically faces the Eiffel Tower
Right and below: north façade with ground-floor plan

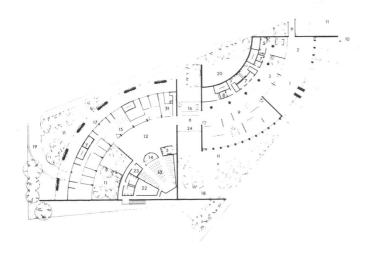

1977

Zeidler Roberts Partnership, *The Eaton Centre*, Toronto, Canada, 1977 (1974–77)
Right: interior of the shopping mall
Below: site location plan and air view with, bottom foreground, Eaton Centre superimposed on site

SITE Architects, *The 'Notch' Project*, Best Products, Sacramento, USA, 1977 (1976–77)
Right: the 14ft high 'notch' serves as main entrance
Below: the opened 'notch'

One of the truly mature design attempts to produce a shopping centre as a convenient and conducive space with architectural ambitions, the Toronto Centre succeeded with distinction and has been successfully extended in the late 1980s. The huge hall space echoes the great interior of the Crystal Palace even to the point of using trees and a static flock of birds!

In contrast, the small, 'notched' entrance, box-like Best Showroom raised merchandising to the level of an art experience. Widely publicised, the SITE project encapsulated James Wine's 'De-Architecture' idea. It used the moving corner as an entrance device thus focusing all attention on the cantilever formed by the two broken brick-work edges. Otherwise it, like many of its successors, remains a fairly ordinary 70m × 60m shed.

The most important postwar international competition produced the Pompidou Centre. When first seen it was considered one of the wonders of the modern world with its exposed fretwork but clearly expressed structure and services and its great diagonal circulation escalators, as well as its brightly coloured features and open planning. It has been referred to as a built piece of *Archigram* architectural design, deriving therefore from the British avant-garde rather than the French at a time when Paris was still largely under the shadow of Le Corbusier. That it has been totally subsumed into Parisian popular culture and life would seem to justify the faith the two designers had in its technology as fictional but buildable fact. Practically, the design achieved a new standard in open-space flexibility. The structural and services functions were expressed in the perimeter walls of the building and the inside could be freely subdivided to provide for a multitude of institutional and public uses. It was designed to reflect change and to encourage change which allows people the freedom to do their own thing. It was conceived as a giant Meccano set rather than a static building and put together with the precision of a steelrigger. The rectangular plan of the Pompidou Centre was divided into 13 bays of 12.8m widths, each supported by standard frame beams spanning onto the generates which rest on the columns and are restrained by the ties. Each frame supports six floors and

is simply connected to the next one. Through this ingenious methodology a neat repetitive façade emerged which acts as a perfect foil to the newly created external courtyard.

Renzo Piano, Richard Rogers, *Centre Pompidou*, Paris, France, 1977 (1970–77)
Top right: the 'street' façade of the Pompidou Centre
Right: courtyard façade detail
Above: interior showing entrance level galleries

1977/78

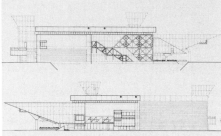

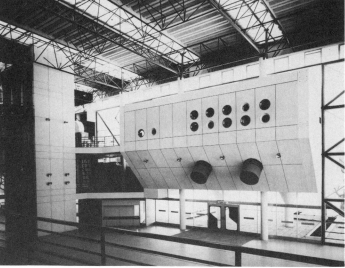

Sumet Jumsai Associates, *The Science Museum*, Bangkok, Thailand, 1977 (1975–77)
Top right: the dramatic cut back main entrance to the west, with drawn elevation to the left of picture
Middle right: main exhibit hall
Above: general view of south side of building

This Bangkok museum, apart from its normal function, is also used as a national science teaching centre. The building was conceived as a technological 'gadget' standing next to a 'science park' which is used for open-air exhibits. The concept of the park stems from the need for open spaces in Bangkok. The site has an existing planetarium which is now linked to the new building. Entry to the 'see-through' museum is from the science park under a giant 15m cantilevered concrete canopy. The public enter a 4-storey main exhibit hall with receding mezzanines so that a general view of all the display areas can be seen all at once. Space trusses above provide supports from which large objects can be

suspended. A central staircase connects the hall to the auditorium (used for orientation classes) and classrooms located above the main entrance, followed by a library, an audiovisual room, and a teacher's room. The latter are grouped into a single volume that projects from the central exhibition space over an area at a corner of the reflecting pool where refreshments are served.

Peichl's satellite design at Affleur is in great contrast to his compact glass and metal Hi-Tech Radio/TV stations for ORF. It is more site than building and very largely an underground structure with an enormous external signal-tracking satellite dish.

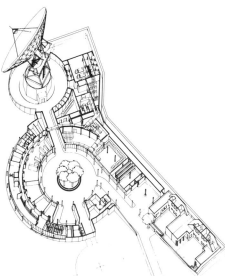

Gustav Peichl, *Earth Station*, Affleur, Austria, 1978 (19 – 78)

Top: the great satellite dish hovers over the partially underground buildings, a dramatic contrast in the winter snow

Above: cut-away axonometric plan with satellite to top left and 2-storey administrative offices to the right

Right: main entrance court

1978

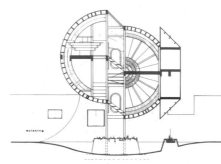

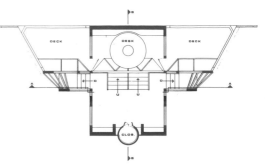

Bart Prince, *Robert Hanna Studio*, 302 Rio Grande
Boulevard, Albuquerque, NM, USA. 1978 (1977–78)
Right: section and upper floor plan
Below: street elevation
Bottom: interiors, the living room on the left in Goff idiom,
and on the right a detail of the glass stairs to the roof

Bart Prince is a talented former student of Bruce Goff who has now more or less assumed his master's mantle. His own architecture is, however, somewhat differently conceived from that of Goff but still as individualistic. It is much less concerned with 1950s Kitsch; more with formal inventions. Prince's Hanna Studio was designed as a multi-use work and entertainment space. It is constructed of wood with a steel frame, and the exterior is covered with ceramic tiles. Technically it is an addition built above a group of 'adobe-like' stucco-finished framed buildings, and the addition stands as a sculptural element apart from the rest.

Set in a formerly prosperous and major mining town in Japan, this new Town Hall by Isozaki was introduced in order to stimulate and activate the life of the area. It is in a sense an anti-Japanese design, although an early design competition entry indicated a quiet, traditional and contextual solution that would easily have fused into the dark city streets. The citizens, however, wanted something new, and they got it. His built design is in the shape of pure forms, a strict and functional composition based on modernist ideas. The mayor's parlour is placed in a cubic frame; the council chamber is the upper part of a cylinder, and the entrance is placed at its base. All is in aluminium-clad curtain walling.

Arata Isozaki, *Town Hall*, Kamioka, Japan, 1978
Left: detail of the metal finished curved wall surfaces
Below: main entrance
Bottom left: site plan with isometric below
Bottom: the entrance façade at dusk

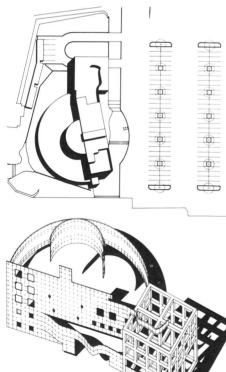

345

1978

Hugh Stubbins and Associates, *Citicorp Office Building*,
New York, NY, USA, 1978 (1976–78)
Right: the cutback roof line of the skyscraper added a
distinctive mark to the New York skyline; the open stilts
carry it above the shopping atrium and the new church
Below: street-level plan and sectional elevation

One of the most successful urban schemes
in New York in the 1970s, 'Citicorp'
brought new life to a downtown Manhattan
city block that had been largely filled by a
popular but far too big Lutheran Church. It
created an exciting new internal plaza for
people with shops, restaurants and performance spaces on a number of levels at the
base of a rather uninteresting square-
format, smooth-faced office tower, chopped
off at 45 degrees at the top, ostensibly to
facilitate solar collection devices. On the
second storey, the old church has found a
spacious, comfortable new home devoting
its services to God and jazz.

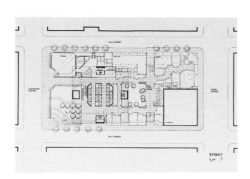

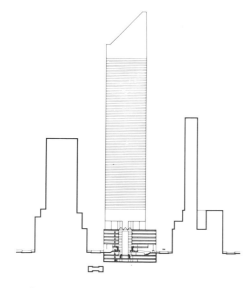

Completed in time for the World Cup Soccer competition in 1978, the linear pavilion scheme colour TV production centre in Buenos Aires was designed under the supervision of Rafael Vinoly. It took 18 months to design, build and furnish and provides 265,000 sq ft of space including 7 soundproof studios, the largest of which seats 400 persons for public performances, and technical, administrative and facility spaces. Built on the edge of a public park, it is separated into 12 blocks, and links effectively with the landscaping. The whole of the interior is carried out in shades of grey with colour introduced only through the TV set monitors. Only the tops of four great studio pavilions obtrude above ground, together with a few well-placed sculptures and sculpted objects, including air-conditioning exhausts and a transmitting tower set in a reflecting pool. Basically it is a single-storey development that integrates beautifully the concrete blocks, well-lighted public entrances and the overall, flat but rich landscape.

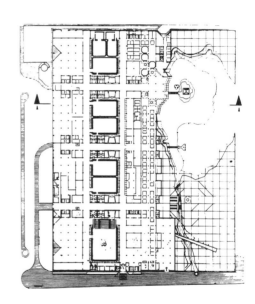

A change in SITE's approach to the Best building programme led them into environmental sculpture for this ghost parking lot at Hamden. Perhaps somewhat limited in architectural significance, it did, however, have a wide influence on the work of public art sculptors.

Manteola, Sanchez Gomez, Santos, Solsona, Vinoly, *TV Studios*, Buenos Aires, Argentina, 1978 (1976–78)
Top: the four main TV studio blocks
Above: the landscaped area and the new pool with, far right, the general plan of the site

SITE Architects, *Ghost Parking Lot*, Best Products, Hamden, Kt, USA, 1978 (1977–78)
Right: car forms in varying states of transformation with Best Store beyond parking lot

1978

Alvar Aalto, *Church*, Riola, Italy, 1978 (1969–78)
Right: exterior of church
Below: architect's original drawing
Middle: ground-floor plan

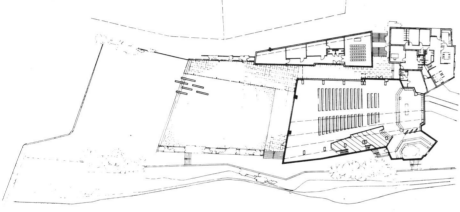

Towards the end of his life Aalto's work outside Finland proved fascinating. The form characteristics which had become familiar in the Finnish examples were exported whole although, as in this case, the detail was never as good and the interior lacked the kind of subtlety in the use of materials associated with his Finnish work. However, it indicated (as had Mount Angel, USA, earlier) the strength of the Aalto design and countered the criticism that his brand of modernism was specific to the Nordic regions and without wider application.

There is a most welcoming simplicity and charm to Tigerman's 2-storey highly coloured steel-faced social welfare building in Chicago. It serves as a haven for the physically handicapped and the blind with common areas for the use of both groups. The plan form is largely triangular with play-school uses on the second storey. The yellow painted structure is made of circular steel columns with beams and a cable tension system for lateral restraint. The external panels are enamelled red.

Stanley Tigerman, *The Illinois Library for the Blind and Physically Handicapped*, Chicago, Ill., USA, 1978 (1976–78)
Right: a slash of window cuts into the road façade
Below: ground-floor plan
Bottom far left: entrance to library

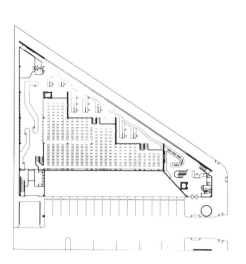

Hans Scharoun and Edgar Wisniewski (Hermann Fehling from 1972–), *Staatsbibliothek Preussischer Kulturbesitz*, Berlin, 1978 (1964–78)
Above: the National Library in the foreground with Scharoun's Philharmonic beyond and Stubbins' convention hall in the distance
Left: ground-floor interior with staircase detail above

A huge urban project that forms part of the cultural plaza in Central Berlin off the Tiergarten, the National Library houses archival material, research facilities, book libraries and upper stackrooms. It was designed by Hans Scharoun but, after his death in 1972, was largely completed by his colleague Edgar Wisniewski. Its area of 38,000 sq m includes many thrilling internal volumes of space very much in the Scharoun mode, although the somewhat compromised and bulky external treatment leaves much to be desired both from an architectural and urban context point of view. It also includes exhibition, study and display spaces, a cafe, a lecture-hall and the Ibero-Amerikanisches Institut.

1978

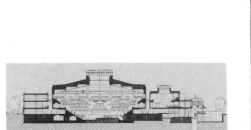

Hermann Hertzberger, *Music Centre*, Vredenberg, Utrecht, The Netherlands, 1978 (1973, 1976–78)
Above: the multi-faceted exterior of the Music Centre
Left: interior of concert hall with section above

Set in the centre of Utrecht, Hertzberger's Music Centre is articulated into a number of parts to reflect a smaller urban scale than the heavy adjoining shopping block. Hardly an anonymous building, it has not sought to become autonomous. In a design sense it might be described as an arbitrary, relaxed music-hall in form, with supporting services, bars, restaurants.

Richard Meier, *The Atheneum Visitor Center*, New Harmony, Indiana, USA, 1979 (1975–79)
Right: the three-storey cubic, white-faced Visitor Center
Below: cross section through lecture hall

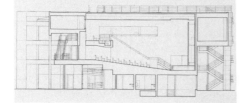

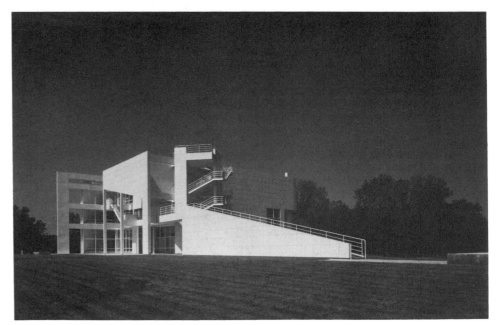

Meier's visitor centre, the 3-storey Atheneum, is probably his best-known transitional building. It comes in his work cycle between the rationalist villas and his later museum work. A gleaming white metal block set on a green lawn, it takes up the idea of the route from Le Corbusier's earlier platonic villas. However, there is less clarity between the relationship of exterior and interior than one would expect to find in the Master's work, although the resulting articulation of solid and void, projecting terraces, recessive space and folded stairs make a memorable, if not exactly monumental, image.

Byker was one of the first major attempts in Britain to create a dialogue between community and architecture. Erskine oversaw the development of this famous project allowing for tenant co-operation and architectural innovation on a large scale to provide housing protected from motorway noise and the rebuilding of a whole estate near the city centre.

The IRCAM Centre situated adjacent to the Pompidou Centre, Paris was the love child of composer Pierre Boulez. It was developed by Mike Davies from the Rogers' office as an underground, soundproofed and highly-tuned laboratory for musical sound.

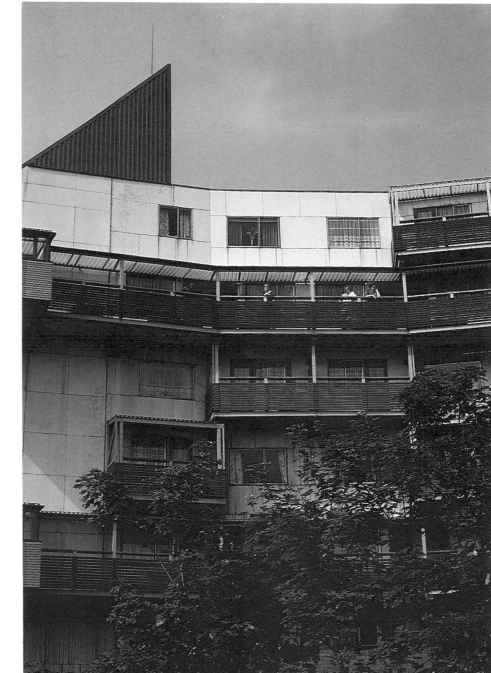

Ralph Erskine *et al, Housing Development*, Byker, Newcastle-upon-Tyne, UK, 1978 (1973–78)
Right: the dramatic shapes of the roofs of the block alongside the motorway with development layout plan below

Richard Rogers & Partners, *IRCAM, Centre Pompidou*, Paris, France, 1978 (1970–78)
Below: the flexible interior of the sound-proofed musical performance space of IRCAM

1978/79

Reima Pietilä, *Congregational Centre*, Church and Market Halls, Hervanta, Tampere, Finland, 1978 (1976–78)
Right: the market halls
Middle left: the entrance to the church
Middle right: side wall of congregational centre
Below: architect's elevation drawing of congregational centre

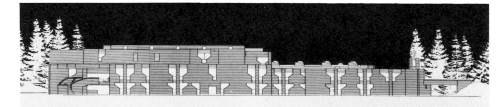

Based on a quadrant open-floor plan (*cf.* Hertzberger's Centraal Beheer, 1974) Hillingdon is arranged around a centrally placed circulation zone on four floors. This was an attempt to create a conducive, friendly, forward-looking, office community of 1,300 staff for the local authority within a very solid, almost Teutonic, brick-faced building. It also has to provide the interface between the local voting public and the elected council and their officers but whether the 'friendly' intentions of the design have been achieved is questionable due to matters of scale and magnitude

rather than the warm and nostalgic materials, the gardens and the dominating pitched roofs.

The huge, rectangular, low-scale shopping mall in Britain's Milton Keynes New City is one of the most imaginative schemes of its type in Europe. It covers some 130,000 sq m. It provides for all levels of accessibility including pedestrians and vehicular traffic, with car parks set out around the centre, and goods and services. The spacious open-air car parks are under constant supervision and over 2,000 car spaces were originally designated as part of the 12 hectare develop-

Robert Matthew Johnson-Marshall & Partners, *Town Hall*, Hillingdon, London
Above: general view of the brick Town Hall with its great pitched roofs

ment. The Centre's structural steel system is simplicity itself with bays of 12m × 6m and 6m × 6m and a variety of column sizes dependent on positions. The first and second floors are in ribbed precast concrete slabs with structural in situ topping. The division walls are blockwork throughout. The roofs are of lightweight corrugated metal decking spanning 3m on steel purlins and beams. The external curtain-walling is ambitious with large glazed walls. Above the first floor these are in stock steel section, angles and tees directly glazed with 6mm heat-resistant mirror self-cleaning glass, set into the legs of the sections with structural neoprene gaskets. The steelwork of the curtain-walls and all exposed stanchions is painted.

Derek Walker MKDC architect, Christopher Woodward & Stuart Mosscrop, *Shopping Centre*, Milton Keynes, UK, 1979 (1974–79)
Above: interior of shopping mall
Right: aerial view of the whole shopping complex

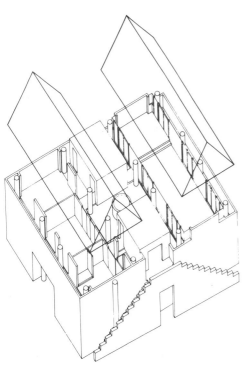

Takefumi Aida, *The Toy Block House*, 'Tomo' Dental Office, Yamgushi, Japan, 1979 (1978–79)
Top: exterior night-time view of west façade
Middle: east elevation
Above left: interior at first floor with axonometric above
Right: ground- and first-floor plans

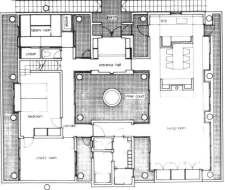

The Toy Block House is concerned with 'remembered images of houses', which it records, according to its architect, in a representational manner. It has, however, been simplified with reference to the artlessness and anonymity of building blocks. The child can assemble such toys uniquely. So can the architect, Aida indicates, in a reinforced concrete project that consists of a dental clinic on the ground floor and an apartment above. The external treatment follows the simple clean theme and with sprayed tiles.

The traditional terrace and semi-detached brick faced housing of the London inner suburbs offered an inspirational source for the Dixon's public housing scheme in Westminster. It makes a useful contribution to the street architecture of Maida Vale.

Won in competition by the Pietiläs, this axial shopping, church and market scheme is part of the neighbourhood centre of the new suburb of Hervanta in Tampere (planned by Aarne Ruusuvuori). Based on the nineteenth-century market hall and arcade principle, it also uses traditional brick finishes to the full with many special details.

It takes as its point of departure the character of the surrounding residential streets, a part of London that is a melting-pot of styles. Priority was given to avoiding the destruction of the pattern of streets with terraced houses and gardens that characterises the English urban estate tradition. Two narrow houses are paired above a single-aspect flat to make a larger 'house' that approximates to the scale of its neighbours. The front façade uses elements of style and

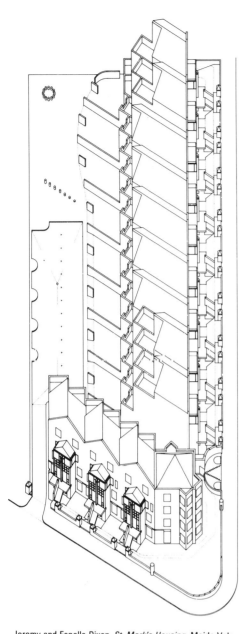

Jeremy and Fenella Dixon, *St. Mark's Housing*, Maida Vale, London, 1978 (1976–78)
Above right: semi-detached block with entrance steps
Above: axonometric

decoration extracted from the surrounding streets – porches, bay windows, stairs, gate posts – exploiting, particularly, features at right angles to the façade in order to produce in perspective the rhythms associated with a street. Each house has a door to the street, a garden and a rear elevation distinct and different from the front façade. The exterior materials are dark stock bricks with details picked out in red brick and white pre-cast concrete.

With a number of hiccups in the commissioning of the Louvain development architect Kroll relentlessly continued to enhance his project with, in 1979, the completion of a major landscaping phase.

Lucien Kroll, *Development of Medical Faculty and settlement*, University of Louvain, Woluwé St. Lambert, Brussels, Belgium, 1979 (1969–79)
Right: the landscaping of the medical faculty living accommodation

Neave Brown's Alexandra Road housing estate in London was a long time in the making. Begun in 1969, it was not completed until ten years later. Situated on a site bounded on the one side by a busy main line railway and on the other by a blocky, limited-access housing project, the peninsular site was developed as two urban streets – one nearly 1km long – with housing along their edges. The public realm penetrated the street – at the pedestrian level – in the traditional manner. There are no artificial setbacks. The proximity to the railway system demanded special constructional techniques to obviate noise and vibration. Thus, the nearest 6-storey terrace of houses was elevated on reinforced-concrete cranked beams and set on anti-vibration foundations. Designed initially for over 1,600 persons in some 520 dwellings, it has underslab car parking and community buildings, including a centre, pub, school for the handicapped as well as a four-acre neighbourhood park. The density was 200 persons per acre in the blocks and thus reverted to the kind of Continental ratios admired by architects at the time. Each dwelling also had at least 100 sq ft of garden or terrace. Occupation commenced in 1978, although it was not fully in use until the following year. The whole project was built using in situ concrete which added to the

unity of the scheme although it was by no means universally popular with the local authority tenants.

The first phase of Erickson's commercial and civic buildings for Vancouver indicated a rather more lightweight approach to covering huge blocks of streets than the Camden scheme. It, too, had a widespread international impact on subsequent developments.

Camden Architects' Dept, (Neave Brown *et al*), *Housing scheme*, Alexandra Road, London, 1979 (1961–79)
Below: detail of balcony
Bottom: the main pedestrian 'street'

Arthur Erickson, *Offices and Courthouse Complex*, Vancouver, B.C., Canada, 1979 (1974–79)
Left: aerial view of first phase

Decade 1980

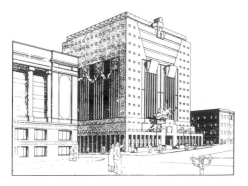

Michael Graves, *sketch for Public Service Building*, Portland, Oregon, USA; an early 1980s excursion into post-Modernism

Bart Prince, *Own House*, Albuquerque, New Mexico, USA, 1980 (1979–80)

Miguel A. Roca, *Arms Square*, Cordoba, Argentina, 1980. Pedestrianization of the city's historical core

The decade of the 1980s was obsessed with fads and fashions. At the beginning of the decade architects were speaking positively about a new 'Post-Modernism'. It gradually took hold during the Modern Movement's menopause. The new fashion took over as a way of designing in architectural schools and results were soon to be seen in practice. It created a new buoyancy. Initially Post-Modernism looked hopeful; eventually it induced boredom, proving to be little more than a fashionable mood and lacking in any real substance. Perhaps it failed because it wanted to change the direction of history? Its advocates had judged the earlier Modern Movement dead. This view was based more on the foibles and failures of Modernism's fellow-travellers rather than on the value (often excellent) of the buildings that had been created. In other words, Modernism was debunked for propaganda reasons. But what was to replace it? History, decoration, applied art were to be part of the new vocabulary. Soon new designs appeared. It proved all too easy to plagiarise these few examples created in a new architectural hyper-style. They certainly made an instant impact. Post-Modernism, however, created a confusion of aims and many architects soon became obsessed with analogy, ornamentation and pastiche. It led to weird distortions and bizarre displacements and eventually, it would seem, to the idealisation of an amalgamated 'historio-graphical' collage. It became ever more academic and pedantic in its intentions, largely for its own sake. One aspect of this fashionable style was soon renamed 'Post-Modern Classical'. It too has proved lifeless.

Post-Modernism was clearly an intellectual hoax but a large number of talented and creative architects fell for it. As a component in the transformation of ideas from the revisionist Modernism of the 1960s to the hedonistic pluralities of the 1970s, PoMo designs did not achieve the special place they were expected to find among architects and designers. Some architects, such as the British designer and urbanist Terry Farrell, with a certain lightness of touch and a sense of fun, managed to raise the tendency above the average by witty renovations like 'TV-AM', a national media fodder company whose breakfast shows were symbolised by egg-in-cup finials on a converted garage building. But Michael Graves's swags and colour scheme for the exterior of the Public Service Building in Portland, Oregon, USA – one of the key examples of Post-Modern design – somehow failed to live up to the hype it generated as a competition-winning project; its final appearance resembled a decorated biscuit tin. However, it fitted snugly into Portland's urban street grid pattern and as a piece of new urban architecture looks particularly interesting. Portland was, momentarily at least, on the world architecture map, basking in the reflected glory, too, of those consistently high-standard contemporary works of architecture it possessed by Belluschi, SOM and Halprin.

The architect-planner Lawrence Halprin is not introduced here in any way as a parenthetical figure but as one whose own participatory and interventionist architecture has consistently proved effective. He was one of the first designers to show that even in such an ambitiously capitalistic society as the United States the involvement in architecture of the community by means of landscape and town-planning projects could be a most effective means of achieving good results. Halfway through the decade Halprin was invited, with a number of other American and European architects, including Johansson, Hollein, Piano, Lasdun, Rogers, Erskine and others, to tackle a different kind of architectural problem, the renovation, rescue, recycling, refurbishment, transformation, revitalisation – anyone of these words might do – of a canonical monument of modern architecture. In the processes of change that accompany modern mass-production manufacturing industries the Fiat Company in Turin had moved into a new type of flat-floor serial production for their cars and found new premises. As a result one of the biggest and most exciting of Modern Movement buildings was up for grabs, or demolition. The Fiat factory, Lingotto, designed by Dr Matte Trucco in 1923, with its famous test-track roof, was larger than Versailles. How could it be re-deployed? Could it be saved? If so, for what? It became the subject of an imaginative international feasibility competition sponsored by Fiat with a programme directed by Bruno Zevi. This programme led to the creation of a new affectionate and romantic mood directed towards new uses for significant modern buildings such as this one.

By the end of the decade a new group of conservationists was established in Eindhoven to document the 'monuments and sites' of the Modern Movement, helping to bring into line the continuity of the ideas and the projects that Modernism itself had sought in the 1920s. DOCOMOMO was inaugurated in Eindhoven in September 1990 although mooted a year before.

The 1980s also saw the emergence of a whole new critical attitude to architecture. This helped create a much greater general awareness of disparate critical issues, from the authentic bases of regional architecture to a wide and lively international debate on Modernism, Post-Modernism and the so-called 'New Classicism', although the latter proved neither new nor, for that matter, very Classical. It also

Right: Clorinda Testa, *National Library*, Buenos Aires, Argentina; still incomplete in the 1980s

Below: The controversial 'traditional' design for the *Bhong Mosque* by R. G. Mahammad (Karachi), 1982, that received an AKAA in 1986

Above: Terry Farrell, *Clifton Nursery's temporary greenhouse*, Paddington, London, c.1985; an ingenious short-life building

Left: William Lim Associates (Mok Wei Wei, project architect), *Tampines North Community Centre*, Singapore, 1983. A witty, highly coloured and popular building set in a high-density housing estate

Above: K. Yeang and Hamzah, *IBM Tower*, Kuala Lumpur, Malaysia, *c*.1988; an example of the local 'Tropical Skyscraper' with green planters to exterior
Right: Glen Murcutt, *model of proposed Mineral and Mining Museum*, Broken Hill, Australia, c.1988

Below: A return to nature: sketches for a tree cathedral by Konrad Chmielewski, *c.*1988

Right: HRH The Prince of Wales *et al*, 'A Vision of Britain' exhibition at the Victoria and Albert Museum, London, 1989. Architects: RMJM London Ltd

led, through the research and critical abilities of a number of architectural historians and writers (particularly those from the United States, Britain, Italy, France and Germany), to a thorough reassessment of modern architectural achievements and principles. In addition, a large number of new biographical assessments and critical analyses of architects' work, both major and minor, were published. The value of such work can be seen in Boyd White's detailed work on Bruno Taut and the Activists, Andrew Saint's study of British post-war school building, DeLong on Goff and Francesco Dal Co's painstaking study of the work of Carlo Scarpa.

Architectural periodicals and academic journals also had a particularly important part to play in this critical reassessment and older, well-established publications were supplemented by a whole new series of journals and a shoal of desk-top publications. All of this contributed to an enormous information explosion. The main instigator of Post-Modernism was Charles Jencks whose books had broken all previously known publishing records for works on architecture. But even Jencks was usurped when the Prince of Wales brought out his *A Vision of Britain* which sold some 100,000 copies in less than three months. His rambling, chauvinistic text set out ten new architectural principles, the Prince's personal code of good design. It met with a mixed reception and has been largely ignored by practising architects. In terms of the international debate on architecture it seems to have shed little light on current issues. Its relevance, apart from the good commonsense it enshrined

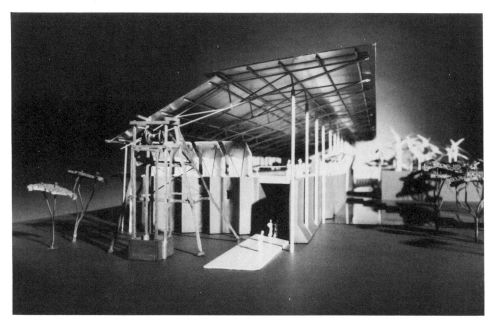

about certain civic issues, will perhaps be judged in the way it brought the whole public debate (and interest) in architecture to a head in Britain and elsewhere. Meanwhile, for architects themselves the indefatigable doyen of American architecture Philip Johnson was once again on the scene, this time associated with reflections on the Structuralist notions of Jacques Derrida and his so-called 'Deconstructionist' position.

By the end of the decade there were clear signs of a wide variety of new attitudes and positions being adopted. Many of these represented a growing concern and respect for the natural world. This was reflected in a reassessment and re-establishment of the so-called organic strain in modern architecture, a further clear indication that the ideas of the PoMo – as they were called – had proved far less fruitful than had been originally imagined and that the continuity of the creative impulse of Modernism was still very much alive albeit in modified forms.

From the current vantage point it would seem that a decade before the new millennium we have come full circle. The architecture of the twentieth century is the architecture of modernity, of the international Modern Movement. That movement was never merely a stylistic one. It grew up as part and parcel of the sensibility of an age which – in its most creative moments at least – was optimistically concerned with innovation, with science and experiment, social progress and personal well-being, as well as artistic endeavour.

Above: I. M. Pei, Cobb and Partners, *Bank of China*, Hong Kong, 1989–

Left: Ralph Erskine, *'Ark' office project* for Ake Larsen, Hammersmith, London, 1991 (1989–91)
Below left: SOM *et al*, proposals for the development of London's Canary Wharf, 1980–90s; the Fall Central building is by Cesar Pelli
Below: Martorell, Bohigas, *Mackay Olympic Village complex and waterside developments*, Barcelona, Spain, 1985–

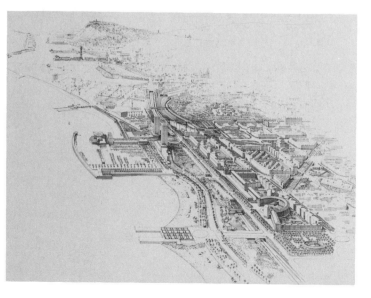

1980

Aldo van Eyck *et al. Humbertus House*, Home for Single Parents and their Children, Plantage Middenlaan, Amsterdam, The Netherlands. 1980 (1976–80)
Right and right below: two general views of the House

Gustav Peichl. *Extension to the Radio House*, Vienna, Austria. 1980 (1979–80)
Below: detail of the extension facade with its glass block walls
Bottom left: general view of the *Funkhaus* extension
Bottom right: library and archive

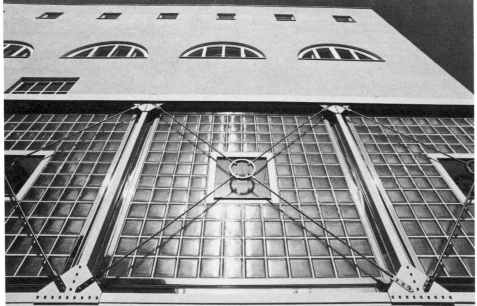

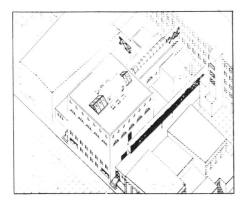

Helmut Jahn. *Xerox Center*, Chicago, Ill, USA. 1980 (1977–80)
Right: the 45-storey Xerox Center rises dramatically from its city lot on the S. Dearborn and W. Monroe corner
Below: roof-top view with ground level plan beneath

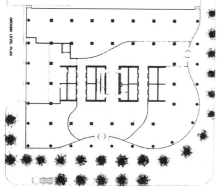

Van Eyck's work lies in line with that important tradition of humanitarian modernism central to 20th century Dutch architecture. The 6-storey Humbertus House cannot be viewed in isolation, although its social success is clearly a result of the way its particular design was carried out. It is concerned with the spirit and the establishment of a comfortable scale for a building of this type and size – an open 'home' for single parents and their children – with the creation of a non-stressful environment, in a block that seems to say 'house'. Like so many of Van Eyck's schemes, it was a co-operative effort, with contributions from Hannie van Eyck and Theo Bosch in particular.

Gustav Peichl's extension to the Radio House in Vienna can be seen as a marked contrast to his other high tech and most original work. Indeed, it had to be. He was extending a building designed by his own teacher. It is a remarkably well-controlled exercise in conservation, which sympathetically fuses old with new elements that less overtly pursue technological ends.

The sleek Xerox Center by Murphy/Jahn is a fine addition to the Chicago skyline. A typical speculative office development it is situated on a site along Dearborn-Vark. Its sleek exterior contrasts with earlier craggy traditional skyscrapers but 'fits in' with the more recent neighbouring examples, although its taut curving aluminium and glass facade is a break with the rectangular 'freestanding tower' idea much liked by Chicago designers. It has an area of 880,000 sq ft.

1980

Domenig's quite extraordinary six-storey bashed-in façade of the *Zentralsparkasse* on the Favoriten was designed for a seemingly conventional branch banking operation. It is, of course, a defiant gesture, a slap in the face of the prosaic solution. Its Neo-Expressionist – even bizarre – metallic forms are wild and riotous yet underpinned by a determined rational seriousness that brings character and chaotic goodwill to a rather dull commercial area in the city. At the rear a great glass roof tumbles over into a small courtyard.

Günter Domenig, *Savings Bank*, Favoriten, Vienna, Austria, 1980 (1975–80)
Right: the Favoriten façade
Below: section
Bottom left and right: details of interior of the Savings Bank

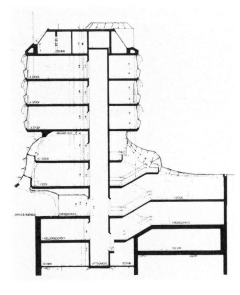

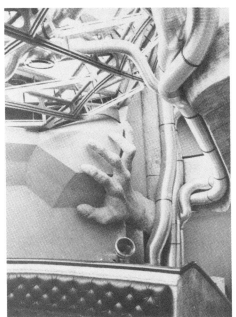

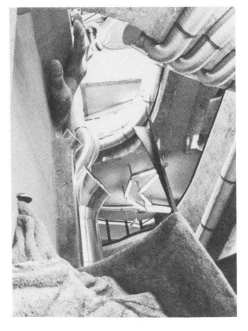

Philip Johnson and John Burgee, *Garden Grove Community Church*, Garden Grove, Los Angeles, Calif., USA, 1980 (1978–80)
Right: the glazed interior of the 'Crystal Cathedral' in use with the sole preacher to the right
Below: the large doors of the church opened up like an airship hangar
Centre: entrance elevation
Bottom: section and plan

Described as the world's first drive-in church, this spectacular, strongly Expressionistic and totally glass environmental building attempts to tie a religious experience to the transparency of nature. Philip Johnson, its architect, claims that he has designed 'a perfectly sensible church', as client-preacher Schuller believes that 'God is in the sky'! Criticised at the time of opening for offering a view of parked cars, Johnson perfunctorily replied that as people live in their cars all day long why should they be ashamed of them, and queried, 'is God not in the car?' The original plan is basically a 4-pointed star, some 406ft by 200ft, reaching up to 128ft at its apex and thus bigger than Notre Dame in Paris. It is constructed with a triodetic steel frame, which serves as a gigantic chimney to provide natural cooling. The chancel, clad in white marble, can accommodate up to 3,000 people. The glass is reflective, allowing only 8 per cent of light and heat to penetrate and giving an atmosphere that has been described as subaqueous.

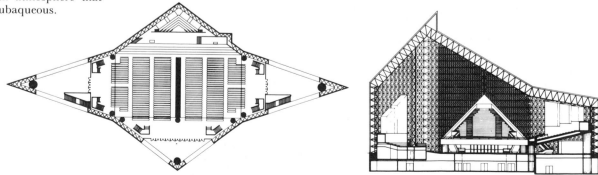

1980/81

Denys Lasdun, Peter Softley and Partners, *European Investment Bank*, Luxembourg, 1981 (1979–81)
Right: entrance front of the EIB

Michael Hopkins and Partners, *Schlumberger Centre*, Madingly Road, Cambridge, UK, 1981 (1979–81)
Below: the research laboratory in the Cambridgeshire cow field, with night view below

The European Investment Bank (ETB) stands among a rather undistinguished group of Euro-bureaucratic institutional buildings on the Kirchberg Plateau just outside Luxembourg city centre. Its precipitous clifftop site provides a pleasant foil to the strict geometrical arrangement of Lasdun's fine and sturdy cruciform-shaped plan. Low-lying wings emphasize the building's relationship to the site building up to an impressive diagonally angled entrance hall. This focal hall gives a sense of direction to the whole complex, which is further unified by the high-quality finishes of the precast concrete clad layers.

The Hopkins single-storey Schlumberger Research Laboratories are situated in the flat Bedford Plain outside Cambridge City near Madingly. They resemble a three-tent

circus complex that sits comfortably amidst its vertical masts and tension wires in a semi-rural setting. Indeed, it is an attractive and exciting addition to a countryside dominated by much heavier structures and a lesson for every conservationist to note that newness can also be a virtue. Unfortunately the mindless accumulations and accretions that often accompany such developments have also occurred here, and even an architect as good as Hopkins has not dealt very expertly with the ubiquitous car park.

Ever resourceful in design terms, Peichl's design for ORF (Radio Station Eisenstadt) (his sixth) is clearly still one of a family of such buildings but now grown more distinctive, more outgoing and innovative. The symbolism (perhaps the playfulness?) has increased, and Eisenstadt has become – with its conical features – a white and silver symbol of the communications age. Yet its basic iconography is still derived from 'the machine' and the various Soviet Constructivist schemes of the early twenties.

This two-storey semi-circular community centre is one of Team Zoo's most popular public buildings. It is complex and seeks to operate at many levels of interest, employing local and regional metaphors and symbols yet retaining its place within the continuity of modern ideas. It houses an auditorium, lecture and conference halls, all of which are served from the crescent shaped concrete colonnade that also works as an emphatic entrance porch adjacent to the old town hall building.

Team Zoo (Koichi Otake), Shinshukan Community Centre, Miyashiro, Japan, 1981
Left: a sense of fragmentation is apparent in Team Zoo's community building

Gustav Peichl, *ORF-Radio and TV Studios*, Eisenstadt, Austria, 1972 (1971–72).
Top: aerial view of the ORF Studios
Middle: entrance roadway to administrative offices
Right: the roof area of the studios

1981/82

The historical interests of Post-Modernist architects like Ricardo Bofill and Peter Hodgkinson of *Taller d'Arquitectura* (or 'Workshop' for Architects) were prominent at the turn of the 1980s decade. The idea of relating urban landscape planning to the exigencies of new town expansionist housing developments was a new one. So was the elementary idea of relating concrete mass-production techniques to pseudo-Classical detailing on a grand scale! 'Culture' – and French Culture at that (from an Anglo/Spanish practice) – provided the source for a scheme focused on a huge new artificial lake that incorporates a modern pastiche of a pier based on Chenonceaux Château, in bare, spartan concrete panels with tiny window openings and called *Le Viaduc*. It links to a duller, dense urban housing courtyard complex, creating a scenario of order and monumentality.

Ricardo Bofill and the Taller d' Arquitectura. *Les Arcades du Lac and Le Viaduc*, St. Quentin-en-Yvelines, France, 1981 (1978–81)
Above: the stark concrete exterior of the Viaduc on a damp day
Centre left: looking from the new artificial lake to the new housing
Bottom: views of the 5-storey 'finger' bridge

Mario Botta. *Single family house*, Stabio, Ticino, Switzerland, 1982 (1981–82)
Left: the circular shaped brick house in the countryside
Centre left: the entrance staircase
Below: main entrance elevation

Botta's small, single family 'Round House' is a beautifully simple architectural statement. It achieves a formal brilliance of expression, a fact that often eludes other architects working out their designs with circular plans. Mario Botta knows his geometry well and readily acknowledges in his use of form the influence of one of his mentors, Louis I. Kahn, on work such as this. This cylindrical brick-built house has two levels and is in complete contrast to the standard countryside dwellings of this small town in which it resides – to the extent of making it look as if all the other previous buildings have been misplaced!

1982

Falké Barmou (Master Mason), *The Yaama Mosque*,
Tahoua, Niger, 1982 (1962–82)
Right: the new Mosque serves a widespread community
Below: interior of Mosque

Hans Hollein, *Schullin Jewellery Shop*, Vienna, Austria,
1982 (1981–82)
Bottom: the Schullin shop interior

The introduction of the Aga Khan Award
for Architecture in 1976 brought worldwide
notice to a procedure that seeks to find a
new, rich seam of excellent architectural
designs specifically related to the Islamic
world. The Awards were valued at £250,000
in 1980 when the first prizes were made.
Every three years each award involves an
elaborate selection process that has brought
to the surface unique buildings and community projects such as the Yaama Mosque
in Niger. It would probably not have been
widely noticed without its 1986 Award. It is
a remarkable structure, noteworthy for its
innovative approach to the use of traditional
materials and building techniques. It uses
sun-dried mud brick and wood. Its simple
volumes and external masses were described
by the AKAA jury as 'breathtaking'. The
building, which took so long to build, is the
focus of village life in the whole Sahel
Region.

A small compact, keyhole of a shop in the
busy central tourist/shopping area of
Vienna, the Schullin shop is typical of
Hollein's meticulous attitude to design.
There are other shops by him, but in this
one the strength of his work is to be found
in its theatrical effects, in detailing that is as
precisely facetted as any of the jewellery on
display and analogous to it.

A neat machine box for modern research
and manufacture may be a way of describing Richard Rogers's colourful hi-tech shed

Richard Rogers and Partners, *INMOS Research Centre*, Monmouth, Gwent, UK, 1982 (1981–82)
Above: Hi-tech in the Welsh countryside
Centre left: corner supports detail, entrance side
Left: the centre access corridor
Below left: rear elevation

Philip Johnson and John Burgee, *The AT&T Building*, New York, NY, USA, 1982 (1978–82)
Below: architects' original design sketch showing full frontal view of building

in South Wales for the government company Inmos. As tight as a chain-link fence, this symmetrical building, the main entrance and corridor of which line up to provide a main service core, provides a series of research laboratory spaces on each side. The whole metal roof structure is suspended from structural mast supports.

The adoption of a broken – or Chippendale – pediment by Johnson for his widely published and controversial skyscraper in New York brought the stylistic arguments in architecture at the time to a head. Here was an approved Modernist playing with

the styles, and in New York where he had worked with Mies van der Rohe on Seagram. It was an astute move on Johnson's part. This maverick designer brought the architecture debate centre-stage and far beyond the arrogantly hyped-up East Coast *mafia*. The building's profile was one thing (which, incidentally, can hardly be viewed from the streets nearby and therefore really was a rooftop gesture); the other aspects of traditional 'newness' included heavy masonry wall construction and a return to monumental, even symmetrical, entrances and lobbies.

1982

Drawing on earlier urban housing models, Rewell's Asian Games Village in New Delhi used a network of streets and squares with vehicular access at either end of the site. Its morphology resembles a traditional village, with cubic solids and voids that are characteristic of the Indian urban fabric (compare with cities such as Jaisalmer and Old Delhi). They offer shade and yet remain vitally alive to the pressures and pleasures of the people who live there. Entrance gateways with linked upper terraces punctuate the sequence of courtyard and garden spaces.

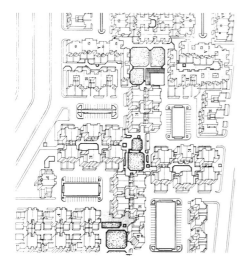

Raj Rewell, *Asian (Olympic) Games Village*, New Delhi, India, 1982 (1980–82)
Top: the compact morphology of the village reflects earlier Indian settlements
Centre and right: general views of the village
Above: a section of the planned layout

Hollein's informal and artificially landscaped Museum Abteiberg at Mönchen-Gladbach was a surprising departure by an architect whose work had hitherto tended towards organizational preciseness, even a continuation, of the geometrical framework of the Viennese school. The problems set by the museum offered scope for a totally different approach, which brought out an exciting combination of disparate elements, including large cubic volumes of museum space and an organic architectural treatment that never lost sight of the problem of 'artistic' display and the stimulation of visual interest. If, still after all the years of work entailed in its development, it remained less coherent than it should have, it has had wide repercussions throughout the world on museum design and layout.

Hans Hollein, *Abteiburg Museum*, Mönchen-Gladbach, Germany, 1982 (1972–82)
Top right: a night view towards the Museum's pavilion
Right: the sculptural forms of the well-lit interior
Above: the parts of the Museum are together on a cultural Acropolis

Michael Graves, *Public Service Building*, Portland, Ore., USA, 1983 (1980–83)
Left: the PSB nearing completion
Below: architect's original model

Benjamin Thompson and Associates, *Fulton Market*, New York, NY, USA, 1983 (1981–83)
Right: Fulton Market renewed
Bottom: the renovated building on the old quayside

The Public Service Building (PSB) in Portland, Oregon, was one of the most talked about competition successes in North America in the late 1970s. In 1983 it became a somewhat watered down reality but not without the residual virtues extolled by Philip Johnson and others that it heralded the reawakening in America of the urban block. It certainly fulfilled its block function, creating a boundary condition on all sides as neatly as a drawer in a filing cabinet. It also brought back the solid wall in a city which, through the work of Belluschi a few decades earlier, had pioneered the seamless glass curtain envelope. But there was also a stylistic dimension here that had no precedent in this city except perhaps in the remnants of the French-inspired Art Deco, and this was advertized as being of a Post-Modernist tendency, although it smacked of the Beaux-Arts just as much. Swags and flags were to enliven the proceedings in a three dimensional sense, as were pastel shapes and mini-windows. It was undoubtedly an exciting moment but soon faded as reality took over the hype and as paint replaced what was thought by many to be marble and Viennese-type materials. It was, after all, a public service building, and economy rather than manners took charge.

After their success a decade ago with the Faneuil Building in Boston and Quincy Market, Benjamin Thompson and Associates turned their attention to 'rebuilding' an old historic seaport area in 1983 in New York. The new Fulton Market is a 3-storey brick and granite structure that reflects the earlier nineteenth-century markets. It is the focus of a multi-block restoration and master-plan development on this East River site, giving some 50,000 sq ft of space and a whole new pedestrian area. Internally the four-square traditionally expressed building has open light wells throughout the retail spaces, and the steel columns combined with slate and glazed tiles give it an industrial feel.

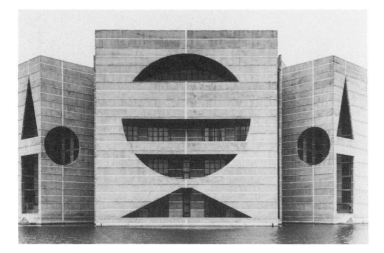

Louis I. Kahn, *The Parliamentary Building Complex (Sher-E-Bangla Nagar Capitol)*, Dacca, Bangladesh, 1983 (1967–83)
Above: detail of the masonry walls rising from the surrounding water pools
Far right: interior of Assembly
Right: general view of the complex
Below: internal street and ground-floor plan

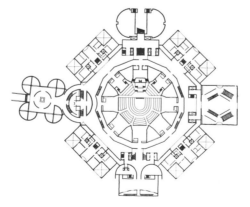

Louis I. Kahn's most ambitious and grand concept was for the Parliamentary complex at Dacca finished many years after his untimely death of a heart attack in New York in 1974 when returning from a site visit to Bangladesh. Profoundly influenced by his love for Roman architecture, he planted in this poverty-ridden country (it became Bangladesh in 1971) a touch of its spatial grandeur. The complex was commissioned in 1962 and consists of simply presented massive curved and square forms wrapped around a central circular one to create a sun-protected environment and a monumental build-up of complicated and suggested – if not fully apprehended – shapes. The great masonry walls of the National Parliament, which itself is a single-storey space, seal it off from the surrounding corridors and ancillary functional accommodation, which in turn is cut into to provide stark shaped circles, triangular tree-form and eyebrow openings. The whole complex consists of two citadels arranged at each end of an axis with the Citadel of Institutions at the northern end and the Citadel of Assembly at the south end. The Assembly was given an Aga Khan Award in 1989.

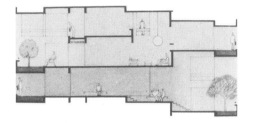

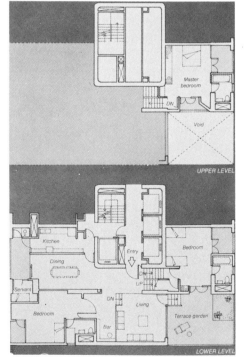

Charles Correa, *Kanchanjunga Apartment Block*, Bombay, India 1983 (1970–83)
Top and left: general view of the apartment block and section
Left: detail of the flank wall and garden recesses
Above: the double height plan

Gordon Bunshaft of SOM, *National Commercial Bank HQ*, Jeddah, Saudi Arabia, 1983 (1981–3)
Above: interior of board room
Right: the tall block in foreground with the smaller offices to the right

These tall apartments draw on the traditional principles of Indian bungalow design. The Kanchanjunga development, which took more than a decade to realize, consists of 32 luxury apartments with a duplex section that basically interlocks 3–4 bedroom units. A series of verandahs, studies, dressing rooms and external living spaces create a kind of high rise 'verandah' zone. The east and west façades of each apartment are protected by the verandahs and bathrooms, and there is continuous cross-ventilation throughout.

Bunshaft's high-rise, high-density AKAA-winning prestige corporate office block for the National Commercial Bank makes a series of oblique, 'abstract' references to the Islamic tradition on a grand, fortress scale. It combines the anonymity of plain exteriors with a conspicuous internal arrangement which, in this case, presents a great rectangular hole cut across a triangular plan in the middle of the block for controlling sun, air circulation and protection as well as aesthetics.

Glen Murcutt, *Artist's House and Studios*, N. Sydney, Australia, 1983 (1982–3)
Top right: the open terraced end of the house
Above top: detail of cladding with roof
Above: the side elevation with terrace

Originally designed as a weekend house and situated in the bush countryside of North Sydney, this artists' house is now used for permanent living, with the two artists it was designed for having built their own studios in the grounds. Today, with the ever-increasing expansion of Sydney, there are many new houses and roads nearby, although the sense of isolation and uniqueness has diminished little. The house is situated on a rugged, rock-strewn site amidst the local vegetation. The house is a

long, low, single-storey column-and-beam platform house entirely constructed in steel with a corrugated curved roof and timber terraces. It sits poised above the undulating ground level on its six I-section columns protected from bush fires with complete coverage from an external sprinkler system. The house was designed, according to the architect, to provide the minimum interference with nature and the existing site. A small open-sided platform bridge runs from the car parking enclosure to the house itself, another precarious reminder of the vulnerability of living in the countryside. Adjacent to the house are two commercial farmyard Dutch barns purchased straight out of a catalogue but ingeniously converted into spacious and waterproof artists' studios.

Farrell's TV-am is really a refurbishment of an old garage building in an attractive if somewhat neglected backwater of north London, although one would hardly detect that from current appearances. It is one of the few flamboyant examples of the fashionable craze for what was euphemistically called Post-Modernism that came off (Lim's converted Church Cinema in Singapore was another). It succeeds where others failed, in my view, because it brought life, colour and humour to an otherwise witless neighbourhood and thus through the regenerative power of the

Terry Farrell and Partners, *TV-am*, Camden Lock, London, UK, 1983 (1981–83)
Above: general view of entrance elevation

O. M. Ungers, *German Architecture Museum*, Frankfurt am Main, Germany, 1983 (1981–83)
Above: the main façade of the 'double villa' museum
Right: plan and axonometric

ever-optimistic entertainment industry – who were the clients for this venture – it put the canal it faces on a new channel. TV-am is, as its name implies, a 'Breakfast' serial and originally the wit and humour ran within the legitimate boundaries of PoMo realism to egg cup finials and lacey gates. Inside the dramatic elements were further hyped up with Egyptian sets and full-blown trees set beside the latest media technology.

The old house in which Ungers's new German Architecture Museum is situated has little more than nostalgic value but, the architect claimed, 'this value justifies preserving the house'. A relatively small development, the new part of the museum was inserted within the existing house walls, the result of which produced a new museum within a house. The visitor is taken through a variety of inter-related spaces, which the architect sees as having special significance as paradigms for the city.

The new East Wing extension to the National Gallery, Washington DC sits on a difficult triangular site. However, Pei was able to exploit this feature, giving his wedge-shaped building a marvellous sense of presence and sculptural purpose. A post-tensioned concrete structure, this extension to Washington's major art gallery follows the triangular shape of its Fourth Avenue site. It is situated on an 8.8 acre site with some 110,000 sq ft of main exhibition space and 16,000 sq ft of temporary exhibition areas. This building helped to shape attitudes to museum building throughout the United States in the 1970s and later. It provides fine public facilities at a lower level which presage the same architect's work at the Louvre, Paris many years later.

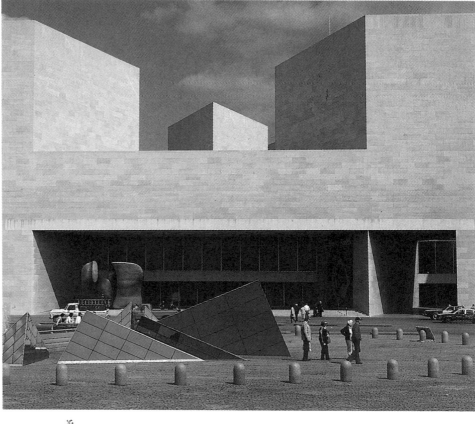

I. M. Pei and Partners, *National Gallery of Art*, East Building, Washington DC, USA, 1983 (1981–83)
Right: main entrance

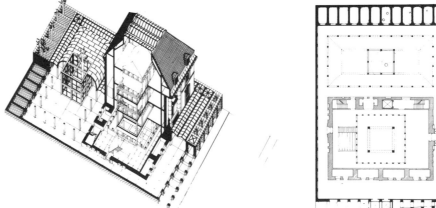

1984

Henning Larsen, *Ministry of Foreign Affairs*, Riyadh, Saudi Arabia, 1984 (1981–84)
Right: detail of façade
Centre: general view
Below: interior street; site plan and section

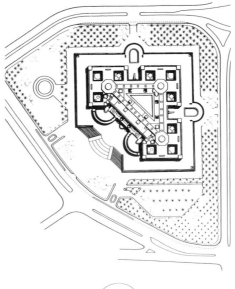

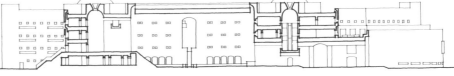

The Ministry of Foreign Affairs reflects Islamic culture as seen by a western architect. Henning Larsen's intentions are embodied in the relation between the fortresslike exterior, the somewhat anonymous facades and the vast open interior arrangements. The utility, orientation and closeness of the interior is in strong contrast to the outside. It is based on the characteristic ideas of the Islamic house. Internally the Islamic concept of urban architecture has been adopted in order to integrate the freestanding building into its local context, producing a series of coherent spatial impressions in a clearly readable building complex. The triangular, four-storey enclosed lobby is characterized by massive enclosing walls, which stretch vertically beyond the level of the 'floating' ceiling. Horizontally their thickness is visually

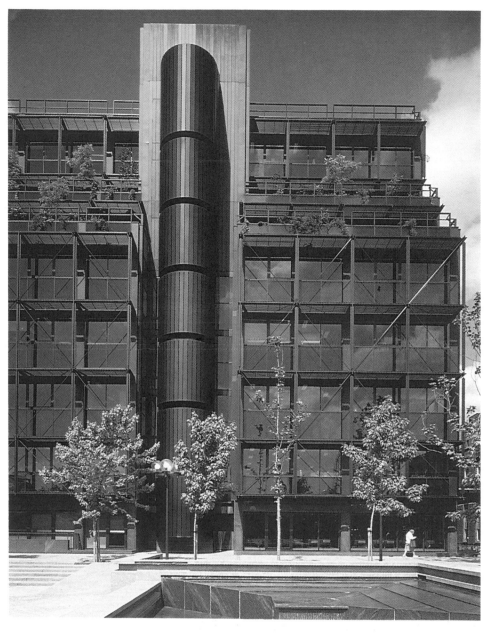

emphasized through the pierced oblique openings. Huge doors lead to the top-lit circulation spine of the complex, which has been inspired by the Islamic bazaars. At the junctions of the isosceles triangle formed by the three streets, where the octagonal light towers are situated, 'twin vistas' further enhance the identity of the interior. Three octagonal spaces form the cores of the individual blocks with flexible office areas grouped around nine courtyards. These offices receive controlled daylight through double outer walls and trellises.

At Broadgate, No 1 Finsbury Avenue set the aesthetic standard, almost single-handedly, for a new breed of speculative office buildings. Its elegant, open, well-lit atrium brought an unusual element in speculative offices but provided the building with, as it were, an internal series of façades. Offices were grouped around the internal glazed courtyard, the steel and glass roof over which brought daylight to all these users. High ceilings in these offices were also an unusual and welcome feature and were a direct response to the new requirements of raised floors for the highly sophisticated and complicated services required by the new technology. Suspended ceilings contain the ductwork for the lighting and air condition-ing. The dark metallic appearance of the exterior of the building with its sunbreakers and diagonal rods provides a telling contrast to the well-lit and light appearance of the interior. The façades have been landscaped with trees and shrubs in a careful and well thought out manner.

Merida was one of the most important Roman cities in Spain at the end of the Empire. This new simply-shaped but mas-sive masonry Museum has been erected over a portion of the Roman remains, thus becoming itself a kind of cultural maus-oleum. Almost a 'Roman' building itself, it does not stoop to pastiche but achieves a remarkable unity and a strong sense of what a modern museum should be like, with a sombre exterior and a well-lit, spacious and atmospheric interior. Light filters through unobtrusive skylights revealing nuances in the white marble sculpture highlighted by the plain Roman brick surfaced walls.

Arup Associates, *Offices*, No 1 Finsbury Avenue, London, UK, 1984 (1982–84)
Above: main street elevation
Above left: section and atrium roof

Rafael Moneo, *National Museum of Roman Art*, Merida, Spain, 1984 (1980–84)
Below: exterior and interior views

1984

Philip Cox, Richardson and Taylor, *Yulara Tourist Village*, Uluru Park, Ayers Rock, NT, Australia, 1984 (1982–84)
Right and below: general views across the village and towards Australia's navel, Ayers Rock
Bottom right: the auditorium
Bottom centre: site plan and section

Situated in the shadow of that amazing red geological lump, Ayers Rock, which lies at the great 'navel' of Australia, this tented tourist resort looks from the air like a fly on the earth's crust. Closer to, it appears a pleasant oasis for Australia's most popular attaction. It is a simple solar energy system. It incorporates a major Inter-Continenal Hotel surrounded by a number of pleasant water features, a further downmarket hotel and various types of tourist accommodation and an open-air performance space. There is nothing particularly Australian about its elegant lightweight, hi-tech steel support structures or the pleasantly coloured fabric awnings, although it makes a lot of sense to build in this manner in this area. The magic it creates in this rather inhospitable environment makes up for a lack of regional emphasis in a place in which any building can only pale into insignificance in the presence of nature's incredible pulling power.

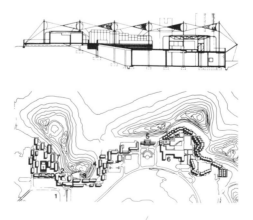

382

Fumihiko Maki, *Gymnasium*, Fujisaiwa, Japan, 1984 (1980–84)
Right: interior of the main arena
Centre: the main arena in the distance with training gym and entrance in foreground
Bottom left: interior of gym
Bottom right: rear elevation

Maki's Fujisaiwa multi-purpose Gymnasium is one of the most dramatic buildings in Modern Japan. It has often been used as an illustration of the state of the art in modern Japanese architecture. Basically, it is a huge public sports hall with smaller spaces for Judo and Kendo as well as changing rooms, restaurants, etc. The great roof over its main arena has an unsupported span of 80m, and is made up of a network of steel H-girders, which support a stainless steel external envelope approximately 0.4mm thick. Maki is seen as one of the main contenders for Japan's highly acclaimed crown of architecture after years of domination by Kenzo Tange. He is probably best known for his original approach to architectural form making, which he claims to relate to some of the major architectural movements in Europe including De Stijl, and the Bauhaus as well as to the formal qualities to be found in the work of Frank Lloyd Wright and Alvar Aalto. But there is another popular dimension to Maki's work, which sees it as amusing and sometimes witty, and which is related as much to

empathy as to abstraction. Of the Gymnasium he has himself said that 'many people say it looks like a helmet or a frog or a beetle or a space ship'. Maki himself denies this, arguing that the development of the form is as much a result of the processes of planning and the exigencies of construction as anything else.

1984/85

Santiago Calatrava, *Railway Station*, Zurich, Switzerland, 1984 (1983–84)
Right and below: the platform canopies

The young Spanish designer Santiago Calatrava sprang to prominence in the 1970s as an architect and engineer in the tradition of Candela and Nervi. Trained in Zurich, where he later set up practice, he has been responsible for a number of bridges and buildings such as the renovation and redevelopment of the railway stations at Lucerne and Zürich (an example which conveys his engineering capabilities). He is concerned with the repetition of invented formal elements.

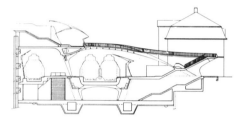

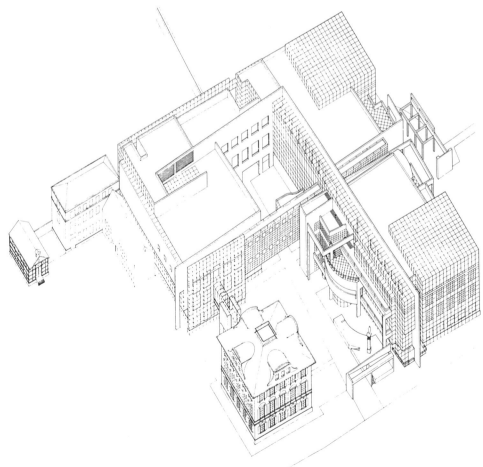

A key building that was erected in the German museum building boom in the 1980s, the Arts and Crafts Museum was also won in a competition run by the city authorities. Situated on a landscaped park site on the south bank of the Main, it provides 7,800m^2 of space. Local fire codes discouraged the use of a steel frame, so the building is in reinforced concrete with load-bearing walls. Windows are on a 110cm module. The museum also incorporates a restaurant, library, offices and an education department. In this building Meier pays tribute to the rise of Modernism before it was banished by Hitler and the Third Reich; his 'white' architecture has proved to be a cleansing force. However, it still acknowledges changes in scale and type and is not just a surface style. Here the pavilions, or departments, of the museum interact, urban elements that modify and control scale but sit on the grass.

Richard Meier, *Decorative Arts Museum*, Frankfurt am Main, Germany, 1984 (1980–84)

Won in an invited competition in 1977, Stirling and Wilford's *Staatsgalerie* at Stuttgart began construction two years later. It opened in March 1984 and proved an instant popular and architectural success at home and abroad. It is considered one of the major architectural achievements of the decade and one of the few buildings that, within its own design, provides a summary of the various architectural positions being adopted by designers at the time. It is also remarkably inventive. The main entrance to the museum is marked by a tall, blue and red painted, centrally placed steel pavilion. It is approached to front right by a staircase and to the left by a ramp dominated by oversized coloured hand-rails. A car park is situated below the main reception area, which is itself dominated by a bright green rubber floor, and this reflects in all the surrounding glazed surfaces. Glimpsed through small windows in this area, the central, scalped stone-faced rotunda can be seen. In it classical references abound. On the first floor lie the 15 top-lit and rather traditional rooms that serve as the galleries and contain some splendid examples of German and foreign art.

James Stirling and Michael Wilford, *Staatsgalerie*, Stuttgart, Germany, 1984 (1977–84)
Top: the entrance plinth to the Museum
Left: the internal sculpture court
Below: the connected gallery route

Harry Seidler and Partners, *The Hong Kong Club*, Hong Kong, 1984 (1980–84)
Right: the Hong Kong Club faces the War Memorial and an open public square
Below: the open feeling of the interior is exemplified in this staircase

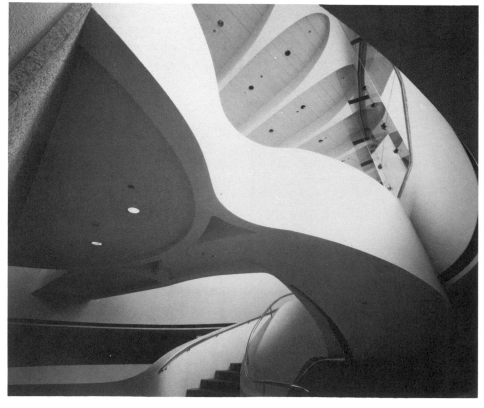

One of the oldest and most exclusive establishments on the island, the Hong Kong Club had outgrown its existing premises but not its role in this burgeoning city. It was incorporated into an inclusive 4-storey element in a new 22-storey office block in its original position on one of the most magnificent and valuable sites (adjacent to Norman Foster's Bank) overlooking the harbour. The new club podium is a spatial *tour de force* over which straddles the wide spanning T-beams (developed with P. L. Nervi) that give the exterior its distinctive wave-like appearance. Independent huge corner columns act as wind braces. Internally the building is free of columns and gloriously spatial.

A convinced Modernist, Ciriani had to fit on to a restricted site a central kitchen to serve St Antoine. In this surprisingly interesting kitchen Ciriani continues his creative exploration of themes from Le Corbusier's work. In it he develops an elaborate architectural promenade and makes the kitchen a world of spatial transparency. It has glass brick walls in the recreation space and masonry facing to the main façade in the Parisian street.

This remarkable structure in Chicago's chief business district resembles a great steel

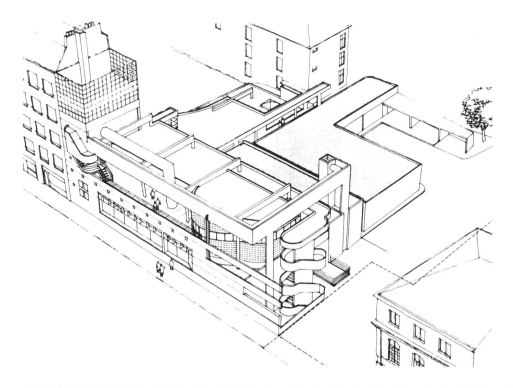

Henry Ciriani, *St. Antoine Hospital Central Kitchen*, Paris, France, 1985 (1983–85)
Left: architect's sketch
Above: external street view

and glass *vol au vent*. It is 17 storeys in height, offering up approx. 1.2 million sq ft of municipal office space plus some 150,000 sq ft of ancillary accommodation including shops and transit facilities. This Rotunda building breaks away from the grid street pattern of the North Loop. It introduces a huge, set-back concave façade on to a city lot – thus providing it with a skylit atrium, as an alternative to the regular street and plaza layout. However, it has presented enormous energy problems as its façade faces south. Setbacks divide the building into three tiers with floor areas ranging from 77,000 to 48,000 sq ft. In contrast to many other monotone buildings in Chicago, it introduces sickly pink and grey granite for the arcades. The vast atrium interior is in blue. The building houses 56 State agencies and is used by 4,600 employees. The construction is a simple structural steel frame on caisson foundations with a composite metal deck and concrete floor system.

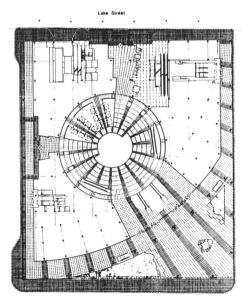

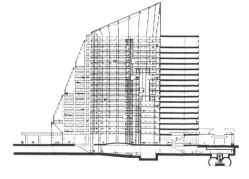

Helmut Jahn, *State of Illinois Center*, Chicago, Ill., USA, 1985 (1980–85)
Above: the building in its urban context
Bottom: section and site plan

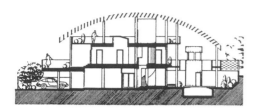

Kenneth Yeang, *'Roof Roof' House*, Selangor, Malaysia, 1986 (1985–86)
Above and right: section through house and general view

Fariburz Sahba, *The Baha'i Temple*, Delhi, India, 1987 (1975–87)
Below: the 'lotus petal' Temple rises from an impressive podium
Bottom: section

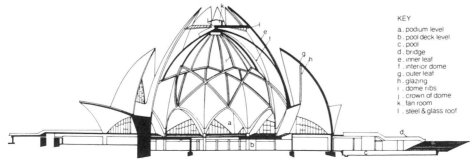

KEY
a . podium level
b . pool deck level
c . pool
d . bridge
e . inner leaf
f . interior dome
g . outer leaf
h . glazing
i . dome ribs
j . crown of dome
k . fan room
l . steel & glass roof

Yeang's small concave concrete experimental house was designed for the architect's own use. It introduces a number of filtering devices to protect the domestic accommodation from the fierce heat of the afternoon sun. It is orientated east-west to reduce solar insolation into the hot sides of the building. A swimming pool is located on the windward side over which cool breezes flow into the building under the roof house filter. The extraordinary concave roof is constructed in concrete panels. It allows for a further terrace area to the top of the two-storey dwelling.

Known as the 'Mother Temple' of the Bahá'í faith, its main hall accommodates 1,200 persons. Its architect was only 27 years old when commissioned in 1975. It is surrounded by water pools, and an ancillary building built into the pool surrounds provides a library and administrative offices. The building represents a geometric lotus flower in bloom, a motif that has a close association with all Indian religions and is considered by many the most beautiful flower in the world. The Temple itself is conceived as 'a fragile flower enshrining an idea'. The 34m high building is constructed from reinforced concrete and covers 8.22ha. The general arrangement consists of a central worship hall, a reception hall surrounded by a free standing 'outer leaf' sun protective podium, which is glazed in a series of arches. The outside walls are clad in white Greek marble.

The Hong Kong and Shanghai Bank by Norman Foster is probably the best known, and most widely publicized building of the decade, largely because it was claimed to have cost more money than any other building to erect. Notwithstanding that kind of publicity and the building's subsequent overshadowing by far inferior competitors, it remains a unique architectural achievement and a small wonder of the modern age.

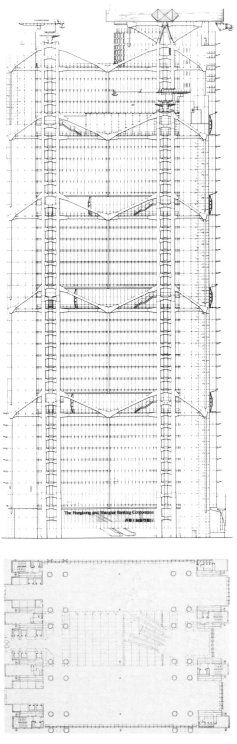

Foster Associates, *Hong Kong and Shanghai Bank*, Hong Kong, 1986 (1979–86)
Top left: the familiar Hong Kong and Shanghai Bank exterior and ground floor entrance
Left: the entrance escalator leading up to the huge atrium
Above: architect's façade drawing and Level 3 Banking Hall

Richard Rogers and Partners, *Lloyds Building*, London, UK, 1986 (1984–86)
Right: the Lloyds' City crown from the south west
Below: close up of the atrium and service towers from the south

The City of London is a most conservative place. It is full of history but tarnished by the insensitive and inept redevelopment in the confused period after the Second World War. It had not seen anything as visually exciting in its recent history as the new building, Lloyds. Perhaps not since Wren's St Paul's Cathedral and his evocative church spires has anything changed so radically the silhouette of this compact city, particularly at night. The new Lloyds is situated at the very heart of London and provides a splendid gesture to freedom in architectural terms, to expression and to originality of concept and bold intentions. The main twelve-storey structure is a simple rectangle circumvented by six service towers. Inside the main tower uninterrupted floors allow the maximum flexibility, with a central atrium and a series of concentric balconies that rise through the entire building. Twelve glazed lifts zip up and down the external face of the building complex, giving it a vital and dynamic visual presence in an area in which buildings are very private and closed in upon themselves. The building is mainly constructed from reinforced concrete with stainless steel cladding and much reflective glazing.

The 'Hysolar' Institute is devoted to research into solar energy and is part of Stuttgart University. It is an experimental building in its own right. With its stainless steel structure, strangely angled fenestration and external solar collectors, it has all the characteristics of a laboratory – which, of course, it is. But it is also a particular kind of architecture, a type that has been advocated by Behnisch in many earlier schemes

and which he often refers to as an accidental – even chaotic – but certainly cheap 'improvisational' design. Architecturally it appears to defy logic, but it possesses a rationale that allows a double use on plan with university facilities on one side and those of an independent institute on the other.

The old Gare d'Orsay was designed by Victor Laloux. It opened in 1900. In 1975 the French President Georges Pompidou directed that it should be turned into a museum, and it was re-opened in December, 1987. Its contents cover art from the second half of the nineteenth century and the early years of the twentieth century. The competition held in 1979 was won by ACT (Art Bardon, P. Colboc, J. P. Philippon) who later were joined, in 1980, by the Italian architect Gae Aulenti, who had been nominated as the winner of the second prize for the interior. The vast exhibition spaces cover some 47,000m² and the cost was estimated as 1,500m FFrs. Aulenti in her interior design built up an exhibition framework that emphasises the division between the existing and the new elements in the old railway station. Her design incorporated a museum circuit of a 'street' of artefacts. This 'stress' is flanked by temple-like galleries with Romanticism and its academic successors to one side and Manet on the other. In the attic of the building the Impressionists are displayed in the Galerie des Hauteurs.

Gunter Behnisch and Partner, *Hysolar Research Building*, Suttgart Technical University, Germany, 1987 (1986–87)
Top: the Hysolar Institute on its open site
Centre: elevation and façade detail

Gae Aulenti *et al, Musée d'Orsay*, Paris, France, 1987 (1980–87)
Left: the interior of the old station transformed into a museum of the nineteenth century

Mario Botta, *André Malraux Cultural Centre*, Chambèry, Le Bas, France, 1987 (1982–87)
Right and centre: general external views of the theatre
Bottom left: theatre auditorium

James Stirling and Michael Wilford, *Clore Building*, Tate Gallery, London, UK, 1987 (1986–87)
Bottom right: main entrance to the Clore Gallery with reflecting pool

The Chambery Theatre complex by Mario Botta links a modern architectural expression to historical forms in an area dominated formerly by military buildings just outside the city's historic core. It was won in limited competition, and Botta linked his theatre to the restored Curial barracks renovated by J-P. Fortier, part of which now serves as an entrance foyer to the 950-seat theatre itself. Again, as with so much of Botta, clear geometrical shapes dominate and the theatre and its cinema below are housed in a half-cylinder shaped block. This auditorium block then joins a rectangular shaped stage and fly tower, all unified by the horizontal striated treatment of the concrete and stonework exterior. The military medieval analogy of the area is again taken up with deep slit windows into the largely blank walls.

Michael Hopkins and Partners, *The Mound Stand*, Lords Cricket Ground, St. John's Wood, London, UK, 1987 (1985–87)
Right: view from the Mound Stand to the hallowed pitch
Centre: an attentive crowd in the new stand
Bottom right: the new street façade

Akitek Tenggara, *Chee Tong Temple*, Singapore, 1987 (1985–87)
Bottom left: the Temple interior

Stirling and Wilford's Clore Gallery, an extension to the prestigious Tate Gallery in London, houses the famous Turner Collection. It is a neat, subdued, if not modest addition to a none too distinguished academic building that gains much from its deep, cheese-cut doorway. The ground-floor area contains public lecture and reception facilities while the main galleries are situated upstairs with a connection back to the main Tate floors. The external re-entrant with the Portland stone faced entrance wall works well, as does the rusticated base. Unfortunately the same cannot be said for the fretwork or grid of coloured facing materials, which looks somewhat arbitrary.

Generally popular with the public, the rebuilt Mound Stand at Lord's, the cricket world's Mecca, by Hopkins is often cited as an example of the way in which a simple inclusive project can also improve local environmental conditions. This it has done by taking the old arched structures to the earlier stand and extending them to form a new street façade. The new stand – which retains the form of the earlier one – is itself a highly sophisticated structure, which allows for large spans to provide expansive views. It rests on six columns and is topped by a white tented ('nautical sail') roof structure that not only provides an efficient and visually exciting space but echoes the origins of village green cricket. The same architects were later commissioned to rebuild the Nursery End stand.

When the Chee Tong Temple was built at the centre of a new high-rise housing estate in Singapore, it created some controversy. Many people felt that the essence and trappings of the old Chinese temple had been lost. Others, including the architect, Soon, felt it worth experimenting with new and innovatory ideas without drawing upon the traditional trappings of older temples. The external appearance of the main temple roof is that of the more traditional temple, although internally the bright red steel frame, which incorporates a system of mirrors mounted on the rooftop, provides a dramatic element of surprise as light is reflected down on to the huge altar area with its religious images and gold leaf. The temple area is situated above a multipurpose room and hall and is approached by a formal staircase. The sequence through the temple spaces themselves is therefore directed in an entirely symmetrical order.

1987

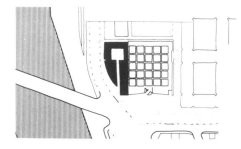

Jean Nouvel, *L'Institut du Monde Arabe*, Paris, France, 1988 (1987–88)
Top: the Institut from the Seine and site plan
Centre: view into southern courtyard and Library interior
Left: the reflected patterns from the ocular devices
Below: typical floor plan

Set on a prominent site in the central part of Paris a short distance from the Church of Notre Dame, the Arab Institute is one of the *Grands Projets* encouraged by the French President during the 1980s. It is an urban scheme of great character. It was won in competition and houses a Franco-Arabian 'World' Institute representing 19 countries. Its purpose is to foster knowledge of Arab world culture by the exchange of information on the arts, sciences and modern technologies. It incorporates some well lit exhibition areas, a museum, library, a 300-

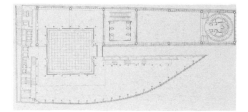

seat hall and a restaurants, as well as offices and car parking. Internally a superb feature is the glass and steel stairs and lift enclosure, which can be seen from most parts of the building. The actual building concept was a simple one and remains little changed from the original competition design. The Institute is composed of two parallel, interconnected and interrelated blocks, one curved to reflect the building's quayside context and the other rectangular and facing a large open courtyard with sculptures and a tented feature. The huge south-facing garden courtyard wall has been described as a 60m 'Venetian blind', although its appearance is more patently Islamic in decorative terms. It is, however, an ocular device of striking originality, made up of numerous and variously dimensioned metallic diaphragms set in pierced metal borders. These diaphragms operate like a camera lens to control the sun's penetration into the interior of the building. The changes to the irises are dramatically revealed internally while externally a subtle density pattern can be observed. Thus the whole effect is like a giant Islamic pierced screen, giving significance and an audacious brilliance to this remarkable building.

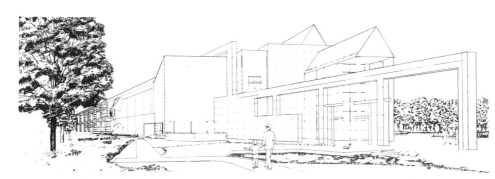

Kisho Kurokawa, *City Art Museum*, Nagoya, Japan, 1987
Left: sketch of the entrance to the Museum
Centre left: interior of lobby with sculpture by J. Borofsky
Below: SW elevation and exhibition space for outdoor events
Bottom: Calder sculpture in entrance approach

Situated on a triangular site in Shirakawa Park Kurokawa's Museum enjoys a position within a mature natural setting. Due to local regulations it had to respect the existing tree heights and the architect has taken his galleries down one floor below ground and provided two above. It runs on a north-south axis. A great undulating glass wall welcomes visitors into the well ordered sequence of exhibition galleries and open spaces. A Calder mobile occupies the entrance courtyard. Externally the building is a composition in pale and dark grey tiles set into aluminium frames to emphasize the structural subdivisions. Inside, the museum is completely white.

Ton Alberts (Alberts and Van Huut), *NMB Bank*,
Amsterdam, The Netherlands, 1988 (1983–88)
Top left: site plan and section
Top right: the main staircase
Centre: general view
Right: corner block

NMB is a German Bank, one of the three
biggest German banks. It decided to locate
its new HQ in a vast new Amsterdam
suburb in order to achieve a better balance
between organizational and technical requirements and the needs of its 2,500 staff.
Designed like a town within a building, it
provides some 50,000m² of floor space in 10
linked pavilions and towers connected by
350m of walkways. The complex also includes 4 restaurants, conference rooms, and
a small theatre. It is naturally ventilated,
constructed from prefabricated concrete
slabs and clad in hand-made bricks.
Albert's design is a rational one, based on
concepts of prefabrication and industrialization. It is a low-energy complex and, owing
to the shape of the blocks, nobody works
more than seven metres from a window.
Everything – colours, furniture, scale – takes
into account the comfort and well-being of
the workers and users.

The small design museum that fronts the more conventional factory sheds at the Vitra Company's headquarters looks as if it has been hit by a tornado and its parts transposed and rapidly re-assembled bit by bit. Its geometric, cubic, stucco-faced forms make up a tidy, facetted whole. This building is a dynamic reminder of Frank Gehry's ruthless American West Coast approach to form-making. It is a further exciting addition to a site that already has buildings by many international architects including Ando, Grimshaw and Jiricna. As with other examples of Gehry's work, the interior is a welcoming, well-controlled, smooth, curved, spacious response to the angular irregularities of the outside. In its calm spaces, chairs are suspended from the ceilings and the walls, creating a balletic impression of inanimate objects vested with a life of their own: a chaise longue here by Le Corbusier, a Jacobsen chair there, sharing the limelight with Rietveld's red, yellow and blue chair and examples by Tonet and Breuer, all set in the naturally lit interior displaying the strength of the owner's collector's choice.

Frank Gehry, *Vitra Furniture Design Museum*, Weil-am-Rhein, Gerany, 1988 (1987–88)
Top right: floor plans
Right: detail view of Museum
Left below: the Chair Museum
Bottom: the fragmented parts of the Museum seen across the surrounding countryside

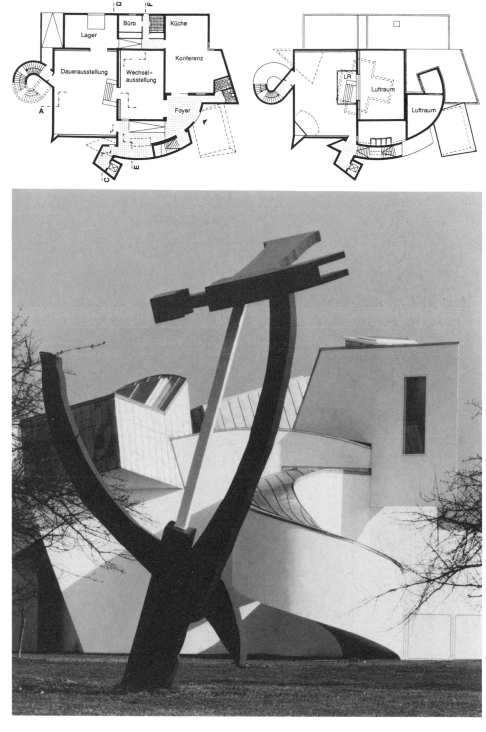

1988

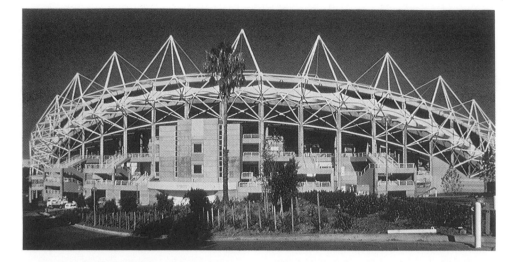

Philip Cox, Richardson and Taylor, *Sydney Football Stadium*, Sydney, Australia, 1988 (1986–88)
Right: the stadium's ribbon roof is held on a network of steel supports
Below: inside the arena
Bottom: plan and elevational perspective

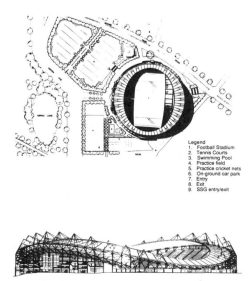

Legend
1. Football Stadium
2. Tennis Courts
3. Swimming Pool
4. Practice field
5. Practice cricket nets
6. On-ground car park
7. Entry
8. Exit
9. SSG entry/exit

Built adjacent to the world-famous Sydney Cricket Ground, this spectacular stadium accommodates all types of football at national and international level. It is described locally as the Sydney 'roller coaster' and is one of Cox's most visually exciting structures. It can hold almost 40,000 spectators. Its curved forms – developed by Arup's – are accentuated by the giant ribbon of steel sheet roof that sweeps up above the 3- or 5-storey boxed stands and then down over the lower-level terraces. The roof is supported on a series of steel trusses, which in turn carry the weight of the roof down concrete-encased stanchions. The ribbon roof itself is continuous and sweeps up over the east and west enclosure stand, dipping down over the lower terraces to the north and south of the ground. The grandstand seating, angled at 30 degrees, is supported on a 3- or 4-storey concrete substructure in which are housed the various

ground facilities including restaurant, bars, toilets and clubrooms. Adjacent to the pitch and below these structures, a concrete terraced slab of seating has been dug into the earth, the last row of which comes right up to the elegant grass playing surface. There are no barriers between spectators and sport. The huge cantilevered steel roof is supported by a series of steel trusses which transfer vertical loads downwards to the perimeter Universal Steel columns. Steel-to-steel connections were made possible throughout the project for simplicity of construction, although they have now been concrete-encased for fire-proofing purposes.

The major NSW Bicentennial project for 1988 in Sydney was the Darling Harbour redevelopment. Cox's firm produced three major structures. Amid a veritable armada of tall buildings, the small, unusual, and exciting Sydney Aquarium looks like a beached whale or some prehistoric sea

Philip Cox, Richardson and Taylor, *Darling Harbour Redevelopment and Museum Area*, Aquarium and National Maritime Museum, Exhibition Halls and Congress Centre, Sydney, Australia, 1988 (1986–88)
Left: Darling Harbour with the new Aquarium
Centre: the Aquarium under construction
Bottom: details of the construction and supports for the exhibition halls

beast, shiny and full-scaled. It differs from all the other buildings in that it was a privately funded building and focuses on an activity below the water rather than on top! In fact it is part building, part barge. It has three sections: an earthbound display; an exhibition and visitor centre; and a restaurant. To its north are three floating and semi-submerged freely moving tanks in which an Oceanarium is situated, allowing spectators to walk literally through walkways surrounded by water and varieties of sea life. The third structure, the Maritime Service Board Wharf No 10, also to the north, houses the support services and labs. The tanks, looking like small barges or ships moored to the wharf are covered by fabric roofs hung from masts and steel cables, all of which further extend in terms of maritime metaphors. The sensation of walking in a boat rather than on hard land is an important feature of this enterprising exhibition.

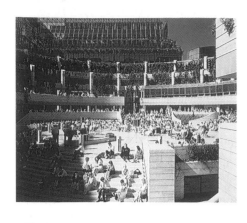

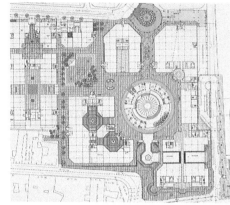

Arup Associates, *Ice Rink and Offices*, Broadgate, London, UK, 1988 (1982–88)
Above and top left: the arena and surrounding offices with plan

Frei Otto, *Wilkhahn Production Pavilions*, Bad Münder, Germany, 1987 (1985–87)
Left and below: the light funnels and interior

The first major building to be completed in London's new Broadgate development was No 1 Finsbury Avenue by Arup Associates, which was featured in the section of this book on 1986. That building was, however, just a fragment of a much larger urban planning project, one of four atrium office buildings that were built between 1985 and 1988. The complete scheme, which in its later stages includes the work of other architects, is one of the most significant new urban developments in Europe. It covers a site area of almost 9 acres, with Finsbury Avenue forming one boundary and the renovated Liverpool Street station acting as a focus for pedestrian access into the scheme. A remarkably high level of space between buildings is incorporated and given over to public use, leisure and recreational enjoyment. New streets and squares are defined by the new buildings, and facilities include shops, pubs and restaur-

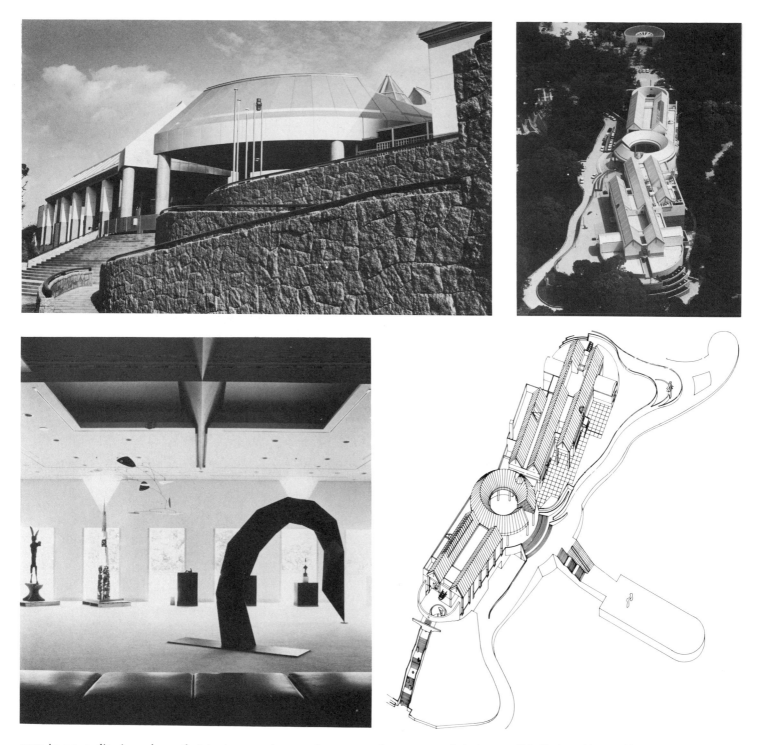

ants in an auditorium shape that in turn centres on the new all-year skating rink. The 'in between' spaces also contain some fine pieces of art including sculptures by Lipchitz, Serra and Segal, and the buildings themselves are adventurous architectural projects with fully glazed atria and much use of reflective glass and transparent surfaces. Disappointingly, in the later stages of the project there was a tendency to introduce heavy masonry materials and rather more dogmatic curved shapes, which results in a somewhat confused aesthetic appearance. However, this is not as bad as some of the adjoining blocks, which assume an altogether different quality of enclosure and introduce a quite unacceptable pseudo-Classical monumentalism in a debased Chicago style.

For Wilkhahn, the German furniture manufacturer, Frei Otto produced an innovative building employing a concept draw-

ing on the company's own use of timber technology. Workstations in the factory are represented by the simple timber-clad pavilions, thus providing a kind of heavyweight version of the more familiar Otto lightweight structures. The architect himself describes the building as a 'new prototype with regard to both its form as dictated by structural design and its lighting and ventilation'. The four major tented workstation pavilions front a large open factory floor.

Designed by Kurokawa, the Hiroshima Museum is based on what he calls his 'philosophy of symbiosis'. His symbiotic process is rooted in an architecture of humanity in which nature plays a part both inside and outside the building. In this design the combined roofs express something much deeper than simple linked spaces: they suggest a group of dwellings or a village connecting, symbiotically, the parts to the whole. They also achieve a scale

Kisho Kurokawa, *Museum of Contemporary Art*, Hiroshima, Japan, 1988 (1986–88)
Top left: looking up towards the entrance plaza
Top right: bird's eye view from south
Below: exhibition foyer and axonometric view from north

that does not dominate in the natural surroundings. The building is situated on the ridge of a hill and never rises above the existing tree heights, while the main exhibition spaces are to be found largely underground. Externally, by the use of materials, the architect draws a further evolutionary analogy that is expressed in the structure: the natural foundations give way to rough stone, to polished stone, and finally to tile and aluminium, thus creating, the architect claims, a further symbiosis from ground to sky.

1988/89

Mitchell/Giurgola and Thorp, *New Parliamentary Buildings*, Canberra, ACT, Australia, 1988 (1981–88)
Right: the verandah entrance wall surmounted by the flag
Below right: view towards Mount Ainslie
Below: ground-floor plan, foyer to the Great Hall and sketch of Members' Hall

A pre-ordained Parliamentary site is the key element to this building. The architects accepted Walter Burley Giffin's generating circular form for the Parliament complex. Within the circle a linear axis is formed and framed by two amazing concrete curvilinear walls whose arcs enclose the Parliamentary chambers. The complex has four major elements: the House of Representatives; the Senate; a central Forum; and an Executive Government area. The vast space of the building nestles into the 'hilltop', creating a new, low, horizontal profile above which flies at the apex the Australian flag supported by a steel mast rising through the Members' Hall.

There is a symbolic sequence of spaces off the Forecourt where the public enter the building to mix, meet and mingle with the politicians. Visitors proceed through the theatrical, post-Modernist but well-articulated Great Verandah before entering the group of buildings that contain as much art work as the average national museum.

Safdie's design was won in limited competition in 1983 and developed in conjunction with Parkin, who had themselves won an earlier competition for a National Gallery in 1976. The building's basic L-shaped plan has along its entrance side an added glass and concrete ramped colonnade. It joins ceremoniously the partly enclosed entrance pavilion to the main focal point of the whole development, Great Hall. From this enormous, multi-level crystal pavilion, 'streets' radiate out from a symmetrical plant to the various public galleries, each of which has an identifiable entrance. The galleries have a nice feeling of unity, are generally well-lit and have an enviable spaciousness about them compared with some more recently designed European galleries. Tucked into the project too is the complete Gothic-revival nineteenth century Rideau Chapel salvaged from an Ottawa convent.

The CCA is a splendidly unique institution founded in 1979. It is a study centre, library, museum and gallery devoted entirely to architecture. It was built for its client owner, who is also its director, and the building's consultant architect, Phyllis Lambert, who collaborated closely with the design architect, Peter Rose. The building itself is a mélange of architectural intentions, partly a restoration (incorporating the Shaunessy House supervised by D. St-Louis, which has stood on the site since the nineteenth century), and part new building as well as a dramatic piece of urban landscaping. Based on a loose and somewhat stark assimilation of classical architectural vocabularies, the CCA presents itself as a tight-knit, formally organized building designed and constructed for long-term use. It is a modern version of a monumental public building, and a consistent modern masonry aesthetic runs through the design

Moshe Safdie, *National Gallery*, Ottawa, Canada, 1988 (1986–88)
Top left: the glazed Great Hall
Top right: colonnade and corridor to Great Hall
Right: ground floor plan

Peter Rose and Phyllis Lambert, *Canadian Centre of Architecture*, Montreal, Canada, 1989 (1986–89)
Below: exterior of the CCA

both inside and out. The French eclectic façades of the Shaunessy provide a real challenge which, in my view, has not been satisfactorily resolved architecturally, although its internal spaces provide a splendid contrast to the new. The landscaped areas include Baile Park, designed by the architect's own team, and the CCA Garden, designed by Melvin Charney in order to 'metaphorically re-represent the Centre' with its overt references to site history and architectural analogies in its sculptural features.

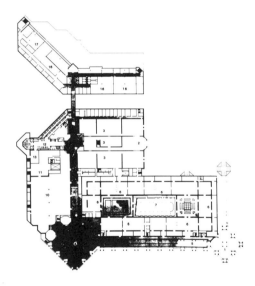

1989

Two much talked about Scandinavian buildings during 1990 were the neat and distinctive Planetarium by Kristoffersen built in the northernmost University in the Norwegian city of Tromsø and the rather less successful, huge shiny spherical 'sporting Globe' that dominates part of modern Stockholm. The former building attracts small audiences, mainly tourists, while the latter provides a leisure, recreational and sporting base for major international events as well as venues for more local cultural activities.

Grimshaw's Sainsbury's is a giant hangar of a store, meticulously detailed and cleverly planned. It provides bold, urban street façades, and around an internal parking court are workshops, stores and access to the new housing. The underground car park is connected directly to the store by a moving pedestrian ramp. The store itself is covered by a spectacular steelwork roof providing a clear span of 40m. It consists of a number of large arched main beams supported by smaller webbed beams at either side. These are counterbalanced and tied down to huge peripheral tie rods, the foundations of which are held in mass concrete blocks. Along the sides of the canal, twelve residential units are situated. These are certainly some of the most advanced and innovative urban housing schemes in London. They grace the side of the calm and pleasant (but woefully neglected) canal. Internally they are rather small, offering little more than a pied-à-terre type of accommodation, but they give a great feeling of space and openness with electronically controlled 'roll up and over' metal windows and internally split-level balconies.

The Austrian originals, Co-op Himmelblau, were into 'Deconstructivist' architecture while the masonry paint was still drying on Johnson's AT&T Building. Their startling, aggressive gestures were well known throughout Europe, sharing the limelight of contemporary relevance with Joseph Beuys and Hundertwasser. Their rooftop remodelling in Vienna is more than a meaning-ridden fashionable gesture. Rather, it is a real attempt to enliven a boring roof space and pervert the relationship between the inside and out by the creation of dynamic, uplifting forms in tension. How difficult it is for us all to ignore such bold, audacious gestures; how easy to say 'just crazy'.

Berg Arkitekkontor AB, *The Globe Arena*, Stockholm, Sweden, 1989 (1987–89)
Above: the enormous Globe project in context
Right: interior of main arena with left elevation

John Kristoffersen, *Nordlys Planetarium*, Tromsø, Norway, 1989 (1988–89)
Below: the Planetarium

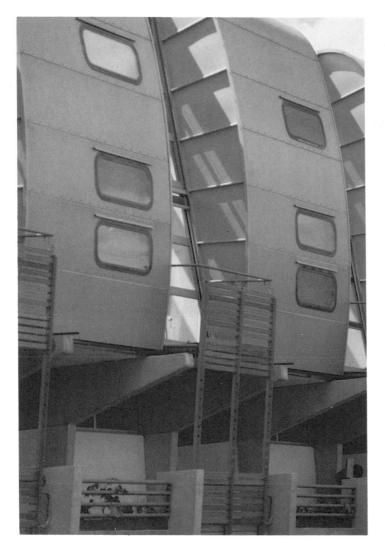

Nicholas Grimshaw and Partners, *Sainsbury's Housing and Superstore*, Camden Lock, London, UK, 1989 (1987–89)
Top: two views of the housing at Sainsbury's

Co-op Himmelblau, *Office Extension*, Vienna, Austria, 1989 (1988–89)
Left: interior of one of the small lawyer's offices
Above: the new roofscape

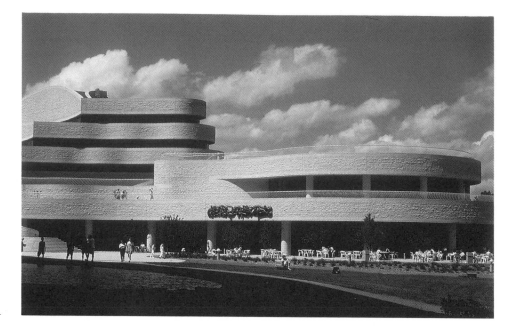

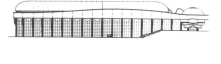
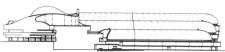

Douglas Cardinal and Associates, *Canadian Museum of Civilization*, Hull, Quebec, Canada, 1989 (1986–89)
Top and above: aerial view and general elevational views
Centre right and below: the bulbous entrance pavilion
Below: ground-floor plan

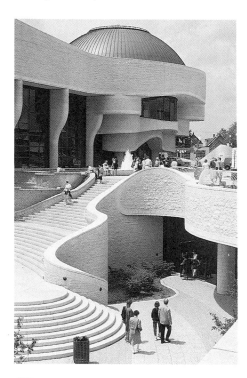

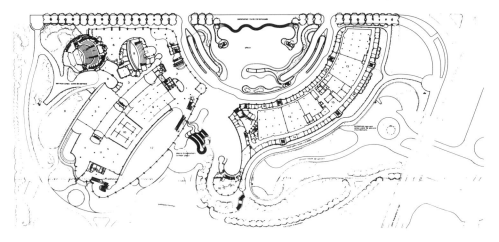

The fluid geometrical waves of the Canadian Museum can be found on a 9.6ha site in Hull, Quebec, adjacent to the River Ottawa. It lies opposite the Canadian Parliament buildings, Ottawa. It is a long, low, amorphously shaped structure interconnected at a level below ground but above ground shaped in such a way as to allow for clear view cones through to the other side of the river. Its forms look as if they have been blown about the expansive site in some prehistoric redistribution of landscape features. It is divided into two major parts, the 'Glacier Wing' and a 6-storey curatorial/ research wing. Pedestrian access between the wings leads from the main street to the parks and river edges. The building covers 100,000m² and the whole building structure is divided into 12 separate compartments to combat earthquake forces. The design, and all draughting work, was done by computer software: 15,000 drawings were produced. The consistency of the design is enhanced externally by the use of a beautiful external facing material, a split-faced, honey coloured Tyndall Stone, a fossil-rich limestone older than any exhibit in the Museum's less well considered interior galleries.

I. M. Pei, Entrance Pyramid, *Le Grand Louvre*, Paris,
France, 1989 (1984–89)
Above: the main entrance pyramid
Left: the staircase sweeps down to the ticket area
Left below: section, site plan and sketch

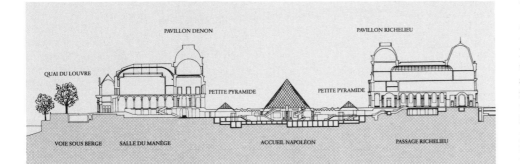

PAVILLON DENON — PAVILLON RICHELIEU

QUAI DU LOUVRE — PETITE PYRAMIDE — PETITE PYRAMIDE

VOIE SOUS BERGE — SALLE DU MANÈGE — ACCUEIL NAPOLÉON — PASSAGE RICHELIEU

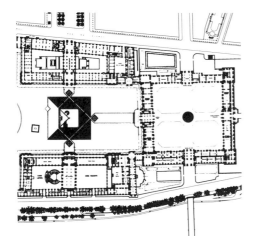

The group of buildings in Paris known as
the *Grands Projets* are of major architectural
interest. Most were officially inaugurated
during the Bicentennial celebrations in
1989, although this did not necessarily
imply the full completion of the project.
Thus, firm completion dates remain proble-
matical.

Of all the *Grands Projets* in Paris, none
created such a stir as the Pei Pyramids in
the courtyard of the famous Louvre
Museum. Spectacular in concept and form,
they provide a startling reminder of the
audacious ability of modern architects to
invigorate and re-circulate traditional architectural forms. In a sense, however, nothing
is more static (or monumental) than the
pyramid shape, which is most familiar in its
most solid form in Egypt with the ancient
pyramid of Cheops at Gizeh (480ft high). I.
M. Pei's scheme depended on the creation
of a different kind of pyramid, a visually
exciting, transparent effect in steel and glass
that is comparable in some ways to other
modern and spectacular structures such as
the Eiffel Tower and Poelzig's Water Tower
at Posen. The main Pyramid is basically
a complex inter-linked steel structure
sheathed in reflective glass. In fact it is an
entrance doorway providing a long-overdue
entrance portico to the main galleries of the
Louvre. As one descends into the interior
entrance foyer, the dramatic nature of the
intervention becomes apparent. The main
Pyramid, which certainly disturbs the
balance of the old Louvre courtyard, is
countered by two smaller pyramids, which
provide further light and ventilation to the
subterranean spaces.

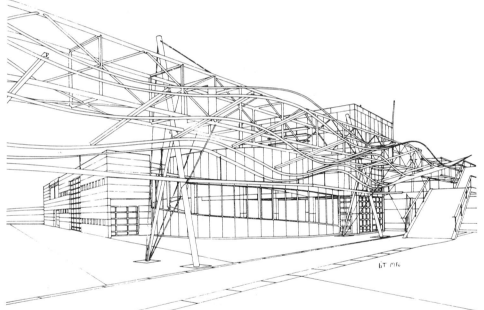

Bernard Tschumi, *Pavilions*, Parc de la Villette, Paris, France, 1989 (1987–89)
Top and centre right: a number of different red pavilions in the park
Above: perspective of the gallery and folie
Far right: the *'Geode'* by Fainsilber

As early as 1983, Bernard Tschumi won an unscheduled run-off for the new Parc de la Villette in collaboration with François Barré. The first series of small, bright red pavilions (or *folies*) situated at the intersections of an invisible grid across the park were inaugurated in 1987. Erected on a site that once accommodated Parisian abattoirs and which eventually will provide 35h of parkland, some 42 coloured *folies* have been planned. These *folies* have no specific function although they imply numerous potentialities. They validate the idea of 'Deconstructivist' architecture and philosopher Jacques Derrida, who has supported their cultural meaning. The architectural detail is deliberately mechanical/industrial. Tschumi has written that 'each *folie* is the result of intersection between spaces, movements and events'. All of this is a remarkable contrast to the formal shape of Fainsilber's *'Geode'*, a container for the new Imax System's 'Omnimax' cinema that dominates the site.

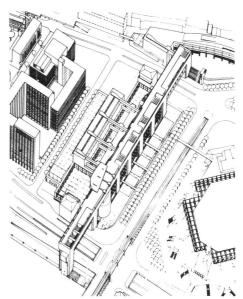

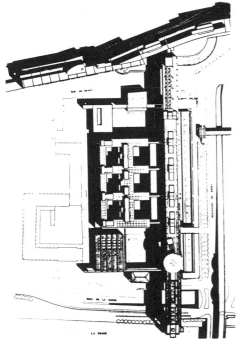

Paul Chemetov, Borja Huidobro, Christian Devillers (with
Emile Duhart-Harostegvy, Atelier d'Urbanisme et
d'Architecture) *Ministry of Economy and Finance*, Paris,
France, 1989 (1982–89)
Top: general elevational view of the Ministry
Top right: architect's drawing and, left, site plan
Right: the urban landscaping incorporates sculptures
specially commissioned

The competition for the new Ministère de
l'Economie et des Finances building was
announced in 1982. The Chemetov and
Huidobro scheme was chosen from 137
projects submitted. A well-controlled, confident building, it is the same length as the
old Treasury at the Louvre, which it re-
places in functional terms. The 9-storey
main building, with its great end bridge
structures, reaches from the River Seine to
the Gare de l'Est where it terminates in a
lower storey, concave building. It provides
150,000m^2 and accommodation for 4,700
staff including four Ministries.

1989/90

Echoing the form of the Arc de Triomphe, Danish architect Von Spreckelsen's arch was the winning design in a competition held by President Mitterrand in 1982 to see how De Gaulle's 'modern mess' at La Défense could be better related to Haussmann's great axis from the Louvre. It was chosen from over 400 projects, and Mitterrand said in 1983 that it was 'remarkable for its purity'. A 100m² office cube, it is constructed of squares of white Carrara marble with splayed walls on each end width. It rises to a height of 110m and contains 35 floors of offices. The elegant fabric 'cloud' under the arch, designed by engineer Peter Rice in stretched fabric, is envisaged as a canopy. Notre Dame could fit within the cube.

The new Opera House at the Place de la Bastille was won in competition in 1984 by the Uruguyan-born Canadian architect Carlos Ott. His smooth-faced scheme fitted the difficult, cramped site like a glove and was one of the few schemes that strictly adhered to an almost impossible programme. Based on a drum within a drum, a massive glass and granite façade wraps itself around the corner site, revealing an adventurous three-dimensional multi-level foyer behind which lies the huge volume of the opera house auditorium.

Johann Otto von Spreckelsen, *La Grande Arche*, Place de la Defense, Paris, France, 1990 (1982–90)
Right: the arch

Carlos Ott, *New Opera House*, Place de la Bastille, Paris, France, 1989 (1982–90)
Below: the new Opera exterior and interior, under construction, 1988–9

The 100-acre Stockley Park is a spectacular example of the new Business Park concept. It is located five minutes from Heathrow and adjacent to motorway connections to London and the rest of Britain via the M25. A derelict 350 acres gravel extraction site filled with 12.5m deep landfill, it had all the attendant pollution problems of methane and leachate. In 1984, 3.5 million cubic metres of rubbish were moved to the north of the site, gravel extracted from below the landfill to ceate a platform for the business park site, using London Clay. Speed of construction was of utmost importance. Inspiration for the park came from the Syntex Labs Inc. in Stamford Park, Palo Alto and Rohm Corporation near San Jose – low rise buildings with pitch roofs set in superbly landscaped parkland. Landscaping, parking and good access to road and air networks were the essential elements of the brief.

The predominant character of most of the buildings is a 2- to 3-storey lightweight steel-framed structure with dark slated pitch roofs and white cladding panels. Sun shading devices give the buildings their individuality – Richie's fretted planar glazing cladding with fritted patterns with an arcade of brise soleil and Troughton McAslan's wavy line of polyester shades are some of the most innovative examples. Structurally the Foster 'BP Exploration' building is one of the most exciting with a dramatic cantilevered entrance.

Arup Associates (Co-ordinating Architects and Planners), *Stockley Park Business Park*, Hillingdon, London, 1989 (1984–89)
Right and below: the whole business park is landscaped and individual buildings designed by various architects
Top: General view of the Business park: The Amenity and Club facilities are set apart in a Lakeside complex: The estate was inaugurated by HRH The Prince of Wales in 1986: Details of Foster's glazed wall

1990

A major refurbishment of a pleasant looking Edwardian crescent-shaped 5-storey building in Store Street, London, has long been overdue. However, not everything is as meets the eye. This refurbishment is only skin-deep – a new façade was not allowed on historic conservation grounds – but behind its familiar face is a completely new structure. What might have been a fussy and perhaps even laughable revamp has turned into an architectural *tour de force* and one of the most talked about designs in London at the turn of the decade. A private development, it houses the offices of 'Imagination' together with other lettable space. The architects reinstated the somewhat mannered Edwardian façade in order to build a designers' world behind it, with studios in the basement and studio conference rooms, exhibition areas and restaurant above. All is dominated by white finishes and big lettering. The most spectacular element in the whole design is the new atrium space between the front building and the rear 4-storey structure, which has been carved out of an existing mews-like light and ventilation well. This provides the core of the new circulation to the building. Windows have been punched into white painted brick walls and the various levels connected by an exciting, almost futuristic, ambience of catwalks and steelwork walkways topped by an elegant, undulating lightweight steel and translucent polyester membrane roof.

The Inclosure School's uncompromisingly modern aesthetic relies on the simplest of structural statements – two shallow curved barrel vaulted roofs are separated by a central top-lit spine. These two roofs serve as sun reflectors to direct the sun's rays back through simple horizontal projecting brise soleil or sun scoop blinds on the north side; the south side reversed the process. The barrels also define the major areas devoted to open teaching. The simple steel structure is unobtrusive but performs its structural purpose in an elegant and inventive manner. Set on the edge of dense woodland, the tall windows offer magnificent views. The building is seen as a contrast to surrounding nature and as a simple, unobtrusive, low-profiled structure that effectively uses the surrounding Queen's Inclosure Woodland as a backdrop. It has also been designed in such a way that it can be easily extended as

the school itself grows. It received a major RIBA National Award in 1990 and the RIBA President's Medal,1991.

With great skill at the end of the decade Austrian Gustav Peichl again accomplishes a *coup d'elegance* at Frankfurt with this small but effective extension to the Städelmuseum. The masonry façade is a powerful medium punctuated by carefully placed features.

The extension to the Städel Museum in Frankfurt, of 1878, was won in open competition by Peichl. His entry demonstrated a 'continuity of architectural design without reverting to an historical language'. The three-storey annexe is connected to the existing building by a bridge on the first floor and is clad in white natural stone.

Herron Associates, *The Imagination Building*, Store Street, London, UK, 1990 (1989–90)
Above: the atrium is situated on the lines of the old mews

C. Stansfield Smith, Hampshire County Architect, *Queen's Inclosure Middle School*, Cowplain, Hants., 1990
Below: entrance to the low-slung school building

Gustave Peichl, *Städel Museum Extension*, Frankfurt am Main, Germany, 1990 (1987–90)

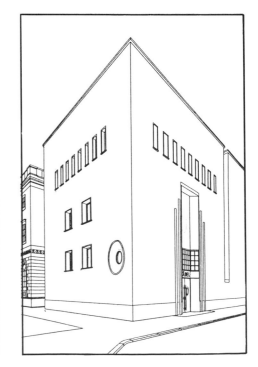

CHRONOLOGY

1900
Binet, René – Château d'Eau, World Fair, Paris, France
Guimard, Hector – Métro Entrances, Paris, France
Horta, Victor – Hôtel Aubecq, Brussels, Belgium
Horta, Victor – Hôtel Solvay, Brussels, Belgium
Voysey, C. F. A. – The Orchard, Chorley Wood, Herts, England

1901
Behrens, Peter – Own house, Darmstadt, Germany
Horta, Victor – L'Innovation Store, Brussels, Belgium
Olbrich, Josef-Maria – Ernst-Ludwigs-Haus, Darmstadt, Germany

1902
André, Emile – Maison Fernbach, Nancy, France
D'Aronco, Raimondo – Central Pavilion, International Exposition of Decorative Arts, Turin, Italy
Townsend, C. H. – Horniman Museum, Forst Hill, London, England
Van de Velde, Henri – Folkwang Museum (alterations), Hagen, Germany

1903
Berlarge, H. P. – The Exchange, Amsterdam, Netherlands
Chédanne, G. P. – 'Le Parisien' Offices, Rue Réaumur, Paris, France
Guimard, Hector – Castel Henriette, Sèvres, France
Perret, Auguste – Apartment Block, 25bis Rue Franklin, Paris, France
Wood, Edgar – Christian Scientist Church, Victoria Park, Manchester, England

1904
Sullivan, Louis H. – Carson, Pirie & Scott Department Store (State Street addition), Chicago, Ill., USA

1905
Wright, Frank Lloyd – Larkin Building, Buffalo, NY, USA

1906
Mackintosh, Charles Rennie – Scotland Street School, Glasgow, Scotland
Perret, Auguste – Garage, Rue de Ponthieu, Paris, France
Wagner, Otto – Post Office Savings Bank, Vienna, Austria

1907
Gaudi, Antonio – Casa Battló (remodelling), Barcelona, Spain
Greene & Greene – Blacker House, Pasadena, Calif., USA
Olbrich, Josef-Maria – Hochzeitsturm and exhibition buildings, Darmstadt, Germany
Wagner, Otto – Church of St Leopold, Am Steinhof, Vienna, Austria
Wright, Frank Lloyd – Unity Church, Oak Park, Ill., USA

1909
Behrens, Peter – AEG Turbine Erecting Shop, Berlin, Germany
Behrens, Peter – Schröder House, Hagen-Eppenhausen, Germany
Gaudí, Antonio – Parochial School, near the Sagrada Familia, Barcelona, Spain
Mackintosh, Charles Rennie – Glasgow School of Art, Library Wing, Glasgow, Scotland
Wright, Frank Lloyd – City National Bank and Hotel, Mason City, Iowa, USA
Wright, Frank Lloyd – Robie House, Chicago, Ill., USA

1910
Gaudí, Antonio – Casa Milá, Barcelona, Spain
Maybeck, Bernard – Christian Science Church, Berkeley, Calif., USA
Pompe, Antoine – Clinic for Dr van Neck, Brussels, Belgium

1911
Hoffmann, Josef – Palais Stoclet, Brussels, Belgium
Loos, Adolf – Steiner House, Vienna, Austria
Poelzig, Hans – Milch Chemical Factory, Luban, Germany (now Poland)
Poelzig, Hans – Water Tower, Posen (Poznan), Germany (now Poland)
Van de Velde, Henri – Art School, Weimar, Germany

1912
Gočár, Josef – The Spa Building, Bohdaneć, Austria (now Czechoslovakia)
Poelzig, Hans – Office Building, Breslau (Wroczlaw), Germany (now Poland)

1913
Berg, Max – Centennial Hall, Breslau (Wroczlaw), Germany (now Poland)
Chochol, Josef – Three houses at Prague-Podoli, Austria (now Czechoslovakia)
Chochol, Josef – Villa, Vyšehrad, Prague, Austria (now Czechoslovakia)
Gropius, Walter & Meyer, Adolf – Fagus Factory, Anfeld an der Leine, Germany
Steiner, Rudolf, & others – Goetheanum I, Dornach, near Basel, Switzerland
Taut, Bruno – Steel Industries Pavilion, Leipzig, Germany

1914
Berlage, H. P. – Holland House, London, England
Gaudí, Antonio – Parc Güell, Barcelona, Spain
Groplus, Walter & Meyer, Adolf – Model Factory, Werkbund Exhibition, Cologne, Germany
Saarinen, Eliel – Railway Terminus, Helsinki, Finland
Steiner, Rudolf – Haus Duldeck, Dornach, near Basel, Switzerland
Taut, Bruno – Glass Industries Pavilion, Werkbund Exhibition, Cologne, Germany
Van der Velde, Henri – Model Theatre, Werkbund Exhibition, Cologne, Germany
Wright, Frank Lloyd – Midway Gardens, Chicago, Ill., USA

1915–16
Gaudí, Antonio – Colonia Güell Chapel, Barcelona, Spain
Gill, Irving – Dodge Residence, Los Angeles, Calif., USA
Van't Hoff, Robert – Villa, Huis ter Heide, near Utrecht, Netherlands
Van der Meij, J. M., & others – Het Scheepvaarthuis, Amsterdam, Netherlands

1918
Kroha, Jiři – Montmartre Night Club, Prague, Czechoslovakia
Staal, J. F., & others – Park Meerwijk, Bergen, Netherlands
Willis Polk – Hallidie Building, San Francisco, Calif., USA

1919
Poelzig, Hans – Grosses Schauspielhaus (remodelling), Berlin, Germany

1920
Brinkman, Michiel – Spangen Housing, Rotterdam, Netherlands
Oud, J. J. P. – 'Tussendijken' Workers' Housing, Rotterdam, Netherlands

1921
De Klerk, Michel – 'Eigen Haard' Housing, Amsterdam, Netherlands
Mendelsohn, Erich – Einstein Tower, Potsdam, Germany

1922
De Klerk, Michel – Apartments, Henriette Ronnerplein, Amsterdam, Netherlands
Kahn, Albert – Glass Plant, Dearborn, Detroit, Mich., USA
Korn, Arthur & Weitzmann, S. – Villa for Dr Goldstein, Berlin, Germany
Le Corbusier – Ozenfant House, Paris, France
Perret, Auguste – Church of Notre Dame, Le Raincy, France
Wiebenga, J. G. – Technical School, Groningen, Netherlands
Wright, Frank Lloyd – Imperial Hotel, Tokyo, Japan

1923
Asplund, Gunnar – Skandia Cinema, Stockholm, Sweden
Freyssinet, Eugène – Airship Hangars, Orly, France
Höger, Fritz – Chile House, Hamburg, Germany
Kramer, Piet – De Dageraad Housing, Amsterdam, Netherlands
Le Corbusier & Jeanneret, Pierre – La Roche House, Paris, France
Matté-Trucco, Giaccomo – Fiat Works, Turin, Italy
Mendelsohn, Erich – Herrmann Hat Factory, Luckenwalde,

Germany
Östberg, Ragnar – Town Hall, Stockholm, Sweden
Wright, Frank Lloyd – Mrs G. M. Millard house, Pasadena, Calif., USA

1924
Gropius, Walter & Meyer, Adolf – Theatre reconstruction, Jena, Germany
Häring, Hugo – Farm Buildings, Gut Garkau, near Lübeck, Germany
Rietveld, Gerrit – Schröder House, Utrecht, Netherlands

1925
Behrens, Peter – IG Farben buildings, Hoechst, Frankfurt-am-Main, Germany
Berlage, H. P. – Christian Scientist Church, The Hague, Netherlands
Bourgeois, Victor – La Cité Moderne, Bercham-Sainte-Agathe, Brussels, Belgium
Kroha, Jiři – Technical School, Mlada Boleslav, Czechoslovakia
Le Corbusier – Pavillon de l'Esprit Nouveau, Exhibition of Decorative Arts, Paris, France
Le Corbusier & Jeanneret, Pierre – Houses, Pessac, Bordeaux, France
Melnikov, K. – Soviet Pavilion, Exhibition of Decorative Arts, Paris, France
Oud, J. J. P. – Café de Unie, Rotterdam, Netherlands
Sauvage, Henri – Flats, Rue des Amiraux, Paris, France
Staal, J. F. – Netherlands Pavilion, Exhibition of Decorative Arts, Paris, France

1926
Behrens, Peter – New Ways, Northampton, England
De Koninck – House and Studio, Uccle, Belgium
Gropius, Walter – Bauhaus Buildings, Dessau, Germany
Gropius, Walter – Housing at the Bauhaus, Dessau, Germany
Mies van der Rohe – Monument to Carl Liebknecht and Rosa Luxemburg, Berlin, Germany
Pompe, Antoine – House, Uccle, Brussels, Belgium
Schindler, R. M. – Beach House for Dr P. Lovell, Newport Beach, Calif., USA

1927
Bonatz, Paul & Scholer, E. F. – Railway Station, Stuttgart, Germany
Brinkman & van der Vlugt – Van Nelle Shop, Leiden, Netherlands
Gropius, Walter – Prefabricated housing, Weissenhofsiedlung, Stuttgart, Germany
Le Corbusier & Jeanneret, Pierre – Villas and apartment block, Weissenhofseidlung, Stuttgart, Germany
Loos, Adolf – Tzara House, Paris, France
Mallet-Stevens, Robert – Apartments, Rue Mallet-Stevens, Passy, Paris, France
Mies van der Rohe – Apartment block, Weissenhofsiedlung, Stuttgart, Germany
Oud, J. J. P. – Housing, Hook of Holland, Netherlands
Oud, J. J. P. – Terrace Housing, Weissenhofsiedlung, Stuttgart, Germany
Stam, Mart – Three terrace houses, Weissenhofsiedlung, Stuttgart, Germany

1928
Asplund, Gunnar – City Library, Stockholm, Sweden
Bartning, Otto – Steel Church, Press Exhibition, Cologne, Germany
Buys, J. W. E., & J. B. Lürsen – De Volharding Store, The Hague, Netherlands
Duiker, Johannes – 'Zonnestraal' Sanatorium, Hilversum, Netherlands
Easton & Robertson – Royal Horticultural Hall, Westminster, England
Fuchs, Bohuslav – Exhibition Pavilion, Brno, Czechoslovakia
Golosov, Ivan P. – Zuyev Club, Moscow, USSR
Gropius, Walter – Dammerstock Housing, Karlsruhe, Germany
Kysela, Ludvik – Bata Store, Prague, Czechoslovakia
Le Corbusier & Jeanneret, P. – Les Terrasses, Garches, France
Luckhardt, Hans & Wassili (with Alfons Anker) – House, Am Rupenhorn, Berlin, Germany
Mendelsohn, Erich – Schocken Department Store,

Stuttgart, Germany
Mendelsohn, Erich – Universum Cinema, Berlin, Germany
Mies van der Rohe – Hermann Lange House, Krefeld, Germany
Oud, J. J. P. – Kiefhock Housing Estate, Rotterdam, Netherlands
Rietveld, Gerrit – Garage and chauffeur's quarters, Utrecht, Netherlands
Steiner, Rudolf – Goetheanum II, Dornach, near Basel, Switzerland
Tait, Thomas – Crittall Housing Estate, Silver End, Essex, England
Van Doesburg, Theo, & others – Cabaret, Cinema and Café, L'Aubette, Strasbourg, France
Wils, Jan – Olympic Stadium, Amsterdam, Netherlands

1929
Barsch, Michael with Sinyavski, Michael – Planetarium, Moscow, USSR
Bernard, Oliver – Strand Palace Hotel Foyer, London, England
Gray, Eileen & Badovici, Jean – Sea-side House, Roquebrune, Cap Martin, France
Krantz, Josef – Café Era, Brno, Czechoslovakia
Laprade, Albert & Bazin, L. E. – Le Marbeuf Garage, Paris, France
Le Corbusier & Jeanneret, P. – Villa annexe, Ville d'Avray, Seine-et-Oise, France
Luckhardt, Hans & Wassili (with Alfons Anker) – Telschow House, Berlin, Germany
May, Ernst – Suburban development, Frankfurt-am-Main, Germany
Melnikov, K. – Own house, Moscow, USSR
Melnikov, K. – Rusakov Workers' Club, Moscow, USSR
Mendelsohn, Erich – Schocken Department Store, Chemnitz (now Karl-Marx-Stadt), Germany
Mies van der Rohe – German Pavilion, Barcelona, Spain
Neutra, Richard – Lovell Health House, Los Angeles, Calif., USA
Scharoun, Hans – Rest Home (Hostel Building), Breslau (now Wroczlaw), Germany (now Poland)
Van Doesburg, Theo – Studio House, Meudon-val-Fleury, Paris, France

1930
Asplund, Gunnar – Stockholm Exhibition, Stockholm, Sweden
Brinkman, J. A. & van der Vlugt, L. C. – Van Nelle Factory, Rotterdam, Netherlands
Connell, Amyas – High and Over, Amersham, Bucks., England
De Koninck, L. H. – Canneel Cottage, Brussels, Belgium
Dudok, W. M. – Town Hall, Hilversum, Netherlands
Duiker, Johannes – Open air School, Amsterdam, Netherlands
Ehn, Karl (City Architect) – Karl-Marx-Hof, Vienna, Austria
Gropius, Walter – Housing, Siemensstadt, Berlin, Germany
Gropius, Walter & Breuer, Marcel – Werkbund Exhibition, Paris, France
Korn, Arthur, & Weizmann, Siegfried – Fromm Rubber Factory, Friedrichshagen, near Berlin, Germany
Loos, Adolf; Lurçat, André; Rietveld, Gerrit – Werkbund Exhibition, Vienna, Austria
Meyer, Hannes – German Trade Unions School, Bernau, near Berlin, Germany
Mies van der Rohe – Tugendhat House, Brno, Czechoslovakia
Oud, J. J. P. – Kiefhoek Housing, Rotterdam, Netherlands
Scharoun, Hans – Apartments and shops, Siemensstadt, Berlin, Germany
Stam, Mart, & Moser, W. (with F. Kramer) – Budge Home for the Aged, Frankfurt-am-Main, Germany

1931
Behrens, Peter – House in the Taunus Hills, Cronberg, Germany
Dudok, W. M. – Bijenkorf Store, Rotterdam, Netherlands
Emberton, Joseph – Royal Corinthian Yacht Club, Burnham-on-Crouch, Essex, England
Le Corbusier & Jeanneret, P. – 'Les Heures Claires' (Villa Savoye), Poissy-sur-Seine, France
Mendelsohn, Erich – Columbushaus, Berlin, Germany
Taut, Max – Trades Union House, Frankfurt, Germany

1932
Adams, Holden & Pearson – Arnos Grove Underground Station, London, England
Chareau, Pierre & Bijvoet, Bernard – Maison de Verre (Dalsace House), Paris, France
Connell, Amyas & Ward, Basil – 'New Farm', Grayswood, Surrey, England
Ellis, Herbert & Clarke, W. L. with Williams, Owen – Daily Express Building, London, England
Haesler, Otto – Old People's Homes, Kassel, Germany
Howe, George & Lescaze, William – Philadelphia Savings

Fund Society Building, Philadelphia, Penn., USA
Le Corbusier & Jeanneret, P. – Swiss Students' Hostel, Cité Universitaire, Paris, France
Nervi, P. L. – Giovanni Berta Stadium, Florence, Italy
Williams, Owen – Boot's Factory, Beeston, Notts., England

1933
Aalto, Alvar – Tuberculosis Sanatorium, Paimio, Finland
Brinkman & Van der Vlugt – Sonneveld House, Rotterdam, Netherlands
Le Corbusier & Jeanneret, P. – Cité de Refuge (Salvation Army Hostel), Paris, France
Lucas, Colin – 'The Hopfield', St Mary's Platt, Kent, England
Lurçat, André – School, Villejuif, France
Scharoun, Hans – Schminke House, Löbau, Germany

1934
Berlage, H. P. – Gemeente Museum, The Hague, Netherlands
Burnet, Tait & Lorne – Curzon Cinema, London, England
Coates, Wells – Lawn Road Flats, Hampstead, London, England
Coates, Wells, & Pleydell-Bouverie – Sunspan Exhibition House, Olympia, London, England
Duiker, Johannes – Handelsblad-Cineac Cinema, Amsterdam, Netherlands
Fischer, Josef – Villa Hoffman, Budapest, Hungary
Lubetkin, Drake and Tecton – Penguin Pool, Zoological gardens, London, England
Roth, Alfred & Emil, with Breuer, Marcel – Flats, Doldertal, Zürich, Switzerland
Williams, Owen – Empire Swimming Pool, Wembley, England

1935
Aalto, Alvar – Municipal Library, Viipuri, Finland (now USSR)
Coates, Wells – Embassy Court, Brighton, Sussex, England
Le Corbusier & others – Centrosoyus Building, Moscow, USSR
Mendelsohn, Erich & Chermanyeff, Serge – De la Warr Pavilion, Bexhill-on-Sea, England
Serafimov, S. & Kravets, A. – Dept. of Industry and Planning, Kharkov, USSR
Syrkus, Helen & Szymon – Skolimow House, Warsaw, Poland
Tecton with Lubetkin, B. – Highpoint I Flats, Highgate, London, England
Torroja, Eduardo & others – Zarzuela Hippodrome, Madrid, Spain
Williams, Owen – Peckham Health Centre, London, England

1936
Fry, Maxwell & Gropius, Walter – House, Chelsea, London, England
Fry, Maxwell – The Sun House, Hampstead, London, England
Mendelsohn, Erich & Chermayeff, Serge – House, Chelsea, London, England
Papadakis, Stamo – House, Glyfadha, near Athens, Greece
Terragni, Giuseppe – Casa del Fascio (Cada del Popolo), Como, Italy

1937
Aalto, Alvar – Finnish Pavilion, World Exposition, Paris, France
De Knoninck, L. H. – Cottage Berteaux, Uccle, Brussels, Belgium
Goff, Bruce – Colmorgan House, Glenview, Ill., USA
McGrath, Raymond – House, Chertsey, Surrey, England
Sert, José Luis – Spanish Pavilion, International Exposition, Paris, France
Tecton – Highpoint II Flats, Highgate, London, England
Wright, Frank Lloyd – Falling Water, Bear Run, Penn., USA

1938
Chermayeff, Serge – Own House, near Halland, Sussex, England
Gropius, Walter & Breuer, Marcel – Gropius House, Lincoln, Mass., USA
Gardella, Ignazio – Anti-tuberculosis Clinic, Alessandria, Italy
Tait, Thomas with Launcelot Ross – Empire Tower and Restaurant, Empire Exhibition, Glasgow, Scotland
Wright, Frank Lloyd – Taliesin West, near Phoenix, Arizona, USA

1939
Aalto, Alvar & Aino – Finnish Pavilion, New York World's Fair, USA
Aalto, Alvar & Aino – 'Mairea' Norrmark, near Björneborg (Pori), Finland
Bel Geddes, Norman – 'Highways & Horizons' exhibit (General Motors) New York World's Fair, USA
Coates, Wells – Flat, 10 Palace Gate, London, England

Goodwin, P. & Stone, E. – Museum of Modern Art, New York, USA
Gropius, Walter & Fry, Maxwell – Village Cottage, Impington, Cambs., England
Maillart, R. – Cement Hall, Swiss National Exhibition, Zürich, Switzerland
Sharon, Arieh – Co-operative Housing, Tel Aviv, Palestine (now Israel)

1940
Asplung, Gunnar – Forest Crematorium, Stockholm, Sweden
Clarke-Hall, Denis – Secondary School, Richmond, Yorkshire, England
Mies van der Rohe – Illinois Institute of Technology, Chicago, Ill., USA
Nervi, Pier Luigi – Aeroplane Hangar, Orbetello, Italy
Reinhard & Hofmeister, & others – Rockefeller Center, New York, USA

1941
Bryggman, Erik – Cemetery Chapel, Turku (Åbo), Finland
Goff, Bruce – 'Triaero' vacation house, Louisville, Kentucky, USA
Moser, Werner – Protestant Church, Altstetten, Zürich, Switzerland

1942
Gropius, Walter & Breuer, Marcel – Defense Housing, New Kensington, Penn., USA
Niemeyer, Oscar & Costa, Lucio – 'Casino Pampulha' and Yacht Club, Belo Horizonte, Brazil

1943
Costa, Lucio; Niemeyer, Oscar; Reidy, Affonso (Consultant: Le Corbusier) – Ministry of Education and Health, Rio de Janeiro, Brazil

1946
Mies van der Rohe – Alumni Memorial Hall, IIT, Chicago, Ill., USA
Niemeyer, Oscar – Church of St Francis of Assisi, Pampulha, Belo Horizonte, Brazil

1947
Breuer, Marcel – Breuer House I, New Canaan, Conn., USA
Herts County Architect's Dept. – Junior Mixed and Infants' School, Cheshunt, Herts., England
Neutra, Richard – Kaufmann Desert House, Palm Springs, Calif., USA

1948
Belluschi, Pietro – Equitable Savings & Loan Association Building Portland, Oregon, USA
Neutra, Richard – Tremaine House, Montecito, Calif., USA

1949
Aalto, Alvar – Student dormitory block, MIT, Cambridge, Mass., USA
Eames, Charles & Ray – Case Study House, Santa Monica, Calif., USA
Ellwood, Craig – Hale House, Beverly Hills, Calif., USA
Goff, Bruce – Samuel Ford Residence, Aurora, Ill., USA
Johnson, Philip – Glass house, New Canaan, Conn., USA
Nervi, Pier Luigi (Nervi & Bartoli) – Exhibition Halls, Turin, Italy
Saarinen, Saarinen & Associates – Christ Church (Lutheran), Minneapolis, Minn., USA
Twitchell & Rudolph – Healy guest house, Sarasota, Florida, USA
Wright, Frank Lloyd – V. C. Morris Gift Shop, San Francisco, Calif., USA

1950
Goff, Bruce – Wilson House, Perdido Bay, Florida, USA
Gropius, Walter (TAC: The Architects' Collaborative) – Harvard Graduate Center, Cambridge, Mass., USA
Jacobson, Arne – Soholm Housing Estate, Klampenborg, Denmark
Mendelsohn, Erich – Maimonides Health Center, San Francisco, Calif., USA
Mies van der Rohe – Farnworth House, Fox River, Plano, Ill., USA
Wright, Frank Lloyd – Helio Laboratory & Research Tower (second phase), Racine, Wisc., USA

1951
Candela, Felix, & Reyna, J. G. – Cosmic Ray Pavilion, University City, Mexico City, Mexico
LCC Architect's Department – Royal Festival Hall, South Bank, London, England
Mies van der Rohe – 860-880 Lake Shore Drive, Chicago, Ill., USA
Montuori, Eugenio & others – Rail Terminus, Rome, Italy

Tubbs, Ralph – Dome of Discovery, Festival of Britain, London, England
Wright, John Lloyd – Wayfarer's Chapel, Palos Verdes, Calif., USA

1952
Aalto, Alvar – Civic Centres, Säynätsalo, Finland
Architects Co-Partnership (ACP) – Rubber Factory, Brynmawr, Wales
Breuer, Marcel – Harry A. Caesar Cottage, Lakeville, Conn., USA
Harrison, Wallace K. & Abramovitz, Max – UN Headquarters, New York, USA
Le Corbusier – Unité d'Habitation, Marseille, France
Lindegren, Yrjö & Jäntti, Toivo – Olympic Stadium, Helsinki, Finland
O'Gorman, Juan – Library, University of Mexico, Mexico
Revell, Viljo, & Petäjä, Keijo – Teollisuuskeskus Building (Palace Hotel), Helsinki, Finland
Skidmore, Owings and Merrill – Lever House, New York, USA
Soleri, Paolo & Mills, Mark – Desert House, Cave Creek, Arizona, USA

1953
Aalto, Alvar – Rautatalo Office Building and Coffee Bar, Helsinki, Finland
Erskine, Ralph – Cardboard Factory, Fors, Sweden
Fuller, R. Buckminster – Ford 'Rotunda' Dome, Dearborn, Mich., USA
Harrison, Wallace & Abramovitz, Max – Alcoa Headquarters, Pittsbug, Penn., USA
Reidy, Affonso Eduardo Apartments, Podrogulho Estato, Rio de Janeiro, Brazil
Soleri, Paolo & Mills, Mark – Solimene Ceramics Factory, Vietri-sul-Mare, Italy
Van den Broek & Bakema – Lijnbaan Shopping Centre, Rotterdam, Netherlands

1954
Atbat-Afrique (Bodiansky, Candilis & Woods) – Flats, Casablanca, Morocco
Candela, Felix – Church of the Miraculous Virgin, Mexico City, Mexico
Kahn, Louis – University Art Gallery and Design Center, Yale University, New Haven, Conn., USA
Le Corbusier – Millowners' Association Building, Ahmedabad, India
Smithson, Alison & Peter – Secondary Modern School, Hunstanton, Norfolk, England

1955
Bernasconi, G. A., with Fiocchi, A., & Nissoli, M. – Olivetti Headquarters, Milan, Italy
Bill, Max – Hochschule für Gestaltung, Ulm, Germany
Goff, Bruce – Bavinger House, Norman, Oklahoma, USA
Le Corbusier – Pilgrimage Chapel of Notre-Dame-du-Haut, Ronchamp, Vosges, France
Saarinen, Eero – General Motors Technical Center, Warren, Mich., USA
Studer, André – Low-cost Apartments, Casablanca, Morrocco

1956
Aalto, Alvar – National Pensions Institute, Helsinki, Finland
Anshen & Allen – Chapel of the Holy Cross, Sedona, Arizona, USA
Candela, Felix – Celestino's Warehouse, Mexico City, Mexico
Hellmuth, Leinweber & Yamasaki – Terminal Building, Lambert-St Louis Airport, Miss., USA
Jacobsen, Arne – Munkegaards School, Copenhagen, Denmark
Jacobsen, Arne – Rødovre Town Hall, Denmark
Le Corbusier – The Courts of Justice, Chandigarh, India
Le Corbusier – Maisons Jaoul, Neuilly-sur-Seine, France
Le Corbusier – Shodhan House, Ahmedabad, India
Mies van der Rohe, & others – S.R. Crown Hall, IIT Chicago, Ill., USA
Smithson, Peter – House of the Future 'Ideal Home' Exhibition, London, England
Tange, Kenzo & Others – Peace Centre, Hiroshima, Japan

1957
BPR (Belgiojoso, L. B., Peresutti, E., & Rogers, E.) – 'Velasca' Tower, Milan, Italy
Figini, Luigi & Pollini, Gino – Olivetti Factory, Ivrea, Italy
Jacobsen, Arne – Carl Christensen Motor Works, Aalborg, Denmark
Nervi, P. L. & Vitlozzi, A. – Palazzetto dello Sport, Rome, Italy
Sirén, Heikki & Kaija – University Chapel, Otaniemi, Finland
Tange, Kenzo & others – Sogetsu Art Centre, Tokyo, Japan

1958
Aalto, Alvar – House of Culture, Helsinki, Finland

Aalato, Alvar – Vuoksenniska Church, Imatra, Finland
Breuer, Marcel, Nervi, P. L. & Zehrfuss, B. UNESCO Headquarters, Paris, France
Candela, Felix & Ordoñez, J. A. & F. A. – Restaurant and Floating Garden, Xochimilco, Mexico City, Mexico
Candela, Felix & Madaleno, J. S. – La Jacaranda Night-club, Acapulco, Mexico
Eiermann, Egon & Ruf, Sep – West German Pavilion, World Exposition, Brussels, Belgium
Fuller, R. Buckminster – Union Tank Car Co. Dome, Baton Rouge, La., USA
Le Corbusier, with Janis Xenakis – Le Poème Électronique (Philips Pavilion), World Exposition, Brussels, Belgium
Le Corbusier – Secretariat, Chandigarh, India
Mies van der Rohe, with Johnson, Philip & others – Seagram Building, Park Avenue, New York, USA
Niemeyer, Oscar – President's Palace of the Dawn, Brasilia, Brazil
Saarinen, Eero, with Orr, Douglas W. – David S. Ingalls Skating Rink, Yale, New Haven, Conn., USA
Tengbom, Anders – Pedagogical Institute, Miljö, Sweden
Yamasaki, M. – McGregor Conference Center, Wayne State University, Detroit, Mich., USA

1959
GLC Architect's Department – Alton West Estate, Roehampton, London, England
Le Corbusier – Monastère Sainte-Marie-de-la-Tourette, Eveux-sur-Arbresle, near Lyon, France
Ponti, Gio, Nerbi, P. L. & others – Pirelli Centre, Milan, Italy
Scharoun, Hans, with Frank, Wilhelm – Romeo and Julia Apartment blocks, Stuttgart-Zuffenhause, Germany
Ungers, Oswald – Own house, Cologne, Germany
Vigano, Vittoriano – Marchiondi Spagliardi Institute, Baggio, Milan, Italy
Wright, Frank Lloyd – Solomon R. Guggenheim Museum, New York, USA

1960
Atelier 5 – Halen Housing Estate, Kirchindach, Berne, Switzerland
Hentrich, Helmut & Petschnigg, Hubert – Phoenix-Rheinrohr Co; Office Tower, Düsseldorf, Germany
Johnson, Philip – Shrine, New Harmony, Indiana, USA
Kahn, Louis – Richards Medical Research Building, University of Pennsylvania, Philadelphia, Penn., USA
Lasdun, Denys & Partners – Cluster Block, Bethnal Green, London, England
Nervi, P. L. – Palazzo dello Sport, Rome, Italy
Niemeyer, Oscar & Costa, Lucio – Plaza of the Three Powers, Brasilia, Brazil
Roth, Alfred – Own house, Zürich, Switzerland
Saarinen, Eero & Associates with Yorke, Rosenberg & Mardall – United States Embassy, London, England
Sheppard, Robson & Partners – Churchill College, Cambridge, England
Skidmore, Owings & Merrill – Chase Manhattan Bank, New York, USA
Skidmore, Owings & Merrill – Union Carbide Corp Building, New York, USA
Tange, Kenzo – City Hall, Kurashiki, Japan
Van den Broek & Bakema – Reformed Church, Nagele, Netherlands

1961
Breuer, Marcel, with Smith, Hamilton – Lecture Halls Wing, Bronx Campus, New York University, New York, USA
Crosby, Theo – IUA Conference Pavilion, London, England
Greene, Herb – Greene Residence, Norman, Oklahoma, USA
Johnson, Philip – Nuclear Reactor, Rehovet, Israel
Lasdun, Denys & Partners – Flats, 26 St James' Place, London, England
Mayekawa, Kunio, & Associates – Metropolitan Festival Hall, Tokyo, Japan
Nervi, P. L. & Ponti, Gio – Palace of Labour, 'Italia 61' Exhibition, Turin, Italy
Saarinen, Eero & Associates – T.W.A. Terminal Building, Kennedy (formerly Idlewild) International Airport, New York, USA
Valle, Gino & Nani – Offices for A. Zanussi Rex Factory, Pordenone, Italy

1962
Aalto, Alvar – Cultural Centre, Wolfsburg, Germany
Cadbury-Brown, H. T., Casson & Gooden – Royal College of Art, South Kensington, London, England
Martin, Leslie & Wilson, Colin St. J. – Harvey Court, Gonville & Caius College, Cambridge, England
Saarinen, Eero & Associates – Terminal Building, Dulles International Airport, Chantilly, Virginia, USA

1963
Gropius, Walter, (TAC) & Belluschi, Pietro – PanAm Building, New York, USA
Le Corbusier & others – The Carpenter Center for the

Visual Arts, Harvard University, Cambridge, Mass., USA
Neumann, Alfred, Hecker, Zvi, & Sharon, Eldar – Municipal Building, Bat Yam, Israel
Roth, Alfred – 'Riedhof' School, Zürich, Switzerland
Rudolph, Paul – Art & Architecture Building, Yale University, New Haven, Conn., USA
Rudolph, Paul – Parking Garage, New Haven, Conn., USA
Scharoun, Hans – Philharmonic Concert Hall, Berlin, Germany
Stirling, James & Gowan, James – Faculty of Engineering, Leicester University, England
Tange, Kenzo – Cultural Centre, Nichinan, Japan

1964
Castiglioni, Enrico – Technical High School, Busto Aruzio, near Milan, Italy
Lasdun, Denys & Partners – Royal College of Physicians, London, England
Martin, Leslie & Wilson, Colin St. J. – St Cross Library, Oxford, England
Neumann, Alfred & Hecker, Zvi – Faculty of Mechanical Engineering, Technion, Haifa, Israel
Smithson, Alison & Peter – Economist Buildings, London, England
Tange, Kenzo, with URTEC – Olympic Sports Halls, Tokyo, Japan
Tange, Kenzo, with Schlombs, Wilhelm – St Mary's Cathedral, Tokyo, Japan
Venturi, Robert & Rausch, John – House, Chestnut Hill, Philadelphia, Penn., USA
Zanuso, Marco – Olivetti Factory, Buenos Aires, Argentina

1965
Aalto, Alvar – Polytechnic Institute, Otaniemi, Finland
Ahrends, Burton & Koralek – Theological College, Chichester, Sussex, England
Casson, Conder & Partners – Elephant & Rhinoceros Pavilion, Zoological Gardens, London, England
Foster, Norman & Wendy with Richard Rogers – Electronics Factory, Swindon, Wilts., England
Kahn, Louis – Salk Institute for Biological Research, La Jolla, Calif., USA
Kiesler, Frederick, with Bartos, Armand P. – Shrine of the Book, Jerusalem, Israel
Lyons, Israel & Ellis – Wolfson Institute, London, England
Matthew, Robert, Johnson-Marshall & Partners – University of York, Heslington, Yorkshire, England
Neumann, Alfred, Hecker, Zvi & Sharon, Eldar – Dubiner Apartment House, Ramat Gan, Israel
Otani, Sachio – International Conference Hall, Kyoti, Japan
Revell, Viljo, & others – City Hall, Toronto, Canada
Roche, Kevin, Dinkeloo, John, & Associates – Cummins Engine Co. Factory, Darlington, England
Sheffield City Architect's Department – Housing, Park Hill and Hyde Park, Sheffield, England
Snowdon, Lord, Price, Cedric & Newby, Frank – Northern Aviary, Zoological Gardens, London, England

1966
Abramovitz, Max, Harrison, Wallace K., Johnson, Philip, & Saarinen, Eero – Lincoln Center for the Performing Arts, New York, USA
Andrews, John with Page & Steel – Scarborough College, University of Toronto, Canada
Architects' Co-Partnership – Dunelm House, University of Durham, England
Gillespie, Kidd & Coia – St Peter's College, Cardross, Scotland
Moore, Charles, Lyndon, Donlyn, Turnbull, William & Whitaker, William – Sea Ranch, Gualala, Calif., USA
Urbahn, Max, & others – Vehicle Assembly Building (VAB), Cape Kennedy, Florida, USA
Van den Broek & Bakema – Auditorium, Technical University, Delft, Netherlands

1967
Affleck, Desbarats & others – Place Bonaventure, Montreal, Canada
Fuller, R. Buckminster (Fuller & Sadao Inc.) – US Pavilion, Expo 67, Montreal, Canada
GLC Architect's Department – Queen Elizabeth Hall and Purcell Room, South Bank Arts Centre, London, England
Goldberg, Bertrand – Marina City, Chicago, USA
Le Corbusier – Centre Le Corbusier, Zürich, Switzerland
Otto, Frei & Gutbrod, Rolf – West German Pavilion Expo 67, Montreal, Quebec, Canada
Roche Dinkeloo Associates – Ford Foundation Headquarters, New York, USA
Safdie, Moshe, with David, Barrott & Boulva – Habitat, Expo 67, Montreal, Canada
Tange, Kenzo, with URTEC – Yamanashi Communications Centre, Koufu, Japan
Wilson, Hugh, Leaker, Dudley & others – Town Centre (phase I), Cumbernauld New Town, near Glasgow, Scotland

1968
GLC Architect's Department – Tower Block Housing (SF I), Elgin Estate, London, England
Kallmann, McKinnell & Knowles – City Hall, Boston, Mass., USA
Lasdun, Denys, & Partners – University of East Anglia, Phase I, Norwich, England
Prouvé, Claude & Jean – Palais des Expositions, Grenoble, France
Roche Dinkeloo Associates – Oakland Museum, Oakland, Calif., USA
Schipporeit-Heinrich Associates – Lake Point Tower, Chicago, Ill., USA
Stirling, James – History Faculty Library, University of Cambridge, England

1969
Lasdun, Denys, & Partners – Extension to Christ's College, Cambridge, England
Moore, Charles – Faculty Club, University of California, Santa Barbara, Calif., USA
Skidmore, Owings & Merrill – John Hancock Center, Chicago, Ill., USA

1970
Aalto, Alvar – Mount Angel Benedictine College Library, Oregon, Ore., USA
Johannsson, John – Mummers Theatre, Oklahoma, Ok., USA
Skidmore, Owings and Merrill, John Hancock Center, Chicago, Ill., USA
Tange, Kenzo & others – Expo 70, Osaka, Japan
Utzon, Jørn – Opera House, Sydney, NSW, Australia
Wurster, Bernardi & Emmons (SOM) with Belluschi, Pietro – Bank of America, San Francisco, Calif., USA

1971
Aalto, Alvar – Finlandia Hall, Helsinki, Finland
Baer, Steve – 'Zomeworks' Solar House, Orrales, New Mexico, USA
Kroll, Lucien – Housing renovation, refurbishment and reorganisation, Alencon, Normandy, France
Meier, Richard – Old Westbury, Long Island, NY, USA
Zeidler Roberts Partnership – Ontario Place, Toronto, Canada

1972
Kurakawa, Kisho – Nakagin Capsule Tower, Tokyo, Japan
Leo, Ludwig – Circulation Tank, Institute for Waterways and Shipbuilding, Berlin, Germany
Peichl, Gustav – Radio and TV Studios, Innsbruck, Austria
Pelli, Cesar – Pacific Design Center, Los Angeles, Calif., USA
Stirling, James & Partners – Foley Building, University of Oxford, England

1973
Architects Design Partnership (William Lim et al) – Golden Mile Shopping Centre, Singapore
Botta, Mario – Family House, Riva san Vitale, Ticino, Switzerland
Hertzberger, Hermann – Centraal Beheer, Apeldoorn, Netherlands
Meier, Richard – Douglas House, Harbour Springs, Mich., USA
Moore Turnbull & Partners, Kresge College, UC: Santa Cruz, Calif., USA
Portman, John and Associates – Hyatt Regency Hotel, San Francisco, Calif., USA

1974
Asmussen, Erik – Music Room, Rudolf Steiner Seminary, Järna, Sweden
England, Richard – Church of the Holy Trinity, Malta
Gutbrod, Rolf, Frei Otto et al – Inter-Continental Hotel and Conference Centre, Mecca, Saudi Arabia
Hertzberger, Hermann – 'De Drei Hoven', Elderly Persons' House, Amsterdam, Netherlands
Isozaki, Arata – The Gunma Prefectural Museum, Japan
Kahm, Louis – Institute of Management, Ahmedabad, India
Martorell/Bohigas/Mackay – The Thau School, Barcelona, Spain

1975
Bofill, Ricardo and the Taller d'Arquitectura – Walden 7, nr Barcelona, Spain
Bofill, Ricardo and Taller de Arquitectura – The Cement Factory, San Justo, Barcelona, Spain
Foster, Norman & Associates – Willis Faber & Dumas Office Building, Ipswich, Suffolk, England
Graves, Michael – Schulmann House, Princeton, NJ, USA
Isozaki, Arata – Central Library, Kitakyusha, Japan
Kikutaki, Kiyonori – Aquapolis, Okinawa, Japan
Lasdun, Denys & Partners – National Theatre, South Bank, London, England

Legorreta, Ricardo – Hotel Camino Real, Cancún, Mexico
Makovecz, Imré – Mortuary Chapel, Budapest, Hungary
Michelucci, M. – Church of the Autostrada, Langasone, Italy
Moore, Charles – Place d'Italia, New Orleans, La., USA
Otto, Frei et al – Garden Pavilion, Mannheim, Germany
Seidler, Harry – MLC Office Tower and Theatre Royal, Sydney, Australia
Sert, Jose Luis – Miro Centre, Montjuic, Barcelona, Spain
Snozzi, Luigi – Casa Bianchetti, Ticino, Switzerland
Zabludorsky, A., Gonzalez, De León – Colegio de Mexico, Mexico City, Mexico

1976
Botta, Mario – Detached House, Lignornetto, Ticino, Switzerland
Kurokawa, Kisho – Sony Tower, Osaka, Japan
Kroll, Lucien – Medical Faculty Housing, University of Louvain, Belgium
Lawrence Halprin & Associates, Freeway Park, Settle, Wash., USA
Levitt Bernstein & Associates, Royal Exchange Theatre, Manchester, England
Thompson, Benjamin and Associates – Quincy Market and Faneuil Hall, Boston, Mass., USA
Utzon, Jørn – Lutheran Church, Bagsveard, nr Copenhagen, Denmark

1977
Asmussen, Erik – Library and Eurhythmy Halls Rudolf Steiner Seminary, Järna, Sweden
Foster, Norman & Associates – Sainsbury Centre, University of East Anglia, Norwich, England
Rogers, Richard, Renzo Piano, Centre Pompidou, Paris, France
Seidler, Harry – The Australian Embassy, Paris, France
SITE Architects – The Notch Project, Best Products, Sacramento, USA
Sumet Jumsai Associates – The Science Museum, Bangkok, Thailand
Zeidler Roberts Partnership – The Eaton Centre, Toronto, Canada

1978
Aalto, Alvar – Church, Riola, Italy
Erskine, Ralph et al – Housing Development, Byker, Newcastle-upon-Tyne, England
Hertzberger, Hermann – Music Centre, Vredenberg, Utrecht, Netherlands
Isozaki, Arata – Central Library, Kitakyushu, Japan
Manteola Sanchez Gomez, Santos Solsona Vinoly – TV Studios, Buenos Aires, Argentina
Pei, I. M. – East Wing, National Gallery, Washington DC, USA
Peichl, Gustav – Earth Station, Affleur, Austria
Prince, Bart, Robert Hanna Studio, Albuquerque, N.M., USA
Rogers, Richard & Partners (Mike Davies) – IRCAM, Centre Pompidous, Paris, France
Scharoun, Hans and Edgar Wisniewski (Hermann Fehling (1972–) – Staatsbibliothek Preussischer Kulturbesitz, Berlin, Germany
SITE Architects – Ghost Parking Lot, Best Products, Hamden, Kt., USA
Soleri, Paolo – Arcosanti, Cordes Junction, Ariz., USA
Stubbins, Hugh – Office building for Citicorp, New York, NY, USA
Tigerman, Stanley – The Illinois Library for the Blind and Handicapped, Chicago, Ill., USA

1979
Aida, Takefumi – The Toy Block House, 'Tomo' Dental Office, Yamgushi, Japan
Brown, Neave et al, Camden Architects' Dept. – Housing, Alexandra Road, London, England
Dixon, Jeremy and Fenella – St Mark's Housing, Maida Vale, London, England
Matthew Johnson Marshall & Partners – Town Hall, Hillingdon, London, England
Meier, Richard – The Atheneum Visitor Center, New Harmony, Ind., USA
Pietila, Reima – Congregational Centre, Church and Market Halls, Hervanta, Tampere, Finland
Walker, Derek, MKDC Architect, Christopher Woodward & Stuart Mosscrop – Shopping Centre, Milton Keynes, England

1980
Domeniq, Günther – Savings Bank, Favoriten, Vienna, Austria
Jahn, Helmut – Xerox Center, Chicago, Ill., USA
Johnson, Philip and John Burgee – Garden Grove Community Church, Los Angeles, Calif., USA
Peichl, Gustav – Extension to the Radio House, Vienna, Austria

Team ZOO, Community Centre, Miyashirocho, Japan (1978–80)
Van Eyck, Aldo et al – Humbertus House, Home for Single Parents and their Children, Plantage Middenlaan, Amsterdam, Netherlands

1981
Bofill, Ricardo and the Taller de Arquitectura – Les Arcades du Lac and Le Viaduc, St Quentin-en-Yvelines, France
Hopkins, Michael and Partners – Schlumberger Centre, Cambridge, England
Lasdun, Denys, Softley and Partners – European Investment Bank, Luxembourg
Peichl, Gustav – Austrian Radio Station, Steiermark, Austria

1982
Barmou, Falké (Master Mason) – The Yaama Mosque, Tahoua, Niger
Botta, Mario – Single family house, Stabio, Ticino, Switzerland
Hollein, Hans – Abteiburg Museum, Mönchengladbach, Germany
Hollein, Hans – The Schullin Jewellery Shop, Vienna, Austria
Rewell, Raj – Asian Games Village, New Delhi, India
Rogers, Richard and Partners – INMOS Research Centre, Monmouth, Gwent, Wales

1983
Bunshaft, Gordon of SOM – National Commercial Bank HQ, Jedda, Saudi Arabia
Correa, Charles – Kanchanjunga Apartments, Bombay, India
Farrell, Terry and Partners – TV-am, Camden Lock, London, England
Graves, Michael – Public Service Building, Portland, Ore., USA
Isozaki, Arata – Tsukuba Civic Centre, Tsukuba Academic New Town, Ibarangi, Japan
Kahn, Louis I – The Parliamentary Building Complex, Dacca, Bangladesh
Murcutt, Glen – Artists' House and Studios, N. Sydney, Australia
Pei, I. M. and Partners – National Gallery of Art, East Building, Washington DC, USA
Thompson, Benjamin and Associates – Fulton Market, New York, NY, USA
Ungers, O. M. – German Architecture Museum, Frankfurt, Germany

1984
Arup Associates, Offices at No 1 Finsbury Avenue, London, England
Calatrava, Santiago – Stadelhofen Station, Zürich, Switzerland
Cox, Richardson and Taylor, Yulara Tourist Village, Uluru Park, Ayers Rock, NT, Australia
Larsen, Henning – Ministry of Foreign Affairs, Riyadh, Saudi Arabia
Maki, Fumiko – Fujisaiwa Gymnasium, Fujisaiwa, Japan
Moneo, Rafael – National Museum of Roman Art, Merida, Spain
Prince, Bart – Own House, Albuquerque, New Mexico, USA

1985
Ciriani, Henry – St Antoine Hospital Central Kitchen, Paris, France
Jahn, Helmut – State of Illinois Center, Chicago, Ill., USA
Meier, Richard – Museum für Kunsthandwerk (Arts and Crafts Museum), Frankfurt-am-Main, Germany
Seidler, Harry and Partners – The Hong Kong Club, Hong Kong
Stirling, James and Michael Wilford – Staatsgalerie, Stuttgart, Germany

1986
Foster, Norman and Partners – Hong Kong and Shanghai Bank, Hong Kong
Yeang, Kenneth – 'Roof Roof' House, Selangor, Malaysia

1987
Akitek Tenggara – Chee Tong Temple, Singapore
Alberts, Ton – NMB Bank, Amsterdam, Netherlands
Aulenti, Gae et al, Musée d'Orsay, Paris, France
Behnisch, Günther and Partner – 'Hysolar' Research Building, Stuttgart Technical University, Germany
Botta, Mario – André Malraux Cultural Centre, Chambery, Le Bas, France
Hopkins, Michael and Partners – The Mound Stand, Lords Cricket Ground, St John's Wood, London, England
Rogers, Richard and Partners – Lloyds Building, London, England

Sahba, Fariburz – The Baha'i Temple, Delhi, India
Stirling, James, Michael Wilford and Associates – Clore
Building, Tate Gallery, London, England

1988
Arup Associates – Ice Rink and Offices, Broadgate,
London, England
Cox, Richardson and Taylor – Darling Harbour
Redevelopment and Museum Area: Aquarium, National
Maritime Museum, Congress Centre, Sydney, Australia
Cox, Richardson and Taylor – Sydney Football Stadium,
Sydney, Australia
Gehry, Frank – Vitra Furniture Museum, Weil-am-Rhein,
Germany
Kurokawa, Kisho – City Art Museum, Nagoya, Japan
Kurokawa, Kisho – Museum of Contemporary Art,
Hiroshima, Japan
Mitchell/Giurgola and Thorp, New Parliamentary Buildings,
Canberra, ACT, Australia
Nouvel, Jean – L'Institut du Monde Arabe, Paris, France
Otto, Frei – Wilkhahn Production Pavilions, Bad Münder,
Germany
Safdie, Moshe – National Gallery, Ottawa, Canada

1989
Cardinal, Douglas and Associates – Canadian Museum of
Civilization, Hull,, Quebec, Canada
Co-op Himmelblau – Office Extension, Vienna, Austria
Grimshaw, Nicholas and Partners – Sainsbury's Superstore
and Housing, Camden Lock, London, England
Kristoffersen, John – Nordlys Planetarium, Trømso,
Norway
Pei, I. M. – La Grande Pyramide, The Louvre, Paris, France
Rose, Peter and Phyllis Lambert – Canadian Centre of
Architecture, Montreal, Canada
Tschumi, Bernard – Pavilions, Parc de la Villette, Paris,
France

1990
Arup Associates (Co-ordinating Architects and Planners) –
Stockley Park Business Park, Hillingdon, London, England
Chemetov, Paul, Borja Huidobro, Christian Devillers with
Emile Duhart-Harostegvy (Atelier d'Urbanisme et
d'Architecture) – Ministère de l'Economie et des Finances,
Paris, France
Herron Associates, The Imagination Building, Store Street,
London, England
Ott, Carlos – New Opera House, Place de la Bastille, Paris,
France
Stansfield Smith, C. Hampshire County Architect – Queen's
Inclosure Middle School, Cowplain, Hants, England
Von Spreckelsen, Johann Otto – La Grande Arche, Place
de la Defense, Paris, France

ACKNOWLEDGEMENTS

A book as wide-ranging and complex as this would not have materialised without the help of a great number of people working in various institutions, exhibition galleries, and photographic studios as well as colleagues and friends. Many of these are acknowledged in the individual credit lines but I would like to record my special thanks to the following whose help has been invaluable in producing this new edition and who, in many cases, have made useful comments on the new texts and provided pictures: Prof. Jeffrey Cook; Roger Connah; Bob Bowlby; Bart Prince; Ian Latham; Anthony Tischhauser; Toshio Nakamura; Kisho Kurokawa; Alan Blanc; Brian Carter; William Lim; Kenneth Yeang; Peter Isnenghi; Louise Noelle; Prof. Peter Cook; Jorge Glusberg; Arne Klingborg and Abbe Asmussen; Prof. C. Norberg-Shulz.

The earlier edition was designed by Brian Trodd. Picture research was by Susan Mayhew and captions by Neil Steedman.

With a great sense of sadness the enthusiastic and knowledgeable involvement in this new project of the late Chris Fawcett is gratefully acknowledged. His valuable contribution on Japanese modern architecture was only a part of a much greater involvement with this revised edition. Yasmin Shariff coordinated early research work on the buildings of the 1970s. Mrs Nancy Jackson, who acted as secretary for the whole revision project, did her work with such quiet and effective efficiency and tact that I shall be eternally grateful – not least for the skill with which she transferred the whole new text onto disk. No mean feat when the words were constantly changing! My thanks also to John Taylor for all his help in getting the book together again editorially and to David Gibbons and Anthony Evans for putting it all together. Ted Hastings brought the existing index up to date.

All other photographs are by the author.

PICTURE CREDITS
The acknowledgements for the use of new illustration material in this expanded, second edition are now combined with photo credits from the previous edition for which permissions have already been granted. Whilst every possible effort has been made to clear and acknowledge copyrights of the pictures used it is possible that some attributions/ownerships have been omitted, or may be incorrect. As much of the material was supplied by individual architects, firms or practices represented in the publication additional photographic credits have not been included unless these were specifically requested or indicated.

The author will be pleased to correct any errors and add credits if required in any subsequent editions.

The author is also most grateful for the helpful co-operation of a number of magazine and publications editors who have kindly loaned material either commissioned for their publications or in their possession. This material has been used in good faith and acknowledged if and as requested. It shall not be the subject of any outside claim. In the event that any other material has been used that is subject to copyright and this has inadvertently not been cleared notification should be given to the author.

Key: t=top; c=centre; b=bottom; l=left; r=right

Max Abramovitz, 238t
Alvar Aalto, 217tl, b
ACL Brussels, 16tr, b
Kamran Adle, 370t, tl
Ahrends, Burton & Koralek, 266c
Akademie der Künste Berlin, 37; 45bc; 46c, b; 49t; 52t, tl; 53b; 58t; 93t; b; 95bl, br; 115cl; 120c, bl; 121bl, br
AKAA, 380t, c, b; 394t, cl, cr; 370tl, tr; 375tl, tr, c
Mokhless Al-Hariri, 316b
John Andrews, 278tl, tr, c
T. & R. Annan & Sons, 33t
Masao Arai, 332tl, tr, t; 327tr; 345b; 384t, cl, cr
F. Arborio Mella, 139c
J. G. Archer, 24tl
Architetti Dott. L. Figini – G. Pollini, 203t
Archigram, 236t, tc, lc, b
Architect & Building News, 235br
Architectengemeenschap, Van den Broek & Bakema, 117t
Architectural Association, 39lc; 41b; 49c; 70b; 74t; 74c; 77tl; tr; 96c, b; 119tl; 129cr; 149t; 152t; 156bl; 162t; 168t; 174t, cl; 179t; 197t, c, bl, br

The Architectural Press, 131cl; 138bl; 156bl; 157b
Architecture & Landscape Library, 75t; 87t; 181tl, br; 185t; 288t, b
L'Architecture Vivante, 105tl, br
Architects' Co-Partnership, 190t, bl, br
Archives d'Architecture Moderne, Brussels, 16tl; 18tl, r, bl; 43t, cr, b; 78tl; 81t; 83tl, tr; 111b; 140t, c; 223t
Archives Photographiques Paris, 122b
ARCOP Associates, 284tl, tr
The Arkansas Office, 379t
Arkitekturmuseet Skeppsholmen, Stockholm, 123tr
Arkkitehtitoimisto Alvar Aalto, 348b
Arup Associates, 381tl, tr
Atelier d'Architecture et d'Urbanisme, Brussels, 305
Australian High Commission Photo Library, 402br
Australian News & Information Service, 110c; 297bl
'A&U', 364c, bl, br; 381bl, br

Morley Baer, 311
Steve Baer, 307t, cr
Barnaby's Picture Library, 208b; 219c
Bauhaus-Archiv, 45br; 74b; 80c; 83b; 115bl, br
BCA, 99
Beata Bergström, 336t, cl, cr
Behr Photography, 264bl
Pietro Belluschi, 167t, b; 257tl, tr; 297t
Bellwood Photography Co., 268c
Ralph Benziger, 91tr, b
Luc Laurent Bernard, 373
Ralph Beyer, 64tr; 120br; 137bl; 189bl
Alan Blanc, 391b
P. Blundell Jones, 34t
O. Bohigas, 142tr
Book Art, 6A, B; 7E; 8B
Boudot-Lamotte, 68tr; 122cr
Robert Bowlby, 358c
Brazilian Embassy, 163t, b; 224t
Brecht-Einzig, 309tr
Marcel Breuer & Associates, 160cr; 164t, c, b; 188bl, br; 246bl
British Museum, 19b
Richard Bryant, 366c, bl; 385t, b, br; 392br; 397cl, cr, b
BT, 235t
Builder & Architect, 187tr; 217tr
Building Centre, London, 9F
Building & Design, 40tc, t
Sir John Burnet Tait & Partners 131tl, tr; 145bl
H. T. Cadbury-Brown, 25t, b
Sherban Cantacuzino, 28bl; 32b; 90tl, tr, cl; 124c, b; 141b; 144c; 146t, c; 180c, b; 201t, c, bl, br; 238cr; 252tr, b
Casson Conder & Partners, 270b
F. Catala-Roca, 319b; 321tl, tr, c
cb Foto, 319t, c, br
Cement & Concrete Association, 23r; 63b; 68cl; 73b; 113b; 118cr; 129b; 135b; 143b; 157tc; 158tl; 160cl, b; 161; 172t, c; 184c; 187b; 192c, bl, br; 194tl, tr; 196tl, tr; 199tl; 207c, b; 209b; 213t, c, b; 218t, b; 219bl; 220t, b; 223c; 226bl, br; 231lcl; 236b; 239t, c; 243tc, b; 244b; 257bl; 329
Martin Charles, 295, 341t, b, c; 355t; 356b
The Chase Manhattan Bank, 240tr
Professor Serge Chermayeff, 134t; 137tl, br; 138br; 149br
Chicago Architectural Photographing Co, 25b; 28cl; 185cl; 204t
Konrad Chmielewski, 360b
City Architect, Vienna, 30tl, tr; 39bl, br; 45c
City Planning Officer & Architect, Sheffield, 268t, c
Laura Cohn, 132b; 134br
Douglas Cole, 19tr; 51tl; 65t, b; 70tl, tr; 86c; 97t, c; 200t, cl, cr
Collection CCA, Montreal, 403b
Jeffrey Cook, 189t, b; 307t, c, br
Donald Cooper, 329
Jan Coppens, 64bl; 76t
Arrigo Coppitz, 331t, c
Trewin Copplestone, 24cl; 25t; 51bl; 82t; 175; 257c
Cosanti Foundation, 297t, b; 337c
Simon Cronley, 360c
Cumbernauld Development Corporation, 282t, c, b
Country Life, 110b

Dell & Wainwright, 146t, c
Dennis De Witt, 77c, b; 117cr, bl, br; 263t; 287b
Jan Derwig, 396tl, b
Carlos Diniz Associates, 361br

E. Dobiecki, 351b
John Donat, 254b; 266t; 277lc; 326c, b; 338t, c; 366t
Dulitzky, 347t, c
Max Dupain, 324t, bl, br; 339c, b; 378tr

Charles Eames, 170t, cl, cr, b
Easton Robertson Preston & Partners, 88t
Hein Engelskirchen, 88c
Richard England, 315
Ralph Erskine, 194b
Esto Photographics, 175
Aldo van Eyck, 9H

Harry S. Fairhurst, 38tc
Farbwerke Hoechst 76tr, b
Felipe Ferré (EPOB), 410bl
Fiat, 73t, c
B. Finlayson, Flint & Neill Partnership, 338c
Museum of Finnish Architecture, 8D; 303tl, c, cr; 304t; 348t, tl, c
Folkwang Verlag, 20br
Ford Foundation, 286t
Ford Motor Company, 191lcl, cr
Foster & Foster, 273t
Foto Hyderbrand, 47t, b
Fox Photos, 153
Fratelli Fabbri, 39tc
Reinhard Friedrich, 349cr, cl, b
Fry Drew & Partners, 132c; 138c; 139t; 150c

Antonio Garbasco, 328c
Gaudi Archives, 31t; 50t, 54t, b
John Gay, 270tl
General Motors Inc., 201t, c, bl, br
Alexandre Georges, 3
Keith Gibson, 27tr; 353t
Janet Gill, 390t, b
Bruce Goff, 142c, b; 159cl, b; 183c, b; 203bl, br
Bertrand Goldberg, 285bl, br
Greater London Council, 187tl, c; 209 bl; 229tl, tr, b
Herb Greene, 248t, br
Spencer de Grey, 28cr; 32t; 253br; 281t, br

Lawrence Halprin, 335tl
Hamlyn Publishing Group, 25b; 26b; 27t, b; 28cl; 31br; 33b; 42b; 44t, c; 68tr; 85tl; 98tr; 108lc; 122cr, b; 169bl, br; 185cl; 242tr; 254b; 264bl; 265bl; 266t; 268c, b; 270tl, cl, cr; 276tl; 277lc; 288; 292tl, tr
Harrison & Ambramovitz, 195tl; 278b
Robert Häuser GDL, 325cl, t
Zvi Hecker, 259b
Hedrich-Blessing, 32b; 142c, b; 162b; 168b; 180t, c, b; 285bl
Hertfordshire County Council, 166tr, b
Architectenburo Hermann Hertzberger 317t; (Beton-Verlag/Menk), 317c
Lucien Hervé 11; 15cr; 104t, cr, b; 205b; 292b
David Hicks, 141tr; 169t; 202lc, b; 227cl; 277t; 279t, br; 280t; 284b; 295tl, tr
HMSO, 154tc
Horniman Museum, 20t
Edvard Hueber, 331b
Pat Hunt, 371bl

Keith Ingham, 235bl
Allan Irvine, 67t, c, b; 136tr, c; 144b; 174cr; 210c; 259tr; 261t, c
Yasuhiro Ishimoto, 318t, b
Israel Government Tourist Office, 267t
The Italian Institute, 243c

Arne Jacobsen, 183t; 211t
Edward Jacoby/Hugh Stubbins Associates, 345r
The Japan Architect, 249t, b, c; 272t, b
E. R. Jarrett, 112t, cr
Philip Johnson, 173t, c, b; 206b; 222; 241tl; 246t
S. C. Johnson, 189tr

Albert Kahn Associates, 69c, b
Kallmann, McKinnell & Knowles, 289tr, cr
Malti Karjanoja, 352cl, cr
Akio Kawasumi, 255c
Kersting 17t; 133t; 235t; 269b
Romi Khosla, 208t; 219t, b
G. E. Kidder-Smith, 238cr

Ken Kirkwood, 338b; 371cl, t
Arne Klingborg, 299
Balthazar Korab, 302b, 306br, 340t
Arthur Kom, 116t, c
Margherita Krischanitz, 370b

Ian Lambert, 317
Landes Bildstelle, 14c
Denys Lasdun & Partners, 242tl, c; 247lc, b; 264t, bl; 290t, c, b; 295b
Randolph Largerbach, 289tl, b
Monica Lehmann, 244t
Dieter Leistner, 379c
Christopher Litte, 298b
Frank Lloyd Wright Foundation 28br; 144c
Colin Lucas, 127t, c

Raymond McGrath, 143t
McGraw-Hill World News, 177b
Magyar Epitóvúvészek Szovetsége, 130cr
John Malthus Ltd, 296b
Bildarchiv Foto Marburg, 19c; 34c; 44t, c
Sir Leslie Martin, 251t; 263cb
MAS, 31br; 41b
Robert Matthew, Johnson-Marshall & Partners, 273cr, b
Millar & Harris, 108lc
MKDC, 353b
Charles W. Moore Associates, 279bl; 294t
Moscow Institute of Architecture, 88cr, br; 135t
O. Murai, 234t
Musée Horta, 16tr, b
Musées de la ville de Strasbourg, 90c, b
Mucoum of Finnich Architocturo, 23tr; 31bl; 104tl; 50c; 126tr, b; 136t; 140b; 150t; 151t; 159tr; 169c; 191b; 196bl; 205t; 212t, b; 217cl; 224bl, br; 269t
Museum of Modern Art New York, 98tr
Pino Musi, 392t, c

NASA, 237t; 277tc
National Employers' Mutual General Insurance Assoc. Ltd., 51br
National Film Archive, 59; 108tc, bl
National Monuments Record, 17c, b; 101c; 123tl
Richard & Dion Neutra Architects & Associates, 165t, c, b
Nippon Bunka Film Co. Ltd., 296t, c, b
Chr. Norbeg-Shulz, 113tl
Nordisk Pressefoto, 154b
Novosti Press Agency, 100bl, br; 101t; 125cl

Taisuke Ogana (*Japan Architect*), 327c; 338t, c, bl, br
Tomio Ohashi, 309, c, cr; 330t, c; 345t; 395cl, cr, b; 401tl, tr, c

Olivetti, 215t; 260c
Ontario Government Office, 260t, b; 267c, b
Cas Oorthuys, 132cl

Marechaux Pascal, 375c; 377; 380c, bl; 394tr, bl
William Pereira, 296t
Photo Cracknell, 149bl
Pictorial Press, 136b
Picture Coverage Ltd, 332b
Monica Pidgeon, 244br
Popperfoto, 176bl; 186b; 224c; 193tl, c; 245cl, cr; 259tl; 297br
The Prairie School Press, 24bl; 35t, b; 179b

Heinz Rasch, 62t; 87cl, b; 86bl
Regie Autonome des Transports Parisienne, 15t
Gunay Reha, 375tr
Jo Reid and John Peck, 359c
RIBA, 13bl; 14tc; 22b; 24br; 26t; 29t, b; 36c, b; 45t, bl; 46t; 48tr, br, bl; 50b; 57t; 60c, b; 64tl, cr; 71t, b; 78c, bl, br; 79tl, b; 84t, c, b; 89t, cl, b; 92t; 96t; 99tl; 101bl, br; 101bl, br; 103bl, br; 105tl, tr, c, br; 106t; 108t; 110b; 112cl, b; 114b; 118b, cr; 119tr, b; 122t; 123bl, br; 132tl; 135cr; 145r; 146; 147bl; 154lc, b; 155t; 156tr; 158tr; 160t; 178bl; 184t; 185br; 191t; 196br; 209tr, c; 210t, b; 211b; 214l, r; 217cr; 226tr, c; 265t; 273cl; 276b; 277tc; 412tb
Kevin Roche, John Dinkeloo & Associates 274t; 286c, b; 291t, c, b
Roger-Viollet, 23br
Aristides Romanos, 138t
John A. Rose, 266b
Steve Rosenthal, 334t, cl, cv; 374l, b
Professor Alfred Roth, 130tr; 230tr, c, br; 255t
Jean Roubier, 85tl
Paul Rudolph, 171cl, cr, b; 253t, bl; 258t, c, b
Roberto Ruiz, 359t

Eero Saarinen & Associates, 168b; 225c, t; 245t, b; 252tl
SAM, Amsterdam, 8C
Ali Schafler, 367t, b
Professor Hans Scharoun, 102t, cl, cr, b; 111tl, tr; 128t, cl, cr, bl; 228tl, tr, bl, br; 256t, c, b
Gordon H. Schenck, 365tl, c
Arieh Sharon, 109br; 151c, b; 275tl, tr, br
Melanie Sharp, 361tr
Schipporeit-Heinrich, 293b
Richard Sheppard, Robson & Partners, 242b
Julius Shulman, 165t, b; 174bl, br; 184bl, br; 189c; 206t, b; 248c, bl, br; 322t, b; 323t; 344tl, c
Skidmore, Owings & Merrill, 240b
Alison & Peter Smithson, 99b; 198t, c, br; 204c, b; 265br
Henk Snoek, 270cl

Soleri, 195tr, b
A. Staal 38b; 56t, c, b
Staatsbibliothek Berlin, 30b
Fotobureau ''t Sticht', 350c
Stichting Architectuurmuseum, 63cb
James Stirling, 254tr
Ezra Stoller, 28bl; 167t; 171cr, b;) 201t, c, bl, br; 240tl; 245t; 252b; 253t; 258c; 286t; 297t; (Richard Meier), 306t, c; 313tb; 350c
Tim Street-Porter, 332bl
Strüwing Reklamefoto, 333tl
Sveriges Arkitekturmuseum, Stockholm, 72tl, tr; 114tr; 157t
Professor Helen Syrkus, 134bl

TAC, 83lcl; 147tl, tr; 182t, b
Kenzo Tange, 207t; 215b; 241tr, b; 255b; 259cr; 261b; 287t
Tate Gallery, 186t
K. Teigen Foto, 148l
Edward Teitelman, 41t; 55t; 106c, b; 274bl; 294b
Anders Tengbom, 221tl, tr, b
Ralph Tubbs, 186t

Ullstein Bilderdienst, 20bl; 34t; 125t; 202t, tc
Professor O. M. Ungers, 230t, c
Union of the Architects of CSSR, 57bl, br; 79c; 95tl, tr; 103t; 113t, c
Union Tank Car Company, 216tl, b
United Nations, 193tr
USIS, 141tl; 199b; 216tr; 280b
US Travel Service, 156br

Gino Valló, 246c, br
Venturi & Rauch, 262t, c, b
Visual Publications, 80t
Visionnaires de l'Architecture, 237c, b
Vittoriano Vigano, 232t, c, b
Volkswagenwerk, 251b

Basil Ward, 124t
Sir Owen Williams & Partners, 125cl, c, cr, b
Wilkhahn Pressfoto, 400cl, b
Dick van Woerkom & Plan Magazine, 55c; 66b; 68b; 75br; 85tr; 92b; 97b, 100t, 115tl, tr; 116br; 121t; 129t; 243t; 277b
F. R. Yerbury, 13t

Zeidler Roberts Partnership/Architects, 306b
Bruno Zevi, 110t

INDEX

Page numbers in italics refer to illustrations

426